Literary Lives

Literary Lives

Selected by **John Sutherland**

OXFORD
UNIVERSITY PRESS

OXFORD
UNIVERSITY PRESS

Great Clarendon Street, Oxford OX2 6DP

Oxford University Press is a department of the University of Oxford.
It furthers the University's objective of excellence in research, scholarship,
and education by publishing worldwide in

Oxford New York

Auckland Bangkok Buenos Aires Cape Town
Chennai Dar es Salaam Delhi Hong Kong Istanbul Karachi
Kolkata Kuala Lumpur Madrid Melbourne Mexico City Mumbai
Nairobi São Paulo Shanghai Singapore Taipei Tokyo Toronto
with associated companies in Berlin Ibadan

Oxford is a registered trade mark of Oxford University Press
in the UK and in certain other countries

Published in the United States
by Oxford University Press Inc., New York

© Oxford University Press 2001

Database right Oxford University Press (maker)

First published 2001

First issued as an Oxford University Press paperback 2002

British Library Cataloguing in Publication Data
Data available

Library of Congress Cataloging in Publication Data
Data available

ISBN 0-19-860642-7

10 9 8 7 6 5 4 3 2

Typeset in DanteMT
by Alliance Phototypesetters, Pondicherry, India
Printed in Great Britain
by T. J. International, Padstow, Cosnwall

Preface

'The best record of a nation's past that any civilization has produced': G. M. Trevelyan's view in 1944 of the *Dictionary of National Biography* highlights the achievement of its first editor Leslie Stephen. Between 1885 and 1900 quarterly volumes rolled out from the presses in alphabetical order by subject. A national institution had come into existence, making its distinctive contribution to the national aptitude for the art of biography.

In his initial prospectus for the *DNB*, Stephen emphasized the need to express 'the greatest possible amount of information in a thoroughly business-like form'. Dates and facts, he said, 'should be given abundantly and precisely', and he had no patience with the sort of 'style' that meant 'superfluous ornament'. But he knew well enough that for 'lucid and condensed narrative', style in the best sense is essential. Nor did he content himself, in the many longer memoirs he himself contributed to the *DNB*, with mere dates and facts: a pioneer in the sociology of literature, he was not at all prone to exaggerate the individual's impact on events, and skilfully 'placed' people in context.

Stephen's powerful machine was carried on by his work-horse of a successor Sidney Lee, who edited the first of the ten supplements (usually decennial) which added people who died between 1901 and 1990. It was in these supplements that all of the memoirs published in this series first appeared, so they were often written soon after the subject died; their authors were frequently able to cite 'personal knowledge' and 'private information'. In such cases there is always a balance to be struck between waiting for written sources to appear and drawing upon living memory while still abundant and fresh. Stephen had no doubts where he stood: he published book-length biographies of his Cambridge friend Henry Fawcett and of his brother Fitzjames within a year of their deaths, and cited Boswell's *Johnson* and Lockhart's *Scott* as proof that the earliest biographies are often the best. Furthermore, memoirs of the recently dead were included in the *DNB* right up to the last possible moment, the press often being stopped for the purpose. Roundell Palmer, for example, died on 4 May 1895 and got into the 43rd volume published at the end of June.

Preface

So the memoirs published in this series are fully in line with what was *DNB* policy from the outset. Furthermore, all have the virtue of reflecting the attitudes to their subjects that were taken up during their lifetimes. They may not always reflect what is now the latest scholarship, but as G. M. Young insisted, 'the real, central theme of history is not what happened, but what people felt about it when it was happening'. So they will never be superseded, and many are classics of their kind—essential raw material for the most up-to-date of historians. They have been selected by acknowledged experts, some of them prominent in helping to produce the *New Dictionary of National Biography*, which will appear in 2004. All are rightly keen that this ambitious revision will not cause these gems of the *DNB* to be lost. So here they are, still sparkling for posterity.

Brian Harrison
Editor, *New Dictionary of National Biography*

Literary Lives—selections from the twentieth-century DNB

Introduction

The *Dictionary of National Biography* is the work of many learned hands but, essentially, the idea of one self-made man who left school to be apprenticed into the book trade at the age of 14. A precocious publishing genius, George Smith was running the family firm (Smith, Elder & Co.) at the age of 19. He earned himself the title 'Prince of Publishers' four years later, in 1847, when he published the first novel of an unknown Yorkshire woman, Currer Bell.

Jane Eyre was the first of innumerable publishing coups for Smith. In what he modestly called 'a long and busy life' he published and mixed socially with a galaxy of Victorian authors. Literary men and women were always his boon companions: Matthew Arnold; Charlotte Brontë; John Ruskin; W. M. Thackeray, and his daughter, Lady Ritchie, 'the lesser Thackeray' (Anthony Trollope); George Eliot, 'Mr George Eliot' (G. H. Lewes); Wilkie Collins; Charles Reade; the Brownings; Mrs Humphry Ward. No Victorian publisher had a more distinguished list of clients. And most of his clients became bosom friends.

Smith, Elder & Co. was (for a leader in the British book trade) unusually diversified in its operations. The firm ran an Indian agency, had shipping and banking interests, and owned the franchise for a popular mineral water, Apollinaris. Buoyed up by his diverse profit stream, George Smith launched what became the most successful of Victorian political newspapers, the *Pall Mall Gazette*, in 1865. He also conceived and launched, with huge fanfare, the most spectacularly successful of the century's monthly miscellanies, the *Cornhill Magazine* (named after the firm's premises in the City of London).

Everything Smith touched turned to gold. In 1882, aged 59, he conceived the plan for his great work, his monument—an English equivalent to the

Biographie universelle. It would be a labour (a Herculean labour) of love. Nor would it be, in what remained of his lifetime, remunerative. It was designed as a service to the nation. An imperial mark.

Among all 'his' authors, Smith had always most valued his connection with Thackeray. After the novelist's premature death in 1863 the publisher formed a close bond with Thackeray's son-in-law (Virginia Woolf's father, 'Mr Ramsay', as we tend to think of him), Leslie Stephen. Stephen (1832–1904), ten years younger than Smith, was the archetypal Victorian man of letters. After a brilliant career at Eton and Cambridge, he backed away from an academic career on grounds of religious agnosticism (and, less intellectually, a desire to marry—college fellows were still enjoined to celibacy. Had he taken a more dutiful route we would never have had *To the Lighthouse*).

Stephen earned his bread as a higher journalist. He became a lead contributor to the *Saturday Review* and Smith's *Pall Mall Gazette*. He edited *Cornhill* from 1871 to 1882. It was Stephen who sagaciously persuaded George Smith to narrow down his proposed 'universal' biographical cyclopaedia into something specifically 'national' (he may have been influenced by the English Men of Letters volumes which he was currently writing for John Morley at Macmillan). And it was Stephen (author of the Shandyan literary essays 'Hours in a Library') who came up with the owlish 'Dictionary' prefix.

Stephen was appointed editor-in-chief of the project. It was a perfect union. 'Mr Smith', as Charlotte Brontë once said, 'is a practical man'. Stephen, was learned, fluent, and equally practical. Years of periodical editing had ingrained a Pavlovian reverence for deadline into his professional makeup. The volumes pulsed out at the factory-production rate of four a year (sixty-three in all) between 1885 and 1900 (the standard reprint is compressed into a mere twenty-two volumes).

Even after retirement from the firm, in the late 1880s, Smith fondly retained the *DNB* as his personal property. On his death, in the fateful year 1901, he bequeathed this great Victorian achievement to his wife. Stephen, who had precipitated ill health and surely hastened his death by his work for the dictionary handed over the reins of editorship in 1899. He had written the lion's share of the literary contributions: some 378 in all, including the massively authoritative entries on Dickens, Scott, Pope, Thackeray, Milton, and Wordsworth.

Smith's widow transferred the property to Oxford University Press in 1917, when Smith, Elder & Co. was wound up as a firm (the university publishers wryly regarded themselves as a sanctuary for such 'white elephants', having earlier taken over the Philological Society's 'English Dictionary', the *OED* as it became; the *DNB*'s great stable-mate).

The twentieth-century 'Supplements' to the *DNB* (from which the contents of this book are compiled) came under the general editorship of Sir Sidney Lee. As he himself pointed out, Lee's task was different from Stephen's, which had been essentially historical. Lee was charged with creating a 'living organism': making what amounted to snap judgements— almost with the speed of the obituary editor on a daily newspaper. With the substantial nucleus of literary entries, there was another urgent pressure on the compilation as it grew (by decennial supplement volumes) in the twentieth century: notably the professionalization of critical taste with the formation of English schools at Oxford, Cambridge, and London. The tone was less cosy, and occasionally donnish.

The following reprinted entries from the twentieth-century supplements to the *DNB* offer, among other good things, a fascinating register of changing literary standards over the century in which those standards were effectively formed. Who now, for example, would rank Lascelles Abercrombie as 'the leading poet of the new generation'—practically, it is implied, in the Robert Bridges class? ('"The Testament of Beauty" is a great poem', we are serenely assured in the Bridges entry).

In his terse entry on Eric Blair (George Orwell), Richard Rees has little sense of how massive his friend's last novel will loom posthumously. For Rees *Nineteen Eighty-Four* is merely 'an apocalyptic vision of doom'. Nothing special. Certainly not a book to change the post-war world. And for Richard Aldington (in a somewhat spiteful assessment of D. H. Lawrence) *Lady Chatterley's Lover* is 'the least satisfactory' of the novelist's books. Perhaps. But with hindsight we see it as the most influential on English literary culture.

The stress in these pieces, naturally enough, is biographical. That is where the *DNB* is always coming from. The entries insist, categorically and aggressively, that there is more to life, even a literary life, than literature. Vera Brittain is 'writer, pacifist, feminist'. Vita Sackville-West is 'writer and gardener'. Winifred Holtby is 'novelist, feminist, and social reformer'.

Myopia—closeness to the subject—has obvious critical liabilities. 'How to assess him?', Michael Denison despairingly asks himself in his entry on Noël Coward. It would be 'rash to attempt a verdict' on A. E. Housman's poetry so soon after his death, D. S. Robertson cautiously decides. But closeness also has its compensating apostolic virtues. The writers of these pieces (how often 'private knowledge' and 'personal information' appear) typically *knew* their subjects, as closely as we know our friends, family, and colleagues.

Max Reinhardt, who writes the warm assessment of Georgette Heyer, was her publisher (as was Ian Parsons of Aldous Huxley). Paul Johnson knew J. B. Priestley for years as a contributor to the *New Statesman*, of which Johnson was editor (this, incidentally, is for my money the bluffest entry in this selection). Sean Day-Lewis contributed the entry on his father (how much it must have cost him to write that the incurably philandering Cecil Day-Lewis 'loved women and was always vulnerable to them').

Sometimes, as in obituaries, shock at recent loss can be palpably felt. When John Lahr writes of Joe Orton, 'no playwright in living memory had met a more gruesome end', one shares the country's horrified shudder in 1967 when it learned, from screaming newspaper headlines, of the young writer being battered to death by his demented lover. The only writer here whose end rivals Orton's in gruesomeness is Erskine Childers, shot by Irish firing squad. Most lived quiet lives and died in their beds. Pedantically the *DNB* always gives the place of death. My favourite is that of Shiva Naipaul, who expired in 'an airy flat in Belsize Gardens' (at the tragically early age of 40).

Of particular interest are those entries where, as posterity would see it, a younger (or happily longer-lived) writer writes about an equal he or she admires: Kingsley Amis on Betjeman and Ian Fleming (about whom he is defiantly laudatory); Philip Larkin on Barbara Pym; John Wain on Philip Larkin (compare his generous judgements on the great English poet with his short, xenophobic dismissal of the great Scottish poet Hugh Mac-Diarmid); Julian Symons on Geoffrey Grigson (the most 'ferocious' critic of his time); John Lehmann on Cyril Connolly; Percy Lubbock (the greatest of Jamesians) on the Master, Henry James.

Unsurprisingly, given the fact that many of these pieces were written soon after death, there is much *nil nisi bonum* and occasional decent reticence. The reader oblivious to undertone will not apprehend, in the entry on Aleister Crowley, that this was the leading diabolist of the century. In his measured appreciation of Joe Ackerley (who died in 1967, the year of the liberating Sexual Offences Act) Peter Parker does not too openly allude to his subject's homosexuality. Writing about Auden, six years later, Stephen Spender has no such inhibition. He refers frankly (and bitterly) to the 'agony' inflicted on Auden by the wanton infidelities of his lover, Chester Kallman. Sex apart, there is often a pleasing outspokenness in the entries, as when we are informed that G. K. Chesterton betrayed his genius by 'overworking, overeating, overdrinking'. And, after the 1960s, even sex is dealt with frankly. For Arthur Koestler, Woodrow Wyatt informs us, 'friends' wives were fair game'.

The principal strength of the following entries is their somatic ability to evoke the physicality of their subjects, 'to the life', as portrait painters say. One feels the vivid power of eyewitness testimony. Margery Allingham, we learn, had 'infectious exhilarating charm'. 'In her prime', Enid Blyton was 'a woman of striking appearance'. John Betjeman's 'expression in repose was timid'. Elizabeth Bowen 'never lost her stammer'. J. G. Farrell had 'a mock-gloomy way of telling anecdotes'. James Joyce, Stuart Gilbert tells us—rather enigmatically—had 'an agreeable presence'. W. E. Johns (creator of the Brylcreem Boy, Biggles) had unsurprisingly 'well-groomed grey hair'. Evelyn Waugh, one is gratified to learn, 'was of less than average height'. Of Robert Graves John Wain recalls: 'one often felt in his presence a certain otherness, a wind blowing from an undefined quarter of the spirit.' The same breeze wafts, vicariously, over the reader.

Readers will select their particular favourites from this collection. My own preference is for the urbane, wonderfully concise, and incorrigibly precious entries by David Cecil (Max Beerbohm, Lytton Strachey, Virginia Woolf). Alan Hollinghurst's cameo on Ronald Firbank strikes one as a beautifully written miniature ('He was known for the refined dandyism of his appearance, the flutterings and oscillations of his bearing, his heavy drinking, and his intense shyness'). Richard Ellmann's piece on T. S. Eliot is a model of what biographically based literary criticism should be. One could continue the catalogue. The styles of judgement and description are as varied as the subjects themselves.

All these 100 entries will be superseded (revised and in many cases totally rewritten) in the forthcoming *New Dictionary of National Biography* (*New DNB*), due to roll out in paper and electronic form in 2004. The lumps will be ironed flat, warts removed, reticent omissions filled in, and a generally higher standard of notation imposed. That is as it should be. And, in course of time, there will be even newer *DNB*s. But those readers who want a less formal, livelier portraiture will be grateful for this *litterateurs'* gallery and memorial to the first heroic age of the our national biographical register.

JOHN SUTHERLAND

January 2001

Contents

Contents

Contents

Contents

Contents

Contents

Contents

Contents

ABERCROMBIE Lascelles

(1881–1938)

Poet and critic, the fifth son, and the eighth of nine children, of William Abercrombie, stockbroker, of Ashton-upon-Mersey, by his wife, Sarah Ann Heron, was born at Ashton 9 January 1881. Even in boyhood he was devoted to music and letters; his taste was fostered at a preparatory school, and also at Malvern College, where he read Greek and Latin eagerly. From 1900 to 1902 he read science at the Owens College, Manchester, but then turned to journalism for a living and to poetry for his vocation. He reviewed much in the Liverpool daily press; his first poem, 'Blind', appeared in 1907 and his first volume of verse, *Interludes and Poems*, in 1908. In 1909 he married Catherine, daughter of Owen Gwatkin, surgeon, of Grange-over-Sands; they had three sons and one daughter. After a stay of more than a year in Birkenhead he and his wife migrated first to Herefordshire and then (1911) to Gloucestershire, where, inspired by happiness and by the noble scenery, he published some of his best verse. It included *Mary and the Bramble* (1910), *The Sale of St. Thomas*, Act I (1911), and also some poetic plays in *New Numbers*, i–iv (1914), a periodical privately issued in partnership with Rupert Brooke, John Drinkwater, and Mr. Wilfrid Gibson.

Abercrombie now came to be recognized as a leading poet of the new generation, distinguished for his lyrical power and speculative daring. He was praised by Robert Bridges for his lucid exposition of difficult themes. He responded profoundly to natural beauty; his love-poetry was ardent and exalted; and the mystical and 'metaphysical' strain was never far away. It is heard again in the prose of *Speculative Dialogues* (1913), with its musings on life and love and on the Last Things; and also in several dramatic poems, such as *Deborah* (1912), which were not designed for the stage. But several were acted; of these the most notable is *The End of the World* (published in *New Numbers*), in which some homely folk are terrified by a false alarm that doomsday has arrived.

Abercrombie was still to write his best verse, but his richest period of poetic production was over. The war of 1914–1918 came as a grievous interruption. Although a keen patriot he was not strong enough for military service and laboured in Liverpool as an examiner of munitions. When peace came he was at a loss for employment, but after a while funds were found for a lecturership in poetry at Liverpool University; this appointment, which he held from 1919 to 1922, was an event that was to affect his whole career. He spoke upon his own craft; he held public audiences, not least by his rare gift for reading aloud; and he taught small classes the outlines of literary criticism and of its history. Abercrombie now devoted himself chiefly to prose, and published many critical studies, often based on the public lectures which he gave at Cambridge, at Baltimore, to the British Academy, and elsewhere. They include *An Essay towards a Theory of Art* (1922), *Principles of English Prosody* (1924), and *Romanticism* (1926). *Poetry, its Music and Meaning* (1932) is a felicitous statement of his artistic and critical convictions. The article on Thomas Hardy in this DICTIONARY is eloquent of a lifelong admiration.

A very active professor, Abercrombie rose quickly in the academic world. He occupied the chair of English literature at Leeds University from 1922 to 1929 and was Hildred Carlile professor of English literature in London University, at Bedford College for Women, from 1929 to 1935. In 1935 he became Goldsmiths' reader in English at Oxford and a fellow of Merton College. He received honorary degrees from the universities of Cambridge, Manchester, and Belfast; held several special lecturerships, including the Clark lecturership at Trinity College, Cambridge, in 1923, and was elected a fellow of the British Academy in 1937. But his health declined, and he died in London 27 October 1938.

In 1930 the Oxford University Press published (in 'The Oxford Poets') Abercrombie's collected *Poems*, all but one, the richest and maturest of all, the completed *Sale of St. Thomas* (1931). Here, in a style which often rises to grandeur, he proclaims his faith in an omnipresent divine spirit embodying the law of ideal beauty. Abercrombie deepened and ennobled English 'metaphysical' poetry. He charged it anew with his passionate feeling for the essential beauty of nature and of human nature. The symbolism may be now and then excessive, or too difficult; yet again and again, as in some of his early lyrics, in the stately choruses of 'Peregrinus', in 'Marriage Song', and never better than in 'The Death of a Friar', he achieves either beauty, or strength, or magnificence, or all these in harmony.

[*The Times*, 28 October 1938; Oliver Elton, *Lascelles Abercrombie, 1981–1938* in *Proceedings* of the British Academy, vol. xxv, 1939 (portrait and bibliography); Wilfrid Gibson in *English*, vol. ii, No. 10, 1939; private information; personal knowledge.]

OLIVER ELTON

published 1949

ACKERLEY Joe Randolph

(1896–1967)

Writer and editor, was born 4 November 1896 in Herne Hill, south London, the younger son and second of three children of Alfred Roger Ackerley, fruit importer of London, and his mistress, Janetta Katherine Aylward, an actress. His parents married in 1919. He was educated at Rossall School and Magdalene College, Cambridge, where he obtained a third class in English in 1921, having abandoned law after a short time. His education had been interrupted by the war of 1914–18, in which he served on the western front as an officer in the 8th battalion of the East Surrey Regiment. Twice wounded, he was captured in May 1917, and subsequently exchanged into internment in Switzerland. These experiences, and the death in action of his elder brother, Peter, resulted in a pronounced strain of melancholy in his character.

In 1922 he received an appreciative letter from E. M. Forster about his long meditative poem, 'Ghosts'. This led to an enduring friendship, the closest of Ackerley's life. It was at Forster's suggestion that Ackerley spent five months in India as companion-secretary to the eccentric Maharajah of Chhatarpur.

The anthology *Poems by Four Authors* (1923) contained ten poems Ackerley had written while an undergraduate, and in 1925 the play based upon his experiences as an internee, *The Prisoners of War*, was produced in London. Its 'difficult' themes (the war and homosexuality) made it a *succès d'estime*, but although Ackerley was hailed as a coming dramatist, he never completed another play.

In 1928 he became an assistant producer in the talks department of the BBC. Through Forster he had acquired a wide circle of literary acquaintances, many of whom he recruited to make broadcasts on the radio. In 1932 he edited *Escapers All*, derived from a series of talks given by men who had escaped from prisoner-of-war camps. That same year he also published *Hindoo Holiday*, based on his Indian diaries. In spite of many excisions on the grounds of libel and obscenity, the book's sly humour and brilliant character-drawing ensured excellent sales and consolidated Ackerley's reputation.

In 1935 he became literary editor of the *Listener*, a post he held for twenty-four years. He wanted the magazine to be 'in the vanguard of contemporary thought, the forefront of the battle', and commissioned reviews, articles, stories, and poems which reflected this. 'I think that people *ought* to be upset,' he wrote; 'I think that life is so important and, in its workings, so upsetting that nobody should be spared.' This was a policy which led to many disagreements with his timid employers, and he waged a vigorous guerrilla campaign against the prudery and philistinism of the BBC hierarchy. His integrity, charm, tact, and an insistence upon the highest standards, led to his being widely considered the finest literary editor of his generation.

Ackerley flouted convention both in and out of the office. Strikingly good-looking and energetically homosexual, he conducted a long but conspicuously unsuccessful search amongst working-class men for 'the Ideal Friend'. His father's life had been similarly unorthodox, for he had kept a second mistress and three daughters, whose existence was revealed only after his death. Ackerley's crusade to tell the truth, however uncomfortable and inconvenient that might be, arose from his belief that his relationship with his father had been compromised by their inability to confide in each other.

In 1956 Ackerley published *My Dog Tulip*, a shockingly frank and funny portrait of his Alsatian bitch, Queenie. The story of how he acquired her from a petty criminal and gradually transferred his love from man to dog is told in his novel *We Think the World of You* (1960), which won the W. H. Smith award. Although unconsummated, this relationship was undoubtedly the most satisfactory of his life and resulted in his passionate advocacy of animal rights.

In retirement Ackerley revised what was to be his masterpiece, a 'family memoir' begun in the 1930s which was eventually published as *My Father and Myself* (1968). He lived in considerable squalor and acrimony in a small Putney flat with his 'three bitches': Queenie, his ageing Aunt Bunny, and his emotionally unstable sister, Nancy. After the death of Queenie in 1961 he became increasingly morose. Although disenchanted with the human world, he turned his misanthropic gloom to good account in witty and self-deprecatory letters. He died from a coronary thrombosis, 4 June 1967, at his home in Putney.

[Peter Parker, *Ackerley: A Life of J. R. Ackerley*, 1989; *The Times*, 6 June 1967; Neville Braybrooke (ed.), *The Letters of J. R. Ackerley*, 1975; Francis King (ed.), *My Sister and Myself* (a selection from Ackerley's diaries), 1982.]

PETER PARKER

published 1993

ALDINGTON Edward Godfree ('Richard')
(1892–1962)

Writer, was born at Portsea, Portsmouth, 8 July 1892, the eldest of the two sons and two daughters of Albert Edward Aldington, a clerk articled to a solicitor, and his wife, Jessie May Godfrey. Educated at Dover College and at University College, London, which he was forced to leave, for financial reasons, before taking his degree, he rapidly established for himself a reputation as an avant-garde poet. Although for a while he became a sports journalist he decided to concentrate upon a literary career when, having had some poems accepted, he was introduced to influential writers such as Ford Madox (Hueffer) Ford, W. B. Yeats, Harold Monro, and Ezra Pound.

Through Pound, Aldington also met his future wife, H. D. (Hilda Doolittle, 1886–1961), an American poet. H. D., daughter of Charles Doolittle, mathematician and later professor of astronomy at the university of Pennsylvania, shared Aldington's love of the classics and of European language and literature. In the autumn of 1912, Aldington, H. D., and Ezra Pound became the original 'Imagists': poets who consciously broke with current diction and prosody in order to present 'an intellectual and emotional complex in an instant of time'. Aldington's verse, through the influence of Pound, was soon being published on both sides of the Atlantic and, on the strength of his growing reputation, he spent most of the following year travelling in Italy with H. D., whom he married in London 18 October 1913.

By now, and again through Pound's influence, Aldington had become literary editor of *The New Freewoman*, to be renamed in 1914 *The Egoist*. Moreover, between 1914 and 1917 the Aldingtons contributed to *Des Imagistes*, edited by Pound, and to three anthologies, *Some Imagist Poets* edited by Aldington and Amy Lowell (1915, 1916, and 1917), while Harold Monro's Poetry Bookshop in 1915 published Aldington's first book of verse, *Images 1910–1915*. During 1914, as a European war threatened, Aldington also worked for a while as secretary to Ford and took down by dictation in longhand the first draft of *The Good Soldier* (1915). However, although Aldington volunteered as soon as war began in 1914, for medical reasons he was not allowed to begin his service until mid 1916 when he enlisted as a private in the Royal Sussex Regiment. He was later commissioned, as a lieutenant and subsequently an acting captain, and saw front-line service in France and Flanders. The war marked a permanent change in Aldington's life. Not only did it cause him physical damage—he suffered for some time from the effects of gassing and shell-shock—but undoubtedly there were other reactions of an emotional nature that affected his personal and creative life. By the autumn of 1919 Aldington, now staying in a cottage at Hermitage, Berkshire, lent to him by D. H. Lawrence, had agreed to live apart from his wife. He had become attached to another resident at their lodgings at 44 Mecklenburgh Square, Dorothy Yorke, who was called Arabella and who joined him in Berkshire. He was also trying to concentrate upon a career as a writer and editor, which exposed him to increasingly varied literary experiences. In addition to publishing poetry and articles he became a regular reviewer of French books for the *Times Literary Supplement* and in 1921 assistant editor of T. S. Eliot's *Criterion*. During this period of renewed interest in French and Italian literature Aldington began to blossom not only as a critic but also as a translator. These activities were to continue throughout his life and he was ultimately to produce over twenty works of criticism and biography and thirty books of translation.

By 1926, despite his growing success (he had been expected to succeed (Sir) Bruce L. Richmond as editor of the *Times Literary Supplement*), Aldington seems to have become disenchanted with the life he was leading and though for the next two years he retained a cottage in Berkshire his thoughts and travels took him increasingly abroad. In 1928 he left England for France and, although he returned periodically until 1939, he never again regarded England as his home. Indeed, Aldington considered 1928 as 'a watershed'. That autumn, while with D. H. Lawrence and his wife on the Mediterranean island of Port Cros, Aldington was writing his first novel *Death of a Hero* (1929), the anti-war book which made him almost overnight a best-selling and internationally known author. During the next ten years he published seven novels, some books of short stories, three long poems, four editions of poetry, and many critical works.

It has frequently been said, especially by critics of his later biographical work, that Aldington's writing became possessed, even obsessed, with a bitterness which, however obscure in origin, was directed against the British literary establishment, which included many of his former colleagues and associates. It is true that *Death of a Hero* and 'Stepping Heavenward' (a satirical short story in *Soft Answers*, 1932) contain harsh lampoons—the latter is about T. S. Eliot and his wife—and it seems undeniable that Aldington's departure from England in 1928 occasioned, and was perhaps caused by, an expatriate resentment (the militantly satirical tone is particularly apparent in *The Colonel's Daughter*, 1931, although here it is directed at English village life). However, Aldington retained throughout his life the affection of friends and relatives who say that he had great personal warmth and generosity. None the less, the undoubted sharpness and anger of some of his writing—most notable perhaps in his well-known war novel—may show evidence both of literary power and of a kind of hard honesty: a quality which comparatively few writers possess.

Between 1935 and 1947 Aldington regarded the United States as his headquarters though until 1939 he still made frequent visits to Europe. In 1936 Aldington met Netta Patmore (1911–77), daughter-in-law of his mistress Brigit Patmore and the daughter of James McCulloch, a lawyer, of Pinner, Middlesex. Having obtained their divorces, Aldington and Netta were married in London on 25 June 1938; they had one daughter, Catherine, who was born a week after the marriage and who was educated primarily in France where she married and practised as a child psychiatrist. Following the adverse publicity about his marriage, Aldington found a new publisher in America and in 1941 his autobiography, *Life for Life's Sake*, appeared. In that year he edited *The Viking Book of Poetry of the English-Speaking World*. Between 1942 and 1946 he worked as a freelance film writer in Hollywood, where he had sold the rights to his novel *All Men Are Enemies* (1933) ten years earlier for a film which was never made. He also wrote during this period a good deal of biography (including *Wellington*, 1946, which won the James Tait Black memorial prize of 1947) and editions and anthologies of verse and prose. Although Aldington had said that he would 'never return to Europe' he finally tired of Hollywood and returned to France. By 1947 they were at Le Lavandou, and Aldington declared himself 'home after a long absence'.

The next few years, in which his work reflected a renewed zest and energy, were to prove crucial to his literary and personal life. He produced the major biographies, *Portrait of a Genius, But . . .*, a *Life of D. H. Lawrence* (1950), *Pinorman, Personal Recollections of Norman Douglas, Orioli, and Prentice* (1954), and *Lawrence of Arabia* (1955). These books mark a progression in the extent of controversy which they aroused. The frankness and honesty that had already made Aldington enemies in the writing and publishing world were now directed, with perhaps a certain relish, at these important figures—two of whom had become internationally admired, even idolized. If open discussion of, for example, (George) Norman Douglas's homosexuality caused wild hostility, such a reaction was utterly mild compared to that which his biography of T. E. Lawrence received. It is ironical that only in the latter case was the individual discussed not known personally, that as always Aldington was meticulous in checking his facts, and that he had initially set out to write a book confirming his belief in a justified national hero. His conclusion, however, that Lawrence was a liar and a fraud, attracted to Aldington a quite extraordinary wrath—and it was a wrath that could hurt. Indeed, it appears that there was a plot by powerful members of the British literary establishment to discredit the book before its publication in an attempt to keep it unpublished, and that the net effect of *Lawrence of Arabia* and *Pinorman* was to cause Aldington's life's work, 'some seventy titles in all', to go out of print.

This was a time when, perhaps as never before, Aldington needed the support of his friends. In 1950 his wife returned to live in England but he still had a daughter, who remained with him, to support. He had, however, in 1947 met Alister Kershaw, an Australian writer, who was to remain for the rest of Aldington's life his loyal friend. And despite all his problems—in particular the war waged against him as a controversial author which soon occasioned acute financial difficulties—he continued to write and to publish, notably his biography of the French poet Frederic Mistral (1956) which was awarded the *Prix de Gratitude Mistralienne* in 1959. From 1957, and for the last five years of his life, Aldington's situation became increasingly happy and secure. Alister Kershaw made available a house near Sury-en-Vaux in the Loire Valley; Aldington's books began to come back into print; he helped to translate the *Larousse Encyclopaedia of Mythology*; he contributed his significant knowledge of D. H. Lawrence to a new work on that author. The last years were especially contented because of the continued friendship and loyalty of those whom he had known for half a century. For example, in 1959 he visited Zurich to see H. D., his first wife, and Annie Winifred Ellerman, who wrote under the pseudonym 'W. Bryher', and whom he had first known as a soldier in the war of 1914–18. One of the most remarkable events of this time was an invitation for him and his daughter to spend three weeks in Russia as guests of the Soviet Writers' Union to honour his seventieth birthday. He had become well known there ever since the publication of *Death of a Hero*. This was his final journey for he died suddenly 27 July 1962 in Maison Sallé near Sury-en-Vaux only ten days or so after returning from Russia.

Aldington lived through, and was intimately associated with, the development of modernism in English literature. Moreover, few other writers have covered such a wide range of literary activity, published in some 200 titles. Indeed, Aldington's versatility has given rise to criticisms of superficiality and plagiarism (such as the claim that his long poem 'A Fool i' the Forest', 1925, is derivative of T. S. Eliot's 'The Waste Land'). He had two major assets. One was his passion for truth which, when threatened by hypocrisy or suppression, burst into formidably explosive utterance. The other was a sensitivity to beauty, especially of shape and colour as revealed in classical and Mediterranean art, and in the natural beauty of the human form, animals, and plants. It was a combination of these talents which created the first Imagist poet just as they were later to produce the angry novelist and biographer. When he saw beauty and truth attacked Aldington combined all his resources to create his most memorable and potent work.

[Richard Aldington, *Life for Life's Sake*, 1941; Brigit Patmore, *My Friends when Young*, 1968; Norman Timmins Gates, *A Checklist of the Letters of Richard Aldington*, 1977; Alister Kershaw and Frédéric-Jacques Temple, *Richard Aldington; an Intimate Portrait*, 1965; private information.]

J. A. MORRIS

published 1981

ALLINGHAM Margery Louise

(1904–1966)

Crime novelist, was born in Ealing 20 May 1904, the eldest child of Herbert John Allingham, editor of the *London Journal* and the *Christian Globe* and prolific writer of serial fiction, by his wife, Emily Jane Hughes. John Till Allingham was among her forebears. She was born to be a writer and wrote all her life. 'My father wrote,' she said, 'my mother wrote, all the weekend visitors wrote and, as soon as I could master the appallingly difficult business of making the initial marks, so did I.'

She was educated at a private school in Colchester and at the Perse High School, Cambridge, where she wrote and acted in her own play, but left at fifteen determined to earn by her pen. She wrote a great deal of fiction for magazines such as *Sexton Blake* and *Girls' Cinema* and in 1923 *Blackkerchief Dick*, a swashbuckling romance. Before long she turned to crime as her theme with a serial for the *Daily Express* in 1926 and *The Crime at Black Dudley* (1929), into which stepped her running-hero Albert Campion. It was followed by *Mystery Mile* (1930), her first considerable success, into which she introduced Campion's manservant, Lugg, the truculent ex-burglar. In the next ten years she wrote many stories for periodicals like the *Strand* and another ten mysteries, among them *Sweet Danger* (1933) and *The Fashion in Shrouds* (1938).

In 1940 she was asked by her American publisher for a factual book on wartime England: *The Oaken Heart* appeared in 1941. During the war years, which were heavily occupied with ARP and first-aid duties, she produced a 'mainstream' novel, *Dance of the Years* (1943), but it had to be finished too hastily and is only a shadow. With peace, however, a new writer emerged, more conscious of evil and the great issues, although she had as early as *Flowers for the Judge* (1936) produced a murder story which kept the dull bits a whodunit writer normally omits, infusing them with a novelist's life-giving art. The change is interestingly reflected in her treatment of Albert Campion. Originally a caricature in the mode of the Scarlet Pimpernel of Baroness Orczy, he was soon found a considerable hindrance as such and was skilfully turned into little more than a pair of eyes. With the wartime break his creator seized the opportunity to make him yet more mature. In *More Work for the Undertaker* (1949) she introduced in addition the 'pile-driver personality' of Charles Luke of the CID.

The post-war books contain her best work, among it *The Beckoning Lady* (1955), her own favourite. Freed of urgent commercial pressures, she was able to write a first draft, dictate a second, rewrite that, and finally dictate all again at speed to restore colloquial raciness. The qualities which had developed over a writing lifetime came to ripeness. There was first a re-markable energy of expression and thought. She had the gift of seeing with a passion which plucked from their everyday context into a startling and rich light things and ideas, people and places, particularly here both the salt-marshes of Essex, where she had grown up, and where from 1934 she lived in the attractive agglomerated D'Arcy House at Tolleshunt D'Arcy, and a romantic yet real London of fog 'like a saffron blanket soaked in ice-water'.

The energy expressed itself as a splendid certainty in everything she wrote. Pen in hand, she was afraid of no one. She could cheerfully label a county family as 'frightful females who smell like puppies' breath' and she could at the end create a figure of true evil like the criminal Jack Havoc of *The Tiger in the Smoke* (1952). Thus armed, she could write without strain of love and of death. She could if necessary compose a poem for one of her characters and a string of genuine *bons mots* for another. With it she brought distinction to the detective story and it enabled her to celebrate an unlikely but entirely harmonious shotgun marriage between truth and romance. Increasingly it permitted her to give rein to a strong intuitive intelligence and say much both penetrating and wise about men and es-pecially women. This in turn gave her pictures of her day a universality which, often forty years after writing, made them still eagerly read in reissued editions in the libraries and as ubiquitous paperbacks.

Margaret Allingham married in 1927 Philip Youngman Carter (died 1969), artist, whom she described as 'a lank youth', a physique the very opposite of her own 'figure designed for great endurance at a desk'. He was the son of the late William Robert Carter, headmaster of Watford Grammar School (1884–1914). He provided dust-jacket illustrations for many of her books, completed her last, *Cargo of Eagles* (1968), and wrote a short memoir which well conveys her 'infectious exhilarating charm'. She died at Colchester 30 June 1966.

[P. Youngman Carter, memoir in the collection *Mr. Campton's Clowns*, 1967; private information.]

H. R. F. KEATING

published 1981

ARDIZZONE Edward Jeffery Irving

(1900–1979)

Artist, illustrator, and author, was born 16 October 1900 at Haiphong in (then) French Indo-China. He was the eldest child of Auguste Ardizzone, a Frenchman of Italian parentage, who was an employee of the Eastern Extension Telegraph Company, married to Margaret, the daughter of Edward Alexander Irving, assistant colonial secretary at Singapore. Margaret's mother was born Christianna Margaret Kirby, and unsubstantiated family tradition traces her back to John Joshua Kirby. Auguste and Margaret Ardizzone had four further children, two daughters and two sons, all French by birth; Edward Ardizzone became a naturalized Englishman in 1922.

Brought to England in 1905, Ardizzone spent his childhood in East Anglia at various residences, often under the charge of his maternal grandmother. His early schooling was at East Bergholt and the junior division of Ipswich Grammar School, and in 1912, when the family moved to Wokingham, he became a boarder at Clayesmore School. This slightly unorthodox, undenominational school has been seen as an odd choice for one who was brought up, and remained, a Roman Catholic, but it was here that his growing interest in drawing and painting was encouraged. Furthermore, his housemaster, the writer and connoisseur Desmond Coke, was later to play a useful role in helping him to find commissions as a free-lance artist.

After leaving school in 1918 Ardizzone spent six months at a college of commerce and for several years he worked as a clerk. His lengthiest employment was with the Eastern Telegraph Company in London, where his father had bought a house at 130 Elgin Avenue which was to become the family home for over fifty years figuring frequently in Ardizzone's illustrations and on the personal Christmas cards which he liked to design. During his period of clerkship he attended evening classes at the Westminster School of Art, devoting his weekends to painting, and in 1926 he gave up his job to concentrate upon a career as a professional artist. In 1929 he married Catherine Josephine Berkley, the daughter of William Cuthbert Anderson, who was chief auditor of the Great Indian Peninsular Railway. They had two sons and a daughter.

In the years up to 1939 Ardizzone worked hard as both painter and graphic artist. In a series of one-man shows, first at the Bloomsbury Gallery and then at the Leger, his very personal, domestic vision received considerable praise. Working chiefly in his favourite medium of watercolour, but also in oils and lithography (for monochrome prints), he celebrated the local life of his quarter of London: recreations in its parks and along the Regent canal, the bonhomie of its pubs and its night-life. He brought to these scenes a mixture of affection, wit, and gentle satire which places him firmly in the tradition of Thomas Rowlandson.

His deep appreciation of the values of narrative art is reflected too in his illustrations of this period: the lengthy suite of pen-drawings for his first major commission *In a Glass Darkly* by J. Sheridan Le Fanu (1929), drawings for the *Radio Times* (which, with *Punch*, was to be a regular source of income), advertising copy for the whisky merchants Johnnie Walker, and picture books which he wrote and illustrated himself. The first of these, *Little Tim and the Brave Sea Captain* (1936), arose from stories told to his own family. It draws on memories of the harbour at Ipswich and upon his liking for ships and the sea, and in its bold integration of word and picture it stands out as one of the most significant picture-books of the age. (It was too an early example of colour offset lithography, its spacious folios being printed in the United States, where the text was hand-lettered by Grace Allen Hogarth, an editor at the Oxford University Press's New York office.)

At the start of the war in 1939 Ardizzone was serving in an anti-aircraft regiment but in 1940 he was appointed an official war artist and was attached to the British Army's GHQ at Arras. A published record of his experiences during the German invasion of France is to be found in his book *Baggage to the Enemy* (1941), just as his further work during the North African and Italian campaigns is recorded in his *Diary of a War Artist* (1974). Nearly three hundred water-colours from this time are housed at the Imperial War Museum.

After the war Ardizzone resumed his freelance career with great energy. He regularly exhibited drawings, water-colours, and lithographs at the Leicester Gallery and at the gallery of his friend Freddy Mayor; he undertook a variety of commissions, ranging from a water-colour portrait of Sir Winston Churchill to a notable series of covers for the *Strand* magazine, and advertising brochures for Ealing Studios and Messrs Guinness; and he illustrated nearly two hundred books, winning the Library Association's Kate Greenaway medal in 1957 for *Tim All Alone* (1956). His chosen medium for these varied from the line and wash drawings which he made for his own picture-books, to pure line, as in his intensely imagined drawings for poems by Walter de la Mare and by his friend James Reeves, and to more elaborate processes, such as the lithographs and stencilled drawings done for the Limited Editions Club of New York.

The foundation for this prolific output was Ardizzone's complete mastery of the drawn line. Although he claimed that 'the born illustrator' should work from copies rather than from life, the existence of some fifty-three sketch-books testifies to his continuous dedication to catching with his pen the significant moments of the life around him. Out of such constant practice there grew a body of finished work that pictures with grace and with a deceptive ease the scenes and incidents of anything from mechanized war to a child's dream of toyland. Only towards the end of his life was there any slackening of his fluent control of the drawn line.

In addition to his creative work Ardizzone served as an instructor in graphic design at the Camberwell School of Art. Then, after a tour of south India for Unesco in 1952, training students in silk-screen printing, he became visiting tutor in etching and lithography at the Royal College of Art. Such variety of occupation was congenial to him, for (despite the hours devoted to his art) he loved company and was held in much affection by a wide circle of friends. He also loved good food and wine, a taste reflected in his designing of menu covers for restaurants and catalogues for wine-shippers, and in his writing and illustrating wine notes for the Royal College.

In 1960 Ardizzone retired from teaching and began to spend more time in Kent, where he bought a house at Rodmersham Green, and in 1972 he and his wife moved there permanently after selling the house in Elgin Avenue. He had a studio built in his garden and, despite declining health, he continued to work at painting and illustrating down to his death at Rodmersham, 8 November 1979.

Ardizzone was elected ARA in 1962 and RA in 1970, and he served on the hanging committee in 1969 and 1971. Among the many honours he received were CBE in 1971 and Royal Designer for Industry in 1974. Numerous self-portrait sketches and drawings are scattered through his graphic works; there is also a portrait by Henry Carr at the Imperial War Museum, and a self-portrait and a portrait drawing by Brian Robb in the possession of the family.

[E. Ardizzone, 'The Born Illustrator', *Motif*, vol. i, November 1958, and *The Young Ardizzone*, 1970; Brian Alderson, 'Edward Ardizzone, a preliminary handlist of his illustrated books', *The Private Library*, vol. v, no. 1, spring 1972; Gabriel White, *Edward Ardizzone*, 1979; private information.]

BRIAN ALDERSON

published 1986

ARLEN Michael

(1895–1956)

Novelist, began life as Dikran Kouyoumdjian, son of an Armenian merchant, Sarkis Kouyoumdjian. He was born at Rustchuk in Bulgaria 16 November 1895, and with an elder brother was educated at Malvern College. In 1922 he was naturalized in the name under which he had begun to publish novels and short stories. With these he was soon to achieve considerable, if temporary, fame. His first novel, *The London Venture*, was published in 1920 on the recommendation of (Sir) Edmund Gosse. Surprisingly George Moore was his early model; but his mannered and ornamented style had certainly a reminiscent tang of the nineties. Three more books in the next three years established him on the literary scene, and in 1924 came *The Green Hat* which was acclaimed, attacked, parodied, and read, to the most fabulous degree of best-sellerdom; and made him a comfortable small fortune. It was a romance suited to its decade—cynical, sophisticated, yet sentimental, highly coloured, and glittering. If the colours have now faded, and the glitter seems mostly tarnished tinsel, the book cast a spell in its day and influenced many young writers. The character of the heroine, Iris Storm, that wanton of quality, 'shameless, shameful lady', gallantly crashing to her death in her great yellow Hispano-Suiza—'for Purity'—set a new fashion in fatal charmers; and the pictures of London café society were exact as glossy photographs. 'The Loyalty'—recognizable as the Embassy Club, at which the smartest people, including young princes, then danced to the blues—was depicted almost table by table, with a mixture of mockery and romanticism which delighted those who read of themselves.

Perhaps because he was a foreigner, who while mingling among them viewed them from outside, Michael Arlen had free licence to mock these people. Rather as English society had petted the young Disraeli, it forgave Arlen his cleverness and his exuberant elegance. Even when poor and

COLLEGIUM
SANCTISSIMAE·TRINITATIS
·APUD·TORONTONENSES·
A·D·MCMXXIII
·JOHANNES·STRACHAN·
FUNDATOR
A·D·MDCCCLI

trinity

TRINITY COLLEGE
University of Toronto
6 Hoskin Ave., Toronto, ON M5S 1H8

10 WAYS TO LEAVE A LEGACY TO TRINITY COLLEGE

1. **Prepare** a will to ensure your estate plans are fulfilled.

2. **Decide** if you want your legacy to support the College as a whole or a specific purpose such as a scholarship or bursary.

3. **Arrange** for your gift to be a specific dollar amount or a percentage of the assets in your will.

4. **Consider** donating assets other than cash, such as stocks, bonds, mutual funds, term deposits, real estate, art or jewellery.

5. **Designate** Trinity College as a beneficiary of your RRSP/RRIF.

6. **Name** Trinity College as the beneficiary of a new, an existing, or a paid-up life insurance policy.

7. **Establish** a charitable remainder trust with Trinity College as beneficiary.

8. **Purchase** a charitable gift annuity through Trinity College.

9. **Remember** your loved ones and friends with memorial gifts to Trinity College.

10. Contact **Analee Stein** for more information at 416-946-7426 or analee.stein@utoronto.ca

struggling this young man had contrived to be elegant; and in prosperity, it was said that his white waistcoat always seemed to be whiter than anybody else's; but Arlen himself was forestallingly ready to disarm criticism—describing himself as 'Every other inch a gentleman', 'The one the Turks forgot', or 'A Case of Pernicious Armenia'. His wit not being above the heads of his fashionable hearers, they found him the best of company; moreover, he was a man of whom his friends spoke with lasting regard.

Arlen took a hand in several plays, published collections of his short stories and, among further novels, *Lily Christine* (1929), *Men Dislike Women* (1931), *Hell! said the Duchess* (1934), and finally *Flying Dutchman* (1939). All had the professional touch of the born story-teller; but he never believed himself an important writer, and in after years steadily declined to have his 'rubbishy' best-sellers reprinted. His gains were well invested; and when he was happily married in 1928 to Atalanta, daughter of Count Mercati, they presently settled in the south of France. They had one son and one daughter. At the outbreak of war in 1939 Arlen returned to England to offer his services and was injured in the bombing of the city which had formed a background to his most successful fictions. The world of which he had written was destroyed in the flames of that bombing; but it can still be resurrected from his pages; and his name, whenever remembered, connected with that coign of Mayfair, that 'collection of lively odours' called Shepherd's Market. Eventually settling in New York he died there 23 June 1956.

[*The Times*, 25 June 1956; private information.]

M. Bellasis

published 1971

(1907–1973)

Poet, essayist, teacher, and collaborator in writing plays and libretti, was born in York 21 February 1907, the third and youngest son (there were no daughters) of Dr George Augustus Auden and his wife, Constance Rosalie Bucknell. In 1908 Dr Auden was appointed school medical officer of the city of Birmingham, to which the Auden family then moved. Dr Auden was a classicist in Greek and Latin and also had a strong interest in psychology. His wife, who had been trained as a hospital nurse, was a high

Anglican, and was musical. Auden was brought up in a home where there were books on scientific subjects, English literature, and Nordic sagas. It may have been important to his own emotional development that his father was away from home (in the Royal Army Medical Corps) from 1914 to 1918. All his life the mother figure was dominant for him.

Clergymen, schoolmasters, and antiquarians were among Auden's forebears. From childhood onward he was interested in limestone landscape, superannuated mining machinery, and place names. Late in life he said that if ever there were to be a school for poets courses in geology should be obligatory. Stimulated perhaps by the Nordic sound of his surname and his Anglo-Saxon Christian name, Auden cherished the belief that he was of Icelandic origin, and made several trips to Iceland; after one of these he published, in collaboration with Louis MacNeice, who had accompanied him, *Letters from Iceland* (1937).

He was educated first at St. Edmunds, a preparatory school at Hindhead in Surrey, where a fellow schoolboy was Christopher Isherwood—who became his lifelong friend, collaborator in writing plays, and, intermittently, lover; then at Gresham's School, Holt, a self-consciously 'modern' school where the emphasis of the teaching was on science (though Gresham's was also distinguished in music and drama); and, finally, at Christ Church, Oxford. His tutor there was Nevill Coghill, to whom, early on, he confided that it was his intention to become not just a poet but a great poet.

The decisive influence on Auden's poetry when he was at Oxford was *The Waste Land* of T. S. Eliot. He also derived from Eliot's early critical essays the view that the poet should be a kind of scientist of language who made, with detached objectivity, poems which were verbal artefacts rather than vehicles for expressing the poet's personality and feelings. Yet his early poems contain images of barriers, impassable frontiers, broken bridges, which seem to express his feelings of personal isolation, but in impersonal guise.

After leaving Oxford with a third class in English literature in 1928, Auden went, in August of the same year, for a year to Berlin. There he met John Layard, an ex-patient of the American psychologist and guru Homer Lane, who interested him in Homer Lane's teaching. This aimed at liberating the forces of the unconscious in the individual without applying moral censorship to whatever behaviour resulted from such release. The healing power of uninhibited love became a theme of the poetry of Auden's Berlin period.

In 1929 the allowance which his parents had given him at Oxford ceased and Auden was obliged to return to England to earn his living. For a year he did this by private tutoring in London. In 1930 he embarked on a five years' period of school-mastering; first at Larchfield Academy in Helens-burgh; and then, from autumn 1932, three years at the Downs School, Colwall. Known to his pupils as Uncle Wiz, Auden's performance as a schoolmaster was later described by one of his pupils as a non-stop fire-work display; but through his psychological knowledge, his empathy for the very young, and his self-discipline as a writer he was a wise educator, both of the boys and his colleagues.

His first book, privately printed by Stephen Spender in an edition of about forty-five copies, was *Poems* (1928). There followed (published by Faber) *Poems* (1930), *The Orators* (1932), and numerous articles and reviews. Periodicals, pre-eminent among which were *New Verse* and the anthologies *New Signatures* and *New Country*, usually incorporating in their titles the epithet 'new', seemed to spring up in response to a new movement in poetry presumably associated with Auden. The names most often cited together with his were Cecil Day-Lewis, Stephen Spender, and (a year or two later) Louis MacNeice.

That brilliant though obscure *tour de force*, *The Orators*—a medley of prose and verse—through wit, strangeness, surrealist effects, beautiful poetry, and uninhibited high spirits, communicated its excitement to a whole generation of Auden's young English contemporaries, often public schoolboys, who discovered in it exhilarating answers to the question posed in its first section: 'What do you think about England, this country of ours where nobody is well?'

Because of Fascism's increasing threat to individual liberty, Auden's poetry began to reflect his growing awareness that the individual was largely conditioned by the society in which he lived and that he had to defend his freedom against Fascism. In his private ideology he now added Marxism to Freudian psychoanalysis (he was later to add Christianity to both). He became involved in work and causes which were anti-Fascist. In mid-1935 he gave up schoolmastering and went to London. He joined the GPO Film Unit, where he worked with his friend the painter (Sir) William Coldstream and the producer John Grierson. In collaboration with Christopher Isherwood he wrote for the Group Theatre *The Dog Beneath the Skin* (1935) and *The Ascent of F6* (1936).

On 15 June 1935, at the instigation of Isherwood, he married Erika, daughter of Thomas Mann, who was a potential victim of Nazi per-secution—and whom, before the marriage, he had never met—in order to provide her with a British passport. This particular union was never consummated.

In 1937 he visited Spain, having volunteered to drive an ambulance for the Republican side, a visit which resulted in his most politically com-mitted poem: 'Spain' (1937). From January to July 1938 Isherwood and he travelled together to China and produced jointly *Journey to a War* (1939), a book which certainly showed that their political sympathies lay with the invaded and occupied Chinese. Its sonnet sequence about the war contains some of Auden's greatest poetry. They returned from China by way of America, a detour which changed their lives: for it was now that they decided that America was the country where they would take up residence.

The poetry Auden wrote when he was an undergraduate might be said to be well within the tradition of the modern movement; in it there were influences of James Joyce, Gertrude Stein, and T. S. Eliot, as well as of Anglo-Saxon and Norse sagas. But the poetry he wrote during the thirties was a departure from symbolist and imagist purism. He renounced *vers libre* and the search for new forms and wrote with virtuosity in a wide variety of traditional forms. He unabashedly introduced into poetry many elements of journalism and declared that poetry, to be interesting, had to contain news. When he wrote, during his visit to Iceland, the dazzling 'Letter to Lord Byron', it was the newsy, gossipy and satiric aspects of *Don Juan* that appealed to him in Byron, not the romantic.

On 18 January 1939 Auden and Isherwood left England for New York, having every intention of taking up residence in America and becoming American citizens, though, at the time, they did not tell their friends of this decision. After the outbreak of war in September of that year they were much criticized in the English press for not returning to England. On various occasions Auden produced reasons for his leaving England and it seems clear that the England which he had loved in his childhood and youth—an England of private values and pleasures and Edenic landscape—had in his mind ceased to exist. Moreover a result of his involvement with anti-Fascist politics and the public activities connected with them, was that he found himself regarded as leader of a movement called 'the Thirties'. This role, though flattering to him, was false to his vocation. Had he remained in England, he would have almost inevitably found himself becoming the public poetic voice of wartime England, which would have been alien to his gift.

America also meant for him Chester Kallman, a young poet whom he first met in New York in the spring of 1939 and in whom, within a matter of weeks of meeting him, he saw his destiny. In the relationship with Kallman lay his future and nothing would ever alter this. He thought of the relationship as a marriage, to which he was wholly committed. Kallman was in fact congenitally incapable of being faithful within a partnership and this brought Auden (and perhaps Kallman too) much agony.

Paradoxical as it may seem it was in America that Auden was able to reinvent the conditions necessary to his vocation, as the poet with a private voice who could 'undo the folded lie' and as teacher. After a brief spell at St. Mark's School in Massachusetts he taught undergraduate and graduate students at a whole series of universities and colleges (among them Michigan, Swarthmore, Bennington, Barnard, and Virginia). At the end of the war (April to August 1945), with the rank equivalent to major, he was one of a team of researchers into the effects of the bombing of German cities on their inhabitants (the morale division of the US Strategic Bombing Survey). He regarded New York as his home in America and would describe himself not as an American but a New Yorker. It might be said that after 1939 his true homeland was an island called Auden since he owed to New York the opportunity it offered him of being alone.

But after the end of the war he resumed, at least in part, his European life. He rented a house on the island of Ischia to which he went every spring and summer from 1949 to 1957. With the proceeds of an Italian literary prize in 1958 he bought a house in the village of Kirchstetten, near Vienna. His delight in possessing this modest home was such that on first arriving there from New York, he would sometimes stand in the garden with his eyes filled with tears of gratitude.

It is widely held, especially in England, that Auden's poetry declined after his arrival in America. Admittedly the poems written after 1938 rarely communicate the exuberance and restless vitality of some of the earlier work. In *The Double Man* (1941), *The Age of Anxiety* (1947), *The Sea and the Mirror* (1944), *Nones* (1951), and *The Shield of Achilles* (1955) the poet seems to have withdrawn into deeper levels of his consciousness, where he is much preoccupied with working out a system of religious ideas which will enclose and illuminate lived and observed experience. He now rejected utterly the idea that poetry could exercise the slightest influence on politics. Nevertheless, Auden's greatest poems are surely those of the American period, precisely because they transform into the terms of his theology and in his unique language so much of the surrounding life of our time. Moreover, several poems—notably, the title poem of *The Shield of Achilles* volume and 'In Praise of Limestone'—equal, if they do not surpass, the greatest poems of the thirties period. In America Auden also wrote highly individual and imaginative essays and lectures—themselves sometimes a kind of prose poetry—contained in *The Enchafèd Flood* (1950) (based on the 1949 Page-Barbour lecture at the University of Virginia), *The Dyer's Hand* (1962), and *Forewords and Afterwords* (1972).

Auden's collaboration with Chester Kallman in writing the libretto— *The Rake's Progress* (1951)—for Igor Stravinsky's music celebrated for him the fusion of their loves through their gifts: as did also their work together on libretti for operas by Hans Werner Henze and Nicolas Nabokov.

Auden

In 1956 Auden was elected professor of poetry at Oxford University. In his inaugural lecture, *Making, Knowing and Judging* (1956), he discussed autobiographically his experience of writing poetry. As poetry professor, Auden would go every morning to the Cadena café in Cornmarket in Oxford and make himself available for consultation and advice to whatever undergraduate poets chose to discuss their work with him. The advice he was most willing to give was about technique.

Probably his life did begin to take a downward curve in the 1960s. In October 1964 he spent six months in Berlin under an 'artists-in-residence' programme there, sponsored by the Ford Foundation. But he did not get on well with those German writers he met—who knew little about him—and he was not happy.

In the early 1970s he lobbied privately to have himself given rooms in Christ Church, his old Oxford college, on terms similar to those granted to E. M. Forster by King's College, Cambridge. In 1972 he was granted residence in a 'grace and favour' cottage in the grounds of Christ Church. That he ever wished for such an arrangement, and that he persisted in it when difficulties arose, are symptoms of loss of self-confidence. His isolation in his New York apartment had begun to have terrors for him. He had visions of falling dead there and his body not being discovered for a week. The return to Oxford was also an attempt to return to his origins by one whose view of his own life was perhaps cyclical. Through no-one's fault, the arrangement did not work out well. Industrialized, tourist-trodden, hooting and hustling modern Oxford did not correspond to Auden's memory of Peck Quad where, as an undergraduate, he had rooms and met his friends. The Students (fellows) of Christ Church, when they found that he was repetitive at high table and often drunk, did not extend to him the amused and admiring tolerance which he had enjoyed in New York. Auden was not in Oxford but Vienna when on 29 September 1973, after a very successful reading of his poems, he died in a hotel bedroom. He was buried in his much loved Kirchstetten on 4 October of that year.

Friends, English and American, whom Auden had known for a long time, formed a kind of constellation of smiled-at presences in his mind, an accompaniment throughout his life. That he had quarrelled with one of them—Benjamin (later Lord) Britten—was a source of grief to him. Despite his magnanimity and his many acts of generosity, there was a streak of inconsiderateness for others in his behaviour. This was one reason why he never found anyone to live with him. He was obsessively punctual and complained loudly if a meal, or a visitor, was five minutes late. He imposed his idiosyncrasies on others as a regime. These minor faults, which created an isolation for him, were outweighed by greater virtues. He had a sense that being a bachelor did not absolve him from family responsibility.

When he was young he was excessively funny, often in an outrageous way, and he remained greatly amusing all his life. His funniness consisted partly in his playing so uncompromisingly his own uniqueness, expressed already in his dress—the crumpled suit and the carpet slippers which he wore in later life—and even in his face, with its skin which, smooth in youth, became in age like crinkled parchment.

He was grateful for his own success and considered himself happy, though to friends it seemed that in old age he was an illustration of whatever is meant by the term 'broken-hearted'. Probably the happiest period of his life was when, a colleague among colleagues, he taught at the Downs School: as that superb poem of undiluted happiness beginning with the line 'Out on the lawn I lie in bed' would seem to testify.

Many people have found it difficult to take his religion seriously because, in irreligious company, he was inclined to 'camp it up' with references to 'Miss God' etc. But in fact theology provided the culmination of his intellectual life-explaining system; and, in the simplest way, in his benign attitude to others, his forgiveness of those who sinned against him, and the centrality of his feeling of love he was Christian and, in a quite old-fashioned sense, a Christian gentleman.

A portrait of him by (Sir) William Coldstream (1937) is in the Humanities Centre, Houston, Texas; there is a pencil drawing by Don Bachardy (1957) in the National Portrait Gallery; in private hands there are three drawings done by David Hockney (1968). There are also sketches by Maurice Field (1932–5) when he was at the Downs School, Colwall, and a page of sketches done by the Viennese artist Anton Schumich at the reading Auden gave in Vienna on the night of his death.

[Humphrey Carpenter, *W. H. Auden: a Biography*, 1981; Edward Mendelson, *Early Auden*, 1981; Stephen Spender (ed.), *W. H. Auden, a Tribute*, 1975; private information; personal knowledge.]

STEPHEN SPENDER

published 1986

(1872–1956)

Author and cartoonist, was born in London 24 August 1872, the youngest child of Julius Ewald Beerbohm, a man of good Baltic family who had settled in England as a corn merchant, and of his second wife, Eliza Draper. Max Beerbohm was educated at a preparatory school in Orme Square, at Charterhouse, and at Merton College, Oxford. Gifted and precocious, by the time he left Oxford Beerbohm was already an accomplished personality, delicately dandified in looks and manner, and a detached, ironical observer of the human comedy. In 1893 he met young (Sir) William Rothenstein who, struck by his talent as a cartoonist, introduced him to the literary and aesthetic circle in London which revolved round the Bodley Head and whose most famous member was Aubrey Beardsley. By this time Max was also friendly with Oscar Wilde. He contributed 'A Defence of Cosmetics' to the first number of the *Yellow Book* in 1894; this had the distinction of being attacked angrily in *Punch*. In 1895, after going down from Oxford, Beerbohm made a short visit to the United States as secretary to his half-brother (Sir) Herbert Beerbohm Tree, the actor. During this journey Max became engaged to Grace Conover, a member of Tree's company. He then settled in London, living with his sisters and widowed mother, drawing and writing: he contributed to various periodicals, notably the *Yellow Book*, the *Savoy*, and to the *Daily Mail*. In 1898 he succeeded G. B. Shaw as dramatic critic for the *Saturday Review*, a post which he held for twelve years. For the rest he occupied himself in social life, artistic and fashionable, where he was much in demand as a charming and witty talker. He became a friend of various distinguished persons including Henry James, Swinburne, Meredith, Conder, G. K. Chesterton, Gordon Craig, and, later, (Sir) Desmond MacCarthy. *The Works of Max Beerbohm*, a volume of essays, appeared in 1896, followed by *The Happy Hypocrite* (1897), *More* (1899), *Yet Again* (1909), and three volumes of drawings: *Caricatures of Twenty-five Gentlemen* (1896), *The Poets' Corner* (1904), and *A Book of Caricatures* (1907).

Meanwhile his love life followed an uncertain course. His engagement with Miss Conover ended in 1903 to be followed by a brief engagement to the well-known actress Constance Collier. She broke it off and a few months later Max began a romantic friendship with yet another actress, Florence Kahn, an American known for her performances in the plays of Ibsen. In 1910 he married her. Partly because they were poor and Italy was cheap, partly because Max had grown tired of the pressure of London social life, they retired to Rapallo which was to be Beerbohm's main home for the rest of his life. In 1911 Max published his prose fantasy *Zuleika Dobson*; in 1912 *A Christmas Garland*, a book of parodies; in 1911 the cartoons *The Second Childhood of John Bull*; in 1913 *Fifty Caricatures*. But his life was passed mainly in humorous and leisurely contemplation, only interrupted by an occasional visit to England to superintend an exhibition of his drawings. In 1915, however, too keenly concerned for his country's fate in the war to stay abroad, he returned to England. Here he remained until 1919. During this period he produced *Seven Men* (1919), much of the work embodied in *And Even Now* (1920), and a memorial volume (1920) to his half-brother Herbert. His drawings were published in *A Survey* (1921); *Rossetti and his Circle* (1922); *Things New and Old* (1923); *Observations* (1925); and *Heroes and Heroines of Bitter Sweet* (1931). A selection of his dramatic criticisms entitled *Around Theatres* appeared in two volumes in 1924.

Two exhibitions, in 1921 and 1923, met with a more mixed reception than hitherto. His caricatures of Labour in 1921 led left-wing critics to rebuke him as a reactionary, whereas in 1923 his caricatures of royalty made Conservative writers attack him as an iconoclast. Amused but unwilling to cause scandal, Beerbohm agreed to withdraw some of the royal caricatures. Meanwhile, back in Italy, he had settled down into his old routine. *A Variety of Things*, his last volume of essays, appeared in 1928. Failing energy combined with a rigidly high standard of performance to make him write very little: and for the most part he set up as a figure from the past, happily resigned to the fact that his day was done. He continued now and again to visit London, notably in 1930 (when he was awarded an honorary LL.D. at Edinburgh), and in 1935 when his wife made a return to the stage in *Peer Gynt* at the Old Vic. In 1935 he was persuaded to broadcast on the subject of 'London Revisited'. He applied himself to the task with his usual high standard of perfection as regards both the text and the performance, with the result that in this wholly modern medium he made an extraordinary success. During the rest of his life he gave occasional broadcasts, some of which were published in *Mainly on the Air* in 1946. An enlarged edition appeared in 1957, after his death. He was knighted in 1939 and made an honorary D.Litt. of Oxford and an honorary fellow of Merton in 1942. The outbreak of war in 1939 had again kept the Beerbohms in England: but they returned to Italy in 1947. In 1951 Florence Beerbohm died. For the rest of his life Beerbohm was looked after by Elisabeth Jungmann (died 1959), an old friend of himself and his wife, although many years younger than either of them. Beerbohm married her in 1956; a few weeks later, 20 May 1956, he died in Rapallo. His ashes were placed in the crypt of St. Paul's Cathedral, where there is a memorial tablet. He had no children.

Max's character was unique and paradoxical: at once friendly and detached, childlike and prudent, sensible and fantastic. But he was much loved: for beneath his dandy's mask he hid a modest, honourable, and affectionate nature and an easy agreeability, enlivened by the play of a whimsical fancy and a demure, impish humour. The work mirrored the man. He aspired only to entertain; but it was entertainment of classical quality: the expression of a distinguished highly cultivated intelligence and an unfailing sense of style. He was a shrewd if not a profound critic and the best essayist, parodist, and cartoonist of his age. His satire was ruthless and urbane, the manifestation of a civilized and independent conservatism, repelled alike by the work of Kipling and of Wells. Meanwhile, in his masterpieces, *Zuleika Dobson* and *Seven Men*, he discovered an original form of ironical fantasy. The blend of aesthete and comedian in him gave his work a double charm: it is at once exquisitely pretty and exquisitely comic.

A portrait of Beerbohm by J.-E. Blanche is on loan from the Ashmolean Museum to Merton College where there is also a portrait statuette by Lady Kennet and a drawing by Rothenstein; another drawing by Rothenstein is in the Manchester City Art Gallery; the National Portrait Gallery has a portrait by Sir William Nicholson, pencil drawings by R. G. Eves and Rothenstein, and a lithograph by C. H. Shannon; a portrait in oils by Eves is in the Tate Gallery.

[A. E. Gallatin and L. M. Oliver, *A Bibliography of the Works of Max Beerbohm*, 1952; J. G. Riewald, *Sir Max Beerbohm*, The Hague, 1953; David Cecil, *Max*, 1964; private information; personal knowledge.]

DAVID CECIL

published 1971

BEITH John Hay

(1876–1952)

Writer under the pseudonym of Ian Hay, was born 17 April 1876 in Manchester, the third son and sixth child of John Alexander Beith, a cotton merchant prominent in the public life of the city, and his wife, Janet, daughter of David Fleming, also a merchant in Manchester. He was the grandson of Alexander Beith, one of the founders of the Free Church of Scotland in 1843, and his background was passionately old-style Scottish.

From Fettes he went to St. John's College, Cambridge, where he obtained a second class in part i of the classical tripos (1898) and distinguished himself at rowing; later, 'large oars' were to garnish his house. He showed early interest in writing and the theatre, submitting 'pars' to the popular press, and haunting country-houses devoted to amateur theatricals.

In 1901 Beith was a junior master at Fettes before returning to Cambridge for a short period to study science. In 1902 as a junior science master he joined Durham School where he worked supremely hard; he coached the rugby teams and river crews and did house tutoring. A charming companion, with a developed social sense, he was extremely popular. Although not in the plot, Durham featured in one of his best books, *Housemaster* (1936).

In 1906 Beith returned to Fettes. Whilst sharing largely in school life, reviving the debating society, fostering school and house concerts, and helping to form the O.T.C., he spent most of his leisure writing, curiously usually in cynosural spots. He was a resourceful if unconventional teacher—lessons on compound interest might wander into New York's finances and end by stabilizing the national debt, but he knew public-school boys instinctively and enjoyed schoolmastering. When in 1912 he left Fettes to make writing his career his decision was generally regretted, perhaps even eventually by himself.

Beith's first novel, *Pip* (1907), coloured by early Manchester schooldays, had been a best-seller and had been followed by other equally light and humorous novels, among them *The Right Stuff* (1908) and *A Man's Man* (1909). With the publication in 1914 of *A Knight on Wheels* and his *Lighter Side of School Life* which owes much to Fettes, his career as a writer was assured. His humour, family gift for story telling, shrewd observation, sentimentality, and truly 'English' grace of sympathetically conveying eccentric characters perfectly suited the age.

In the war of 1914–18 Beith served first with the Argyll and Sutherland Highlanders, then transferred to the Machine Gun Corps. He reached the rank of captain in 1915 and major in 1918 and was mentioned in dispatches and awarded the M.C. in 1916. In the meantime his most famous book, *The First Hundred Thousand*, had been published in 1915. Written in billets at home and in France, it was effective beyond its apparent literary stature, especially in America, then isolated by war conditions from British thought. It was followed by *Carrying On* (1917) and *The Last Million* (1918). Earlier employed in recruiting, Beith spent 1916–18 in America with the information bureau of the British War Mission where his energy and success were rewarded by a C.B.E. (1918).

In 1919 Beith took up the theatre, living from then on in London, absorbed in its social and theatrical life. He was particularly successful in translating his own novels into plays, among them *A Safety Match* (1921), *Housemaster* (1936), and, perhaps his most successful play, *Tilly of Bloomsbury* (1919, based on his novel *Happy-go-Lucky*, 1913). This has considerable merit and largely through his skill in making small parts interesting has remained an amateurs' favourite. Despite the cynicism and vulgarity of the age, his wit, romanticism, decorous mind, and exceptional theatrical sense kept his plays popular. He proved an excellent collaborator with other writers, among them Anthony Armstrong (*Orders are Orders*, 1932); Guy Bolton (*A Song of Sixpence*, 1930); (Sir) Seymour Hicks (*Good Luck*, 1923); Stephen (later Lord) King-Hall (*The Middle Watch*, 1929, and others); A. E. W. Mason (*A Present from Margate*, 1933); L. du Garde Peach (*The White Sheep of the Family*, 1951); and P. G. Wodehouse (*A Damsel in Distress*, 1928, *Leave it to Psmith*, 1930, and others).

Although Beith's gay theatrical flair was unfaltering, through some curious change in emphasis his later novels never achieved his pre-war success. He eventually failed to adjust and his last works were considered failures. *The King's Service* (1938), an informal history of the army, may have helped him to the directorship of War Office public relations (1938–41) and the rank of major-general, but this and the war cut him off from his public. His tribute to Malta, *The Unconquered Isle* (1943), an attempt at a second *Hundred Thousand*, misjudged the mood of a people who with their own experience of bombing resented his cheerful glossing.

On the lapse of his directorship Beith returned to work in America. After 1945 he wrote semi-official histories, deemed failures, though none is bad; his one serious, and inexplicable, play, *Hattie Stowe* (1947), about Harriet Beecher Stowe, failed, possibly only through an over-large cast.

Beith had apparently enjoyed his London years. He travelled, was chairman of the Society of Authors (1921–4, 1935–9), a member of the council of the League of British Dramatists from 1933, and president of the Dramatists Club from 1937. He was an officer of the Order of St. John of Jerusalem, for long a governor of Guy's Hospital, and gave his services also to St. Dunstan's. A very fine bow shot he was a member of the Queen's Body Guard for Scotland, the Royal Company of Archers, a history of which he wrote in 1951. He was noted for charm, striking personality, equable temperament, after-dinner speeches, and personal austerity. Some observers, however, thought they detected an inner unhappiness; perhaps his essential Calvinism evoked a sense of regret discernible in his own reported remark, bitter though humorously offered, that all his life he had lived on his wits.

In 1915 Beith married Helen Margaret, only daughter of the late Peter Alexander Speirs, of Polmont Park, Stirlingshire; they had no children. He died near Petersfield 22 September 1952. There is a portrait at the Garrick Club by T. C. Dugdale.

[*The Times* and *Scotsman*, 23 September 1952; *The Fettesian*, December 1952; *Fifty Years of Fettes, 1870–1920*, 1931; private information; personal knowledge.]

PATRICK MURRAY

published 1971

BENSON Edward Frederic

(1867–1940)

Author, was born at Wellington College 24 July 1867, the third son of Edward White Benson, afterwards archbishop of Canterbury, by his wife, Mary Sidgwick. He was a younger brother of A. C. Benson and an elder brother of R. H. Benson. He was educated at Marlborough and at King's College, Cambridge, where he was exhibitioner (1888) and scholar (1890); after taking his degree with first classes in both parts of the classical tripos (1890, 1891) he worked in Athens for the British School of Archaeology (1892–1895) and in Egypt for the Society for the Promotion of Hellenic Studies (1895). Latterly he lived for the greater part of each year at Lamb House, Rye, which had been the home of Henry James. He was mayor of Rye from 1934 to 1937. He was elected an honorary fellow of Magdalene College, Cambridge, in 1938. As a young man he was a considerable athlete, particularly as a skater and winter sportsman. He never married; and many of his novels suggest that he had a generalized dislike of women. He died in London 29 February 1940.

As a writer Benson was uncontrollably prolific: he published at least ninety-three books (not counting collaborations), of which about twenty are plays, biographies, sporting or political, and the rest fiction and reminiscences. This was his first misfortune. The second was that his first story, *Dodo* (1893), had a great success. In consequence—because he wrote too much and too quickly, and because the adolescent thrill of being in 'society' matured into a witty and malicious delight in mocking fools and climbers—his genuine talents as a novelist seldom achieved the perfection of form or the permanence of interest of which they were certainly capable. A few of his books are so nearly first rate that the reader becomes regretfully aware that none quite reaches that level. A further result of his easy, careless writing, added to his obsession with the artificialities of socially ambitious women, was that he became repetitive. He would re-use one of his series of groupings, embellishing it with new and amusing dialogue, with new and crushing incidental detail, yet in fact writing the same story two, three, or even four times over.

In one of his books of family recollections Benson claims for himself a retentive, observational memory, even of things hardly noted at the time; and this is perhaps his most remarkable quality. In non-fiction and fiction alike, he shows an extraordinary power of recalling scenes and individuals over the whole period of his adult life. This capacity gives to his works of reminiscence (e.g. *Account Rendered*, 1911; *Our Family Affairs, 1867–1897*, 1920; *As We Were*, 1930; *As We Are*, 1932; *Final Edition*, 1940) real value as sources for social history and personal anecdote, even though the student may hesitate to take them literally. Those of his novels—and they are the majority—which applaud or scarify smart London, or literary, or provincial society, give so strong an impression of carefully distorted portraiture that, just as the 'Dodo' series (*Dodo, Dodo the Second*, 1914, *Dodo Wonders*, 1921) is generally assumed to centre on Margot Tennant, who became Lady Oxford; just as *Secret Lives* (1932), one of his best novels, can hardly have been based on anyone but Marie Corelli; just as the 'Lucia' series (the first two, *Queen Lucia*, 1920, and *Lucia in London*, 1927, are the best) are said to be *romans-à-clef*, so it is natural to suspect real people everywhere. It is hardly worth while to wonder on whom are based the chattering West End exhibitionists in such remembered but inferior books as *Scarlet and Hyssop* (1902), *Sheaves*, and *The Climber* (1908); but the reader might well like to know from whom are derived the more modest provincial *intrigantes* in such far superior stories as *Mrs. Ames* (1912) and *Miss Mapp* (1922).

Apart from social satire Benson made repeated experiments in two other fictional directions. The first comprises stories of public school, university, and immediately post-university life. These are so oversweetened as to be almost intolerable. From the tedious sparkle of *The Babe, B.A.* (1897), an early product of 'dodoism' in undergraduate terms, through the 'Blaize' books to *Colin II* (1925), the tales pile wholesome fun on saccharine sentimentalism, until the reader sickens of the clean-limbed young Apollos, for all the frequent wit with which they are presented. The second group, that of stories of horror and of the supernatural, contains much excellent work. *The Luck of the Vails* (1901) perhaps hardly qualifies, as nearly half of it is a lavish picture of rich, selfish folk, painted with the admiring relish which Benson at this early period undoubtedly felt for persons of the kind; but the second portion of the story is at once dramatic and brilliant, terror and wit being perfectly fused. *The Room in the Tower* (1912) shows him mastering the technique of *macabre* writing, although he still overdoes the details of spendthrift luxury and too often lets the climax of his tale dissolve in sentiment. *Visible and Invisible* (1923) is 'horror' in perfect training, proficient, inventive, but, save in the final story, queerly devoid of feeling. *Spook Stories* (1928) and *More Spook Stories* (1934) mark the closing stages of a highly efficient, coldly unemotional excursion into the realm of ghosts and marvels.

[*The Times*, 1 March 1940; *The Times Literary Supplement*, 9 March 1940; *Final Edition: Informal Autobiography*, 1940; private information.]

MICHAEL SADLEIR

published 1949

BETJEMAN Sir John

(1906–1984)

Poet, writer on architecture, and broadcaster, was born 28 August 1906 at 52 Parliament Hill Mansions, north London, the only child of Ernest Betjemann, a furniture manufacturer, and his wife, Mabel Bessie Dawson. The family name, of Dutch or German origin, can be traced back to an immigration in the late eighteenth century. The poet adopted his style of it about the age of twenty-one.

He attended the Dragon School, Oxford, and Marlborough College and was active at both in school theatricals and in various forms of writing. He entered Magdalen College, Oxford, in 1925 but was rusticated three years later after failing in divinity. To his father's deep disappointment he declined to enter the family business, becoming successively a preparatory school master (at Thorpe House School, Gerrard's Cross, and at Heddon Court, Cockfosters, Hertfordshire), assistant editor of the *Architectural Review* in 1930, and film critic of the London *Evening Standard* in 1933. Shortly after his marriage that year he moved to a farmhouse in Uffington, in the Vale of White Horse, Berkshire, where his wife was able to keep horses.

His first two collections of poems, *Mount Zion* (1931) and *Continual Dew* (1937), showed a poet already fully formed, with the impeccable ear, delight in skill, and assured mastery of a wide range of tones and themes that so distinguished all his subsequent work in verse. In these early volumes, as later, Betjeman moved with perfect assurance from light pieces, *vers de société*, satirical sketches of muscular padres or philistine businessmen (as in the famously ferocious tirade 'Slough') to sombre reflections on the impermanence of all human things. In a remarkable variety of metres and manners the poems make an equally clear-cut impression on the reader, never drifting into obscurity and never once tainted with the modernism then fashionable. Here too he gave glimpses of the world of gas-lit Victorian churches and railway stations, of grim provincial cities and leafy suburbs that he was to make his own, not forgetting the grimmer contemporary developments, shopping arcades, and bogus Tudor bars, that he saw effacing it and strove to resist.

These concerns are reflected in his publication of 1933, *Ghastly Good Taste*, subtitled 'a depressing story of the rise and fall of English architecture', which attracted more immediate attention than either of his first books of poems. In it he attacked not only modern or modernistic trends but also the other extreme of unthinking antiquarianism, nor had he any time for the safely conventional. While still at school he had become interested in Victorian architecture, thoroughly unmodish as it was at the time. His writings on the subject over the years led to a revival in appreciation of the buildings of that era and paved the way for the eventual founding of the successful Victorian Society. Further afield, he showed among other things his fondness for provincial architecture in his contributions to the Shell series of English county guides, of which the most notable is that on Cornwall, another enthusiasm acquired in boyhood. He had joined the publicity department of Shell in the mid-1930s.

Betjeman's poetical career had begun to flourish with the appearance in 1940 of *Old Lights for New Chancels* and continued with *New Bats in Old Belfries* (1945) and *A Few Late Chrysanthemums* (1954). Many of the poems in these three volumes became classics of their time, including 'Pot Pourri from a Surrey Garden', 'A Subaltern's Love-song' and 'How to Get On in Society'. His *Collected Poems* came out in 1958 and went through many impressions. *Summoned by Bells* is dated 1960, a blank-verse poem of some 2,000 lines that gives an account of his early life up to schoolmastering days with characteristic animation, humour, sadness, and abundance of detail.

Both these volumes were widely successful, the first edition of the *Collected Poems* selling over 100,000 copies. Betjeman's poetry has continued to enjoy a popularity unknown in this country since the days of Rudyard Kipling and A. E. Housman. No doubt it was poems like the three mentioned above and the more obviously quaint period pieces that made an immediate appeal. Nor should one underestimate the sheer relief and delight to be felt at the appearance of a poetry of contemporary date that was easy to follow and yielded the almost forgotten pleasures of rhyme and metre expertly handled. Nevertheless it may not be instantly obvious how so strongly personal a poet, one given moreover to evoking characters and places that might seem outside general interest, should have proved so welcome. He is full of nasty jolts for the squeamish too.

The answer must lie in the closeness of the concerns of Betjeman's poetry to the ordinary day-to-day experience of his readers, something else that had been far to seek in the work of his contemporaries. For all the delight in the past, it is the past as seen from and against the present; for all the cherished eccentricities—as such hardly repugnant to British taste anyway—the subject is ourselves and our own world. The point was well made by Philip Larkin, the friend and admirer who best understood his work: 'He offers us something we cannot find in any other writer—a gaiety, a sense of the ridiculous, an affection for human beings and how and where they live, a vivid and vivacious portrait of mid-twentieth-century English social life' (Philip Larkin, 'It Could Only Happen in England', 1971, in *Required Writing*, 1983, pp. 204–18).

In World War II Betjeman volunteered for the RAF but was rejected and joined the films division of the Ministry of Information. He then became UK press attaché in Dublin (1941–3) to Sir John Maffey (later Lord Rugby) and subsequently worked in P branch (a secret department) in the Admiralty, Bath. In 1945 he moved to Farnborough and in 1951 to Wantage where his wife opened a tea shop, King Alfred's Kitchen. By the mid-1950s his main income came from book reviewing, broadcasting, and his poems. He pursued a highly successful career as a broadcaster, and with the help of the image he projected through television, engaging, diffident, exuberant, often launched on some architectural or decorative enthusiasm, he became a celebrated and much-loved figure in national life. He used this position to further zealously the defence of many buildings threatened with demolition. He was able to save many of these, from St Pancras station to Sweeting's fish restaurant in the City of London, though the Euston Arch was lost despite his vigorous campaign. Appropriately, it was at St Pancras, naming a British Rail locomotive after himself, that he was to make his last public appearance on 24 June 1983.

In later years Betjeman continued his work in poetry, publishing *High and Low* in 1966 and *A Nip in the Air* in 1974. The contents of these two volumes reveal no loss of energy; indeed, poems like 'On Leaving Wantage 1972' embody a melancholy, even a tragic, power he had never surpassed. All the same, apart from the ebulliently satirical 'Executive', almost none of them have achieved much individual popularity. They were incorporated entire in the fourth edition of the *Collected Poems* in 1979. Those in *Uncollected Poems* (1982) were such as the poet was content should remain in that state and are unlikely to gain him many new readers, though lovers of his work would not be without any of them.

No account of Betjeman's life could fail to stress his devoted adherence to the Anglican Church, not only for the sake of its buildings, its liturgy, and its worshippers but for its faith. Expressions of doubt and the fear of old age and death are strong and memorable in his poetry, but 'Church of England thoughts' are pervasive too, and one of its chief attractions, seldom given proper weight, has been the sense of an undemonstrative but deep Christian belief of a kind able to contain the harsh, ugly, absurd realities of present-day existence.

John Betjeman was a sociable man, one who loved company and valued it the more for being also a shy man. Although he was renowned for his youthful gregariousness and was endlessly affable with all manner of people, his was a life rich in intimacy. Latterly he was partial to small gatherings and old friends and a sufficiency of wine. His expression in repose was timid, perhaps not altogether at ease, and even at the best of times it was possible to surprise on his face a look of great dejection. But all this was blown away in an instant by laughter of a totality that warmed all who knew him. His presence, like his work in verse and prose, was full of the enjoyment he felt and gave.

He was chosen as poet laureate to universal acclaim in 1972. He received many distinctions besides, being awarded the Duff Cooper memorial prize, the Foyle poetry prize, and in 1960 the Queen's medal for poetry. In that year too he was appointed CBE, in 1968 he was elected a Companion of Literature by the Royal Society of Literature, and in 1969 he was knighted. He was an honorary fellow of his old college, Magdalen (1975), and also of Keble College, Oxford (1972). He had honorary degrees from Oxford, Reading, Birmingham, Exeter, City University, Liverpool, Hull, and Trinity College, Dublin. He was also honorary ARIBA.

In 1933 he married Penelope Valentine Hester, only daughter of Field-Marshal Sir Philip Walhouse Chetwode, first Baron Chetwode, OM, commander-in-chief in India at the time. In latter years they were amicably separated and Betjeman was cared for by his friend Lady Elizabeth Cavendish, sister of the Duke of Devonshire. Lady Betjeman, a writer of travel books (as Penelope Chetwode) and a devotee of Indian culture, died in 1986. There were a son and a daughter of the marriage. From the mid-1970s Betjeman had suffered increasingly from the onset of Parkinson's disease and he died at Treen, his home in Trebetherick, Cornwall, 19 May 1984. He is buried in nearby St Enodoc churchyard.

[*The Times*, 21 May 1984; Bevis Hillier, *John Betjeman: a Life in Pictures*, 1984, and *Young Betjeman*, 1988; personal knowledge.]

KINGSLEY AMIS

published 1990

BLAIR Eric Arthur
(1903–1950)

Author, known under the pseudonym of George Orwell, was born at Motihari, Bengal, 25 June 1903, the only son of Richard Walmesley Blair, of the Bengal Civil Service, and his wife, Ida Mabel Limouzin. On leaving Eton, where he was a King's scholar, in 1921, he went not to a university but to Burma to serve in the Imperial Police, but after five years he returned to Europe and set himself with extraordinary conscientiousness to learn the facts of poverty by experience, as a dish-washer in Paris and as a tramp in England. He described this later in his first book, *Down and Out in Paris and London* (1933). He next worked as a schoolmaster and as a bookseller's assistant and during this period he wrote three novels. The best of these, *Burmese Days* (1935), is an able and bitter analysis of social strains in Burma in the early 'twenties. A later novel, *Coming up for Air* (1939), makes a high-spirited defence of the small man in the toils of big business, standardization, and urbanization.

From 1937 onwards Orwell's political thought, an unorthodox and very individual Socialism, was developed through *The Road to Wigan Pier* (1937), *Homage to Catalonia* (1938), *The Lion and the Unicorn* (1941), and *Animal Farm* (1945) to an apocalyptic vision of doom in *Nineteen Eighty-Four* which was published in 1949. It is on these books and on his literary essays that his reputation chiefly stands. Just as his character combined adventurousness with a love of peaceful country pursuits, so his mind was both libertarian and tradition-loving, but these divergent and sometimes conflicting tendencies were fused together by a passionate generosity and love of justice which illuminate his best work with a flash of genius. Although his books were influential from about 1938 onwards he remained poor until near the end of his life.

Satire was his best medium, although if he had lived longer he might have gone beyond it, for he had also a poetic gift. But the political fable, *Animal Farm*, the form of which was influenced by the *Tale of a Tub*, remains his most technically perfect work. His polemical writing was virile and fearlessly honest, although not without an occasional touch of extravagance and perversity. Among the objects of his attack were capitalism, pacifism, spiritualism, Roman Catholicism, and the servile state, whether Fascist, Socialist, or Communist; and as a result of his experiences in the Spanish civil war, in which he was severely wounded, fighting as a Socialist militiaman, he became one of the most formidable and best-equipped critics of Stalinism. But it is in his literary essays, on Dickens and

Kipling for example (*Critical Essays*, 1946), that the more conservative and traditional aspects of his thought are seen at their best.

Orwell was twice married: first, in 1936 to Eileen Maud (died 1945), daughter of the late Laurence O'Shaughnessy, of the Inland Revenue; and secondly, in 1949 to Sonia Mary, daughter of Charles Neville Brownell, a business man in India. He was survived by an adopted son. He died in London, 21 January 1950, after a long struggle against consumption.

[*The Times*, 23 January 1950; Ian Willison, *George Orwell: Some materials for a bibliography*, in the Library of London University; private information; personal knowledge.]

R. REES

published 1959

BLYTON Enid Mary

(1897–1968)

Writer for children, was born 11 August 1897 at Lordship Lane, East Dulwich, London, the eldest child in a family of one girl and two boys of Thomas Carey Blyton, a businessman of modest means, formerly of Sheffield and then of London, and his wife, Theresa Mary Harrison. He was ambitious for her to be a concert pianist and she studied hard for many years, taking her LRAM at an early age. But after he had left the family house to live with another woman—an event that must have psychologically affected Enid who was then thirteen and loved him deeply—she gradually dropped her studies and took to writing poems and stories. Educated at St. Christopher's School for Girls (1907–15), where she became head girl in 1913, she subsequently spent some months studying music, and in 1916 she began to train as a teacher at Ipswich, where she studied the Froebel and Montessori methods for teaching the young—a training that influenced her writing techniques in later years. Having completed the course by December 1918, in 1919 she went to teach at Bickley Park School in Kent and the following year became nursery governess in Surbiton to a family of four young boys and the children of neighbours.

In the last decade of her life, she often claimed to have papered her bedroom with rejection slips from magazine and book publishers but her surviving diaries of those formative writing years tell a story of early and ever-growing success. At the age of fourteen she had published a poem in one of the children's papers of Arthur Mee, and in March 1917 *Nash's Magazine* published one of her poems. In 1921 and 1922 various short stories and poems appeared in the *Saturday Westminster Review*, the *Bystander*, the *Londoner, Passing Show*, and other magazines of the period. Her first book, *Child Whispers*, a collection of poems, was published in 1922 and in the next year she earned well over £300 from her published work. In 1924 the total exceeded £500 and in 1925 over £1,200—a substantial income for any contemporary author. By then she had given up her teaching work.

In 1924 she married Major Hugh Alexander Pollock, DSO, the son of an antique bookseller in Ayr. After a distinguished army career in the war of 1914–18, in 1923 Pollock had become editor of the book department at Newnes, the magazine and book publishers. Pollock had been married before, but his wife had left him during the war. He submitted Enid's books to his employers and also arranged for her to write and edit *Sunny Stories*, a new weekly publication with which she was to be associated for nearly a quarter of a century. They had two daughters, Gillian, born in 1931, and Imogen, born in 1937. But by the outbreak of war in 1939 the relationship was already under strain and Hugh Pollock's later absences on military duties increased the pressures. In 1942 they were divorced and six months later, in 1943, Enid married a middle-aged London surgeon, Kenneth Fraser Darrell Waters (died 1967). The second marriage was a happy and harmonious one. Darrell Waters, whose first marriage had been childless, looked on Enid's daughters as his own; their names were eventually changed to Darrell Waters by deed poll.

By the mid 1930s, Enid Blyton had got into the prolific stride which she maintained for a further thirty years. In 1935 she published six different titles and in 1940 eleven titles and two under the pseudonym 'Mary Pollock' emerged from her facile pen: or rather, from her portable typewriter. She had the habit of typing on a sunny veranda at her home, Green Hedges, in Beaconsfield, Buckinghamshire, with a portable typewriter on her knees and a shawl around her shoulders. Ten thousand words a day was a good cruising speed and she was known to complete a full-length book for children between a Monday and a Friday of the same week. So vast was her output that her books were rumoured to be created by a team of ghostwriters. The rumours were baseless. With the help of her immense energy, years of practice, and a vast if quiet self-confidence, she would tell close friends that she could sit down with the typewriter on her knees, think of a compelling opening sentence, and then go off into a trance-like state while the story flowed from her imagination through her nimble fingers on to the page. When this became public knowledge, unkind critics maintained that the resulting story read as though the author had indeed been in a trance at the time of writing.

Because of paper-rationing during the war of 1939–45, Enid Blyton's output was too prolific to be confined to one publisher. By the early fifties, she had close on forty British publishers. At the end of her active writing career around 1965, she had published over four hundred different titles, many of which had also appeared in translation in about twenty different languages or dialects—from Afrikaans to Swahili, as she was proud to claim. The English-speaking sales alone (1977) were in excess of two hundred million copies and, nearly ten years after her death, were increasing at the rate of about five million copies per year. She was the first major children's author to appear in paperback editions and in 1977 over one hundred of her individual titles were continually in print. She deliberately wrote, in the language of every age-group, for children from five to fifteen, so that those who discovered her works when very young would remain faithful for the next decade.

She became a well-known author in the 1940s with her *Famous Five* and *Secret Seven* stories, and her *Adventure* series, but in 1949 she became a major public figure with the creation of Little Noddy. One day she called on a publisher and was shown some original line and colour drawings depicting puppet figures by a Dutch artist named Harmsen van der Beek. At once she began to weave names, stories, and a continuing background for the characters depicted—Little Noddy, Big Ears, Mr Plod the policeman, and the other characters of Toyland Village. Noddy and his friends were not only immensely successful in book form—the sales ran into several million copies—but manufacturers rushed to produce Noddy dolls, Noddy toothpaste, Noddy pyjamas, and Noddy drawings on cereal packets. There was a very popular 'Noddy in Toyland' pantomime for children each Christmas and fifty-two Noddy puppet films shown weekly on commercial television.

Such a huge popular success was bound to create an adverse reaction in certain quarters. Literary articles were published which criticized the moral qualities inherent in Enid Blyton's work. Some librarians banned her works from public libraries on the grounds that the simple prose style and black-and-white moralizing in the plots deterred young children from reading books with more subtle literary values. The simple and incontrovertible answer was that the children themselves *wanted* to read her books and continued to do so in ever-increasing numbers.

Although she produced several hundred thousand words every year, conducted an immense correspondence by postcard with her many young fans, edited and wrote the *Enid Blyton Magazine*, actively supported charities for children, and ran the domestic household at Green Hedges, up to the last fifteen years of her life Enid Blyton did not use the services of a literary agent for her voluminous and intricate publishing affairs. She dealt with a variety of British and foreign publishers and with her incisive business mind always drove a good bargain. She would never accept an advance payment on account of royalties but insisted that the minimum printing of each book should be twenty-five thousand copies. She also insisted on having complete control over the choice of artist for the dust-jacket and illustrations: the publisher who erred once in presenting in-different art-work to her never did so twice.

As a famous writer who for many years enjoyed an annual income of well over £100,000, Enid Blyton was quiet and unostentatious in her private life. She shunned publicity and often wrote to literary editors asking them not to review her books but to devote the space to up-and-coming authors. Once her legal advisers took action because of a humorous remark about her in 1952 on the *Take it From Here* radio programme on the BBC. She saw life in simple, unshaded terms and sensed from her early teaching days that young children prefer certainty and the familiar in their reading tastes. Her monument remains on the shelves of bookshops and libraries.

In her prime, Enid Blyton was a woman of striking appearance— somewhat above average in height, with dark, curly hair and eloquent dark eyes, a longish nose, and ruddy complexion. She was handsome in a Spanish gypsy style rather than conventionally pretty and, although she was not well versed in social small talk, she would light up and become the focus of any conversation that settled on her favourite topics—children, her books for and about them, and the publishers who helped to introduce the former to the latter. She died in a Hampstead nursing home, 28 November 1968. There is a portrait in oils by Derek Houston, which is in the possession of the family.

[Barbara Stoney, *Enid Blyton*, 1974; Enid Blyton, *The Story of My Life*, 1952; personal knowledge.]

GEORGE GREENFIELD

published 1981

BOWEN Elizabeth Dorothea Cole

(1899–1973)

Writer, was born 7 June 1899 in Dublin, the only child of Henry Charles Cole Bowen, barrister, of Bowen's Court, Kildorrery, county Cork, and his wife, Florence Isabella Pomeroy, third of the ten children of Henry Fitz-George Colley, of Mount Temple, Dublin. She was educated at Harpenden Hall School, Hertfordshire, and Downe House, Kent.

She spent the summers of early childhood at Bowen's Court—the house completed by her ancestor, Henry Bowen, in 1775. The first Bowen to settle in county Cork had come over from Wales with Cromwell's army. Elizabeth Bowen set down the history of her family and of the house in *Bowen's Court* (1942). Winters were spent in the pre-World War I Dublin nostalgically evoked by her in *Seven Winters* (1942). When she was seven her father suffered a severe nervous breakdown; she and her mother, on his doctors' advice, moved to England. Her lifelong stammer dated from this family upheaval. They lived happily enough in rented holiday houses on the Kent coast, an area for which she retained a lasting affection, until when she was thirteen her mother died of cancer, in Hythe: she never fully recovered from this loss, which is reflected in the sense of displacement experienced by many of the child characters in her fiction. After her mother's death, 'Bitha', as she was known in the family, was brought up by what she called 'a committee of aunts'. The holidays of her adolescence and young womanhood were spent with her father—now recovered and remarried, to Mary Gwynn—at Bowen's Court, a period of her life on which she later drew for her novel *The Last September* (1929), in which the house 'Danielstown' is based on Bowen's Court.

In 1923 she married Alan Charles Cameron, an educationist, then assistant secretary for education for Northamptonshire. Born in 1893, he had seen action on the Somme and in Italy, and had been awarded the MC. Her first book, the collection of short stories entitled *Encounters*, was published in the year that she married, and her first novel, *The Hotel*, in 1927. In 1925 Alan Cameron was appointed secretary for education for the city of Oxford, and they moved to the house called Waldencote in Old Headington. In Oxford she made important friendships with the Tweedsmuirs (John, and Susan Buchan), Lord David Cecil, Sir Isaiah Berlin, Sir Maurice Bowra and his circle, and had a considerable personal success. In 1935, the year she published *The House in Paris*, her husband's work—now with the central council of the BBC's schools broadcasting service—brought them to London. In London, at 2 Clarence Terrace,

Regent's Park, she established herself as a hospitable and frequent party-giver. The dinner guests, like the afternoon callers, were her own friends from the artistic and literary worlds—including Bloomsbury, and with a constant leaven of Colley cousins from Ireland—rather than her husband's. But the marriage was an affectionate and stable one, although childless, and in spite of her greater fame and her close friendships with, at different times, Humphry House, Goronwy Rees, Sean O'Faolain and, lastingly, the Canadian diplomat Charles Ritchie.

The best-known novels of her London period, in which she makes Regent's Park her own literary territory, are *The Death of the Heart* (1938) and *The Heat of the Day* (1949), a war novel that was her greatest commercial success both in Britain and in the United States. She remained in London throughout World War II, working as an ARP warden and returning to Ireland from time to time chiefly to provide reports for the Ministry of Information on the Irish political climate. Some of her finest short stories, many of them touching on the supernatural, are set in blitz-torn London. After the war she was one of the two women members of the royal commission on capital punishment.

In 1930, on the death of her father, she had inherited Bowen's Court, where she entertained English, Irish, and American friends during holiday periods. After the war she and her husband made Bowen's Court their permanent home; and there, in 1952, Alan Cameron died. She had the support of close friends in Ireland—notably at this time Edward Sackville-West (Lord Sackville), who had settled nearby at Clogheen—but she was unable to keep up the big old house on her own in spite of successful lecture tours for the British Council and in the United States, periods as writer-in-residence at American universities, and a great deal of journalism. In 1959, in New York, she was unwell and under stress; on her return, she sold up the property in some haste. The new owner, being interested only in the land and the timber, demolished the house at once.

She returned to live in England—first in Oxford, and then in a small modern house in Hythe. She returned regularly to Ireland, generally staying with Lady Ursula Vernon at Kinsale: she wrote the narrative for a pageant on Kinsale's history, performed there in 1965.

She was a large-boned, handsome woman, classically Anglo-Irish, caught between two worlds; Churchillian in her politics, staunchly Anglican in her religion, conventional in her social attitudes and demeanour. In Headington, she had enjoyed belonging to the Women's Institute. Yet she was also thoroughly Celtic in her imaginative range, her basic secretiveness, and her sense of the spirit of place. She had a love of talk, a talent for intimacy, and a hankering after the bizarre and the vulgar: she described herself as 'farouche'. She enjoyed intense friendships with country neighbours of no social pretension in Ireland just as she did with literati in London and New York, but she kept her relationships in separate compartments. She never lost her stammer and was always a little shy and self-concealing, preferring to be introduced as 'Mrs Cameron'.

She published twenty-seven books in her lifetime, which include travel (notably *A Time in Rome*, 1960), criticism, reminiscence, and history, but it is for her novels and short stories that she will be remembered. She was adept at tracing in her fictions what she called 'the cracks in the surface of life'—the displacements, shocks, and shifts of feeling that take place beneath a controlled, conventional exterior. Sometimes her style is excessively convoluted and 'Jamesian'; sometimes it is subtly precise, taking sensitive perception to a point further than anyone except her friend Virginia Woolf. During and after the war, the class structure and codes of accepted behaviour on which her themes largely depended were eroded, and her preoccupations seemed to lose some of their significance. She charted the disintegration of the world she had known in the wartime short story 'The Disinherited'. *A World of Love* (1955) was the last novel she wrote in her old-established mode; in her final two novels, *The Little Girls* (1964) and *Eva Trout* (1969), which won the James Tait Black memorial prize, she was breaking new ground, but had neither the time nor the strength left to her to consolidate new approaches and techniques.

She was appointed CBE in 1948 and C.Lit. in 1965. She was a member of the Irish Academy of Letters and received honorary D.Litts. from Trinity College, Dublin (1949), and Oxford (1956). In 1972 lung cancer was diagnosed—she was a heavy smoker—and she died in University College Hospital, London, 22 February 1973. She is buried beside her father and husband in Farahy churchyard, which adjoins the Bowen's Court demesne.

[Victoria Glendinning, *Elizabeth Bowen: Portrait of a Writer*, 1977.]

VICTORIA GLENDINNING

published 1986

BRIDGES Robert Seymour

(1844–1930)

Poet laureate, was born at Walmer 23 October 1844, the fourth son and eighth of nine children of John Thomas Bridges, only son of John Bridges, of St. Nicholas Court, Isle of Thanet. His mother was Harriet Elizabeth, third daughter of the Rev. Sir Robert Affleck, at the time of the marriage (1829) vicar of Silkstone, Yorkshire, who in 1833 succeeded a cousin as fourth baronet and afterwards lived at Dalham Hall, Suffolk. The Bridges family had been substantial yeomen in the Isle of Thanet since the sixteenth century, descending from the Rev. John Bridges or Brydges (died 1590), rector of Harbledown 1579–1589. At the end of the eighteenth century the family belonged to the class of which Edward Hasted (*History . . . of Kent*, vol. iv, 291, 1799) says: 'The farms throughout the island are mostly large and considerable, and the farmers wealthy, insomuch that they are usually denominated *gentlemen farmers* on that account, as well as from their hospitable and substantial mode of living.' Most of the family property came into the hands of Robert Bridges's grandfather and so to his father, and was sold under the will of the latter, who died in 1853 at the age of forty-seven when Robert was only nine years old. Thus Robert grew up under no necessity of earning a livelihood.

During Bridges's childhood the family lived at his father's house, Roselands, Walmer, which afterwards became a convent. This period is recalled by two of his poems, 'The Summer House on the Mound' (*New Poems*, 1899) and 'Kate's Mother' written in 1921 (*New Verse*, 1926), and by many pictures and touches, especially in the *Shorter Poems*, of the sea, sky, cliffs, birds, and flowers of the south coast. The year after his father's death his mother became the second wife of the Rev. John Edward Nassau Molesworth, vicar of Rochdale, Lancashire, and the vicarage was thenceforth Robert's home. Meantime, in September 1854, before he was ten years old, he had been sent to Eton, where he remained for nine years, and in his last winter played in the Oppidans' wall and field elevens. Eton, especially its river, trees, and meadows, St. George's chapel at Windsor with its music, and the companionship of eager, high-souled youth, fed and confirmed the inborn aesthetic sensibility and mental energy which distinguished Bridges throughout his life. During his later school years his mind was exercised by religious problems and drawn towards 'Puseyite' views, principally by his contemporary, Vincent Stuckey Stratton Coles, 'pre-eminent' among his schoolboy friends 'for his precocious theological bent and devotion to *the cause*' [Bridges's memoir prefixed to *Poems of D. M. Dolben*, 1911]. In January 1862 Bridges's distant cousin, young Digby Mackworth Dolben, arrived at Eton, already passionately and poetically religious. Bridges was captain of his house and befriended Dolben, who in his turn both intensely admired his elder cousin and eagerly sought to convert him to his own enthusiasms, above all to the dream of founding an Anglican 'Brotherhood', of which Bridges writes: 'He was to decide everything, and I, who was to be the head of the community, could never of course disagree with him.'

Bridges

Bridges was immune to theological dogmas, but equally alive both to the beauty of holiness and to the holiness of beauty; hence his affection for and at the same time independence of such friends as Dolben and Gerard Manley Hopkins, whose acquaintance he made at Oxford, whither he proceeded as a commoner of Corpus Christi College in October 1863. Hopkins entered Balliol College as an exhibitioner the same term, and they both took honours in *literae humaniores* in 1867; Hopkins obtained a first class in Trinity term, Bridges a second class in Michaelmas term. Bridges was a distinguished oarsman, stroked the Corpus boat as second on the river in 1867 and again the same summer in a regatta at Paris, which, to his distress, coincided with the death of Dolben from heart-failure while bathing in the river Welland.

During his undergraduate career Bridges was, as he records (*op. cit.*), 'drifting fast away' from 'the religious sympathies' of his Eton days, and becoming more interested in philosophy and natural science. In February 1866 his younger brother Edward died. They had been mutually devoted. Writing of Dolben's monastic dreams he says: 'The only definite plan of this kind which had seriously influenced me was an understanding between my younger brother and myself that we would always live together; and such was our affection that I think now [1909] that nothing but his early death could have prevented its realization.' Of this event he writes that it 'plunged me into deep sorrow at the time and considerably altered the hopes and prospects of my life'; and it was probably about this time that he resolved to study medicine. He had no intention of making this his lifelong profession; he pursued it mainly for the sake of knowledge and human experience; and he was so far from concentrating on his medical training that he spent much of his time both before and after being entered as a student at St. Bartholomew's Hospital (November 1869) in travel and literary studies abroad. Thus he travelled in Egypt and Syria and then, after an interval at home, spent eight months studying German in Germany with William Sanday, who had entered Balliol as a commoner in 1862, became scholar of Corpus in 1863, and a fellow of Trinity College in 1866. He also made a tour in the Netherlands and was twice in France for some months, spending one winter in Paris. In 1874 he went to Italy for six months with his lifelong friend, Harry Ellis Wooldridge, afterwards Slade professor of fine art at Oxford, and to whose wide and accurate knowledge and discriminating taste in literature and the fine arts, especially music, Bridges gratefully acknowledged his indebtedness.

From his schooldays Bridges had been devoted to music and poetry; but, unlike most young poets, he was in no hurry to take the world into his confidence. He preserved affectionate letters from Hopkins, beginning in 1865, in which the latter writes of religion, music, and even his own poems.

Yet apparently Hopkins was unaware that Bridges wrote poetry at all until, in January 1874, he came upon Andrew Lang's review of Bridges's first published volume [C. C. Abbott, *Letters of G. M. Hopkins*, i, 29]. Bridges writes of his later schooldays: 'My own boyish muse was being silenced [1862–3] by my reading of the great poets. . . . What had led me to poetry was the inexhaustible satisfaction of form, the magic of speech, lying as it seemed to me in the masterly control of the material: it was an art which I hoped to learn' [*Memoir* of Dolben]. The whole passage is most significant for any appreciation of Bridges as a poetic artist. Evidently this hope was one great motive in his studies of French, German, and Italian literature, and the last-named particularly left distinct traces upon his own poetry. But whatever verses he wrote before his thirtieth year, hardly any of them ever saw the light. Of his first volume, published in 1873, he himself wrote that he 'went to the seaside [Seaford] for two weeks and wrote it there'. It was greeted with a long and appreciative review by Andrew Lang in the *Academy* of 17 January 1874; but far from courting the *popularis aura* Bridges issued nothing more in his own name for ten years except a *jeu d'esprit* in Latin elegiacs for his friends at St. Bartholomew's Hospital in 1876 and a contribution to a brochure, *The Garland of Rachel*, privately printed in 1881 by his friend Charles Henry Olive Daniel, afterwards provost of Worcester College, Oxford. Meantime, in 1876, he published anonymously *The Growth of Love; A Poem in Twenty-four Sonnets*, which was in great measure the fruit of his six months in Italy. Of these sonnets ten were dropped from subsequent editions, while six were much rewritten, and many new ones added.

Bridges actually began his medical course at St. Bartholomew's Hospital in 1871 and graduated M.B. in 1874. He was house physician for one year (1875–1876) to Dr. Patrick Black, for whom he had great admiration and to whom he dedicated his Latin poem, of 558 lines, 'De Nosocomio Sti. Bartolomaei'. In 1877 he was appointed casualty physician, a post which he held for two years; and he contributed a trenchant 'Account of the Casualty Department' to the Hospital *Reports* of 1878, in which he recorded that he had seen 30,940 patients in the course of one year with an average of 1·28 minutes given to each case, and had ordered over 200,000 doses of medicine containing iron. In 1878 Bridges was appointed assistant physician to the Hospital for Sick Children, Great Ormond Street, and afterwards to the Great Northern Hospital in Holloway. His skill and acumen would have carried him far, but he intended to retire at the age of forty, and even while in medical practice must have found a good deal of time for his favourite studies. Thus he published in 1879 and 1880 two more sheaves of lyrical *Poems, by the author of the Growth of Love*, which were cordially, though not widely, noticed, the *Academy* reviewer complaining of his 'cryptic, scrappy' method of publication and, while praising his freshness and technical perfection, somewhat deprecating his 'experiments in a new prosody'.

In London Bridges lived first at 50 Maddox Street with Wooldridge, and after Dr. Molesworth's death in 1877 made a home for his mother at 52 Bedford Square. In June 1881 his medical career was ended by an attack of pneumonia and empyema, from the effects of which he did not recover for eighteen months. In November he went to spend the winter in Italy and Sicily, and on his return in 1882 took his mother to live at the Manor House, Yattendon, Berkshire. Here, in 1884, he married Monica, eldest daughter of his neighbour, the architect Alfred Waterhouse—a union in which the poet's charm and spiritual distinction were well mated with his wife's, and his welfare guarded by her unselfish devotion, a devotion extended to the careful editing of his prose writings after his death.

During the next few years Bridges's one son and two daughters were born; and at Yattendon he lived until 1904, pursuing poetry and music and congenial friendships with gusto, and producing, in collaboration with Wooldridge and with the friendly consent of the rector of Yattendon, Henry Charles Beeching, afterwards dean of Norwich, 'The Yattendon Hymnal' (1895–1899), which was influential in the contemporary reform of hymnody and the revival of sixteenth- and seventeenth-century music. Here, too, he wrote his eight dramas and quasi-dramas and his one long narrative poem, *Eros and Psyche* (1885), a version of Apuleius, as well as many lyrics, odes for music such as that in honour of Henry Purcell, and the first of his poems in quantitative verse, 'Now in wintry delights' and 'No ethical system' (1903). In 1887 he contributed an essay 'On the elements of Milton's Blank Verse in *Paradise Lost*' to Beeching's edition of the first book of that poem, and he followed this up in 1889 with a brief pamphlet *On the Prosody of Paradise Regained and Samson Agonistes*. Little noticed at the time, this masterly and original work was republished with additions in 1893, reviewed with insight by Laurence Binyon in the *Academy* of 10 March 1894 and, together with Bridges's practice as a poet, was the real inauguration of a new development of English verse, in which the natural accentuation of the phrase was to reassert itself, producing a fresh flexibility of rhythm, and requiring for success a highly sensitive discrimination of sounds. Bridges constantly discussed these matters with friends, most fruitfully in earlier years with Hopkins and afterwards with W. J. Stone, whose tract on *Classical Metres in English Verse* (1899) excited his keenest interest. After Stone's premature death, Bridges added this tract, together with his own criticism, to an enlarged edition of *Milton's Prosody* (1901); and he further treated the subject in *Ibant Obscuri* (*New Quarterly*, ii,

January 1909 and Clarendon Press 1916), in his edition of the *Poems* of G. M. Hopkins (1918), and elsewhere.

From the first Bridges was justly appreciated by contemporary and younger men of letters, as reviews by Andrew Lang, William Watson, and J. W. Mackail testify. In 1895 he was invited by a strong list of supporters to stand for election to the chair of poetry at Oxford. This he declined to do; and he made no efforts to get his plays acted, although he wrote *Demeter*, a masque, for the students of Somerville College, Oxford, to perform at the opening of their new library in June 1904. In 1905–1906 he spent nine months in Switzerland for the sake of his wife's health, and in 1907 settled at Chilswell House, which he built on Boar's Hill overlooking Oxford. He published little during his earlier years there, but a one-volume edition of his *Poems*, excluding the plays, was issued in 1912. When, in 1913, he was appointed poet laureate, the general reading public was surprised, although little interested in an office reduced again to insignificance by its last holder, Alfred Austin, whose appointment had probably been a mere reward for political journalism. The prime minister, Mr. Asquith, unlike Lord Salisbury, was interested in literature; but certainly the popular voice would have acclaimed Rudyard Kipling—and still more so when only a year later the country was plunged into the European War. Bridges wrote about twenty poems concerned with the War, most of which were collected in his volume *October and other poems* (1920); few of them would be preserved apart from his more congenial work.

Bridges's artistic and musical bent had long inclined him to an interest in English pronunciation and spelling as well as prosody. He experimented in spelling in successive issues of his poetry, thereby delaying the recognition of its real poetic quality while proving the sincerity of his purpose. As early as 1900 he broached to Henry Bradley a scheme for introducing 'an aesthetic phonetic script so like our present literary spelling and writing that any one with common education could read it', and he published his scheme in 1910 (*English Association Essays*, vol. i). In 1926 he began to introduce his new 'symbols' in a series of reprints of his essays, which was continued by Mrs. Bridges after his death. In 1913 he founded the Society for Pure English in concert with Bradley, Sir Walter Raleigh, and Logan Pearsall Smith, though the War postponed its activity until 1919. For the rest of his life this was, after poetry, Bridges's principal public interest. 'From the beginning he planned its policy, chose its collaborators, and guided its destiny, and wrote its most important papers' [*S.P.E. Tracts*, no. xxxv, p. 500]. His principal confidants were Mrs. Bridges (in this as in other matters), Pearsall Smith, and Bradley, whom Bridges called the 'mainstay' of the Society, since 'though he never wrote any entire article for it, he passed and censored all its publications'.

These last words are quoted from a *Memoir* of Henry Bradley, one of the few but, in their kind, perfect appreciations which Bridges wrote. Three of these were memorials of intimate friends, R. W. Dixon (1909), D. M. Dolben (1911), and Bradley (1926), reissued in one volume, *Three Friends* (1932): another of special note was *John Keats, a critical essay*, written in 1894 (privately printed in 1895) as an introduction to G. Thorn Drury's edition of the *Poems* (1896). He wrote other occasional articles and lectures, always in a style which, without affectation, was strongly personal. In 1916 he compiled *The Spirit of Man*, a collection of passages in prose and verse 'designed to bring fortitude and peace of mind to his countrymen in war time'. This admirable and successful anthology was especially remarkable for the prominence given to Aristotle and Shelley, than whom no two authors influenced Bridges more, the one by his robust and magisterial reasoning, the other by his impassioned sense of beauty and joy.

In 1924 Bridges and his wife spent three months at Ann Arbor as guests of the university of Michigan, and in the same year his eightieth birthday was marked by the gift, from a distinguished group of admirers, of a clavichord made for the occasion by Arnold Dolmetsch. At the end of 1925 appeared *New Verse*, mostly written in 1921, 'a volume packed with beauty and humour' (Sir Henry Newbolt in *The Times*) and containing seven poems in the writer's latest manner, viz. 'Neo-Miltonic syllabics'. These are in themselves small masterpieces while serving as studies for the *magnum opus* upon which he embarked in July 1926. This was *The Testament of Beauty*, which was published on the poet's eighty-fifth birthday in 1929, and achieved an instantaneous success both in England and the United States of America. *The Testament of Beauty* is a great poem, demanding too much intellectual effort ever to be popular, but full of passages which carry away any sensitive reader by their eloquence, wit, and beauty of sound and imagery. It is unique as the work of an octogenarian, able to sum up his aesthetic and spiritual experience in a poem surpassing all he had previously written, not only in scope and significance but in vigour and freshness. Fortunate to the end, Bridges had just revised his poem for the second English edition before he died at Chilswell 21 April 1930.

No better portrait could be given of Bridges than that contributed to *The Times* (22 April) by Sir Henry Newbolt: 'In presence Bridges was one of the most remarkable figures of his time; there is no company in which he would not have been distinguished. He had great stature and fine proportions, a leonine head, deep eyes, expressive lips, and a full-toned voice, made more effective by a slight occasional hesitation in his speech. His extraordinary personal charm was, however, due to something deeper than these: it lay in the transparent sincerity with which every word and motion expressed the whole of his character, its greatness and its scarcely less memorable littlenesses . . . none would have wished these away: they were not the flaws but the "grotesque" ornaments of his character. Behind them was always visible the strength of a towering and many-sided nature, at once aristocratic and unconventional, virile and affectionate, fearlessly inquiring and profoundly religious.'

Bridges received the Order of Merit in 1929; he was also an honorary D.Litt. of Oxford University and an honorary LL.D. of St. Andrews, Harvard, and Michigan universities, and from 1895 an honorary fellow of Corpus Christi College, Oxford.

An oil portrait of Bridges, painted by Charles Furse in 1893, and a drawing by Anning Bell, are in the possession of Mrs. Bridges. An oil portrait painted by Lionel Muirhead from a photograph by F. Hollyer (1888), and another by Sir William Richmond (1911), are in the possession of Lt.-Colonel A. Muirhead, Haseley Court, Wallingford. A sketch by William Strang, gold point on pink paper, is in the National Portrait Gallery. Many drawings were made by Sir William Rothenstein, of which examples are published in his *English Portraits* (1897) and *Twenty-four Portraits* (1920), and in *The Portrait Drawings of W. Rothenstein 1899–1925* (1926). A drawing by Richard Troncy (1912) is prefixed to the Oxford one-volume edition of Bridges's *Poetical Works* (1913). A medallion profile was executed by Spicer Simson in 1922.

No complete edition of Bridges's works has yet appeared. The *Poetical Works of Robert Bridges* (1898–1905) contains poetry and plays previous to 1905.

[*The Times*, 22 April 1930; Bridges's published writings; *Letters of G. M. Hopkins*, edited by C. C. Abbott, 1935; private information.]

N. C. SMITH

published 1937

BRITTAIN Vera Mary

(1893–1970)

Writer, pacifist, and feminist, was born at Newcastle under Lyme 29 December 1893, the only daughter of Thomas Arthur Brittain, paper manufacturer, and his wife, Edith Mary Bervon. Her only surviving brother, Edward, less than two years her junior, a cherished companion, was killed in action in 1918. Vera Brittain grew up in Macclesfield and then in Buxton in Derbyshire, amidst provincial restrictions against which she increasingly chafed. Her intellectual powers were stimulated by her brother and his Uppingham friends and at St. Monica's, Kingswood, a school which afforded unusual scope for extra-curricular reading and discussion. When she left, she was already set on one of the paths which she followed to the end of her days, the cause of feminism.

That her awakened mind should seek deeper and more disciplined experience would never have occurred to her kind but conventional parents had not chance brought to their Buxton home a distinguished university extension lecturer in the person of (Sir) John Marriott. With his encouragement, she won an open exhibition to Somerville College and went up to Oxford in 1914. There followed the nightmare years of war. University life became insupportable and she enrolled as a VAD, among the young women who were not trained nurses, but who worked and suffered side by side with them. She served in France and Malta as well as London. In the carnage of trench warfare one by one her gifted fiancé, Roland Leighton (brother of the artist Clare Leighton), their closest friends, and finally her beloved brother were killed or died of wounds.

Post-war Oxford (where she obtained a second in history in 1921) brought frustrations but it enabled her to establish a friendship of remarkable quality with a fellow student from Yorkshire, Winifred Holtby, author of *South Riding*, whose untimely death in 1935 led Vera Brittain to commemorate her in *Testament of Friendship* (1940). Meanwhile, another Oxford graduate had noticed the talented young woman who was beginning to make her way in her chosen career as a lecturer and writer. (Sir) George Catlin (died 1979), of New College, became professor of politics at Cornell University in 1924 at the age of twenty-eight. In 1925 he and Vera Brittain were married at St. James's, Spanish Place. She herself never embraced the Roman Catholic faith, although Roland Leighton, her husband, and her daughter did so.

Marriage posed for Vera Brittain in its sharpest form the dilemma of home and career. She had no doubt that, for her, a career as writer and speaker was essential. Transatlantic correspondence on this necessity preceded marriage. One winter at Cornell convinced her that she could not work there. There followed a long period of what she termed 'semi-detached marriage', with Catlin going each winter to Cornell and later to other universities, while she and their son and daughter remained at home. Despite much physical separation, the bond of affection remained strong and when, in her last years, her strength began to fail, nothing could have exceeded the devotion with which her husband tended her.

It was in 1933 that the book which brought her fame was published. *Testament of Youth* spoke with the most moving eloquence for a whole generation. There had been other war books and much war poetry. But this autobiographical narrative, based on diaries and the letters of a group of exceptionally intelligent, sensitive, and articulate young people, was the first book of note to view the horror and heartbreak of war through the eyes of a woman: 'The world was mad and we were all victims . . .'. The book's controlled poignancy brought immediate and overwhelming response: Vera Brittain awoke to find herself famous. The impression made on the post-war generation as well as on her contemporaries was intense.

She wrote the book to release her deeply felt obligations to the dead, but also with the conviction that, for those who had survived, nothing mattered so much as to persuade the world of the criminal futility of war. Already a socialist, in 1936 she joined the Peace Pledge Union of Canon Dick Sheppard and spoke widely at pacifist meetings. During the war of 1939–45 her courageous denunciation of the saturation bombing of Germany brought much public criticism in the United States as well as Britain.

As a publicist for feminist and pacifist causes, Vera Brittain achieved a fair measure of success. As a novelist, she lacked the humour and skill in characterization of her friend Winifred Holtby. The special interest of a further autobiographical instalment, *Testament of Experience* (1957), lies in the references to her children, especially her daughter who, as Mrs Shirley Williams, was destined to become a leading Labour politician and Cabinet minister, thus fulfilling both her mother's feminist aspirations and her father's unrealized personal political ambitions.

In youth, Vera Brittain's slight figure and 'large, melting dark eyes' were clearly very attractive, although she frequently lamented her lack of stature and 'immature appearance' as handicaps on public platforms. She took a lively interest in clothes. Always reticent and a little formal, within her own circle she could arouse intense devotion. She received an honorary D.Litt. from Mills College, California, in 1946. She died in London 29 March 1970. A drawing and a portrait by Sir William Rothenstein are in the possession of her daughter.

[Vera Brittain, *Testament of Youth*, 1933, and *Testament of Experience*, 1957; private papers; personal knowledge.]

EIRENE WHITE

published 1981

BUCHAN John

(1875–1940)

First Baron Tweedsmuir

Author, and governor-general of Canada, born at Perth 26 August 1875, came of mainly Border lowland stock, being the eldest child in the family of four sons and one surviving daughter (the novelist 'O. Douglas') of John Buchan, minister of the Free Church of Scotland, by his wife, Helen, daughter of John Masterton, farmer, at Broughton Green, Peeblesshire. Buchan's father, who had been brought up in the atmosphere of the Disruption, served congregations at Kirkcaldy and at John Knox's church, in the Gorbals district of Glasgow, and the impression made by these rather different places can be easily traced in his son's writings. Perhaps an even greater influence on Buchan was wielded by his mother, a woman sentimental yet shrewd, contemplative but alert, able to hold her own in any company, who lived to see her son surrounded by the pomp of Holyrood and the splendour of Ottawa. In 1895, after attendance at Hutcheson's Boys' Grammar School at Glasgow and at lectures at Glasgow University, he was awarded a scholarship at Brasenose College, Oxford, and thenceforth his life was bound up with England, South Africa, and Canada. Nevertheless, Scotland always 'haunted him like a passion', and he never lost the impress of his home and native land; he remained throughout his life a Christian who said his prayers, read his Bible, and knew the *Pilgrim's Progress* almost by heart.

At Oxford, Buchan won in 1897 the Stanhope historical essay prize on the subject of 'Sir Walter Raleigh' and in 1898 the Newdigate prize for English verse with the 'Pilgrim Fathers' as its theme. He was president of the Union in 1899 and was awarded a first class in *literae humaniores* that same year. Having one or two books already to his credit, he was commissioned by his college to write its history for the Robinson series of 'College Histories'. It appeared in 1898 while he was yet an undergraduate, and called forth severe criticism from antiquarian reviewers unaccustomed to so unconventional a style of historical writing. Disappointed of a prize fellowship, Buchan went to London, where he widened the large circle of his friends and was called to the bar by the Middle Temple in 1901, earning his living by journalism, and reading with J. A. Hamilton (later Lord Sumner) and (Sir) Sidney Rowlatt. But his legal career was cut short when, after his call to the bar, Lord Milner summoned him to South Africa as one of his assistant private secretaries.

Although Buchan spent only two years (1901–1903) in South Africa, the appointment was the most important step in his career. He gained enormously from daily association with Milner and from his modest tasks in the resettlement of the country, where his warm human desire to make friends with the Boers and bury the hatchet gave him horizon and a sense of size, and his imperialism, cleansed of vulgar jingoism, became elevated above the patronizing 'trust' conception into an association of free peoples in loyalty to a common throne. So Pieter Pienaar, resourceful and true, becomes one of the heroes of his adventure novels. Indeed he was eager for a career in Egypt under Lord Cromer when his work in South Africa was over. For the second time and again for the good he was disappointed. Yet it may be affirmed with confidence that, without apprenticeship in Africa, there would have been no governor-generalship of Canada, for Buchan had there learned to think as statesmen think.

In 1903 Buchan returned to the bar in London, 'devilling' for Rowlatt and 'noting' for Sir R. B. (later Viscount) Finlay who, while assessing his mind as not exact enough for supremacy at the bar, admired his abilities and character. He wrote 'opinions', one, for instance, on the legality of Chinese labour (after the liberal victory of 1906) in which his seniors were Arthur Cohen, Finlay, and Rufus Isaacs (later Marquess of Reading). But this episode was a backwater. In 1907 T. A. Nelson the publisher, a friend from Oxford days, invited him to join the firm as 'literary adviser' and as a limited partner. He was to reside in London and superintend the issue of, *inter alia*, the sevenpenny edition of *The Best Literature*. He accepted and was in his element. He could never have mortified the flesh as he describes Milner doing, nor could he have given himself body and soul to the bar. His admirable, but ephemeral, *Law relating to the Taxation of Foreign Income* (1905), written at the instance of R. B. (later Viscount) Haldane, remains as his testament to the Middle Temple, which elected him a bencher in 1935. He was also engaged to be married to one of that world which had fascinated him since his Oxford days by its ease and grace. With her he enjoyed unclouded happiness for thirty-three years. Being free from drudgery he could, as a man of letters, give scope to the dominating activity of his life. Hitherto his books, some written before he ever came to Oxford (*Sir Quixote of the Moors*, 1895, *Scholar Gipsies*, 1896, *Grey Weather*, 1899, *The Half-Hearted*, 1900, and *The Watcher by the Threshold*, 1902), had contained the freshness of youth and were charming harbingers of even better to come. These had been followed by the African books, *The African Colony* (1903) and *A Lodge in the Wilderness* (1906), more interesting perhaps as autobiography than as literature, while *Prester John* (1910) begins the long series of his books of adventure. Except for the Stanhope essay, *Sir*

Walter Raleigh in dramatic form (1911) is the first sign of his turn towards history, and then, after two more adventure stories, came *The Marquis of Montrose* (1913), now out of print and not included in his collected works. This was Buchan's first serious attempt at writing history and a good deal of it was history, and very good history, the most impressive feature being the power which he exhibited of describing marches and battles and their wild natural settings. But zeal for his idolized 'discovery' (although the tragedy of the 'great Marquess' had pointed many a moral and adorned many a tale) led him to commit so many elementary blunders, all of which invariably told in favour of Montrose and against Argyle and the Estates, tinged with a certain 'acerbity' and an air of omniscience, that he was severely taken to task by D. H. Fleming in a review printed in *The British Weekly* of 12 February 1914. No reply was or could be made. *Montrose* (1928) is the sequel: the blemishes complained of are gone, but whether we have the final Marquess 'in his faults and failings, in his virtues and valour' (Hay Fleming) is open to question among those for whom historic truth is all in all, and brilliant writing no more than decoration.

The outbreak of war in 1914 found Buchan, on the eve of his thirty-ninth birthday, seriously ill for the first time since his childhood, when at the age of five he had fallen out of a carriage and a wheel passing over the side of his skull had left its mark for life. He had then lain for a year in bed and had to learn once more how to walk. He grew to be about 5 feet 8 inches in height, lean, sinewy, well knit, and active as a chamois. A daring and expert cragsman, he had sampled many rock climbs in Skye and Austria, and he had literally climbed into the Alpine Club. He was a keen fisherman but an indifferent shot, and his riding was purely utilitarian, preferring as he did Shanks's mare, a nimble, sure steed which never tired. Games, accomplishments, and parlour tricks were outside his activities.

Compelled to keep his bed, Buchan wrote. He made a start with his well-known *History of the Great War*, which occupied twenty-four volumes of the 'Nelson Library' series; but he also wrote *The Thirty-Nine Steps* (1915) which fairly stormed the reading world with its combination of excitement and sensation, written as only a master of English can write. He was well enough by 1915 to be on the staff of *The Times* on the western front, and by 1916 he had joined the army as a major in the Intelligence Corps and enjoyed confidential innominate duties at general headquarters at Montreuil-sur-Mer, which brought him into personal touch with another Borderer by extraction, Sir Douglas Haig, whom he admired as a great man and soldier. Summoned to London in 1917, he made such a personal success of the new Department of Information that it became a ministry with Buchan as subordinate director until the armistice. With renewed successes his pen consoled him for irritating drudgery and unreasonable people: *Greenmantle* (1916) and *Mr. Standfast* (1919) completed the trilogy on the war opened by *The Thirty-Nine Steps.* In *Poems, Scots and English* (1917) some of the poems are topical of the front, but the book is at once a monument of detachment from ugly actuality and a source of regret that he did not write more verse. Buchan loved poetry and had it in his bones.

Private life resulted in settlement at Elsfield Manor, near Oxford, purchased in 1919 after deliberation of several years. That 'ivory tower' was so unlike Buchan's native land that nostalgia was not aroused, and in this phase of his life there was a copious output of books. *The History of the South African Forces in France* and the memoir of *Francis und Riversdale Grenfell* (1920) were the aftermath of the war, together with the *History of the Great War* which was revised, compressed, and republished in 1921–1922 and the complete regimental *History of the Royal Scots Fusiliers* (1925), a valuable tribute to the memory of his youngest brother, Alastair, killed in 1917.

The excellence of the tribute to the Grenfells may have led to his life of *Lord Minto* (1924) which proved to be the forerunner of the historical biographies, on which he undoubtedly intended that his future fame should rest. By an interesting chance it familiarized him with a stage on which, as a successor to Minto, he was destined to play his part. Meantime novel after novel poured from his pen. *Huntingtower* (1922) opened a new series based on Glasgow memories and the scout movement, with a coy candidature of Peeblesshire. *Midwinter* (1923) was an historical novel linking Elsfield with Samuel Johnson just as Elsfield and Henry VIII were drawn together in *The Blanket of the Dark* (1931). *Witch Wood* (1927) links Tweeddale with Montrose and Philiphaugh and is a by-product of the preparation for *Montrose*. But the majority were the yarns (as he called them) spun easily for his own and an eager public's enjoyment.

It is remarkable that he went on writing in the last phase of his life, when he was a public man. The almost inspired literary criticism of his *Sir Walter Scott* (1932) and the sympathetic understanding of the spiritual side of the Protector in *Oliver Cromwell* (1934) show Buchan at his best. At a by-election in 1927 he was elected conservative member of parliament for the Scottish Universities, and held the seat until his elevation to the peerage in 1935. He fitted the constituency like a glove. He loved the House of Commons and the House listened to him. Moreover he had achieved fame in America chiefly as an historian and a novelist. He was a member of the Pilgrim Trust and in that capacity he did good service to Oxford City and Oxford University. And then, in 1933 and 1934 the elder of St. Columba's church at Oxford was appointed lord high commissioner to the General Assembly of the Church of Scotland. In that illustrious office, eloquent of the history of the struggles between church and state since the Reformation, Buchan was supremely happy both in his manner and in his utterances, as befitted the joint author (with Sir George Adam Smith) of the masterly little treatise *The Kirk in Scotland, 1560–1929* (1930). And it was again Ramsay MacDonald who in 1935 advised the appointment of Buchan to the governor-generalship of Canada, the supreme opportunity of Buchan's life, to show of what mettle he was made.

That Lord Tweedsmuir (the appropriate title conferred upon Buchan) had qualities which fitted him in no common degree for the office was shown by *The King's Grace: 1910–1935* (1935). The auspices, save in the matter of his health, were good. He was a Scot, a Presbyterian, and his wife was descended from the two noble houses of Grosvenor and Stuart-Wortley, and in her ancestry she could count more statesmen than most people. His vigour was undiminished and in 1937 *Augustus* brought to a close his studies in ancient history and the humanities.

As governor-general Tweedsmuir had to face the change in the position of the representative of the crown made by the Statute of Westminster (1931). He therefore requited a warm welcome with unwearied devotion to duty on ceremonial occasions, courts, reviews, the delivery of addresses and lectures, not only in English but in French, for he took a special interest in Lower Canada and the French-Canadian culture. Moreover, he was discreet and tactful, and he possessed charm in both its forms, sympathy with the interlocutor or audience, and sympathy of bearing. He was made a Red Indian chief. The author of *The Last Secrets* (1923) never neglected a chance of exploration and he travelled to visit all sorts and conditions of men throughout the Dominion.

But Tweedsmuir overtaxed his strength, and the anxiety inseparable from the visit of the King and Queen in 1939 strained it in spite of the excellence of the arrangements. Any chance of a needed rest was lost by the outbreak of war in September. His death, which took place at Montreal 11 February 1940, was followed by a spontaneous outburst of sorrow from all quarters of the free world. It was felt in Canada that his public services in voicing the spirit of Canadian loyalty, in promoting recruiting, and showing a gallant front had, as Cardinal Villeneuve said, been a factor in cementing national unity in Canada. Nor was his influence confined to Canada. Since 1937 at least he had been on terms of real friendship with President Roosevelt, and, with Lord Lothian at Washington, another member of Milner's South African 'kindergarten', he played his part in maintaining relations with the United States on the right plane.

Tweedsmuir married in 1907 Susan Charlotte, elder daughter of Captain Norman de l'Aigle Grosvenor, third son of the first Lord Ebury, and had three sons and one daughter. He was succeeded as second baron by his eldest son, John Norman Stuart (born 1911). His honours, public and academic, came freely. He was sworn of the Privy Council in 1937, and was appointed C.H. in 1932, G.C.M.G. in 1935, and G.C.V.O. in 1939. He was elected chancellor of Edinburgh University in 1937 and an honorary fellow of Brasenose College in 1934, and he received honorary degrees from three of the four Scottish universities, and from Oxford, Harvard, Yale, and most of the Canadian universities.

A portrait of Lord Tweedsmuir, by Sholto Johnstone-Douglas (1900), is in the possession of Mr. J. W. Buchan, Bank House, Peebles, who also owns a bust by T. J. Clapperton. A posthumous portrait, by Alphonse Jongers, was presented to Lady Tweedsmuir by the women of Canada.

[*Manchester Guardian*, 12 February 1940; *The Times*, 12 and 15 February 1940; John Buchan, *A Lost Lady of Old Years*, 1899, and *Memory Hold-the-Door*, 1940; Hon. A. C. Murray, *Master and Brother*, 1945; Anna Buchan (O. Douglas), *Ann and her Mother*, 1922; *Unforgettable: Unforgotten* (1945); *John Buchan*, by his wife and friends, 1947; personal knowledge.]

S. A. GILLON

published 1949

CAMPBELL (Ignatius) Royston Dunnachie

(1901–1957)

Poet and translator, known as Roy Campbell, was born in Durban, Natal, 2 October 1901, the grandson of a Scots settler and the fourth child of Dr. Samuel George Campbell by his wife, Margaret, daughter of James Dunnachie, of Glenboig, Lanarkshire, who had married Jean Hendry of Eaglesham. Educated at Durban High School, and in a family of soldiers, farmers, administrators, naturalists, hunters, athletes, and verse-writers, Campbell acquired early that lifelong passion for wild animals, poetry, physical prowess, and a blunt outspokenness which gave colour and verve to all his writings.

At fifteen he ran away from school to join his brothers in the war, but was stopped and brought back to his lessons. Sent to Oxford in 1919, he failed to master Greek for university entrance: 'university lectures', he told his father, 'interfere very much with my work'—which was verse-writing stimulated by avid readings in Nietzsche, Darwin, and the English Elizabethan and Romantic poets. Holidays spent in wandering through France and along the Mediterranean coast in search of the sun, odd jobs, and adventure alternated with periods in bohemian London. Among his early fruitful contacts were (Sir) William Walton, the Sitwells, Wyndham Lewis (many of whose 'blasting and bombardiering' attitudes he adopted), and T. W. Earp, who deserves credit for weaning Campbell from Tennysonian pastiche and arousing his enthusiasm for the French Symbolist poets. In 1922 he married without parental consent and forfeited, for a time, the generous parental allowance.

While living in a small converted stable on the coast of North Wales, Campbell completed his first long poem, *The Flaming Terrapin* (1924), a humanistic allegory on the rejuvenation of man, projected in episodes and images of such flamboyant splendour that the work justly made him famous. Returning to Natal, he started, with William Plomer and Laurens van der Post, a monthly review called *Voorslag* (*Whiplash*), but after two numbers he resigned and returned to England. Beneath the romantic idealism of the *Terrapin* was a promising vein of Byronic satire. This was now opened up with skill and malice in *The Wayzgoose* (1928), a hilarious lampoon, in rhyming couplets, on the cultural limitations of South Africa. But he soon found that the cults and coteries of literary Bloomsbury were as little to his taste as the 'shop-keeping mentality' of Durban; so off he trekked again with his family, this time, in 1928, to the genial warmth of Martigues in maritime Provence. There he lived strenuously as a poet, bon-vivant, casual fisherman, and amateur athlete. The physical activities for which he achieved some local reputation were the dangerous sports of water-jousting, steer-throwing, and snatching the cocarde from between the horns of cows and young bulls in the small arenas of Istres and Fos sur Mer.

Both South Africa and the Midi contributed motives to the passion and luminosity of his first book of lyrics, *Adamastor* (1930), and to the less important *Poems* (Paris) of the same year. Such pieces as 'Tristan da Cunha', 'The Albatross', 'The Zulu Girl', 'The Serf', 'The Palm', 'To a Pet Cobra', and 'Horses on the Camargue' went far beyond Campbell's modest claim to have 'added a few solar colours to English poetry'. Borrowings from Kuhlemann, Mistral, Valéry, and Baudelaire were transmuted into a wholly individual style characterized by firmness of outline, copiousness of images, resonance of tone, symbolic overtones, wit, irony, and a superb mastery of rhyme and versification. This success was quickly followed by his best satire, *The Georgiad* (1931), a comic fantasy which pilloried brilliantly, if somewhat vindictively, the moral and aesthetic follies of Georgian 'Bloomsburies'; it also set deep the foundations of an unpopularity which was exacerbated by the reactionary opinions, and the bark-if-not-bite of fascist attitudes, in his first autobiography, *Broken Record* (1934). Yet in this book he writes with such charm and panache on the wild life of Africa and the carefree life of a 'useless poet' that one forgives or accepts his gasconading and swashbuckling and enjoys (with reservations) his confessedly Münchausen-like anecdotes.

Before leaving France for Spain in 1933, Campbell, always a great *aficionado* and frequenter of the *manades*, published *Taurine Provence* (1932), a book on bull-fighting, and a third book of lyrics, *Flowering Reeds* (1933), which contains the well known 'Choosing a Mast' and 'The Gum Trees' and reveals a new classical restraint and brooding tenderness.

In 1935 the Campbells were received into the Roman Catholic Church and shortly afterwards settled in Toledo. By temperament the poet was aristocratic and traditionalist, and although always a good mixer with peasants, gipsies, fishermen, and door-keepers, he had little sympathy with popular humanitarian movements; hence he watched with distaste the growing revolutionary forces in Spain. At considerable risk he sheltered priests and hid the Carmelite archives in his own house; but on being caught in the bombardment of Toledo he and his family were evacuated to England, where he saw the publication and virtual boycotting of his most religious, subtle, and intensely Spanish book of original poems, *Mithraic Emblems* (1936). Early in 1937 he returned to Spain as war correspondent of the *Tablet*, saw some fighting on the Madrid front, sustained an injury to his left hip, and soon retired to Portugal, where he wrote his longest and least disciplined poem, the virulent anti-Red, pro-Franco *Flowering Rifle* (1939) which horrified the English liberal press.

On returning from Italy to Spain at the end of the civil war, Campbell revised his opinion of the Axis powers. Pulled by old loyalties, and now eager to fight for the democratic principles which he never ceased to criticize, he returned to England, and after launching a popular selection of his best poems, *Sons of the Mistral* (1941), he enlisted as a private in the Intelligence Corps. Later, as a sergeant, he commanded Askari coast-watchers in East Africa; but owing to chronic osteoarthritis in his injured left hip he was discharged as unfit in 1944. Back in London, he was a talks producer in the B.B.C. from 1946 to 1949, and in the former year published *Talking Bronco*, a piquant mixture of pure poems, like 'Dreaming Spires' and 'The Skull in the Desert', and witty near-libellous attacks on the left-wing poets.

His three years as joint-editor of *Catacomb*, a right-wing periodical, initiated his last productive period: *Collected Poems* (1949; vol. ii, 1957); *Light on a Dark Horse* (1951), his racy and at times *ben trovato* recension of his life-story and legend up to 1935; *Lorca* (1952), a critical study with translations; *The Mamba's Precipice* (1953), a boy's tale of adventures in Natal. His masterly translations from Spanish, French, and Portuguese include: *Poems of St. John of the Cross* (1951), awarded the Foyle poetry prize; Baudelaire's

Campbell

Les Fleurs du Mal (1952); *Six Spanish Plays* (ed. Bentley, New York, 1959), the five translated by Campbell having been produced on the Third Programme; Calderón's *The Surgeon of His Honour* (University of Wisconsin, 1960); two Portuguese novels by Eça de Queiroz—*Cousin Bazilio* (1953) and *The City and the Mountains* (1955); *Poemas Imperfeitos* by J. Paço d'Arcos, englished as *Nostalgia* (1960). In the third volume of his *Collected Poems* (1960) there are fine renderings of Camões, Lorca, Horace, etc. Although not an exact scholar Campbell was a born poet. 'He was an amazing linguist', said T. S. Eliot, 'and certainly no one can have equalled his translations of St. John of the Cross and Rimbaud's *Bateau Ivre*.'

In 1952 Campbell made his last move—to Portugal. In the many lectures which he gave in England, Spain, and on two visits to America, he read and discussed his poems in his unpolished accent, and gaily attacked the obscure, 'cross-word-happy' poets (some of whom he had actually punched) and the 'parasitical growths' of modern analytical criticism. The climax of his career came in 1954, when he flew to the university of Natal to receive the honorary degree of D.Litt. On his return to Sintra he wrote his last prose work, *Portugal* (1957). There again we find the great zest for life, the fighting spirit, the passion for heroism and dynamic beauty, the extrovert impatience with doubts and hesitations and the fundamentally pious man's love of earth and of simple agrarian or equestrian peoples; there are also the occasional exaggerations, credulities, prejudices, and tall stories given as fact, which mar the literary quality but not necessarily the readability of his prose. Fortunately his best poetry is quite free from these blemishes.

On 23 April 1957 Campbell was killed outright in a car-crash near Setubal, Portugal, and was buried in the San Pedro cemetery near Sintra. His marriage to Mary Margaret, daughter of Walter Chancellor Garman, a Wednesbury doctor, and sister of the second wife of Sir Jacob Epstein, was a very happy one. He was unswervingly devoted to his 'Mary' and their two daughters, and often said that but for his wife's faith in him and her loyal support he would never have achieved success as a writer.

Six foot two, handsome, with remarkable eyes and every inch a poet, the young South African in a typical broad-brimmed hat was painted by Augustus John (&c. 1924) and the portrait now hangs in the Pittsburgh Art Gallery.

[Campbell's autobiographies and unpublished remains; private information; personal knowledge.]

W. H. Gardner

published 1971

(1888–1957)

Author, was born in Londonderry, Ireland, 7 December 1888, the elder son of Arthur Pitt Chambers Cary and his first wife, Charlotte Louisa, daughter of James Joyce, bank manager, of Londonderry. The Ulster branch of the Cary family was founded by a grandson of Sir Robert Cary of Clovelly Court, Devonshire, George Cary, who went to Ireland in Chichester's administration, became recorder of Derry in 1613, married a sister of Sir Tristram Beresford, bart., built himself a handsome house, Redcastle near Derry, and established a family which was to live the life of Ascendancy landowners in beautiful Inishowen between Lough Swilly and Lough Foyle for 300 years. Joyce Cary's grandfather, Arthur Lunel Cary of Castlecary, lost his estate as an indirect result of the Land Act of 1881. But already the pattern of life had changed: some of the family had acquired professions, some had emigrated—to Illinois, to Canada, to Australia— and one, Dr. Tristram Cary, had established himself in London. This pattern repeated itself in the next generation: one son to Canada, one to the United States, while two sons—of whom one was Joyce Cary's father— and four of their sisters lived mainly in or near London.

Joyce Cary's father trained and practised as an engineer in England. He lived in London with his wife and two sons, first at Nunhead and later in the Kitto Road. Charlotte Cary died in 1898 when Joyce was nine. Shortly afterwards the family moved to Gunnersbury, Middlesex, where Dr. Tristram Cary's home was a centre of intense, affectionate family life for his nephews and nieces and their children, described by Joyce Cary in a piece called 'Cromwell House' (New Yorker, 3 November 1956). There was still a close bond with Ireland, endless talk of the past, and frequent visits: the boys went every summer for their long holidays. When Joyce went to his Cary grandmother he would read omnivorously and dream of the past evoked for him by family portraits and by the stories the country people loved to tell him of his people. But when his grandmother Joyce took a holiday house for all her grandchildren, he with his many cousins would range about the countryside and picnic and bathe and sail. His auto-biographical novel A House of Children (1941) is a radiant evocation of such a summer. He gained from his Irish experience not only the setting and characters for this novel and for Castle Corner (1938) but also a sense of history and tradition alive with the conflicts of religion and politics; a realization of the random injustice of life, from his family vicissitudes; and a deep affection for simple people together with an awareness that dignity is not a class prerogative.

He went to Hurstleigh preparatory school in Tunbridge Wells, then to Clifton College. Fifty years later he recalled, with not uncritical gratitude, two Clifton masters: one, who could communicate his profound love of Shakespeare, another who gave Cary the run of his library and encouraged him to write. At Clifton, Cary met (Sir) William Heneage Ogilvie who was to become not only a lifelong friend but also his brother-in-law. (Sir Frederick Wolff Ogilvie was a younger brother.)

A talent for drawing and painting ran through the Cary family—there are several sketches of Joyce as child and adolescent by his father and by his father's sister, Hessie. Cary resolved to become a painter, and at seventeen, having inherited from his grandmother Helen Joyce property which provided him with about £300 a year, he studied art at Edinburgh, where he spent 1907-9, with occasional visits to Paris. His Edinburgh teacher, devoted to classical art, laid great emphasis on the study of anatomy and drawing; the young Cary accepted that formal skills could be acquired in Edinburgh, but Paris of the Post-Impressionists provided the excitement of creative art.

During his last year at Edinburgh, dissatisfied with his painting, and feeling that this was not the medium in which he could best express himself, Cary turned his thoughts to writing. (A volume of his juvenilia, entitled *Verse* by Arthur Cary, was printed by Robert Grant in Edinburgh in 1908.) But all his life the visual arts remained a constant source of interest and pleasure. Moreover, when he came to write his novels he worked like a painter in that he planned out a rough design for the whole and then lavished his days on any parts of it, not in sequence, but turning happily at will from work on section 10 to section 3, and so on. He came, too, to value his careful training in anatomy and drawing not only for having strengthened his sense of structure and form but also for having made him aware of the sheer hard work involved in acquiring skill in any art.

He next went up to Trinity College, Oxford, ostensibly to read law (in which he got a fourth in 1912) but in practice to spend his time reading widely, writing, arguing and discussing, forming friendships and intellectual interests. Religion and philosophy now assumed an importance for him which they never lost. During his third year he shared digs in Holywell with Middleton Murry, who has described Joyce as carpeting the floor with poems in the making. Paris during the vacations for talk and friendship was an extension of Oxford, but for visual and artistic excitement unique as always. During his final year he met his friend's sister, Gertrude Margaret Ogilvie, who was to become his wife in 1916 and his devoted love until her death in 1949.

After Oxford, years of varied and active experience followed. During the Balkan wars (1912–13) he served as a medical orderly in the British Red Cross attached to the Montenegrin army during two campaigns, an experience recorded and illustrated in his posthumously published *Memoir of the Bobotes* (1964). Dr. Martin Leake, V.C., has attested that Cary 'went into a burning magazine at Antivari at great risk to his own life and helped to rescue two men'. Cary then spent a few months working with Sir Horace Plunkett for the Irish Agricultural Organization Society before joining the Nigerian political service in late 1913. Apart from home leaves, he remained in West Africa from May 1914 until 1920; but part of 1915–17 was spent in military service with the Nigerian Regiment in the Cameroons campaign during which he received a slight wound in an engagement on Mount Mora. After his marriage a long sequence of letters to his wife in England records his daily life in Borgu in vivid detail. The Nigerian experience was to provide the themes and settings for his four African novels: *Aissa Saved* (1932); *An American Visitor* (1933); *The African Witch* (1936); *Mister Johnson* (1939); for an unpublished play, *The King is Dead, Long Live the King*; and for several short stories. It is also the basis of two of his political treatises, *The Case for African Freedom* (1941) and *Britain and West Africa* (1946).

In 1920 Cary left the Nigerian service, and he and his wife settled in Oxford at 12 Parks Road, where they continued for the rest of their lives. Family life with his wife and four sons provided him with joy and anxiety—joy particularly in his wife's love and loyal encouragement, anxiety mainly about his work. His wife's devotion to music gave her an understanding of his stubborn pursuit of his own art, writing. This she needed, for although he had published (under the pseudonym Thomas Joyce) several short stories during and shortly after his African sojourn, he now found himself unable to write the novel he wanted to. He later said that at this time he had not yet arrived at a coherent view of reality and therefore the novel he was engaged on had no form. 'I simply lost control of it.' Ten years were to pass in intensive reading and writing, formulating questions and seeking answers to them, before his creative energies were freed. From then on he wrote easily and quickly, producing after 1932 sixteen novels, many short stories (*Spring Song and other stories*, 1960), and two long poems, *Marching Soldier* (1945) and *The Drunken Sailor* (1947), as well as treatises, autobiographical pieces, and essays.

The African novels were succeeded by *Charley is my Darling* (1940), whose characters are wartime evacuee children from London. After this sympathetic study of the have-nots, he wrote the novel based on his own childhood, *A House of Children* (James Tait Black memorial prize). The two childhood novels are in some sense paralleled by two novels in which the theme is the nature of woman, constant in changing circumstances: *The Moonlight* (1946) and *A Fearful Joy* (1949).

The overriding theme of the novels is man's freedom to shape his idea of the world and so to create his own life: 'from chaos man makes his world'. The main opposition is between the traditional and conserving on the one hand and the dynamic and creative on the other. All the novels are set within the same period, roughly from the end of the nineteenth century up to the second world war years, a period which Cary described as a progress into liberty; he measured freedom of the mind by its ability to accept new truth, and the liberty a society affords not merely by absence of restraint but also by the positive opportunities for freedom it offers in terms of standards of living and education. Each novel is set firmly in its social and historical context of rapidly changing events, of societies in confrontation. All are suffused with the joy of living and all embody Cary's belief that beauty, art, loyalty are as indestructible as life itself. Few twentieth-century novelists have presented such a range of characters— politicians and preachers, artists and witches, lawyers and delinquent children. The novels focus on those areas of life where the creative impulse has most range and potential: art, politics, and religion.

Thus the most complex works, the two trilogies, are concerned, the one with art (*Herself Surprised, To Be a Pilgrim, The Horse's Mouth*, 1941–4) and the other with politics (*Prisoner of Grace, Except the Lord, Not Honour More*, 1952–5). A third trilogy was projected, with religion as its centre, but when in 1956 Joyce Cary realized that he could not live long enough to write it, he settled for treating the theme in a single volume, the unfinished, posthumously published novel, *The Captive and the Free* (1959).

Cary was technically inventive and ingenious, and nowhere more than in his trilogies. He said that he devised this form 'to show three characters, not only in themselves, but as seen by others. The object was to get a three-dimensional depth and force of character. One character was to speak in each book and describe the other two as seen by that person'. The form affords rich opportunity for irony in the divergence between objective truth and the subjective view; between official record and actual event; and most notably between how a character sees himself and how others see him. By the way in which he selects and interprets events, each narrator reveals his own view of reality. It is no accident that the writer who devised this subtle form entitled his aesthetic credo *Art and Reality* (Clark lectures, 1956).

The novels express his own idea of life and its joyful variety. *Art and Reality* derived inextricably both from his experience as novelist and from his perception of life's meaning as he conveyed it in his novels and in his own gay, courageous living until the day of his death, in Oxford, 29 March 1957.

A portrait in oils by Eric Kennington is in the possession of the family; a self-portrait (etching) is in the National Portrait Gallery. Joyce Cary's manuscripts and papers are in the Cary Collection presented to the Bodleian Library, Oxford, by James M. Osborn.

[Andrew Wright, *Joyce Cary*, 1958; M. M. Mahood, *Joyce Cary's Africa*, 1964; Lionel Stevenson, 'Joyce Cary and the Anglo-Irish Tradition', in *Modern Fiction Studies* (Purdue University, Lafayette, Indiana), vol. ix, No. 3, Autumn 1963; unpublished letters and papers; personal knowledge.]

WINIFRED DAVIN

published 1971

CHESTERTON Gilbert Keith

(1874–1936)

Poet, novelist, and critic, was born on Campden Hill, London, 29 May 1874, the elder son of Edward Chesterton, head of the well-known Kensington firm of auctioneers and estate agents. His mother, Marie Louise Grosjean, was of French and Scottish blood, and her maternal ancestors, the Keiths of Aberdeen, gave Chesterton his middle name. He was educated at St. Paul's School from 1887 to 1892. At sixteen he started the junior debating club and a magazine known as 'The Debater' which contains startlingly good work for a boy of that age—a boy, moreover, who was almost two years behind his contemporaries in his school work. The practical side of producing and distributing the paper was altogether beyond Chesterton's powers and was taken care of by one of his most intimate friends, later his wife's brother-in-law, Lucian Oldershaw. He was already the kind of being that he was to remain all his life: absent-minded, good-natured almost to weakness, yet of a rock-like strength in holding and maintaining his ideas. Some of those ideas were inherited: love of freedom, belief in human equality and in all that is generally known as liberalism; others he was now slowly acquiring. As he sat at his desk, a tall, clumsy, unbrushed, untidy scarecrow, drawing all over his blotter and his books, his mind was deeply concentrated, not on his lessons, but on the deepest problems of reality. Of this mental travail he has given some notion in *Orthodoxy* and it is confirmed by his note-books and the memories of his friends.

Chesterton's drawings at this time showed so much talent that it was decided that he should go, not to Oxford, but to the Slade School of Art, continuing at the same time to study English literature at London University. It soon became abundantly clear that writing, not drawing, was his primary talent. But that he could and still did draw may be seen from his illustrations to Mr. Hilaire Belloc's novels: he would often complete the sketches for one of these in a couple of hours: at all times he would draw and paint while he talked or thought. In *The Coloured Lands*, published in 1938 after his death, may be seen a fair sample of his work at different periods.

Although Chesterton's headmaster had spoken of him to his mother as a genius, neither she nor his father dreamed of a livelihood made by writing alone. Obviously unfitted for the career of an estate agent, he worked for a time in two publishing houses and thence moved gradually into journalism. This became his profession, and in later years when his fame was at its height he would claim no other title than that of journalist.

Chesterton in 1899 was working on the *Speaker* with a group of young liberals of the same general outlook as his own. His friendship with Mr. Belloc had begun, and this meant much for his social thinking. He had fallen in love and was engaged to Frances, eldest daughter of George William Blogg, a London diamond merchant. She was an Anglo-Catholic, and this meant much for his religious thinking. His first published volumes were both verse. *The Wild Knight*, financed by his father, won wide acclaim as poetry. *Greybeards at Play*, illustrated by the author, was highly successful fooling. Both were published in 1900. He was married in 1901. Public events were shaping in a fashion that stimulated at once his patriotism and a fierce criticism of the country that he loved. The South African war came like a flash of lightning separating liberal from liberal—Chesterton, for instance, from Mr. Bernard Shaw: separating brother from brother—Chesterton, for instance, from his brother Cecil: and casting a vivid light on thoughts that had not yet been fully outlined even, perhaps, to himself.

Rightly or wrongly, Chesterton thus accepted the war and his own possible unpopularity as a pro-Boer as a test of his social and political views. He hated imperialism: he was what has been called a 'little Englander': and he wrote *The Napoleon of Notting Hill* (1904) in fantastic illustration of this thesis, outlining it more soberly in his long introductory chapter to *England a Nation* (also 1904), a symposium of young liberal thinking with the sub-title 'Papers of a Patriots' Club', edited by Oldershaw.

During the period 1900 to 1910 the whole of Chesterton's philosophy was outlined and illustrated in twenty books and innumerable articles. He published over one hundred volumes in the course of a lifetime, greatly enriching and deepening but in no fundamental altering that philosophy. There were vigorous controversies in the religious field with Robert Blatchford and Joseph McCabe, in the national field with Mr. Bernard Shaw and H. G. Wells; criticism in the national field of Rudyard Kipling and the imperialists made of *Heretics* (1905) a brilliant display of fireworks that drew all eyes. He had long contributed art criticism to the *Bookman*, and in 1904 he published *G. F. Watts*. In the field of pure letters his studies of *Robert Browning* (1903) and of *Charles Dickens* (1906) won him another sort of fame: it seemed that he might choose—poet, fantastic novelist, artist and art critic, political pamphleteer, essayist, sociologist, philosopher, and theologian. He chose them all and he chose, too, to remain in style and manner a journalist, to be careless of his facts and references, to avoid solemnity, to laugh at the experts and at himself, to puzzle his fellow journalists alike by his earnestness and his frivolity, to prove that 'there is foam on deep water'.

Orthodoxy (1908) was called by Chesterton 'a sort of slovenly auto biography'. It was, he said, 'an attempt to utter the unutterable things . . . my ultimate attitude towards life'. As against the various 'prophets' of the period—Ibsen, Mr. Shaw, Wells, Kipling, and the rest, each of whom was stressing some one element or tendency—Chesterton saw the riddle of a vast variety in the universe and he came to see Christianity as its only answer. Christianity made a new balance that was also a liberation: it 'made moderation out of the still crash of two impetuous emotions', 'got over the difficulty of combining furious opposites by keeping them both furious'. It taught 'terrible ideals and devouring doctrines': it managed to make the lion lie down with the lamb and yet keep his royal ferocity. *Orthodoxy* was 'a thrilling romance'. It was not the philosophy created by one man to fit himself, and hence too small even to satisfy that self. 'God and humanity made it and it made me.'

Soon after the publication of *Orthodoxy* the Chestertons moved from their little flat in Battersea and went to live at Beaconsfield where they remained for the rest of their lives, at first in a small rented house, later in one built to suit their ideal, a house with a few small bedrooms and one vast living-room where they could have parties for young and old, act charades, or show plays in Chesterton's favourite toy theatre. He spent much time in painting and cutting out figures and scenery for this theatre and in making drawings for guessing games in the invention of which he showed an endless fertility. Grieved at having no child of their own the Chestertons surrounded themselves with children: nieces and nephews, godchildren and young neighbours. His wife created a lovely garden in which Chesterton took a vague pleasure and which often appears in the background of his stories. He began to write about Father Brown, the little priest-detective (*The Innocence of Father Brown* was published in 1911). He took his wife with him and motored over the King Alfred country planning *The Ballad of the White Horse*. He saw his many friends, sometimes in London, sometimes at Beaconsfield: he appeared in pageants as Dr. Johnson: he grew fatter every year and became more and more a figure of legend, wearing a large flapping hat and an ample cloak, carrying a sword-stick and getting lost on every possible and impossible occasion. Setting out from home to give a lecture in some midland town he telegraphed to his wife: 'Am in Market Harborough. Where ought I to be?'

'Father Brown' was actually Father (afterwards Monsignor) O'Connor who, despite his Irish name, is a Yorkshireman, in whose house part of the *White Horse* was written and who, in long walks over the Yorkshire moors, helped Chesterton to thrash out the ideas that beset him. Both Father O'Connor and Mr. Belloc were deeply concerned with the social angle of Christianity's answer to the riddle of the universe. And as with *Orthodoxy* so, too, with Chesterton's social philosophy the battle against the opposing ideas held by Mr. Shaw and others brought Chesterton's own thoughts into clearer focus. In 1909 he published his brilliant sketch of Mr. Shaw. 'I liked it very much,' wrote Mr. Shaw, 'especially as it was so completely free from my own influence.' This book cleared the ground for *What's Wrong with the World?* (1910) much as *Heretics* and the controversy with Blatchford had cleared it for *Orthodoxy*.

Starting life as a liberal by inheritance Chesterton said in these years: 'as much as ever I did, more than ever I did I believe in Liberalism. But there was a rosy time of innocence when I believed in Liberals.' It seemed to him that while no medical doctor says: 'we've had too much scarlet fever, let's try a little measles for a change', that was precisely what the socio-logical 'doctors' were saying. Capitalism was a failure: he agreed that it was a disease: but when they said: 'let's try a little socialism for a change', it seemed to him that for lack of a clear picture of health one disease was being offered as remedy for another.

In *What's Wrong with the World?* Chesterton suggests some root thought on the nature of man, of sex, of the child and its education. Historically and of his nature man needs the family, for its protection the family needs property which capitalism destroys no less than socialism. 'It is the negation of property that the Duke of Sutherland should have all the farms in one estate: just as it would be the negation of marriage if he had all our wives in one harem.' Property in its true meaning is also a condition for the ordinary man's development: 'Property is the art of the democracy.' He goes on to define 'the functions of father, mother and child as such' and to show the limits that a free family would set to the power of the State.

The book is Chesterton's social credo: later on he wrote *The Superstition of Divorce* (1920), *Eugenics and Other Evils* (1922), *The Outline of Sanity* (1926). These and his essays deepen and enrich his social thinking but they add nothing in essentials to *What's Wrong with the World?*

The Ballad of the White Horse was published in 1911 and in 1912 *Manalive*, which is among the best of Chesterton's fantastic stories, expressing as it does supremely the intense zest which he brought to the business of living. *The Victorian Age in Literature* (1913) showed him still brilliant in the field of pure literature. The same year, goaded by Mr. Shaw, he produced a play, *Magic*, which, despite admiring reviews, was a stage failure.

Then came the war of 1914–1918 and Chesterton's almost mortal illness. He had been overworking, overeating, and drinking ('absent-mindedly' as a friend said, for it was only necessary to fill his plate or glass while he talked for him to empty it again). Cecil Chesterton had stood his trial for a libel action which had worried his elder brother more than himself: the war had come as a final blow. 'I wonder', the doctor heard him murmur as he was lifted into a water bed, 'if this bally ship will ever get to shore.' He lay for many months unconscious between life and death. His wife nursed him devotedly and brought him back to full life and vigour. 'I am afraid', he wrote at once to Mr. Shaw, 'you must reconcile yourself to the dismal prospect of my being more or less like what I was before; and any resumption of my ordinary habits must necessarily include the habit of disagreeing with you.'

In 1917 appeared Chesterton's fascinating, sketchy, and inaccurate *Short History of England*. It exasperated historians, yet 'He's got at something we hadn't got' wryly confessed a professor of history to one of Chesterton's friends. In 1919 came *Irish Impressions* and in 1920 *The New Jerusalem*. These books all mark stages in that mental voyage of discovery in which Chesterton, historically and in the contemporary world, was approaching nearer and nearer to the Roman Catholic Church. Externally he was at once urged forward and held back by the circumstances of his life. Cecil Chesterton had with Mr. Belloc some years earlier started a newspaper, first (1911) the *Eye Witness*, later (1912) the *New Witness*, to combat corruption in public life and to uphold and restore the liberties of the poor against a growing bureaucracy. On Cecil's joining the army in 1916 Gilbert took over the editorship. Cecil died in France in December 1918, and his brother continued to edit the paper until its termination in 1923. It was revived under his editorship in 1925 as *G. K.'s Weekly*, which survived until 1938. Added to all that he already had in hand, this editorship produced a chronic condition of overwork. On the other hand a journey to Jerusalem gave fresh inspiration to his thinking, and lecture tours in Holland and the United States of America strengthened his awareness of the Church's universality. All his thinking—directly religious, philosophical, sociological—brought him to the same conclusion, and in 1922 he overcame the largely physical problem posed for him by over-work, physical lethargy, and the habit of depending on his wife for all practical decisions. Chesterton was received into the Roman Catholic Church by Father O'Connor in July 1922. His wife followed him four years later.

The two best known of the books which quickly followed Chesterton's reception are *St. Francis of Assisi* (1923) and *The Everlasting Man* (1925). Of these the former is by far the more popular, the latter the more important. In *Orthodoxy* Chesterton had traced his own discovery of Christianity, in *The Everlasting Man* he traced rather what that discovery, that revelation, had meant for mankind as a whole. Like Wells writing his *Outline of History*, Chesterton claimed 'the right of the amateur to do his best with the facts the specialists provide'. Unlike Wells: 'I do not believe', says Chesterton, 'that the best way to produce an outline of history is to rub out the lines.' But his own aim was not merely to draw an outline but to show something that seemed stale and dusty and old as it really was, fresh and new everlastingly. He asked men to read the Gospels like their daily paper, not merely as good but as *news*. 'I desire to help the reader to see Christendom from the outside in the sense of seeing it as a whole against the background of other historic things; just as I desire him to see humanity as a whole against the background of natural things. And I say that in both cases when seen thus, they stand out from their background like supernatural things.'

When *The Everlasting Man* was published Chesterton had only eleven years to live. They were years of little external action, of amazing productivity. He travelled: to Europe fairly often, to America once more (1930–1931) where he gave courses at Notre Dame University, Indiana, and lectured throughout the country and in Canada. He wrote another play (*The Judgment of Dr. Johnson*, 1927), essays innumerable, more detective stories, more poems (especially *The Queen of Seven Swords*, 1926), literary works, of which by far the best was his *R. L. Stevenson* (1927), theology and philosophy, books of travel. His *St. Thomas Aquinas* (1933) was called by Etienne Gilson 'the best book on St. Thomas that has ever been written'. The pages of *G. K's Weekly* are littered with brilliant matter never re-printed, but from them and from his scattered papers were gathered posthumously (1940) *The End of the Armistice* which cast, like his *William Cobbett* (1925) written during the same period, an almost lurid light of prophecy on the horrors that have followed. Never did Chesterton give in to the 'rather weakminded reaction', the mood of pacificism and appeasement that followed the war of 1914–1918.

Added to Chesterton's other activities in his last years were several series of radio talks for the British Broadcasting Corporation. Both his own purely literary talks and his contributions to various series ('The Spice of Life', 'Seven Days Hard') were received with rare enthusiasm. In these talks and in his writings down to the hour of his death an element was present that has caused the most fundamental disagreement as to Chesterton's character and his place in history. A note of youth, of high spirits, of fooling, present when he entered letters as a young journalist, was as audible in the mature man broadcasting his last message to his countrymen

> They may go out with a whimper,
> But I will go out with a bang.

'Chesterton the Child' was the supreme attribute given to Chesterton by Walter de la Mare when the sword of the warrior and the pen of the thinker had been laid aside. There was nothing childish in Chesterton, nothing callow in his youthful high spirits. The conception of Chesterton as a Peter Pan who never grew up accords ill with the books and ideas which led philosophers to welcome him as one of their own calibre, poets to give him front rank among themselves, and men of letters to acclaim his *Dickens*, his *Browning*, and his *Stevenson* as showing the insight of genius.

Chesterton died at Beaconsfield 14 June 1936; his wife survived him until 1938.

A painting of Chesterton, Maurice Baring, and Mr. Hilaire Belloc (1932), by James Gunn, belongs to Mr. Hugh Balfour, Foss House, Pitlochry. There is a plasticine medallion, by Theodore Spicer-Simson, in the National Portrait Gallery, which also owns a bronze bust by Maria Petrie.

[G. K. Chesterton, *Autobiography*, 1936; Maisie Ward, *Gilbert Keith Chesterton*, 1944; personal knowledge.]

MAISIE WARD

published 1949

Robert Erskine

(1870–1922)

Author and politician, was born in London 25 June 1870, the second son of Robert Caesar Childers, the Pali scholar, by his wife, Anna Mary Henrietta, daughter of Thomas Johnston Barton, of Glendalough House, co. Wicklow. From his father, the pioneer of Pali literary studies in England, who died of consumption, hastened by devotion to his beloved studies, at the early age of thirty-eight, Childers seems to have inherited his extraordinary powers of concentration on his work; from his mother, his intense love of Ireland, fostered by the fact that until his marriage Glendalough House was his only real home. He was educated at Haileybury and at Trinity College, Cambridge, taking the law tripos and his B.A. degree in 1893, and from 1895 to 1910 was a clerk in the House of Commons. Quiet and reserved in appearance, even in his early days he showed a singular power of rising to the occasion. At Cambridge his re-markable elocutionary efforts as a candidate for the presidency of the *Magpie and Stump* are still remembered as the occasion of the most de-lightful 'rag' there within living memory. Soon after he left Cambridge he began spending a large part of his holidays, either alone or with a friend or two, navigating some tiny little yacht through the storms of the Channel or the North Sea, or threading his way through the complicated shoals of the German, Danish, or Baltic coasts.

When, at the end of 1899, the call came for volunteers in the South African War, Childers was among the first to join the City Imperial Volunteer battery of the Honourable Artillery Company. As a result of this experience there came from his pen a vivid personal record of the war, *In the Ranks of the C.I.V.* (1900); he was also responsible, as a collaborator, for the official volume, *The H.A.C. in South Africa* (1903). But his most popular and lasting book, *The Riddle of the Sands* (1903), was the outcome of his yachting expeditions to the coast of Germany. The story, told with even more charm than his narrative about the C.I.V., and based on exact topographical observations of this coast, was a purely imaginary account of preparations for a German raid on England; but it at once touched the prevalent feeling of suspicion as to German plans, and became even more popular when it was republished in August 1914. In September 1903 he went to Boston with the Honourable Artillery Company on a visit to the Ancient and Honourable Artillery Company of Massachusetts, an offshoot of the London body, the first visit in peace time of an armed body of British soldiers to the United States. In the course of the celebrations he happened one day to sit next to Miss Mary Alden Osgood, of Boston: the two fell in love at first sight, and on 5 January 1904 were married at Boston. On his return to London in that month they established themselves in a Chelsea flat. Of this marriage Childers wrote some years later that it was 'the most wonderful happiness that I know'; indeed, in all his subsequent activities he and his wife were as one mind and soul. Two sons were born to them.

Childers's next literary work was vol. v of *The Times' History of the War in South Africa* (1907)—a task which suggested to him a campaign against antiquated uses of cavalry, through his volumes *War and the Arme Blanche* (with a preface by Lord Roberts, 1910) and *German Influence on British Cavalry* (1911). His summer holidays were, as before, spent yachting, chiefly in the Baltic in the yacht *Asgard*, modelled on the lines of Nansen's *Fram* by Colin Archer, of Larvig; the yacht was one of his wedding presents. In all these trips he was accompanied by his wife, who, though crippled, soon became almost as expert in seamanship as he was himself.

Meanwhile Childers's attention had been more and more concentrated on Irish affairs. Of unionist stock, he came back from the South African War with a growing inclination to liberalism; but in 1902 he still could write, 'I am not a Home Ruler'. It was not until 1908 that, after seeing much of Sir Horace Plunkett's work in Ireland, he wrote in a private letter, 'I have come back finally and immutably a convert to Home Rule'. Thenceforward he thought of little else but Ireland. In 1910 he resigned his clerkship in the House of Commons in order to devote himself to political work, appearing for a short time as liberal candidate for Devonport, a constituency which was little suited to him, and which he relinquished before the election came on. In London he joined a committee to discuss *Home Rule Problems* (the papers, including one of his, read before this committee being published under this title in 1911); and in his own book, *The Framework of Home Rule* (1911), he went farther than most Englishmen of the time in advocating full dominion status for Ireland. In July 1914, after the passage of Mr. Asquith's Home Rule Bill and the subsequent failure of the government to prevent the arming of the Ulster Volunteers, Childers and his wife undertook, on behalf of a small Anglo-Irish committee, to carry a cargo of arms in his yacht *Asgard* into Howth harbour, five miles north of Dublin, for the use of the National Volunteers—a task which he accomplished with complete success.

Immediately afterwards the European War broke out. Childers, with his knowledge of the German coast as displayed in *The Riddle of the Sands*, was naturally pitched upon by the Admiralty for reconnaissance work on the seaplane carrier H.M.S. *Engadine*. As an R.N.V.R. officer he took part in the Cuxhaven raid (November 1914), and during the rest of the War was employed as an intelligence officer and in training officers for reconnaissance work in the Royal Naval Air Service. He also did staff work at the Admiralty, and at the end of the War made an important report on the effects of enemy bombing on protected buildings. He was several times mentioned in dispatches, was promoted lieutenant-commander, and eventually, on amalgamation of the Naval Air Service with the Royal Air Force, held the rank of major; for his services in the War he received the D.S.C.

At the outset of the War Childers had joined up enthusiastically, in the belief that the rights of nationality promised by the Allies would be extended to Ireland; moreover, in 1917 he was seconded for service on the secretariat of the Irish Convention, which, however, failed to secure agreement on Home Rule. Bitterly disappointed in 1918 by the continued delay in giving any form of self-government to Ireland, he determined, on his demobilization in March 1919, to devote the rest of his life to securing, no longer dominion status, the time for which he believed had passed, but complete independence for Ireland as a republic. With this object, in the same year he accompanied the Irish republican envoys sent by Arthur Griffith to Paris to put the case for Ireland before the Versailles Conference, and in the following December settled with his family in Dublin in order to work in the Irish republican ranks. He wrote continually in the English, Irish, and foreign press to protest against the Dublin Castle methods of government and against the employment of the 'Black and Tans', some of his articles being reprinted as a pamphlet, *Military Rule in Ireland* (1920). In May 1921 he was elected to the self-constituted Dail Eireann as member for county Wicklow and was appointed minister of propaganda. After the truce of July in that year he went with Eamonn De Valera on the first delegation to London and was principal secretary to the subsequent Irish delegation which negotiated the Treaty with the British government (October–December 1921). But by this time Childers had become irreconcilable to any form of treaty which did not recognize an Irish republic, and in the Dail debates on the articles of agreement he vehemently opposed Arthur Griffith and Michael Collins, who were for acceptance of the Treaty.

After the establishment of the Irish Free State government, Childers joined the Republican army, and while actually serving in mobile columns in the south edited and published the Republican organ *Poblact na h-Eireann*. On 10 November 1922 his old home, Glendalough House, where he had taken passing refuge, was surrounded by Free State soldiers; he had a pistol, but did not fire it, as one of the women of the house threw herself between him and the soldiers. He was arrested, and court-martialled in Dublin on 17 November by a court which he refused to acknowledge; and on 24 November he was shot at Beggar's Bush barracks by a firing party, with each member of which he had first shaken hands.

At the time Childers's name was branded on both sides of the Channel as that of a traitor and renegade to both Ireland and England. But no one who knew the man believed that, whatever might be thought of his judgement, he had a particle of meanness or treachery in his nature, or that the course of action which he had adopted was based on anything but the prompting of his conscience and sense of honour. By his friends Childers will always be remembered as a man of indomitable courage, of winning modesty, of extraordinary generosity and, in his earlier and happier days, of a most engaging sense of humour.

[Basil Williams, *Erskine Childers* (a pamphlet privately printed), 1926; private information; personal knowledge.]

B. WILLIAMS

published 1937

CHRISTIE Dame Agatha Mary Clarissa
(1890–1976)

Detective novelist and playwright, was born 15 September 1890 at Torquay, the third and youngest child and second daughter of Frederick Alvah Miller, of independent means, formerly of New York, and his wife, Clarissa ('Clara') Margaret Boehmer. She had no schooling at all, not even a governess. But, once having frustrated her mother's current belief that no child should read until the age of eight, she devoured books voraciously, as well as conducting in her mind an endless school story with a vivid and varied cast. She began to write, too. At eleven there was a poem in a local paper ('When first the electric tram did run'). But the notion of being a writer as such, she says in *An Autobiography* (1977), never entered her head.

Her talents were seen to lie in the direction of music. At sixteen she went to Paris and studied both singing and the piano, hoping for a concert career only to learn that her temperament was too reticent for public performance. Her happy, quiet life in Torquay—it was to be reflected in the values that underlay all her books—was plunged into a more dramatic tempo when, rejecting a suitor with whom she had an unannounced engagement, she fell in love with a young officer, Archibald Christie (died 1962), just about to join the Royal Flying Corps. She married him, at two days' notice, in 1914 during his first leave after war had broken out, and then returned to the Voluntary Aid Detachment nursing she had taken up and the dispensary work that followed.

It was during lulls in the dispensary that she began a detective story. Seeking some point of originality for a sleuth in the Sherlock Holmes tradition she thought of the Belgian refugees in Torquay and Hercule Poirot, retired Belgian policeman evacuated to England, was born, though it was not until 1920 and six unsuccessful trips to publishers that he saw the light of day in *The Mysterious Affair at Styles*, a book that shows little indeed of the prentice hand. Once embarked on a writing career, however, books followed in regular succession until in 1926 she produced *The Murder of Roger Ackroyd* which by its daring reversal of the understood conventions of the genre created a considerable sensation.

It was a sensation that in the same year was echoed in her own life. Her husband, now Colonel Christie, had fallen in love with a friend's secretary, Nancy Neele, and at the same time following the death of her much loved mother she undertook the clearing up of the old family home. The strain was too much. Leaving no explanation, she made her way from Surrey to a Harrogate hotel where she registered under Miss Neele's name. The disappearance of a figure associated with crime and a highly popular form of writing caused an immense furore, and when after nine days she was recognized the newspaper brouhaha left her always suspicious of publicity. She divorced Colonel Christie in 1928. There was one child of the marriage, a daughter.

It was as the result of a visit during an impromptu holiday to the archaeological site at Ur then being excavated by (Sir) C. Leonard Woolley, whose wife was a passionate admirer of *The Murder of Roger Ackroyd*, that she met (Sir) Max Mallowan. They were married in 1930 and for the remainder of her life, except for his period of service in the war of 1939–45, she was closely associated with his work, learning to photograph, clean, and register the hundreds of small finds of a dig, to run a camp and pay the many workmen. She accompanied her husband on his expeditions, and a handful of her novels reflect the archaeological life, notably *Death Comes As the End* (1945), ingeniously set in Ancient Egypt, as well as a slim factual account enlivened with humour, *Come Tell Me How You Live* (1946).

But archaeology did not prevent her producing a book a year, sometimes more, and her best work is to be found in the twenty-five novels she wrote up to the end of the war of 1939–45 with two 'last books' written in the war years and consigned to her solicitor's safe to appear, *coronat finis opus*, as *Curtain: Hercule Poirot's Last Case* in 1975 and as *Sleeping Murder* in 1976, which contained the final appearance of Miss Marple, her equally popular sleuth brought from short stories to the novel in *Murder at the Vicarage* (1930), whose intuition replaced the logicality of Poirot's 'little grey cells'.

These books show her two great gifts, ingenuity of puzzle and unhesitating narrative. The ingenuity is to be found both in basic plot and in beautifully skilful minor misdirection. That basic conjuring trick may be exemplified in the idea for *Evil Under the Sun* (1941) in which a character is presented to the reader as the archetypal misused wife only to be revealed finally as co-conspirator with her supposedly arrogantly straying husband. The minor misdirections—there are scores of them—may be typified as either verbal sleight of hand ('I did all that was necessary', neutrally says the character who has in fact been arranging his alibi) or visual trickery (seeping blood that is nail polish with a real wound self-inflicted later).

The narrative skill is always unobtrusive. It consists primarily in a shunning of all irrelevance, even of the fine phrase, that is almost heroic, coupled with a fine sense of timing (perhaps deriving from her musicality). To these two positive factors must be added, in accounting for the enormous success of the books, some more negative ones. Characters are seldom portrayed in any depth or much described, so that readers as far apart as Nicaragua and Bengal can each see them through their own experience. Nor did she often leave the territory she knew best, upper middle-class English life, limiting but safe. Physical description of all kinds is minimal and as much as possible of the story is told through dialogue, easy everyday talk.

These virtues, and these avoidances of the pitfalls awaiting the ambitious, account too for her success as a playwright, artistic in *Witness for the Prosecution* (1953), financial in *The Mousetrap* (1952). Two other aspects of her work should be mentioned, the six romantic novels she wrote as Mary Westmacott, uneven but personally revealing, and the volume of religious stories for children, *Star over Bethlehem* (1965), which speaks a little of the spiritual commitment that sustained her until her death, wheeled in her invalid-chair from the luncheon table by her husband at their Oxfordshire home, Winterbrook House, Wallingford, 12 January 1976.

So popular did her books become that totalling her sales defied all the efforts of her publishers and literary agent. She was translated into 103 languages. Her film rights were sold for record sums. Her play *The Mousetrap* achieved a run on the London stage exceeding a quarter of a century and far outpacing any other. She was honoured with the CBE in 1956 and appointed DBE in 1971. She was a D.Litt. of the University of Exeter.

[Agatha Christie, *First Lady of Crime* (ed. H. R. F. Keating), 1977, and *An Autobiography*, 1977; Janet Morgan, *Agatha Christie*, 1984.]

H. R. F. KEATING

published 1986

(1903–1974)

Author, literary editor, and journalist, was born in Coventry 10 September 1903, the only son of Major Matthew Connolly, a conchologist, of Bath, and his wife, Muriel Vernon, who was Irish. He went up to Eton as a King's scholar, and then in 1922 to Balliol College, Oxford, where he was Brackenbury scholar. He obtained a third class in modern history in 1925. His schooling imbued him with a love of the classical authors, which never left him, and made a powerful imprint on his prose style, in its clarity, balance, and pungent concision of judgement. Connolly was a complex character, a wit, a nostalgic hedonist, a gourmet, and the most entertaining of companions and conversationalists when he was in the mood, but inspiring something akin to terror when the company (or the food) was not congenial to him. He hated all that was philistine or pompously conventional, and was quick in his appreciation of every development that was fresh and original in art as well as literature. He was especially devoted to French literature, both ancient and modern, his taste ranging from La Fontaine to Marcel Proust. He was the coiner of many *bon mots* which have passed into general usage, the best known of which is his remark that 'imprisoned in every fat man a thin one is wildly signalling to be let out'.

After going down from Oxford, Connolly became for a time the secretary of the rich, fastidious Anglo-American man of letters, Logan Pearsall Smith, who allowed him great liberty to develop himself as a writer, while reinforcing his repugnance for the cliché and whatever was woolly and imprecise in prose expression. The great freshness, wit, and conversational ease of Connolly's fully matured prose style owes not a little, one cannot help thinking, to the standards of this early mentor.

Connolly proclaimed that he had a passion for travel, and wrote in *Who's Who* that his recreation was 'travel'; but he had none of the zeal that distinguished some of his contemporaries for exploring remote and little known places where the amenities of civilization were few. He preferred those areas where comfort and good food were available, and characteristically his first book was his short novel about the South of France, *The Rock Pool* (1936). It has spice and charm, and still has its admirers; but it showed, not least one fancies to its author, that he was not born to be a novelist. His next book, *Enemies of Promise* (1938), revealed his true gifts as witty commentator on the contemporary literary scene and analyst of the dangers that lie in wait for the literary aspirant. Not a few of the more sweeping generalizations have dated, but though some of the enemies have inevitably changed their aspect they are still there. The second section of the book, 'A Georgian Boyhood', a candid account of his years at Eton, remains one of the best sustained pieces of writing he ever produced. During the war he prepared a book of aphorisms of his own and observations on the aphorisms of his favourite authors, such as Chamfort. *The Unquiet Grave* (1944, revised edn. 1945) was published under the *nom de plume* of Palinurus, a disguise which deceived nobody and was probably not intended to. It was deeply steeped in nostalgia for the lost pleasures of peacetime, and has the distinction of being the least warlike of all the books produced during that cataclysmic conflict. It revealed for the first time his deep love of the delicate exotic creatures of the lemur family: many of the most touching and haunting passages in the book are devoted to them.

Connolly tempted providence by asserting in the opening paragraph of *The Unquiet Grave* that 'the true function of a writer is to produce a masterpiece and that no other task is of any consequence'. Though *The Unquiet Grave* abounds in felicities of writing and observation that could not have come from any other pen, it is difficult to see it, disjointed in structure and relying as it does so heavily on quotations from his most admired authors, as the masterpiece he longed to achieve. His most enduring monument will almost certainly be his editorship of the literary magazine *Horizon*, which he founded with Peter Watson and (Sir) Stephen Spender in 1939 and edited until 1950. In the first number he announced uncompromisingly 'our standards are aesthetic ones, politics are in abeyance'. He remained true to this ideal throughout the magazine's life, though not without difficulty, as it had its narrow-spirited enemies in the war bureaucracy, who did not consider it sufficiently uplifting to morale, but rather a waste of scarce paper. Connolly was not to be deflected, with the result that *Horizon* was one of the greatest morale-boosters of the war among intellectuals and artists, and came to be a symbol for them of what we were truly fighting to defend. The enormous variety and excellence of its most outstanding contributions in poetry, short fiction, and criticism were superbly illustrated by the selective anthology he published in 1953, *The Golden Horizon*. Connolly had his prejudices and his moods, which were clearly apparent in his editorial comments, and though he showed signs of wearying of his task towards the end, the magnitude of his achievement cannot be denied.

Early on in his career he began writing reviews and articles for the weekly press; he was literary editor of the *Observer* between 1942 and 1943, and during the last phase of his life he became a leading book reviewer for the *Sunday Times*. He collected these reviews, together with longer articles written for other English and American periodicals, into four volumes: *The*

Condemned Playground (1945), *Ideas and Places* (1953), *Previous Convictions* (1963), and *The Evening Colonnade* (1973). In the first of these volumes, he confessed in a typically self-revealing fashion: 'Like most critics I drifted into the profession through a lack of moral stamina: I wanted to be a poet, and to revive the epic; I wanted to write a novel about Archaic Greece— but my epic and my novel fell so short of the standards which my reading had set me that I despaired of them, and, despairing, slipped into the interim habit of writing short-term articles about books.' Nevertheless his reviews were always readable, well informed and beautifully written, and characterized by an individual personal note that made one look out for them with pleasure from week to week, though when he was writing about a book that bored him the lowering of the critical tension was immediately apparent. He had a curiously persistent passion for making lists, the chief example of which is his *catalogue raisonné* of 'one hundred key books from 1880 to 1950', which he called *The Modern Movement* (1965). He was rewarded by a great exhibition of first editions of all the books he had chosen by the University of Texas, in a way the apotheosis of his career as a critic, arbiter of taste, and bibliophile.

Connolly was a chevalier of the Legion of Honour, became FRSL, and was appointed both CBE and C.Lit. in 1972.

In 1930 he married Frances Jean Bakewell, of Baltimore. This marriage ended in divorce and he married, secondly, Barbara Skelton. There were no children of either marriage. After the dissolution of the second marriage he married in 1959 Deirdre, formerly the wife of Jonathan Craven, of the 9th Lancers, and daughter of Major (Patrick William) Dennis Craig, MBE, son of the first Viscount Craigavon, first prime minister of Northern Ireland. They had a son and a daughter. Connolly died in London 26 November 1974.

[Stephen Spender, *Cyril Connolly*, 1978 (reprinted from *Times Literary Supplement*, 6 December 1974); *The Times*, 27 and 30 November and 3 December 1974; David Pryce-Jones, *Cyril Connolly, Journal and Memoir*, 1983; personal knowledge.]

JOHN LEHMANN

published 1986

COWARD Sir Noël Peirce

(1899–1973)

Actor, playwright, composer, lyricist, producer, author, occasional poet, and Sunday painter, was born 16 December 1899 at Teddington, Middlesex, the second in the family of three sons (the eldest of whom died at the age of six) of Arthur Sabin Coward (described as a clerk, but whose passion was music) and his wife Violet Agnes, daughter of Henry Gordon Veitch, a captain in the Royal Navy. His grandfather was James Coward, organist and chorister. Both parental backgrounds had a strong influence on the boy and the man. His mother was also musical—the parents met as members of the local church choir—and was an ardent and knowledgeable theatre-goer. Coward was soon to be a chorister himself, but was frustrated by the absence of applause after his solos. His birthday treats were invariably visits to the theatre; and by the time he was 'rushing towards puberty' he could play accurately by ear numbers from the show he had seen that day. His formal education was sporadic, not helped by a quick temper—he left one school after biting the headmistress in the arm; and though he attended the Chapel Royal choir school at Clapham in 1909, he failed surprisingly, but perhaps providentially, to be accepted for the choir. The start of his professional career was less than a year away—27 January 1911—playing Prince Mussel in *The Goldfish* as one of a 'Star Cast of Wonder Children'. (Indeed, they included Michael MacLiammóir, and (Dame) Ninette de Valois.) His success led to a number of engagements with (Sir) Charles Hawtrey, from whom he learned much about playing comedy, and—quite as important—gained an insight into the anatomy of writing plays. In 1913 he appeared as an angel in *Hannele* by Hauptmann with the fifteen-year-old Gertrude Lawrence. (And so began a very special personal and professional relationship which lasted until her death in 1952.) Christmas 1913 saw a dream realized when he played Slightly in *Peter Pan* with Pauline Chase.

Throughout 1914–15 there was little work and some anxiety about his health. However the period was not uneventful. Worldly-wise for his years, his sophistication was purely theatrical; but in June 1915 an invitation to visit a Mrs Astley Cooper at Hambleton Hall gave Coward a first exciting view of that undiscovered country of high society, in which he would become increasingly at home, as welcome as he was at ease, and from which, both as writer and actor, he was to develop an important element of his comedy. Also from this period comes that distinctive mark of self-awareness—a new and durable signature, described by Sir John Betjeman at the Coward memorial service: 'Noël with two dots over the "e", and the firm decided downward stroke of the "l".' At Christmas 1915 he at last worked again, in *Where the Rainbow Ends*; followed by a tour in the thankless part of Charley in *Charley's Aunt* (1916). After a two-week run in *Light Blues*, singing and dancing with the newly-wed Jack Hulbert and (Dame) Cicely Courtneidge, he had his first solo number in *The Happy Family* (1916), of which one critic wrote: 'He combined the grace of a Russian dancer with the manner of an English schoolboy'. In 1916 he wrote the lyrics and music of his first song; by 1917 he had written three plays. The best of them, *The Rat Trap* (produced in 1924), was described as 'lousy in construction' by American impresario Gilbert Miller. Dialogue is not enough, was Miller's message. Coward took it to heart. Miller was enthusiastic about his acting however, and engaged him for the juvenile lead in a star-studded production of *The Saving Grace* (1917). Before that he appeared in his first film, *Hearts of the World*, directed by the legendary D. W. Griffith.

In the spring of 1918 began a frustrating nine-month 'engagement' in the army. Though at home with the rigorous discipline of the theatre, and already recognizing the no less demanding self-discipline required of the writer, Coward found that the military equivalent actually made him ill. (Would it have been the same, one wonders, if his call-up had been to the navy?) Although personally little affected by 'the war to end war' Coward shared the hectic relief of his contemporaries that it was over; and was soon considered by press and public as typical of the Bright Young Things, and also paradoxically, of the cynically disillusioned minority as well. The epithet 'brittle' was first applied to him now; it was to haunt him and his reputation to the grave and beyond.

Through his friendship with the tragically short-lived Meggie Albanesi he came to know Lorn Macnaughtan, who as Lorn Loraine became his secretary and 'one of the principal mainstays' of his life until her death forty-six years later. (It was she who first called him 'master'—as a joke.) In 1920 he first appeared in London in a play of his own, *I'll Leave It to You*, which, despite good notices, closed in five weeks. Undaunted, he went abroad for the first time, visiting Paris, and going on to Alassio to Mrs Astley Cooper, where he met another lifelong member of his inner circle—Gladys Calthrop, who was to design sets and costumes for a host of his plays. A rapid escape abroad, when his contribution to a production was over (whatever its fate), became hereafter part of the pattern of his life. 'Like a window opening in my head', he called it.

In *The Young Idea* (1922) Coward shamelessly borrowed his brother and sister from the twins in *You Never Can Tell* by George Bernard Shaw. Shaw was not offended, but wrote Coward a most constructive letter, including the advice 'never to see or read my plays. Unless you can get clear away from me you will begin as a back number, and be hopelessly out of it when you are forty'. (In 1941, when Coward had unwittingly breached the currency regulations and received much bad publicity, Shaw was his doughty champion, reminding him that there was no guilt without intention, and telling him to plead 'not guilty' despite his lawyers' advice. He did; and received a minimal fine.) He was composer and part-author of *London Calling* (1923), a revue starring himself and Gertrude Lawrence. As with *The Young Idea* the majority of critics preferred his writing to his performances. The rest would only accept him as a performer in the works of others—a contradiction only explicable by the hostility of both factions to versatility. (Meanwhile in 1921 he had paid his first exciting but impoverished visit to New York, meeting Alfred Lunt—Lynn Fontanne he already knew from London; and also Laurette Taylor and family, whose absent-minded hospitality and parlour games gave him the idea for *Hay Fever*.)

In November 1924 *The Vortex*—his play about drug addiction—put Coward triumphantly and controversially on the map, winning the allegiance of the beau monde led by the Mountbattens; confirming the worst fears of the stuffier elements of society. During its seven-month run—the longest he would ever permit himself—his output included *On With the Dance* (1925), a revue for (Sir) C. B. Cochran, an association which lasted for nine years (to see its Manchester opening Coward left *The Vortex* briefly to his understudy—(Sir) John Gielgud); *Fallen Angels* (1925) with Tallulah Bankhead—another *succès de scandale*; and *Hay Fever* (1925) with (Dame) Marie Tempest, which ran for a year. In September 1925 *The Vortex* took New York by storm, and Coward bought his first Rolls-Royce. *Easy Virtue* (1925) was written and produced while he was there. There were two consequences of this astonishing burst of successful activity, neither surprising. In 1926 he suffered a severe breakdown; and he yielded to the temptation to allow the production of three plays from his bottom drawer. All were failures—the most notorious being *Sirocco* (1927), which starred his great friend Ivor Novello. It was the only time they worked together.

Thanks to Cochran, Coward soon bounced back, with his most successful revue *This Year of Grace* (1928). *Bitter Sweet* (1929) followed—its most famous number 'I'll see you again' being composed in a taxi in a New York traffic jam. Even a Far Eastern holiday was productive. Alone in Shanghai, he had a mental picture of 'Gertie' in a white Molyneux dress in the South of France. Four hours later *Private Lives* had been mapped out; the actual writing took four days. It opened in London in 1930—Laurence (later Lord) Olivier playing a minor role—and was sold out for its three-month season, as it was in New York. Arnold Bennett called Coward 'the

Congreve of our day'. 'Thin' and 'brittle' replied the critics. *Cavalcade* (1931) was his most ambitious production, suggested to his ever fertile mind by a photograph of a troop-ship leaving for the Boer war. It gave him the opportunity to proclaim in a brilliant mixture of pageantry and under-statement his intense patriotism, coupled with a warning that 'this country of ours which we love so much' was losing its way. His enemies found it obscene that the author of *The Vortex* should treat such a subject. The nation and the English-speaking world responded differently. *Design for Living* (1932) was written in South America to redeem a promise made to the Lunts. It was so successful that he broke his three-month rule and played five in New York, using the mornings to write his first volume of autobiography *Present Indicative* (1937). From a Caribbean cruise with the navy he emerged with the libretto of *Conversation Piece* (1934), his last collaboration with Cochran. 1935 saw the writing of the nine playlets, some with music, which were presented in three programmes as *To-night at 8.30* (1936). *Operette* (1938) broke this long run of success, despite the hit number 'The Stately Homes of England'. Coward spent the summer of 1939 writing *Present Laughter* and *This Happy Breed*, but their production was postponed until 1942 by the outbreak of war, and by Coward's prearranged war job in Paris. This and a proposed intelligence assignment in Amer-ica came to nothing, due in part, he believed, to the hostility of Lord Beaverbrook. Angry and frustrated, he turned with relief to his own field. The results included his longest running comedy *Blithe Spirit* (1941); his finest film script *In Which We Serve* (1942) about the sinking of Mount-batten's destroyer *Kelly*; and one of his most enduring songs 'London Pride'.

Cole Lesley, who died in 1980, writer of the best biography of Coward, came to work for him in 1936; Graham Payn joined the resident 'family' in 1947, completing with Joyce Carey, Lorn Loraine, and Gladys Calthrop the inner circle, which apart from Lorn Loraine's death in 1967, remained unchanged until his own. But if the domestic background was serene, Coward for the next twenty years was to endure much professional dis-appointment and disparagement. Between 1946 and 1964 six musicals and two plays fell short of Coward's highest hopes; fortunately *Relative Values* (1951), *Quadrille* (1952), *South Sea Bubble* and *Nude With Violin* (1956), though not his own favourites, were box-office successes.

In 1948, after a disastrous New York revival of *To-night at 8.30*, Coward took Graham Payn, who had starred in it with Gertrude Lawrence, to Jamaica. He fell in love with the island, built a house by the sea called Blue Harbour, and later, on the hill above ('piling Pelléas on Mélisande' he called it) a small retreat—Firefly Hill (where he died, and is buried). Also in 1948 he performed *Present Laughter* (*Joyeux Chagrins* in French) in Paris—a remarkable achievement, which failed dismally. His French was too good, they said, and the humour did not translate.

In 1951 he accepted an engagement which led to lifelong financial security. He appeared singing his own songs in cabaret at London's Café de Paris. Three more sell-out seasons followed; and then one in 1955 at Las Vegas, at 35,000 dollars a week for four weeks. From this in turn came highly lucrative American television and film engagements; and the difficult decision to emigrate, first to Bermuda and later to Switzerland, to mitigate the depredations of the Inland Revenue, and because, intending to perform less in future, 'I might as well do it for double the appreciation and ten times the lolly'. In any case, as Sir Winston Churchill told him, 'An Englishman has an inalienable right to live wherever he chooses'.

In 1953 he had a great success as King Magnus in Shaw's *The Apple Cart*; in 1960 his only novel *Pomp and Circumstance* was predictably more successful in America than Britain.

In 1964 an invitation by Sir Laurence Olivier to direct Dame Edith Evans in *Hay Fever* for the National Theatre marked the beginning of the last sunlit years of Coward's career, demonstrating once again that the British only feel comfortable with talent or genius when their possessors are 'over the hill'. Coward decided to risk his new reputation as 'demonstrably the greatest living English playwright' (Ronald Bryden) by appearing one last time in the West End. The result was *A Song at Twilight* and a double bill *Come Into the Garden, Maud*, and *Shadows of the Evening* (1966). Though seriously weakened by the onset of arterio-sclerosis, and by amoebic dysentery caught in the Seychelles, and for the only time in his life suffering the indignity of occasionally drying up, the season was a triumphant sell-out. There was only one bad notice. 'Good', he said reading it, 'I thought I might be slipping.' Professionally that was the final curtain. What followed was a trip round the world with Cole Lesley and Graham Payn; the seventieth birthday celebrations, culminating in an emotional midnight tribute by his fellow professionals; his long delayed and much deserved knighthood (1970); in America a special Tony award (1970)—his first—for services to the theatre; an honorary D.Litt. from Sussex University (1972); peaceful days in Switzerland and Jamaica with his friends, and finally, without warning, the end in Jamaica 26 March 1973.

How to assess him? His staccato speech, developed, it is said, to penetrate his mother's deafness, became the instrument of both his comedy and of his conversation. A hostile journalist once asked him for what he would be remembered after his death. 'Charm', he replied. T. E. Lawrence called him 'a hasty kind of genius'. In 1930 W. Somerset Maugham predicted that he would be responsible for the manner in which plays would be written for thirty years. He said himself that it was only natural that 'my writing should be appreciated casually, because my personality, performance, music and legend get in the way'. Of his homosexuality Dame Rebecca West, a close and clear-sighted friend, wrote: 'There was impeccable dignity in his sexual life, which was reticent but untainted by pretence.'

A quintessential professional himself, he could be a scathing and witty critic of the second-rate; but he was outstandingly generous in his praise, never standing on dignity because of his position. He had the capacity to inspire great devotion. Gertrude Lawrence's last letter to him ended: 'It's always you I want to please more than *anyone*'—a sentiment that would be widely echoed among those who knew him.

There are portraits of him by Edward Seago in the Garrick Club and the Phoenix Theatre and by Clemence Dane in the National Portrait Gallery. In 1984 a black memorial stone, with the words 'A talent to amuse', was unveiled in Westminster Abbey.

[*Noël Coward Autobiography*, 1986 (ed. Sheridan Morley); Cole Lesley, *The Life of Noël Coward*, 1976; Charles Castle, *Noël*, 1972; Sheridan Morley, *A Talent to Amuse*, 1969; *Who's Who in the Theatre* (15th edn.) for a comprehensive list of his writings and performances; personal knowledge.]

MICHAEL DENISON

published 1986

CRONIN Archibald Joseph

(1896–1981)

Novelist, was born 19 July 1896 at Cardross, Dunbartonshire, the only child of Patrick Cronin, a clerk and commercial traveller, and his wife, Jessie Montgomerie. When he was seven his father died and Cronin and his mother went to live with her family. His mother became a travelling saleswoman and the first woman public health inspector with Glasgow Corporation.

Cronin was educated at Dumbarton Academy and Glasgow University, where he studied medicine. He graduated MB, Ch.B. in 1919. His years at Glasgow were interrupted by service in 1916 as surgeon sub-lieutenant in the Royal Naval Volunteer Reserve and by three months at the Rotunda Hospital in Dublin, where he took his midwifery course. His first practice was in a mining district in Wales. During this period he obtained a diploma in public health (Lond. 1923), an MRCP (Lond. 1924) and an MD (Glasgow, 1925)—a considerable achievement which involved unremitting work. In

1924 he was appointed medical inspector of mines for Great Britain. His work at this time led to two reports on dust inhalation and first aid in mines.

Between 1926 and 1930 he practised in London, but ill health took him to the West Highlands, and there he wrote *Hatter's Castle* (1931). It made him famous overnight; he was able to give up his medical practice and become a full-time writer, as he had always wished to do. The second novel, *Three Loves* (1932), was 'torture to write', as he expressed it, and did not do well. However, *The Stars Look Down* (1935) was an instant favourite with his public. His next book, *The Citadel* (1937), which fiercely attacked the greed in Harley Street, caused a sensation. Launched with a brilliant publicity campaign by his publisher (Sir) Victor Gollancz, it probably played some part in creating the climate of opinion which led to the National Health Service.

In July 1939 Cronin went with his family to the United States. Two of his novels were filmed in Hollywood at about this time (several of his books were made into successful films). Between 1941 and 1945 he worked in Washington for the British Ministry of Information and wrote *The Keys of the Kingdom* (1942) and *The Green Years* (1945). After the war he lived permanently in Switzerland, writing novels at roughly two-yearly intervals, notably *The Spanish Gardener* (1950). He was an honorary D.Litt. of Bowdoin and of Lafayette University.

Cronin's strength as a novelist lay in his narrative skill, his acute observation, and his graphic powers of description. His plots were often overdramatic and his characters were in general unremarkable—he needed, as he himself remarked, to have real people to base them on (the tyrannical James Brodie, in *Hatter's Castle*, is said to be a portrait of his maternal grandfather, which caused consternation in the family). But as a craftsman he was meticulous and highly professional, and there is some refreshing humour in his books. He was not an intellectual, and enjoyed simple pleasures such as watching cricket matches and talking to the people round him, the kind of people who might have been his patients. A very hard worker, he greatly enjoyed writing. He also loved travelling, and this gave him material for his books which he used to good effect. He was a Catholic, and several of his novels are concerned with religion and matters of conscience. Though extremely tough in business dealings, in private life he was a happy, good-humoured person to whom each day was an adventure. His last years, however, after his wife became ill, were lonely, for he had always been a solitary individual, and his wealth cut him off from other people.

Cronin's experience in Dublin and Wales made him keenly aware of the evils of extreme poverty, and his skill in combining romantic, compelling narrative and vivid, realistic portrayal of life among the poorer members of society is one of the most striking facets of his novels. Nearly all his books have a strong autobiographical element, returning again and again to his childhood in Dumbarton, which is thinly veiled under the fictitious name of Levenford. Episodes in his autobiography *Adventures in Two Worlds* (1952) are repeated in his novels, making it difficult to disentangle fact from fiction. The immensely popular television and radio series which he wrote, *Dr Finlay's Casebook*, is also based on his experiences as a doctor.

Although Cronin's powers flagged in his later years, the best of his novels are extremely readable and accomplished, and they had deservedly large sales. He was a middlebrow writer *par excellence*, and above all a masterly story-teller.

He married Agnes Mary Gibson, MB, Ch.B., in 1921. She was the daughter of Robert Gibson, a master baker, of Hamilton, Lanarkshire. They had three sons, the eldest of whom, Vincent, became a writer. Cronin died 6 January 1981 at Glion, near Montreux, Switzerland.

[*The Times*, 10 January 1981; private information; personal knowledge.]

SHEILA HODGES

published 1990

CROWLEY Edward Alexander ('Aleister')

(1875–1947)

Writer, better known by his chosen name of Aleister Crowley (1898), was born 12 October 1875 in Leamington Spa, the only son and elder child (the daughter died in infancy) of Edward Crowley, evangelist and wealthy retired brewer of Crowley's Ales, and his wife Emily Bertha Bishop, who came from a Devonshire and Somerset family. Both parents were committed members of the Plymouth Brethren. After unhappy periods at Cambridge Plymouth Brethren preparatory school and at Malvern College, he was educated by private tutors, interspersed with periods of instruction at Tonbridge and at King's College, London, before attending Trinity College, Cambridge, in 1895 to study chemistry. There he won a half-blue in chess, and left in 1898 without taking a degree. At this time, his principal interests in life were mountaineering, poetry, and magick, his favoured term for varieties of religious experience.

His doubted claims to have been the greatest mountaineer of his generation have foundation in fact, despite the hostility which existed between him and the English Alpine Club. Few have surpassed his climbs on Beachy Head's treacherous chalk cliffs (1893–5). He was a pioneer of guideless Alpine ascents, which included the Eiger. With his partner Oscar Eckenstein, inventor of the crampon, he claimed the majority of available world mountaineering records in 1900, particularly those for pace uphill at high altitude, and these claims have not been convincingly refuted. The Eckenstein–Crowley expedition of 1902 to K2, the first attempt upon the world's second highest mountain, reached a height unsurpassed for over two decades. This was also true of the tragic Crowley expedition to the world's third highest mountain, Kinchinjunga, in 1905.

His poetry, from *Aceldama* (1898) via *The Collected Works* (3 vols., 1905–7) until *Olla* (1947), has consistently aroused extremes of praise and blame from critics. Despite the fact that connoisseurs applauded and collected his sumptuously produced, privately printed editions in terms of the designer's art, his work became unfashionable after 1918, and appreciation was marred by the poet's increasingly vilified personal reputation.

Crowley's principal concerns, however, consisted of his researches into ways of accelerating human evolution through increasing human intelligence by techniques of concentrating the mind one-pointedly, stimulating the central nervous system, and maximizing and mapping hitherto unexplored regions of the brain. This initially led him to ceremonial magick and London's Hermetic Order of the Golden Dawn (1898), members of which included W. B. Yeats, Arthur Machen, and its leader, S. L. Mathers; and to yoga with the former Golden Dawn member Allan Bennett, later Bhikku Anada Metteya, who brought Theravada (Hinayana) Buddhism to Great Britain. Crowley summarized his learning and practice in *The Equinox* (vol. i, 10 numbers, 1909–13) under the motto: 'The Method of Science: the Aim of Religion'. He circled the globe (1900–3), winning also a reputation as an explorer and big-game hunter.

Crowley regarded the most important event of his life as being his 'reception' in April 1904 of *The Book of the Law*, a prose poem which he believed to have been dictated to him by 'a praeter-human intelligence'. He did not accept it until 1909 when he became its proclaimed prophet. Its principal commandment, 'Do what thou wilt shall be the whole of the Law', to him meant not vulgar hedonism but the honest and honourable fulfilment of a person's deepest potential.

Unfortunately, these concerns led to a campaign of vilification in the press and Crowley was called the 'wickedest man in the world' (1923) on account of his endeavour to express his ideas at Cefalu, Sicily (1920–3). Even though he had attempted to make a propagandist contribution to the British war effort in 1915–17, he was slandered as a traitor. He spent the years 1914–19 in America and wrote ludicrous, counter-productive, pro-German propaganda for *The Fatherland*. He was not prosecuted when he returned to England in 1919 and insisted that he had been employed by British Naval Intelligence. He subsequently travelled in France, Italy, Spain, China, Portugal, India, Sri Lanka, Russia, Scandinavia, North Africa, and Germany.

Crowley was colourful, eccentric, flamboyant, and deliberately shocking, always a keen adventurer and womanizer. In 1903 he married Rose Edith, daughter of the Revd Frederick Festus Kelly and sister of his Cambridge contemporary and friend, (Sir) Gerald Kelly. They had three daughters, the first of whom died in 1906. Crowley's wife divorced him on grounds of admitted adultery in 1910. In 1929, in Berlin, he married Maria Teresa de Miramar, of Nicaragua. A mutually agreed separation subsequently ensued. Although excoriated and ignored, Crowley died 1 December 1947 in comfortable circumstances at 'Netherwood', Hastings, a country house turned residential hotel, and was cremated in Brighton 5 December.

[The Yorke Collection, Warburg Institute, University of London, and private conversation with Gerald Yorke; Israel Regardie, *The Eye in the Triangle*, 1970; C. R. Cammell, *Aleister Crowley: the Man: the Mage: the Poet*, 1951; Gerald Suster, *The Legacy of the Beast*, 1988; John Symonds, *The King of the Shadow Realm*, 1989.]

GERALD SUSTER

published 1993

DASHWOOD Edmée Elizabeth Monica

(1890–1943)

Authoress, better known by her pen-name of E. M. Delafield, was born 9 June 1890 at Steyning, Sussex, the elder daughter of Count Henry Philip Ducarel de la Pasture, of Llandogo Priory, Monmouthshire, a member of a noble family which settled in England after the French revolution, by his wife, Elizabeth Lydia Rosabelle, daughter of Edward William Bonham, who, as Mrs. Henry de la Pasture, became known as a novelist. The girlhood of E. M. Delafield was spent in the last days of the Edwardian era, and that formal sheltered society is reproduced with dry fidelity in many of her books. At the outbreak of war in 1914 she became a member of a voluntary aid detachment in Exeter, and there, in snatched moments, wrote her first novel, *Zella Sees Herself*, which was published in 1917. At the end of the war she was working for the south-western region of the

Ministry of National Service, at Bristol; and after two years in the Malay States she and her husband, Major A. P. Dashwood, settled at Cullompton in Devonshire, where Mrs. Dashwood became a magistrate, and a great worker for Women's Institutes.

Meanwhile, no year in the 'twenties or 'thirties passed without the publication of one of her books, often several. These were chiefly fiction, but she also wrote three plays, and was probably most widely and popularly known for her humorous sketches. Had her output been less, her literary reputation would have been higher, as it deserved to be; but even her least-considered work is unfailingly readable. Romance and beauty were outside her deliberately narrowed range; what interested her was the mechanism of human behaviour, particularly the phenomena of vanity and self-deception. Her mood suited the decades when the word 'debunking' gained currency, and her plain style fitted the unsparing common sense and somewhat feline wit of her fiction in general. Perhaps her best novel was *Thank Heaven Fasting* (1932). Typical of her more serious work was *Nothing is Safe* (1937), an indictment of the harm caused to children by easy divorce; and her interest in criminology inspired the earlier *Messalina of the Suburbs* (1923), a reconstruction of a well-known crime. Another hobby, the study of the lesser Victorian novelists, resulted in a book not seen in her list of published works, *The Bazalgettes* (1935), a pastiche of Rhoda Broughton so exact as to deceive many critics. Her gift for mimicry was also evident in her series for *Punch* 'As Others Hear Us': and pre-eminently in the books which gave her the greatest popularity, *The Diary of A Provincial Lady* (1930) and its sequels. The Provincial Lady appeared originally in *Time and Tide*, of which E. M. Delafield was a director; and this lovable creation, always ready to laugh at herself, presents, in the opinion of friends, a better clue to the gentle and generous personality of the writer than does her more satirical work.

In 1919 she married Major Arthur Paul Dashwood, second surviving son of Sir George Dashwood, sixth baronet. They had one son and one daughter. E. M. Delafield died at Cullompton, Devonshire, 2 December 1943. A portrait painted in 1909 by D. A. Wehrschmidt (later Veresmith) is in the possession of the family.

[*The Times*, 3 December 1943; *Time and Tide*, 11 December 1943.]

M. BELLASIS

published 1959

(1904–1972)

Poet laureate and detective novelist, was born 27 April 1904 at Ballin-tubbert, Queen's county (now county Laois), Ireland, the only child of the Revd Frank Cecil Day-Lewis, Church of Ireland curate, and his wife, Kathleen Blake, daughter of William Alfred Squires, civil servant. His mother died when he was four and he was brought up in London by his father and his selfless aunt Agnes Olive ('Knos') Squires. Educated at Wilkie's preparatory school, London, and Sherborne, he entered Wadham College, Oxford, in 1923 with a classics exhibition. He began writing verse as a schoolboy and, sure of his poetic vocation, he chose mainly literary friends and acquaintances at Oxford. During his third year there he met the undergraduate W. H. Auden, the major influence on his early work. Their collaboration continued through 1927–8 when Day-Lewis held a teaching post at Summer Fields preparatory school in Oxford. Together they edited *Oxford Poetry 1927*. Day-Lewis obtained a second class in classical honour moderations in 1925 and a third in *literae humaniores* in 1927.

After his two early slim volumes of verse, more or less 'Georgian' in style, *Beechen Vigil* (1925) and *Country Comets* (1928), Day-Lewis became more rigorous with *Transitional Poem* (1929). This sequence was the first public manifestation of what was to become known as the Auden Gang or, as their unsympathetic contemporary Roy Campbell satirically put it, the MacSpaunday (Louis MacNeice, Stephen Spender, W. H. Auden, C. Day-Lewis) beast. Though this poetic movement was really little more than a convenient pigeon-hole for critics its supposed members were contem-poraries subject to the weather of the times and responding to it with a similar leftish stance. Day-Lewis in particular remained spellbound by Auden's work. Though private themes often provided a framework they were used to question the social order and brimmed with Audenesque images and metaphors drawn from natural science. His sequences from *From Feathers to Iron* (1931) and *The Magnetic Mountain* (1933) to *A Time to Dance* (1935) and *Noah and the Waters* (1936) were exuberant, eclectic, and voguish enough to make him fashionable but delayed the finding of his true voice as a lyric poet of nature and private emotion. At the same time he provided a critical manifesto for the young poets of his generation, *A Hope for Poetry* (1934), claiming Gerard Manley Hopkins, Wilfred Owen, and T. S. Eliot as their immediate ancestors.

He had married in 1928 when he took his second teaching post at Larchfield School, Helensburgh, near Glasgow. His wife was (Constance)

Mary, daughter of one of his former Sherborne form-masters, Henry Robinson King. Two years later he moved to Cheltenham Junior School in Gloucestershire. By 1934 he had two sons as well as a wife to support and it was primarily to make money that he became the detective novelist Nicholas Blake. His *A Question of Proof* (1935), set at a prep. school mixing aspects of those he had taught at, proved to be the first of twenty Blake novels mostly featuring the detective Nigel Strangeways. Its success was a factor in encouraging him to retire from teaching to become a full-time writer and political activist, in December 1935. He joined the Communist Party three months later and there followed two intense years when he wrote three straight novels, two detective novels, weekly book reviews, and many polemical pamphlets and essays. He was in demand as a speaker and lecturer and in the organization of the tiny Gloucestershire branch of the party. By early 1938 he had decided he must make a choice between 'being an amateurish political worker or trying to make myself a better poet'. Poetry won.

In order to break with political and public life he moved with his family to a secluded thatched cottage on an upper slope of Castle Hill above Musbury, a straggling east Devon village, in August 1938. It was a move crucial to his poetic development. In *Overtures to Death* (1938) the verse concerned with the possibilities of heroic action had been overshadowed by that where the political militant retired to wait for the inevitable disaster of war. As Auden sailed for the United States, Day-Lewis found his new and true home close to the Dorset border, and Thomas Hardy country. With his translation of Virgil's *Georgics* (1940) and his own verse collections *Word Over All* (1943) and *Poems 1943–1947* (1948) he achieved his full stature as a poet. The Hardy influence now predominated. He could parody his idol as in 'Singing Children: Luca della Robbia', part of the 'Florence: Works of Art' section of *An Italian Visit* (1953). He could make pastiche as in 'Birthday Poem for Thomas Hardy' in the 1948 collection. More importantly he was able to absorb and transmute the influence into a voice unmistakably his own. His poetry in this period reflected his private concerns, his responses to war, his Devon neighbours and their landscape, his divided emotional life.

After a hilarious period in command of Musbury's Home Guard platoon he went to London in the spring of 1941 to become an editor in the Ministry of Information's publications division. In 1946, soon after his release from the ministry, he became senior reader for the publishers Chatto and Windus, an association that lasted until the end of his life. Increasingly through this decade there was a conflict between the private Devon poet nourished by the countryside and the public London literary figure, the conscientious committee man.

This conflict was echoed in his emotional life. In 1939–41 he took part in a volcanic love affair with the wife of a neighbouring Musbury farmer, dwelt on in several poems and the final somewhat autobiographical Nicholas Blake story *The Private Wound* (1968). They had a son. From 1941 he began a more complete relationship with the novelist Rosamond Lehmann, commuting for the rest of the decade between her and his family at Musbury. She inspired some good poems, she broadened his personality, and she encouraged him to travel abroad and to take on such tasks as the 1946 Clark lectures at Cambridge. Such a divided life was a great strain on all concerned. At the end of 1949 he fell in love again, this time with the twenty-four-year-old actress Jill Angela Henriette Balcon, daughter of Sir Michael Balcon, film producer. The following year he left both Mary and Rosamond for a second marriage with Jill, which took place after the dissolution of his first marriage in 1951. There were two sons (one of whom was to write his father's biography) of the first marriage, and a daughter and a son of the second.

In the last two decades of his life he looked wistfully back towards Dorset, the county of his school-days as well as Hardy, and to his Irish roots. But he settled against becoming the rural regional poet that he might have been and opted permanently for London and the literary life. With every passing year the profile of his public honours and responsibilities moved upwards and the one indicating critical esteem curved in the opposite direction. In 1951, the year in which his translation of Virgil's *Aeneid* commissioned by the BBC was broadcast as part of the Festival of Britain, he was elected Oxford professor of poetry. His five-year term opened a period when he became more preoccupied with public poetry reading, mainly in partnership with his second wife, prestigious lectureships, and his public-spirited work for organizations like the Apollo Society, the Royal Society of Literature (he received its C.Lit. in 1965), and the Arts Council. His taste for public honours was most gratified in 1968 when he was chosen to succeed John Masefield as poet laureate, the first Irish-born holder of that office since Nahum Tate (1652–1715). He also received honorary degrees from Exeter (1965), Trinity College, Dublin, (1968), and Hull (1970). In 1968 he became an honorary fellow of Wadham College and was elected to the Irish Academy of Letters.

Though no longer fashionable and much diverted by this public activity, his work as a publisher, and the raising of a second family, he continued to regard the writing of poetry as the point of his life. His final volumes of verse, *Pegasus* (1957), *The Gate* (1962), *The Room* (1965), and *The Whispering Roots* (1970), were received with woundingly faint praise by reviewers. They nevertheless contain some of Day-Lewis's best poems and display a mature mastery of craftsmanship and a fluency of technique that delighted his discriminating band of admirers. His themes ranged from the public and prosaic to those private explorations of love and living that put him firmly in the poetic family of Hardy, Edward Thomas, and Robert Frost. His health declined after 1969 and he died 22 May 1972 at Lemmons, Hadley Wood, Hertfordshire, the home of the novelists Elizabeth Jane Howard and Kingsley Amis. Appropriately he is buried at Stinsford in Dorset only a few feet from Hardy's grave and less than thirty miles from the Devon border country where he found his voice.

Day-Lewis was a man of considerable generosity, charm, and elegance who laughed easily and was as stylish in his movements as in his dress. In his younger days he had a light lyric tenor voice very effective in the Irish songs of Tom Moore he learned at his aunt's knee, and good enough to be heard several times on BBC radio. If he loved women and was always vulnerable to them he was also good at making and keeping friends of both sexes. He was a tireless advocate of English literature in general and poetry in particular and unsparing in his encouragement of younger writers in whom he found any glimmer of talent.

A 1946 portrait of Day-Lewis by Lawrence Gowing was commissioned by Rosamond Lehmann and is the property of Sean and Nicholas Day-Lewis.

[C. Day-Lewis, *The Buried Day* (autobiography), 1960; Sean Day-Lewis, *C. Day-Lewis: An English Literary Life*, 1980; personal knowledge.]

SEAN DAY-LEWIS

published 1986

DE LA MARE Walter John

(1873–1956)

Poet, novelist, and anthologist, was born 25 April 1873 at Charlton, Kent, the sixth child of James Edward de la Mare, an official in the Bank of England, and his wife, Lucy Sophia Browning. He was educated at St. Paul's Cathedral Choristers' School, where he edited the school magazine, and then entered the service of the Anglo-American Oil Company for which he worked until 1908. He began his literary career with *Songs of Childhood* (1902), followed by the vast *opus* of poems, stories, novels, books for children, and anthologies, all marked by an individual genius which was quickly recognized.

His first prose book, *Henry Brocken* (1904), is a romance using famous figures from the literatures of Europe. It sets the perspective line of all his subsequent work. The background of his view of life was to remain fixed in the world of books. If incongruity threatened, then life had to be refashioned by fantasy to fit that background, whether it was the life of children or adults. Thus, the strange adaptations of fact in *The Return* (1910), *The Three Mulla-Mulgars* (1910), and *Memoirs of a Midget* (1921).

The book which carried his poetry to a wide public was *The Listeners* (1912). Even more popular, perhaps, was the book of poems for children *Peacock Pie* (1913). *Come Hither*, an anthology (1923), finally established his fame as a writer for children. His two most characteristic anthologies, both enriched by long introductions, are *Behold, This Dreamer* (1939) and *Love* (1943). His most sustained poem, a synopsis of his philosophy of life, and a final revelation of his temperament, is *The Traveller* (1946).

Within his own universe de la Mare was a highly complicated organism, compounded of subtly articulated nervous tensions which made his contacts with the outside world oblique, tentative, sometimes even bizarre. His first book, *Songs of Childhood*, was published under the pseudonym of Walter Ramal, an adaptation of de la Mare read in a mirror. Again, in one of his most characteristic prose books, *The Return*, the central figure looks at himself in the mirror, about to shave, and there sees a face only dimly, historically, resembling his own. This horrifying experience was not horrifying to de la Mare; his nature accepted it welcomingly. It was as though he were endowed with several extra sets of eyes, which he was able to set out in strategic positions to get a many-intelligenced view of any given situation, mood, fear, or passion, person, or place. And it was his multiplied curiosity which did the work in the making of a story or a poem, just as it controlled his conversations with fellow mortals.

In his conversation, the climate of discussion began to resemble that of his poetry. Oblique lights shot across the familiar scene, and what was normally visible became an obscured form gradually filling up with horror, while the vacant lots of the commonplace became peopled with dancing shadows which grew more and more concrete and plausible. Size, form, time, and place intervolved, and the de la Marian universe was all around the visitor: strange, thwart, more yet less than human, full of contradictions that resolved with lightning speed into a weird symbolism of desperate faith. For that is what he moved towards, all his life. He was beset by these damaging queries; he could not refrain from the destructive questioning. But out of the breakages resulting from this passionate, devout scepticism, he contrived (and with a childlike simplicity) to build up the poetry which irradiated all his work.

The nature and texture of that poetry are as interwoven as are the meaning and the strange phrasing in the most characteristic of Shakespeare's dialogue; completely a unit as organism, yet more and more miraculous and incredible the more it is analysed. De la Mare's use of poetic inversion, for example, is in itself a study which baffles the critic. It was partly involuntary, because he could not keep himself from this ingrained gesture of turning to the mirror to look out on life in reflection, in opposites, and above all in that weird silence which pervades all reflection. Although he wrote vastly, and usually anonymously, as a critic, he never hesitated to say that he could not be certain how his own work was done, how the moonlight (another reflection) became the chief illuminant of his field of vision. He knew the craft of the poet, and was jealous in the care and use of the medium, the unruly flock of words. In a letter in 1945, he said: 'I often wonder how many people really understand the language. Not a great number, I fancy. There are many good reasons for liking and delighting in poetry, if reasons they can be called; but *the* reason—one could not define it—but that once realized, all else is only addendas.'

His was a mind, a personality, which loved dangerous living. He would not be content to bask by the fireside of accepted values. The certainties of life must always be opened, disrupted by him in his almost irresponsible inquisitiveness. In the most ordinary and innocuous of things and events he saw a force which was always a threat. Atomic fission was his daily practice. He drew again and again towards this brink of the abyss which most people ignored or denied, and there he stood, fascinated, wondering what might be the result if a mortal defied this pervasive latency.

Any old object would serve towards this perilous adventure: a candle-end, a scarecrow, a snatch of mist, a trail of bindweed. The smallest thing was a key into the humming power-house of the Mystery. In the poem called 'The Bottle' he sums up this attitude, as he describes it,

> Of green and hexagonal glass,
> With sharp, fluted sides—
> Vaguely transparent these walls,
> Wherein motionless hides
> A simple so potent it can
> To oblivion lull
> The weary, the racked, the bereaved,
> The miserable.

And he applies to himself, and the ever-questing consciousness within him, the efficacy of the drug in that bottle to reveal the answer,

> Wicket out into the dark
> That swings but one way;

> Infinite hush in an ocean of silence
> Aeons away—
> *Thou* forsaken!—even thou!—
> The dread good-bye;
> The abandoned, the thronged, the watched, the unshared—
> Awaiting me—I!

That may be the way into a fuller understanding of this poet and his work; the realization that always he dallied with danger, was obsessed with the curiosity of what might happen if he should dissociate this material world from its physical coherence and set free the forces which so restrained it.

De la Mare received honorary degrees from the universities of Oxford, Cambridge, London, St. Andrews, and Bristol, and was an honorary fellow of Keble College, Oxford. In 1948 he was appointed C.H. and in 1953 O.M.

In 1899 he married Constance Elfrida (died 1943), daughter of Alfred William Ingpen and sister of Roger Ingpen who married Walter de la Mare's sister. He had two daughters and two sons, the elder of whom, Richard, became chairman of Faber & Faber, Ltd., the publishers of the definitive edition of his father's works.

A drawing of de la Mare by Augustus John was first in the possession of Lady Cynthia Asquith. Of several drawings by Sir William Rothenstein, one is reproduced in *Twenty-Four Portraits* (second series, 1923) and another in *Twelve Portraits* (1929). A chalk drawing of Walter de la Mare in bed by H. A. Freeth was exhibited at the Royal Academy in 1958; and a death mask was made by his family for presentation to the National Portrait Gallery which also has a drawing by Rothenstein and another by Augustus John.

Walter de la Mare died at Twickenham, Middlesex, 22 June 1956. His ashes are buried in the crypt of St. Paul's Cathedral where there is a memorial plaque.

[Private information; personal knowledge.]

RICHARD CHURCH

published 1971

DOUGLAS Keith Castellain

(1920–1944)

Poet, was born 24 January 1920 in Tunbridge Wells, the only child of Captain Keith Sholto Douglas, MC, soldier and chicken farmer, and his wife, (Marie) Josephine, daughter of Charles Castellain, a man of private means. His childhood was spent in Cranleigh, and he was educated at Edgeborough School, Guildford, where he revealed precocious talents as artist, poet, and sportsman, and at Christ's Hospital, London. In 1927 his father left home and, in due course, remarried. Like Lord Byron, who suffered a similar deprivation and whom he would grow to resemble in other ways, Douglas hero-worshipped the absent captain, at twelve beginning an autobiographical essay: 'As a child he was a militarist, and like many of his warlike elders, built up heroic opinions upon little information—some scrappy war stories of his father.'

In 1938 he won a scholarship to Merton College, Oxford, where his influential tutor was Edmund Blunden, soldier-poet of an earlier war than that for which Douglas enlisted in 1940. A year later, now a second lieutenant, he sailed to Palestine to join the Nottinghamshire Sherwood Rangers Yeomanry, a cavalry regiment that had recently exchanged its horses for tanks. Moving with them to north Africa, he was initially held in enforced inactivity behind the lines, a problem which he solved in characteristic style: 'The Battle of Alamein began on the 23rd of October, 1942. Six days afterwards I set out in direct disobedience of orders to rejoin my regiment. My batman was delighted with this manoeuvre. "I like you, sir," he said, "You're shit or bust, you are." This praise gratified me a lot.' So ends the introduction to Douglas's prose memoir of that battle and its aftermath, *Alamein to Zem Zem*. Published posthumously in 1946, with his own illustrations and an appendix of poems, this rendered the war in the Western Desert as graphically as Blunden's *Undertones of War* (1928) had depicted life and death on the western front.

Douglas had an artist's eye for the horrors—and also the absurdities—of battle. Technically, his war poems show the influence of those of Wilfred Owen, but their language is simpler, more direct, and they have nothing of his indignation. There was less cause for indignation in the desert than in the trenches, and Douglas never lost his insatiable appetite for experience. Where Owen's preface to his poems had declared 'This book is not about heroes', Douglas in both his poetry and prose celebrates the last stand of the chivalric hero, men like his colonel, 'Piccadilly Jim'. In his poem 'Sportsmen' he asks: 'How then can I live among this gentle/obsolescent breed of heroes, and not weep?' His language, finely responsive to his theme, fuses ancient and modern: his fellow officers are 'gentle', like the 'verray parfit gentil knight' of Geoffrey Chaucer, and at the same time 'obsolescent'.

Douglas was wounded by a mine in January 1943, but survived the desert campaign. Back in England for Christmas, he wrote some of his finest

poems, collected and copied others, and by the end of March had completed manuscripts of *Alamein to Zem Zem* and a volume of poems.

He commanded a tank troop in the main assault on the Normandy
beaches, and his death outside the village of St Pierre, 9 June 1944, robbed
English literature—as had Owen's death in 1918—of the most individual
and accomplished poet of his generation. He was unmarried.

[Desmond Graham (ed.), *Alamein to Zem Zem*, 1979, *The Complete Poems of Keith
Douglas*, 1978, and *Keith Douglas: a Prose Miscellany*, 1985; Desmond Graham,
Keith Douglas 1920–1944: a Biography, 1974.]

JON STALLWORTHY

published 1993

DOYLE Sir Arthur Conan

(1859–1930)

Author, the eldest son of Charles Altamont Doyle, clerk in the Board of
Works and artist, by his wife, Mary Foley, was born in Edinburgh 22 May
1859. He came of an Irish Roman Catholic family, and one well known in
art and letters. His grandfather was John Doyle, the portrait-painter and
caricaturist, and his uncle was Richard Doyle, the black-and-white artist
who drew for *Punch* in the early years of that journal and designed its well-
known cover.

Arthur Conan Doyle was educated at Stonyhurst and at Edinburgh
University. He qualified M.B. in 1881 and M.D. in 1885, and practised at
Southsea from 1882 to 1890. In 1887 he published his first book, *A Study in
Scarlet*—a novel, of a not more than moderately thrilling type, which is
chiefly noteworthy for introducing to the public a character, Sherlock
Holmes, who became a famous figure in detective fiction. Conan Doyle
followed this tale with *Micah Clarke* (1887), *The Captain of the Polestar* (1889),
The White Company (1890), *The Sign of Four* (1890, another Holmes story),
and other novels of general or historical interest.

But what attracted more attention than these complete works was a
series of short stories which came out under the title *The Adventures of
Sherlock Holmes*. The first of these, 'A Scandal in Bohemia', appeared in the
Strand Magazine for July 1891, and for many months the stories formed an
attractive feature of that periodical. The hero of these exploits was now
handled with greater sureness and fertility of invention. Sherlock Holmes
was represented as a private detective, living in Baker Street with a friend,

Doctor Watson, who describes the cases brought to them by distracted clients, and the manner in which Holmes solved mysteries which baffled everyone else, including the leading officials of Scotland Yard. Holmes's methods consisted in the careful and systematic examination of minute details, and a process of deduction from the points observed. The character is said to have been suggested to Doyle by his recollection of an eminent Edinburgh surgeon, Dr. Joseph Bell, under whom he had worked as a medical student. It was Bell's custom to impress upon his pupils the value in diagnosis of the faculty of close observation of facts and the intelligent interpretation of them.

Conan Doyle made free use of this creation of his fancy in many stories both short and long. Sherlock Holmes, with his clean-shaven face and penetrating eyes, his spare yet muscular frame, his pipe, his dressing-gown, his violin, and the cocaine syringe with which he soothed his nerves, became a familiar figure to millions of readers. Equally appreciated, and in striking contrast, was the simplicity of Doctor Watson, who could be trusted to put the questions necessary for displaying to the best advantage his leader's unusual gifts. All too soon, however, the association of Holmes and Watson was cut short by a fatality which befell the great detective, when he shared the fate of a master-criminal whom he at last brought to account in a life and death struggle on the brink of a precipice. The public was deeply distressed. The Sherlock Holmes stories which had begun, as stated, in July 1891, in the *Strand Magazine*, continued with a break of a few months only until December 1893, when this tragedy occurred. Fortunately, after some time had passed it was discovered that, although in grave peril, Holmes had escaped with his life and was able to embark upon a new series of exploits. These short stories began in October 1903, and the adventures continued to appear at irregular intervals until within a year or two of the author's death. He had published, besides, a longer and rather more elaborate Sherlock Holmes tale *The Hound of the Baskervilles*, which ran in the *Strand* from August 1901 to April 1902, and was afterwards published as a separate volume. Whatever rank may be assigned to Conan Doyle among English novelists, he at least earned the distinction of having created a figure whose name has passed into the language as a synonym for the qualities with which the author invested him.

Conan Doyle did not confine his energies to literature. He was distinguished by a spirit of genuine patriotism, and any Imperial cause attracted him. During the South African War of 1899–1902 he placed his medical knowledge and experience at the disposal of the government, and acted as senior physician to the field hospital maintained and equipped by Sir John Langman. He wrote an account of the earlier stages of the campaign in his book *The Great Boer War* (1900). More important than this book was his pamphlet, *The War in South Africa. Its Cause and Conduct* (1902), which had as its object the justification of England's action in declaring war against the Boers, and the vindication of her method of conducting the campaign. Some exposition of the facts had become essential in order to correct misconceptions industriously spread over the Continent. The pamphlet was translated into twelve European languages, and more than a hundred thousand copies of it were given away. Shortly after the conclusion of the War, Conan Doyle came out as a warm supporter of the proposals put forward in 1903 by Joseph Chamberlain for tariff reform and Colonial preference. He had already stood for parliament in 1900 as liberal unionist candidate for Central Edinburgh, without success; and in 1906 he stood again—this time for the Hawick Burghs as a tariff reformer. Though a capable speaker on his own subjects, and a most vigorous electioneer, he failed to obtain a seat in parliament. He was an active propagandist in fields other than political, and devoted much labour to championing the cause of a man named Oscar Slater, who was sentenced to death (commuted afterwards to penal servitude) for murder and robbery at Glasgow in May 1909. Actuated by a firm belief that this was a case of mistaken identity, Doyle published in 1912 a criticism of the judgment, which led to an official inquiry in 1914. As a result it was announced that no grounds for interference with Slater's sentence had been found, and this announcement was repeated by the secretary for Scotland in 1925. Two years later the introduction of fresh evidence led to the case being remitted to the Scottish court of criminal appeal, and upon 20 July 1928 the sentence was quashed, and Slater, who had already been released from gaol, received an *ex gratia* payment of £6,000 as compensation.

For nearly forty years Conan Doyle continued to write and publish regularly. He chose a hero, Brigadier Gerard, for several stories of Napoleonic times, and his lively imagination played with many different forms of sensation, as in *The Lost World* (1912) and *The Poison Belt* (1913). He also wrote several more books dealing with public topics, such as *The Crime of the Congo* (1910). During the European War he was engaged upon a *History of the British Campaign in France and Flanders* (6 vols., 1916–1920), and he also wrote *A Visit to Three Fronts* (1916). He made a few essays in dramatic authorship, the most successful being *A Story of Waterloo* (1894); in this, a one-act play, Sir Henry Irving gave a remarkable representation of a veteran soldier.

In the later years of his life Conan Doyle became absorbed by the subject of spiritualism, upon which he wrote and lectured not only in England, but in South Africa and Australia. Among his books on this subject are *The Wanderings of a Spiritualist* (1921) and a *History of Spiritualism* (2 vols.,

1926), and most of the writing that he undertook in this period was coloured by his views on the evidence for spirit communication.

Conan Doyle was a big man, strong, and heavily built. He was fond of all sports and games. He was a fair cricketer, and played in many good second-class matches for the Marylebone and other clubs. He was also a regular patron of boxing, and brought the subject of pugilism into one of the best of his novels, *Rodney Stone* (1896). His writings were in keeping with his character. His novels, with no claim to literary distinction, are for the most part capital stories told in a straightforward and vigorous style.

Conan Doyle was knighted after the South African War, in 1902. He received the honorary degree of LL.D. from the university of Edinburgh in 1905 and was a knight of grace of the order of St. John of Jerusalem. He married twice: first, in 1885 Louise (died 1906), daughter of J. Hawkins, of Minsterworth, Gloucestershire, by whom he had one son and one daughter; secondly, in 1907 Jean, daughter of James Blyth Leckie, of Glebe House, Blackheath, by whom he had two sons and one daughter. He died at his home at Crowborough, Sussex, 7 July 1930.

[*The Times*, 8 July 1930.]

A. COCHRANE

published 1937

ELIOT Thomas Stearns

(1888–1965)

Poet, playwright, critic, editor, and publisher, was born in St. Louis, Missouri, 26 September 1888. He was the youngest son in the family of seven children of Henry Ware Eliot, a successful industrialist, and his wife, Charlotte Chauncy Stearns, a woman of literary interests. His mother wrote two books, one a biography (1904) of her father-in-law, William Greenleaf Eliot, who after completing his course at the Harvard Divinity School had gone in 1834 to settle in St. Louis. He founded the first Unitarian church in the city, and was also the founder of Washington University there. But for a humility which he transmitted to his grandson, it would have been named Eliot University. Mrs Eliot's second book (privately printed in London in 1926 at her son's behest) was a dramatic poem about Savonarola. A respect for family tradition and a predisposition to intense religious experience may have come to Eliot through her.

His family, as Eliot wrote, 'zealously guarded' its New England connections. He himself, after spending five years (1898–1903) at Smith Academy (another of his grandfather's foundations) in St. Louis, was sent back to Milton Academy in Massachusetts in 1905, and then in 1906 to Harvard University. He completed in three years the four-year course, and received his BA in 1909. He wrote later that in St. Louis he had felt himself to be a New Englander, but that in New England he felt himself to be a Southwesterner. He was later to experience, with ambivalent feelings, further deracination.

He planned at this time to become a professor of philosophy, and to that end entered the Harvard Graduate School. In 1910 he took his MA and then went to the Sorbonne for a year. On his return to Harvard he began to write a doctoral dissertation on the philosophy of F. H. Bradley. The conception of 'immediate experience' as a means of transcending appearance and achieving the 'Absolute' had an effect upon Eliot's own thought, but other influences had also begun to make themselves felt. At Harvard his principal teacher was Irving Babbitt, who in a notable book excoriated *Rousseau and Romanticism*. Eliot's anti-romantic tendencies perhaps derived from him. Another intense interest came in 1908 when he was introduced to the poetry of Jules Laforgue, of whom he would say that 'he was the first to teach me how to speak, to teach me the poetic possibilities of my own idiom of speech'. A little later he studied intensively the languages Sanskrit and Pali, and read a good deal in Indic religion, admiring especially its concern with diligently working out a means of transcending individual selfhood. Gradually these interests were to coalesce.

While still an undergraduate Eliot had contributed a few poems to the *Harvard Advocate*, the later ones exercises in Laforguian irony. In 1910 he composed his first mature poem, 'The Love Song of J. Alfred Prufrock'. In 1914, after having assisted in philosophy courses at Harvard, he was awarded a travelling fellowship by the university. He went to study for the summer in Marburg, but the outbreak of war in August obliged him to make his way, in a less leisurely fashion than he had intended, to Oxford. He continued there, at Merton College, under the supervision of Harold Joachim, his study of Bradley's *Appearance and Reality*.

The year 1914–15 proved to be pivotal for Eliot. He came to three interrelated decisions. The first was to give up the appearance of the philosopher for the reality of the poet, though he equivocated a little about this by continuing to write reviews for philosophical journals for some time thereafter. The second was to marry, and the third to settle in England, the war notwithstanding. He was helped to all three decisions by Ezra Pound, whom he met in September 1914. Pound had come to

England in 1908 and was convinced (though he changed his mind later) that this was the country most congenial to the literary life. He not only encouraged Eliot to marry and settle, but he succeeded (where Eliot had failed) in having some of Eliot's poems published. The first to appear was 'Prufrock' in *Poetry* (Chicago) for June 1915. This was a bizarre lament for the surrender of deeper impulses to elegant proprieties. The mysterious interstices of this poem, its mixture of colloquialism and elegance, and its memorable ironies were established with great confidence. The portrait of enervation was executed with contradictory energy.

In the same month that 'Prufrock' was published, Eliot married. His wife was Vivien Haigh Haigh-Wood, an Englishwoman with aspirations to be a painter or writer. The marriage proved most unhappy, and unhappiness, fostered by the war, and by what he once described as a lifelong aboulia, became the tenor of much of Eliot's verse. Domestic anxiety may have encouraged him to search out images of ruin and devastation, which joined with the international disasters of the war and the evils of modern industrial society. The witty, humorous side of his nature—well known to his friends—found only sporadic written expression, in the partly satirical cast of his first volumes of verse, in the flamboyant *Sweeney Agonistes* (1932), and, more genially, in *Old Possum's Book of Practical Cats* (1939).

After his marriage Eliot resisted the urgings of his parents that he return with his wife to the safe side of the Atlantic and teach philosophy. They did not cut him off, but, while they wished their son to finish his dissertation, they did not give enough money for full support. To manage at all, Eliot took up schoolteaching. His first position was at High Wycombe Grammar School from September to December 1915, after which he changed to Highgate Junior School and taught until December 1916. During this period he had completed and submitted his dissertation, which was found acceptable, and in April 1916 he was set to return to Harvard for his oral examination. But the ship did not sail and he made no further efforts to secure his doctorate. Teaching did not prove a satisfactory way of life, since it left him no leisure time, and in March 1917 he shifted to a position in the colonial and foreign department at Lloyds Bank in London, and kept at it for eight years, until November 1925. When the United States entered the war he was rejected for active service, on medical grounds, and his subsequent efforts to volunteer for military or naval intelligence were also unsuccessful. After the peace treaty was signed, the bank put him in sole charge of dealing with debts and claims of the bank and Germans. He manœuvred dexterously among the complications.

But his principal work during this period had to be conducted at night: this was the conquest of a position as both poet and critic. As poet he had to create a new style, and as critic to validate it. He wrote many reviews and essays, and, with a sparseness already habitual, a few poems. In 1917 he published *Prufrock and Other Observations*, in 1919 *Poems*, in 1920 *Ara Vos Prec* (which included the two previous volumes). An American edition of his verse to date also appeared in 1920 under the title *Poems*. The same year he collected his prose pieces and published them under the title *The Sacred Wood*.

The combination of careers sapped his strength and kept him on the verge of breakdown. Vivien Eliot's health was also bad, and the drugs which she increasingly required to alleviate her migraine and nervous pains were a new source of tension for her husband. In 1921 Eliot felt ill enough to consult a neurologist, who advised him to take three months' convalescent leave. With the consent of Lloyds Bank, Eliot went in October to Margate and in November, for a psychiatric consultation, to Lausanne. While in Switzerland, where he remained into December, he brought to completion *The Waste Land*, the long poem on which he had been working seriously since late in 1919. The publication in 1971 of the original manuscript of this poem (edited by his second wife, Valerie Eliot), after it had been missing for almost half a century, explained and confirmed Eliot's acknowledgement, in the poem's dedication, of his debt to Ezra Pound. It was Pound who helped him sift the final version from many drafts and false starts.

The Waste Land appeared with considerable fanfare on both sides of the Atlantic late in 1922. Although many readers found it outrageous, it gave Eliot his central position in modern verse. The work brought poetry into the same atmosphere of innovation which characterized music and painting of the time, and as with those arts, its effect was not of tentative but of consolidated experiment. In later life Eliot would speak severely of *The Waste Land* as 'just a piece of rhythmical grumbling', but in fact it broke with traditional structure and prosodic conventions, and if it grumbled, did so for a generation as well as for the poet himself. What appeared to be bits of actuality adventitiously juxtaposed with fragmentary allusions from literature, opera, and popular song, were actually parts of a mosaic with definite outlines. Eliot brought together various kinds of despair, for lost youth, lost love, lost friendship, lost value. Sombre and obscure, the poem also offered some possibilities of renewal (though these were not immediately recognized) in its blend of pagan vegetation rites, Christian resurrection, and exhortations from the *Upanishads*. In spite of many shifts of scene, it was anchored firmly in London, and with all its mustering of past ages, it spoke sharply to its own time.

After *The Waste Land* it was incumbent upon Eliot to choose between immobile lamentation, never his mode, and a new journey of the spirit. His next poems, including 'The Hollow Men' (1925), 'Journey of the Magi'

(1927), and 'Ash-Wednesday' (1930), testified that he had found his direction not in Indic religion but in Christianity. The process had been taking place, he said, 'perhaps insensibly, over a long period of time'. The year 1927 was almost as momentous as 1915: he was confirmed in the Church of England and he became a British subject. Soon thereafter, in his preface to a book of essays, *For Lancelot Andrewes* (1928), he characterized himself as 'classical in literature, royalist in politics, and anglo-catholic in religion'. (He would later regret the phrasing, though not the stances.) His politics became steadily more conservative. To the astonishment of admirers of his early work, in which the Church had played a less dignified role (as in 'The Hippopotamus'), Eliot became active in many church activities, participating as church warden, committee member, and lay apologist. His most resolute effort in this field was his book, *The Idea of a Christian Society*, published just after the onset of war in 1939. The ideal of an organic society had been implicit in his work almost from the beginning, though represented chiefly by depiction of its opposite; but the explicitly Christian form of the society was a summation of his later views.

The more lasting and effective expression of his spiritual quest came in *Four Quartets* (1944), a group of four poems which were interrelated but first published separately, *Burnt Norton* (1935), *East Coker* (1940), *The Dry Salvages* (1941), and *Little Gidding* (1942). Written in conversational and lyrical modes, the poems confront the problems of history, art, virtue, and mortality; the search for religious truth is subtly, expertly blended with the search for aesthetic expression, and both are shown to be the poet's intimate, lifelong pursuit. The language is triumphantly varied and modern; the imagery blends divebombers and the London underground with almost immemorial symbols of spiritual life. *Little Gidding* concludes with a vision of paradisal completeness for which his early verse, with its satirical portrayal of the infernal aspects of modern life, and his middle verse, instinct with purgatorial pain and hope, seem preparatory.

From 1922 Eliot devoted much of his time to work as editor and publisher. He founded in that year a new quarterly review, the *Criterion*, and became its editor, at first not printing his name so as to avoid complications at Lloyds Bank. The review was primarily literary, but its interests extended to social and political subjects as Eliot expanded the range of his own enquiries. He wished, he said, to create a place for the new attitudes to literature and art, and to make English letters a part of the European cultural community. He published work by the leading writers on the Continent as well as in England and America. A crisis ensued in 1925 when the patron of the *Criterion*, Lady Rothermere, withdrew her support. About the same time Eliot left the bank to become a director in the publishing firm of Faber & Gwyer (later Faber & Faber), and shortly

Eliot

afterwards the firm took over the review. It resumed publication as a monthly until June 1927, and then as a quarterly until January 1939, when the last number appeared. Although its circulation was modest, the *Criterion* had a large following among intellectuals. Besides his work for the review, Eliot took responsibility for his firm's selection of poets, and his taste set a standard; to be published by Eliot's firm was the ultimate guarantee. His own work was translated into many languages, and the latest poet in Arabic, Swahili, or Japanese was more likely to sound like Eliot than like earlier poets in those languages. His eminence became, in fact, a hazard to young poets who felt that their fundamental aesthetic problem was to avoid imitating him.

In the thirties Eliot took up seriously a form which had always attracted him, poetic drama. His first efforts were for a Christian pageant, *The Rock* (Sadler's Wells, 1934), and led the following year to *Murder in the Cathedral*, a play about the martyrdom of Thomas à Becket which was produced in Canterbury Cathedral chapter house. Eliot showed great skill in exploring dramatically the psychology of both martyrdom and political assassination. His later plays dwelt, seemingly, on secular matters, but with various degrees of obliquity explored problems of conscience in profane circumstances. *The Family Reunion* (Westminster Theatre, 1939) deals with sin and expiation; its hero returns to England after an absence of many years and believes himself pursued by the Furies for the putative murder of his wife. This play had a great success in the commercial theatre, as did, ten years later, *The Cocktail Party* produced by Henry Sherek (Edinburgh Festival, 1949), a play about ways of existence and redemption. The last two plays were *The Confidential Clerk* (Edinburgh Festival, 1953), in which the search for parentage by three foundlings—a staple of Greek comedy—becomes an existential search for identity; and *The Elder Statesman* (Edinburgh Festival, 1958), in which the title character has gradually to shed his pretences and come to terms with his real self. All these moral comedies were written in verse, which Eliot increasingly brought as close to prose as possible, on the theory that a more obvious metric would seem unnatural and distracting on the modern stage.

Eliot's dramatic talent was not negligible, but it was limited; his criticism, along with his verse, is more certain to last. In *The Sacred Wood* he enunciated certain cardinal principles. The essay, 'Tradition and the Individual Talent', held that a new work of art alters the arrangement of the 'existing monuments', so that tradition is not to be understood as a fixed entity, but as a changing one. He also made here his famous comparison of the writer to a catalytic agent, who joins the literary tradition to the experience and language of his own time. Against the romantic conception of self-expression, Eliot described the creative process as an escape from personality. The writer, he said in his essay on 'Hamlet', has to find an 'objective correlative' for his emotion. This process had become more difficult since the seventeenth century when, as he argued in 'The Metaphysical Poets' (*Homage to John Dryden*, 1924), there took place 'a dissociation of sensibility', so that poets could no longer feel a thought 'as immediately as the odour of a rose'. A mental disjunctiveness had led to what he sometimes regarded as the 'cultural breakdown' of the twentieth century.

Eliot's essays on these matters, on the Elizabethan dramatists, on Milton and the romantic poets, on Dante and Baudelaire, and on such contemporaries as Joyce, Pound, and Lawrence, became focal points of modern criticism. Many of them, as he said, offered a theoretical basis for his poetic practice. He did not wish this basis to be taken as systematic, and often insisted that particular ideas required expression at particular times, and were polemical rather than dogmatic. As his religious bent became more pronounced, both in his verse and in his life, he strove to see literature as part of a larger spiritual enterprise. His book, *After Strange Gods* (1934), based on lectures he gave at the university of Virginia in 1933, bore the subtitle 'A Primer of Modern Heresy', and tried to pick a path among contemporary writers according to the degree of orthodoxy or heterodoxy he found in them, the former being exalted. The result was a simplification of his position which he regretted and afterwards suppressed. But his other critical volumes, such as *Selected Essays* (1932) (expanded later), *On Poetry and Poets* (1957), and *To Criticize the Critic* (1965), have commanded and kept attention. His later criticism is less confidently assertive than his earlier, which he sometimes repudiates, yet it abounds in untrammelled and precise discriminations.

Eliot's later life became rather stately. In 1932–3 he went back to the United States for the first time to give the Charles Eliot Norton lectures at Harvard. (These were published as *The Use of Poetry and the Use of Criticism*, 1933.) At this time he arranged a permanent separation from his wife, and provided for her support. On his return to London he lived with various friends; his longest stay was with the critic John Hayward, who shared Eliot's flat from 1946 to 1957. His wife died in 1947. The following year Eliot received the Nobel prize for literature, and also the Order of Merit. He was to receive eighteen honorary degrees; he was an honorary fellow of Merton College, Oxford, and of Magdalene College, Cambridge; and he was an officer of the Legion of Honour. With his plays on Broadway and in the West End, his best lines on every lip, his opinions cited on all manner of subjects, he was the man of letters *par excellence* of the English-speaking world. He was also a man of generous spirit and firm friendship.

In 1957 Eliot married (Esmé) Valerie, only daughter of James Fletcher, of Headingley, Leeds, with whom he lived in great contentment for the rest of his life. He died in London 4 January 1965. His ashes were buried in St. Michael's church in East Coker, the place from which his ancestors had emigrated to the United States and the scene of the second *Quartet*. A memorial service was held in Westminster Abbey where a stone has been placed to his memory.

In appearance Eliot was tall and a little stooped. His beaked nose encouraged him to describe himself in one poem as an 'aged eagle'. Though even in youth he was an impressive and powerful presence, he had a vein of self-mockery, and was known to play practical jokes. In conversation he spoke with great deftness, and often with fine wit. If seized by an idea, he would follow it to its end, oblivious to others' attempts to interrupt, but he could also be silently attentive. His courtesy, self-abnegation, and kindness in difficult situations were celebrated. In later life his affection for his second wife, to whom he wrote the dedicatory poem of *The Elder Statesman*, was proudly manifest.

There is an early portrait of Eliot by Wyndham Lewis in the National Gallery in Durban, South Africa, and a late one by Sir Gerald Kelly, in the possession of the family. The best photographs are by Edward McKnight Kauffer and by Angus McBean, the latter at the London Library of which Eliot was president from 1952 until his death. The National Portrait Gallery has a bust by Sir Jacob Epstein.

[Introductory matter in Valerie Eliot's edition of the manuscript of *The Waste Land*, 1971; Lyndall Gordon, *Eliot's Early Years*, 1979; private information.]

RICHARD ELLMANN

published 1981

FARNOL (John) Jeffery

(1878–1952)

Novelist, was born in Aston Manor, Birmingham, 10 February 1878, the eldest son of Henry John Farnol, brass founder, and his wife, Katherine Jeffery. Ten years later the family moved to south London; and from Lee and Blackheath the boy explored the unspoilt green fields and white roads of Kent which were to form the background of many of his romances. He was educated privately; and his first job with a Birmingham firm of brass founders ended when he knocked down a works foreman for calling him a liar—showing a taste for fisticuffs which found its way into his books. He then attended the Westminster School of Art; and though he decided that he would never be a good artist, the training was useful; when he found himself in New York, where he went in 1902, and newly married, he was able to earn a living painting scenery for the Astor Theatre. Meanwhile, he began to write and sell stories; and all his feeling for romance, all his homesickness for the fields and woods of England were poured into a long novel of the open road, *The Broad Highway*, set in Kent in the days of the Regency. American publishers found it much too long and 'too English'. After it had vainly gone the rounds it was sent home to England, whither Farnol followed it when it was eventually published in 1910. It was a great success, and was his freshest and probably his best book.

The hero, Peter Vibart, a scholarly young aristocrat who can use his fists, takes to the road, in the manner of Borrow, and has a great many adventures with other wayfarers, highwaymen, tinkers, and ladies in distress, before settling to earn his bread as a village blacksmith. To his woodland cottage comes a superb beauty named Charmian, in flight from a smoothly villainous baronet, who is the hero's cousin and counterpart; there is plenty of love and fighting before all ends well.

In Farnol's next most popular novel, *The Amateur Gentleman* (1913), he reversed the story: a hero from humble life inherits a fortune and cuts a figure in the fashionable world as a Regency buck, winning a spirited and lovely lady. The formula was established and varied little, whatever the period, in the romances which Farnol turned out regularly for the next forty years. The hero was brave and honourable, the heroine innocent and beautiful, the villain properly villainous: nor was the reader ever invited to sympathize with the base rather than with the honest characters. It was the stuff of dreams and archetypal romance: with enough magic in it to capture generations of young people, and do them no harm. Older readers would cherish their taste for these tales through all changes of fictional fashion, reread their favourites, and remember the days when every green wood or winding lane seemed to them likely to produce a gallant adventure or a glorious beauty.

There was thus an appreciative welcome over the years for all Jeffery Farnol's overlarge output, even though many of his later books were hurried and inferior. Among his best and most popular were *The Money Moon* (1911), *The Chronicles of the Imp* (1915), *Our Admirable Betty* (1918), *The Geste of Duke Jocelyn* (1919), *Black Bartlemy's Treasure* (1920), and *Peregrine's Progress* (1922).

As it must be one of the happier lots in life to give a great deal of pleasure to a great many people for a great many years, 'Jack' Farnol had a right to a happy disposition: and is recorded to have been exceptionally gentle, generous, and hospitable. His chief hobby was the collection of swords and armour belonging to the picturesque past of which he wrote.

He had one daughter by his first wife, Blanche, daughter of F. Hughson Hawley, of New York. This marriage was dissolved in 1938 in which year he married Phyllis Clarke. He died at Eastbourne 9 August 1952.

[*The Times*, 11 and 19 August 1952; private information.]

M. BELLASIS

published 1971

FARRELL James Gordon

(1935–1979)

Novelist, was born 23 January 1935 at Liverpool, the second of the three sons (there were no daughters) of William Francis Farrell, accountant, of Liverpool, and his wife, (Prudence) Josephine, eldest daughter of Robert Gordon Russell, timber merchant, of Portlaoise, Ireland. He was educated at Rossall School and Brasenose College, Oxford, where he graduated BA with a third class in modern languages (French and Spanish) in 1960. At school he had been a distinguished games player as well as a notable contributor to the school magazine and it was after playing a game of rugby for Brasenose that he was suddenly taken ill with polio. He used the experience of being in an iron lung as the basis for his second novel, *The Lung* (1965). Only those who knew him well would have noticed that he was partly paralysed in one arm, though his hair turned prematurely white and he liked to suggest that the illness transformed him from a conventional public school 'hearty' into a writer.

After leaving Oxford Farrell spent a rather lonely and unhappy period teaching in Toulouse, where he wrote his first novel, *A Man from Elsewhere* (1963). In 1965 he went to the United States on a Harkness fellowship and his third novel, the last with a contemporary setting, was published in 1967 (*A Girl in the Head*). The American visit had little obvious effect on his writing, though it was on an island off New England that he first saw the ruined hotel which, transferred to Ireland, he used as the setting for *Troubles* (1970), winner of the Geoffrey Faber memorial prize of that year. *Troubles* was his first novel with an historical setting—Southern Ireland in 1919–21—which was also a family setting. His parents were Anglo-Irish and he had been brought up in Dublin. *The Siege of Krishnapur* (1973), which won the Booker prize that year, was based on the siege of Lucknow in the Indian mutiny and *The Singapore Grip* (1978) on the fall of Singapore in World War II. The family connections here were that his parents had married in India and lived there for some years before his birth and that his father had worked in Singapore before meeting his mother.

The common denominator in all his novels after the first was an ironic manner—which in the later books certainly owed something to Thomas Mann, though Stendhal, Malcolm Lowry, and Richard Hughes were earlier influences—and a rich vein of inventive fantasy. The disasters that befall Farrell's characters are ludicrous as well as horrific, comic as well as epic. Observed in long-shot his historical events have a grim dignity, but once he closes with the characters, absurdity tends to prevail. These middle-class imperialists at bay may deserve, because they are essentially innocent, to survive, or at least to be pitied for their experiences, but they also deserve, because they are arrogant, foolish, selfish, and greedy, to suffer and be laughed at. Yet the humour is seldom savage, probably because the events are seen mainly through the eyes of sympathetic, well-intentioned narrators (their doyen is the major in *Troubles* and *Singapore*), whose optimism buoys up the reader if not always the other characters.

The charm of Farrell's narrators came directly from himself. He had many friends and enjoyed being entertained by them or, after he had moved from a single room in Notting Hill to a tiny flat near Knightsbridge (he was unmarried), entertaining them in return. He taught himself to cook and spent part of his Booker prize on buying fine wines at auction, but his outstanding attribute as either host or guest was his self-deprecating, mock-gloomy manner of telling anecdotes. His social life, however, was strictly subordinate to his work as a novelist. He did almost no reviewing and was extremely hard-up until the last year of his life. When, finally, with the accumulating success of *Krishnapur* and *Singapore* and the advance on a new novel, provisionally called *The Hill Station* (published in its unfinished state in 1981), he had some money to spare, he spent it on a cottage beside Bantry Bay in Ireland. Four months after moving there he was drowned on 12 August 1979 while fishing from a rock. He left behind a sense of literary as well as personal loss, for remarkable as his novels are—certainly among the best of his generation—they promise more. His modesty about his own books was not an affectation but a measure of what he still hoped and intended to achieve.

[Private information; personal knowledge.]

JOHN SPURLING

published 1986

FIRBANK (Arthur Annesley) Ronald

(1886–1926)

Novelist, was born 17 January 1886 in London, the second of the three sons and the four children of (Sir) Joseph Thomas Firbank of London, railway contractor and later Unionist MP for East Hull, and his wife Jane Harriette, daughter of James Perkins Garrett, rector of Kellistown, county Carlow, Ireland. Firbank spent the first ten years of his life at his family's new home, The Coopers, Chislehurst—a village whose connections with the exiled Empress Eugénie may have influenced his enduring fascination with both royalty and Catholicism. He was sent in May 1900 to Uppingham, where, suffering from ill health, he stayed only two terms. Subsequent private tuition was taken in England, France, and Spain in 1901–6. His first book, containing two stories, 'Odette D'Antrevernes' and 'A Study in Temperament', was published in 1905; and in the following summer he was at work on his first novel *The Artificial Princess* (published posthumously in 1934): in it he devised the techniques of elliptical narrative and baroque construction, and the manner, at once satirical and lyric, concentrated and fragmentary, that were to characterize his mature work.

In October 1906 he went to Trinity Hall, Cambridge, and left in March 1909, having taken no examinations; on 6 December 1907 he had been received into the Catholic Church by R. Hugh Benson. In October 1909 Firbank went to Rome, where he hoped, but failed, to join the Guardia Nobile, and remained in Italy until October 1910, when his father died and he assumed control of the family's finances. Over the following four years he cultivated the nomadic way of life which, with the exception of the war years, was to be his until he died: he drifted restlessly in southern Europe and North Africa—and when in London was seen at the theatre, the Ballets Russes, the Café Royal, and at the bohemian restaurant, La Tour Eiffel. He was known for the refined dandyism of his appearance, the flutterings and oscillations of his bearing, his heavy drinking, and his intense shyness.

With the appearance of his novel *Vainglory* in 1915 he styled himself Ronald Firbank for the first time, signalling the emergence of the mature writer. Like all his books until *Prancing Nigger* (1924), it was published at his own expense and to negligible acclaim. It was the most experimental modernist novel yet published in England, and its abstruseness was found additionally baffling in the context of the war. Being unfit for service, and to escape the danger of bombing, Firbank moved to rooms in the High Street, Oxford, in October 1915, and remained there until September 1919.

This was a period of intense isolation, in which he sank into nervous apprehensiveness and paranoia. But it was also a period of remarkable creativity, in which he wrote his novels *Inclinations* (1916), *Caprice* (1917), and *Valmouth* (1919). He showed an exceptional and sustaining dedication to his art in the face of personal loneliness and critical indifference; it was only after his death that he emerged as a vital influence on writers of the generation of Evelyn Waugh, W. H. Auden, and Anthony Powell.

Firbank had no close emotional attachments, save with his mother; but in 1919 he seems to have become infatuated with the Hon. Evan Morgan, who rebuffed him by refusing the dedication of his only play, *The Princess Zoubaroff*, days before its publication in 1920. After this Firbank resumed his nomadism, and the settings of his books, too, were henceforth to be fantastic versions of foreign places: Vienna, Havana, Seville. His North African tale *Santal* appeared in 1921, and *The Flower Beneath the Foot*, the first of the three major novels of his last years, in 1923. This book shows a new satirical vigour and contempt for British society, at a time when the American writer, Carl Van Vechten, had begun to promote Firbank's work in the United States. His next novel *Prancing Nigger* (1924) was published first with considerable success in New York, and then under the author's preferred title of *Sorrow in Sunlight* in London. American editions of *The Flower Beneath the Foot* and *Vainglory* followed, but Brentano declined *Concerning the Eccentricities of Cardinal Pirelli* (1926) on religious and moral grounds: Firbank's work after the death of his mother in March 1924 showed a new candour in its treatment of homosexuality. He was working on a novel set in New York, *The New Rythum* (fragments published in 1962), when he died in Rome 21 May 1926.

[Ifan Kyrle Fletcher, *Ronald Firbank: a Memoir*, 1930; Miriam J. Benkovitz, *A Bibliography of Ronald Firbank*, 1963, new edn., 1982; *idem*, *Ronald Firbank: a Biography*, 1969; Brigid Brophy, *Prancing Novelist*, 1973.]

ALAN HOLLINGHURST

published 1993

FLEMING Ian Lancaster

(1908–1964)

Writer, was born in London 28 May 1908, the second of the four sons of Valentine Fleming, who became Conservative member of Parliament for South Oxfordshire in 1910 and was killed in France in 1917, when he was posthumously appointed to the DSO. His mother was Evelyn Beatrice Ste. Croix, daughter of George Alfred Ste. Croix Rose, JP, of the Red House, Sonning, Berkshire. She was ambitious for her sons and her dominant personality was perhaps in some part responsible for Ian Fleming's early lack of confidence. Peter Fleming, the traveller and writer, was his elder, Richard Fleming, merchant banker, a younger, brother. Ian Fleming was educated at Eton where he was overshadowed by Peter's brilliance but proved an outstanding athlete, becoming victor ludorum two years in succession, a feat only once equalled. By the wish of his mother he entered the Royal Military College, Sandhurst, but he withdrew in the following year and continued his education privately in Austria, Germany, and Switzerland.

Having failed to enter the Foreign Office in 1931, he joined Reuters news agency and in 1933 reported the historic trial in Moscow of some British engineers on charges of espionage and sabotage, an experience he was not to forget. Between 1933 and 1939 he worked successively as a banker and a stockbroker in the City of London. Throughout the war he held a key position in the Naval Intelligence Division in Whitehall as personal assistant to the director of naval intelligence, rising to the rank of commander. His particular interest was the organization of 30 Assault Unit dedicated to the task of seizing material of value to intelligence. Soon after demobilization he became foreign manager of the Kemsley group of newspapers, and continued to hold the post after Roy Thomson (later Lord Thomson of Fleet) acquired the concern, resigning finally at the end of 1959. For the last years of his life he worked only as a writer. In 1952 he had married Anne Geraldine Mary, eldest daughter of the Hon. Guy Lawrence Charteris, son of the eleventh Earl of Wemyss, and divorced wife of the second Viscount Rothermere. The Flemings' only child, a son, was born in that year.

The wedding had taken place in Jamaica, where Fleming had built a house in 1946, and where it was to become his habit to spend the winter months working on the successive adventures of his famous creation, the secret agent James Bond ('007'). Beginning with *Casino Royale* in 1953, one of these books appeared every year until 1966. The success of the series, though immediate, was not overwhelming until the publication in 1958 of *Dr. No*, the first of his books to be filmed. Thereafter his economic position and his worldwide fame were assured.

On the publication of *Casino Royale* it was apparent to many that a remarkable new writer had arrived on the scene, in the tradition of Buchan, Dornford Yates, and Sapper, although at that stage almost certainly more promising than any of these had been. Original in construction, the book contained many of the elements which were to become Fleming's hallmark: evident familiarity with secret-service activities (not least those of his country's enemies), portrayal of the kind of rich life to be found in exclusive clubs, smart restaurants, and fashionable resorts, obsessive interest in machines and gadgets and in gambling, an exotic setting, a formidable and physically repulsive villain, a strong sexual component, a glamorous and complaisant but affectionate heroine, and—of course—James Bond himself. Bond, at any rate on the surface, was a carefully constructed amalgam of what many men would like to be—and of what perhaps rather fewer women would like to meet: handsome, elegant, brave, tough, at ease in expensive surroundings, predatory and yet chivalrous in sexual dealings, with a touch of Byronic melancholy and remoteness thrown in.

Some would say that Fleming never surpassed, perhaps never quite equalled, his achievement in *Casino Royale*. Certainly there is a power and freshness about the book which in an age less rigidly hierarchical in its attitudes to literature, would have caused it to be hailed as one of the most remarkable first novels to be published in England in the previous thirty years. Yet, as the series continued, the author extended and deepened his range, attaining a new pitch of ingenuity and technological inventiveness while discovering in himself a gift for descriptions of landscape and of wild life, in particular birds and sea-creatures, pushing out in the direction of a more audacious fantasy, as in *Goldfinger* (1959), and also towards a greater realism, as in *The Spy Who Loved Me* (1962). In *You Only Live Twice* (1964) he produced a striking synthesis of these two impulses, though in narrative and other respects the book was unsatisfactory; and the last volume, *The Man with the Golden Gun*, published in 1965 after his death and written when his health had already begun to fail, was sadly the weakest of the series: it never received his final revision. It was during convalescence from a heart attack that he began to write the children's stories *Chitty-Chitty-Bang-Bang* which were later to be filmed.

It is arguable that *Dr. No* is at least as absorbing and memorable as any of the other books, with its unrelaxed tension, its terrifying house of evil, and the savage beauty of its main setting on a Caribbean island, a locale which Fleming made part of himself and which always excited his pen to produce some of his best writing. But one cannot forget *Moonraker* (1955) for the vivid, rounded depiction of its villain, Hugo Drax, and what is probably the most gripping game of cards in the whole of literature, nor *On Her Majesty's Secret Service* (1963) for its idyllic seaside opening and the vigour of its skiing scenes. Indeed, there is hardly a page in all the 3,000 and more of the saga that does not testify to Fleming's ability to realize a unique personal world with its own rules and its own unmistakable atmosphere. His style is plain and flexible, serving equally well for fast action, lucid technical exposition, and sensuous evocation of place and climate; if it falls here and there into cliché or the language of the novelette, it never descends to pretentiousness. The strength of his work lies in its command of pace and its profound latent romanticism.

Fleming travelled widely from an early age and his interest in foreign places is reflected in his journalism, of which two volumes are collected, as well as in his fiction. His pursuits included motoring, golf, bridge, and underwater swimming, but his reading and his cultural interests generally were wider and deeper than might be thought common in writers of his stamp. He acquired an unusual collection of first editions of books which marked 'milestones of human progress'. His friendships were many and enduring. He was humble about his work and, though totally professional in his approach to his task, did not take himself seriously as a literary figure, perhaps to the detriment of his standing in critical circles.

He died in Canterbury 12 August 1964 less than a month after the death of his mother. A portrait of him by Amherst Villiers was reproduced in the limited, signed edition of *On Her Majesty's Secret Service*.

[Fleming's own writings; John Pearson, *The Life of Ian Fleming*, 1966; *Burke's Landed Gentry*.]

KINGSLEY AMIS

published 1981

FORESTER Cecil Scott
(1899–1966)

Novelist, was born Cecil Lewis Troughton Smith in Cairo 27 August 1899, third son and fifth child of George Foster Smith, schoolmaster and author of elementary Arabic text-books, and his wife, Sarah Medhurst Troughton. Smith took the name Forester for professional purposes in 1923. From an early age he was able to read with ease. With his brothers, he conducted long battles with lead soldiers and naval campaigns with paper ships, drawing up army lists and naval operation orders in Nelsonian style. He frequented the public library, forming the lifetime habit of reading at least one book a day. His omnivorous reading included Gibbon, Suetonius, 'dozens of naval histories', and Harmsworth's Encyclopaedia, besides G. A.

Henty and R. M. Ballantyne, Harry Collingwood and Robert Leighton. This, added to rigorous cramming for scholarships at his elementary school in London, revealed the weakness of Forester's eyesight.

A Christ's Hospital scholarship having been withdrawn at the last moment because of the size of his father's income, Forester, aged eleven, joined the fourth form at Alleyn's School. After an unhappy start, he did well enough to be offered some public-school scholarships, settling for an internal offer of two years' free tuition. He moved next to the sixth form (science) at Dulwich College. He was a good cricketer and keen games player.

Between the ages of twelve and sixteen, Forester grew five inches annually. An army medical examination at seventeen revealed a weak heart, precluding his recruitment in 1917. This was an unhappy time for Forester. His vivid imagination enabled him to picture his contemporaries' sufferings 'with terrible realism', sharpening his distaste for civilian complacency. Overshadowed by his eldest brother who had qualified aged twenty, Forester entered Guy's Hospital as a medical student, but he came to the conclusion that he was unfitted for medicine. His thoughts turned increasingly to writing, and the novelist's instinct triumphed over family opposition.

Forester's first attempts at fiction taught him that 'the better part of the work is done before pen is put to paper'. The artistic standard he set himself (he called it 'beauty') was first met by *Payment Deferred* (1926), a compelling narration of a murderer being accused of a crime he did not commit. In 1931 Charles Laughton acted in a successful stage version, and the story was also later filmed. *Brown on Resolution* (1929) collates the themes of the command of the sea, the service of England, and 'the man alone', which dominate Forester's best work. Yet the story has a curious moral; the heroic death of an illegitimate son, after his mother dies of cancer, advances his father's naval career. Forester's best biography was *Nelson* (1929). *Death to the French* (1932) reveals an acute insight into the British army during the Peninsular War. Rifleman Dodd, separated from his regiment, shows the value of Sir John Moore's training. *The African Queen* (1935) convincingly depicts a dedicated woman's love driving a weak man to heroic efforts on England's behalf. This was later filmed and, although the ending was altered, is generally considered to be the best of the various films made of Forester's books.

The General (1936) is a striking study of Lieutenant-General Sir Herbert Curzon, a professional British officer, whose rapid rise to high command in the war of 1914–18 ends during the German offensive of March 1918. The novel stresses Curzon's devotion to duty and unbending sense of honour, without glozing his narrow outlook and sympathies.

During these years Forester was combining the writing of books with journalism; from 1936 to 1937 he was a correspondent in Spain during the civil war, and he was also in Czechoslovakia when the Germans occupied Prague in March 1939.

In 1937, with the publication of *The Happy Return*, Forester created his best-known character, Horatio Hornblower, a sensitive and gifted individual, the flowering of whose talents within the chain of naval command revealed the author's understanding of Nelson's navy, and of seapower. Forester's command of the historical detail of the period was due to his chance purchase, some time previously, of three volumes of the *Naval Chronicle*, a journal published during the Napoleonic wars. Between 1937 and 1962 appeared twelve Hornblower stories, tracing the rise of the hero from midshipman to admiral. The books were written in a terse, effective style, well suited to the portrayal of the self-doubting but self-disciplined Hornblower, whose complex personality was brilliantly evoked. Hornblower's activities were confined, during the thirty years of the stories (1793 to 1823) to the Atlantic, Baltic, Mediterranean, and Caribbean. In *The Hornblower Companion* (1964), which contains a candid account of the creation and writing of the Hornblower books, Forester explained frankly why this was the case: 'These were the only waters with which Hornblower's biographer was familiar while writing about the closing years of the Napoleonic Wars.' One of the Hornblower novels, *A Ship of the Line*, was awarded the James Tait Black memorial prize for 1938.

During the war of 1939–45 Forester, always conscious of the shared British–American heritage, contributed much to British and American propaganda, producing short stories and articles, illustrating the British war effort, for American publication. When America entered the war he was co-opted as an American propagandist and became a familiar figure in the Pentagon. He accompanied a United States warship on one of its missions. In 1943 he was invited by the British Admiralty to sail in the *Penelope*, an experience which resulted in his writing *The Ship* (1943), of which half a million copies were printed and distributed throughout the fleet. The book was a brilliant portrait of trained individuals working as a team. Forester was also a frequent contributor to the *Saturday Evening Post*, in which *The Commodore* (1945) appeared as a serial.

In 1945 the Allied Governments foresaw the possibility of protracted Japanese resistance. Forester, now settled permanently in the United States, was given the freedom of the Navy Department, Washington, with number two priority on air transport. He busied himself with writing 'logistics for the common man', stories about the Pacific war (*The Man in the Yellow Raft*, published posthumously in 1969).

Forester, a shy man, thin-lipped and high-browed, had a quiet sense of humour. He enjoyed bridge and travel. However, arteriosclerosis curtailed his mobility from 1943 onwards, and a severe stroke in 1964 confined him to a wheelchair. He died in Fullerton, California, 2 April 1966.

In 1926 Forester married Kathleen, daughter of George Belcher, schoolmaster, and had two sons. The marriage was dissolved in 1944. In 1947 he married Dorothy Ellen, daughter of William Foster, ship-broker. A bust by Cynthia Drummond is in the possession of the family.

[C. S. Forester, *The Hornblower Companion*, 1964, and *Long Before Forty*, 1967; *The Times*, 4 and 6 April 1966, private information.]

NEIL HUXTER

published 1981

FRANKAU Gilbert

(1884–1952)

Novelist, was born 21 April 1884 in Gloucester Terrace, London, the eldest of three sons and one daughter of Arthur Frankau, a principal partner of the firm of J. Frankau & Co., wholesale cigar merchants, founded originally in 1837 to import leeches from France. His mother, Julia, daughter of Hyman Davis, wrote novels under the pen-name of 'Frank Danby' and achieved a considerable success as early as 1887 with *Dr. Phillips, a Maida Vale Idyll*; her best-known book was *Pigs in Clover* (1903). Her sister Mrs. Eliza Aria was also a writer and for many years contributed a weekly column to *Truth* entitled 'Mrs. A's diary'.

Frankau won a scholarship to Harrow, but did not take it, then another to Eton and went there, though not as a scholar. He took his first step towards becoming a writer while still a schoolboy when he launched and edited *The X* magazine, with Lord Turnour (later Earl Winterton) as his assistant editor. The magazine, too outspoken about the masters, was suppressed by the headmaster after only four numbers. Frankau immediately found a fresh outlet for his talent with a volume of satiric verse entitled *Eton Echoes* (1901).

He decided, however, to go into the family business and left school shortly afterwards to become a cigar merchant. He went to Hamburg to learn German. His aptitude for learning languages was remarkable; in time he had an equal fluency in French, Italian, and Spanish, then turned to learning Turkish. With concentrated application he quickly acquired a

119

thorough knowledge of the cigar business and became managing director of the family firm at the age of twenty-one. His activities took him to Havana, then on a two-year world tour.

Writing was not altogether neglected. In 1912 he published *One of Us*, a novel in *ottava rima* as used by Byron in *Don Juan*, followed it up with a dramatic poem *Tid'apa* (1915) reprinted from the *English Review*, and two further books of poems—*The Guns* (1916) and *The City of Fear* (1917).

On the outbreak of war in 1914 he had joined up at once, was commissioned in the 9th battalion of the East Surrey Regiment in October, but transferred to the Royal Field Artillery five months later and served at Loos, Ypres, and the Somme. In October 1916 he was sent to Italy as a staff captain to undertake special duties to counter German propaganda against Britain. His activities involved a press and film campaign which he handled most effectively. But delayed symptoms of shell-shock led to his being invalided out of the army in February 1918. The family cigar business had already been disposed of and Frankau, with a wife and two daughters to provide for, decided to seek an income from writing. He embarked on his new career with the same concentration, zest, and efficiency which he had brought to the conduct of his business. Each book was planned with the utmost care, and regular hours were assigned to its writing. His study was his office and he would brook no interruption: no telephone calls were accepted, crises, no matter how grave and pressing, had to wait until he emerged. Strict routine now governed his whole life. Always something of an exhibitionist, he adopted an aristocratic air, engaged in hunting (although, as he admitted later, he was terrified of riding), joined the Cavalry Club where he played bridge, and took up fencing. Many found his arrogance insufferable, but he prided himself on being like the heroes in his books—dashing and tough: such was his outward pose, but to his more intimate friends he confessed that he was haunted by the doubt that underneath it all he was really a coward. Kindness he professed to regard as 'sloppy', but all through his life his deeds were far kinder than his words.

His first prose novel, *The Woman of the Horizon*, was published in 1917. With *Peter Jackson, Cigar Merchant* (1920) he attained both popular acclaim and prosperity. Doors instantly began to open: magazines begged for short stories, newspapers for articles; he was invited to make speeches at literary gatherings. Books now appeared with clockwork regularity: in 1921 *The Seeds of Enchantment*, in which he attacked indiscipline and proclaimed the superiority of the white above the black and yellow races; in 1922 *The Love-Story of Aliette Brunton* making a dramatic plea for divorce law reform. In 1924 his speeches took a political turn. His sympathies were with the extreme Right and one could not fail to discern the influence of Italian fascism.

A number of his novels were filmed, and in 1926, with the publication of *Masterson*, he undertook a long and strenuous tour of the United States, which he described vividly and entertainingly in *My Unsentimental Journey* (1926). An unhappy venture into journalism, his first since he was at Eton, came in 1928 when he launched and edited *Britannia*, a sixpenny weekly with a strongly emphasized imperialist note. It was not a success. The fees paid to contributors made even the recipients gasp. Advertisers held aloof and after ten issues Frankau returned to novel writing.

As a story-teller he had considerable talent. His narrative style was compelling, his characters often larger than life, his imagery inclined to be lavish; but, painstaking in his research and meticulous in detail, he commanded a vast public both in Britain and in the United States. Of his later novels *Christopher Strong* (1932), *Three Englishmen* (1935), and *Son of Morning* (1949) may be singled out. His last book, considered by some as being among his best, was *Unborn Tomorrow* (1953), a vision of the future. Although aware that death was near, his iron resolve and self-discipline enabled him to finish it just before he died at his home at Hove 4 November 1952.

Frankau was thrice married: in 1905 to Dorothea Frances Markham, daughter of Charles Edward Drummond Black, by whom he had two daughters, one of whom, Pamela Frankau (died 1967), won fame as a novelist. The marriage ended in divorce and in 1922 Frankau married the actress Aimée, daughter of Robert de Burgh and formerly wife of Leon Quartermaine. This marriage also ended in divorce. In 1932 he married Susan Lorna, daughter of Walter Henry Harris. A portrait of Frankau by Flora Lion is in the possession of the family.

[*The Times*, 5 November 1952; Gilbert Frankau, *Self-Portrait*, 1939; Pamela Frankau, *Pen to Paper*, 1961; personal knowledge.]

R. J. MINNEY

published 1971

(1892–1981)

Writer, editor, and publisher, was born 9 March 1892 at Brighton, the only child of Edward Garnett, author and publishers' reader, of The Cearne, Edenbridge, and his wife, Constance, distinguished translator of Russian classics. She was the daughter of David Black, coroner. His grandfather was Richard Garnett (1835–1906), prolific man of letters and keeper of printed books at the British Museum. David was educated at University College School and the Royal College of Science, South Kensington, where he studied botany, and fungi in particular. At twelve years of age he paid a memorable visit to Russia with his mother, while through his father's gift for discovering literary talent he became friendly from boyhood with such writers as Joseph Conrad, D. H. Lawrence, and W. H. Hudson. Later he got to know the Stracheys, J. Maynard (later Lord) Keynes, Duncan Grant, and the rest of the Bloomsbury Group, with whom he was associated all his adult life.

During the war of 1914–18 he went to France with the Friends' War Victims' Relief Mission, and afterwards worked on the land. After the war he opened a bookshop in the heart of Bloomsbury with his friend Francis Birrell, but writing had already become his chief interest, and his marriage in 1921 together with the outstanding success of his first serious novel *Lady into Fox* (1922; Hawthornden and James Tait Black memorial prizes for 1923) persuaded him to buy Hilton Hall, a Queen Anne house near Cambridge, and devote himself entirely to literature. His output of over a dozen novels included *The Sailor's Return* (1925), *Aspects of Love* (1955), and *Up She Rises* (1977). Among his autobiographical works were *A Rabbit in the Air*, a delightful account of learning to fly (1932), *The Golden Echo* (1953), and *Great Friends* (1979). Garnett was also responsible for editing *The Letters of T. E. Lawrence* (1938), *The Novels of Thomas Love Peacock* (1948), and Dora Carrington's *Letters and Extracts from her Diaries* (1970), as well as being involved in two successful publishing ventures: the Nonesuch Press—with (Sir) Francis Meynell—in 1923, and Rupert Hart-Davis Ltd. in 1946.

In 1939 Garnett became literary editor of the *New Statesman*, and he continued contributing to it after the outbreak of World War II, when he joined the Air Ministry with the rank of flight-lieutenant RAFVR, and subsequently was an intelligence officer in the Political Warfare Executive, whose secret history he wrote. His was a large and vigorous output, based on a variety of interests and wide reading. On first starting as a novelist he had taken Daniel Defoe as his model, and the same combination of an imaginative or fantastic premiss with a sturdy, objective, and masculine style can be seen in both writers. Many of his plots were markedly original, and have attracted the interest of artists in other media. Ballets founded on *Lady into Fox* (1939, with music by Arthur Honegger) and *The Sailor's Return* (1947) were successfully staged by the Ballet Rambert with Sally Gilmour in the leading roles, while the latter novel and *A Man in the Zoo* (1928) were made into films and shown on television.

As a young man Garnett, known as 'Bunny' to his friends, was good-looking, fair-haired, and blue-eyed. His energy and enterprise—and perhaps a streak of recklessness—found an outlet in learning to fly, among other outdoor activities such as fishing, swimming (he could be seen diving into cold water when he was over eighty), and bee keeping. For a time he kept a small Jersey herd at Hilton, and he took a sympathetic interest in most agricultural processes and liked to describe them. As he said himself: 'I believe I can write about grass growing as well as anyone.' Indeed he had always been more at home in the country than in town, from his days as a rather solitary child exploring the woods around his parents' house and developing an enthusiasm for the wild flowers and creatures he saw there until his discovery in middle age of the attractions of the Yorkshire dales. Travel was another source of pleasure, particularly in France, but he also paid several visits to the United States, where he made many friends and sometimes gave lectures. A life-lover, gregarious, and a genial host, he gave and received much affection and was an excellent letter writer. He spent the last ten years of his life in a modest stone cottage in Charry, Moncuq, Lot, France, surrounded by his fine library and a small collection of Bloomsbury paintings. Here he cooked and bottled wine for his many visitors, and could be seen sitting out of doors under a large straw hat typing away at his latest book until he died there 17 February 1981.

David Garnett was appointed CBE in 1952, was elected a fellow of the Imperial College of Science and Technology in 1956, and became C.Lit. in 1977. In 1977 he received an honorary D.Litt. from Birmingham University.

In 1921 he married Rachel Alice ('Ray'), daughter of William Cecil Marshall, architect, and sister of the author of this notice. She illustrated her husband's books and some others, and died in 1940. In 1942 he married Angelica Vanessa, daughter of Duncan James Corrowr Grant and Vanessa Bell, both painters, of Charleston, Sussex. There were two sons of the first marriage and four daughters, of whom the final two were twins, of the second. His eldest daughter died in 1973.

[*The Times*, 19 February and 4 and 23 March 1981; Carolyn G. Heilbrun, *The Garnett Family*, 1961; David Garnett, *The Golden Echo*, 1953, *Flowers of the Forest*, 1955, and *The Familiar Faces*, 1962 (autobiographies); private information; personal knowledge.]

FRANCES PARTRIDGE

published 1990

(1864–1943)

Novelist, was born in Jersey 17 October 1864, the younger daughter of Douglas Sutherland, a Scottish civil engineer, and his wife, Elinor, daughter of Thomas Saunders (the son of an English father and an aristocratic French mother) who had emigrated to Ontario with his Irish wife. Three months after the birth of his second child Douglas Sutherland died, his ambition to prove himself heir to the seventh Lord Duffus unfulfilled. The young widow returned to Canada where for some years the children were trained by their grandmother in a code of manners modelled on the French aristocracy of the eighteenth century. Elinor never forgot these lessons on the duties and privileges, and the self-discipline required, of those born to high estate. In 1871 Mrs. Sutherland married David Kennedy, an elderly and parsimonious Scot who tyrannized over her but failed to subdue his stepchildren who heartily disliked him. Returning to Europe the family settled in St. Helier where a succession of governesses abandoned the attempt to instruct two rebellious and lonely little girls. Elinor, however, became bilingual in French, read voraciously and precociously in a large library, and lived in a dream-world of her own. Kingsley's *The Heroes* became and remained her favourite work. In later years she profited by her friendships with men such as Lord Curzon, Lord Milner, and F. H. Bradley to fill in some of the gaps in her education. Orthodox Christianity she rejected at an early age, but it was not until later in life that she came increasingly to believe in reincarnation.

Red-headed and green-eyed, Elinor had been brought up to believe that she was ugly, but her first essays into society in Paris and in England soon made her aware that this was untrue. There were some extravagant scenes: four rivals for her attentions at a house party in midwinter threw each other into the lake and then bathed in champagne to ward off chills. Marriage, however, was long delayed by reason of the conflict between her innate romanticism and a streak of practicality and even cynicism traceable to her French ancestry: she sought romance, but there must be money too. In the event, her marriage to Clayton Glyn (died 1915), a personable landowner, into which she entered with high hopes in 1892, brought neither. Her husband's affection waned as he became reimmersed in country interests which Elinor did not share; and he was profoundly disappointed that she bore him two daughters but no son. Nevertheless, marriage gave her an assured position in society and her life with its round of country-house parties interspersed with foreign travel was not unhappy.

That she was a detached and acute observer of her milieu was revealed when during a period of convalescence she embarked on her first book. *The Visits of Elizabeth*, the letters of a young girl to her mother, ingenuously exposing the foibles and philandering of society, was first serialized in the *World*, and then published in book form in 1900. Its success encouraged her to write several more 'society' novels before turning to a passionate romanticism in which her heroines were haughty, her heroes masterful, her settings luxurious, and her plots improbable. Judged by later standards her novels are only rescued from absurdity by her genuine ability to tell a story. In her own time they were much admired. *Three Weeks* (1907), an extra-marital interlude between a Balkan queen and an Englishman, ending in death for the one and regeneration for the other, created something of a sensation, being widely condemned and still more widely read. Curzon and Milner both presented her with a tiger skin, a much publicized feature of the story. For Milner, with whom she discussed the Greek philosophers, she had no more than 'a gentle admiration'; but there was a mutual attraction between herself and Curzon. He was for her the great romantic figure, 'the sun, moon and stars to the end of time'; the announcement of his engagement in 1916 without a word to her before or afterwards was a bitter blow.

It was not the first which she had faced with courage: in 1908 Clayton Glyn had revealed that for years he had been living on capital and was now deeply in debt. Henceforth Elinor Glyn wrote of necessity, and many of her novels were designed merely to entertain her wide public in England and America. The winter of 1909–10 was spent by invitation at the court of St. Petersburg which provided a brilliant and well-observed background for *His Hour* (1910), one of her ablest romances. Of her more serious character studies may be mentioned *Halcyone* (1912), with its recognizable portraits of Bradley and Curzon, *The Career of Katherine Bush* (1917), in which her heroine for once was not well-born, *Man and Maid* (1922), and *It* (1927). The last, a short novel in an American setting, made the word 'It' for many years synonymous with personal magnetism. A new career as a script writer began in 1920 in Hollywood where a number of her own novels were filmed, including *Three Weeks* and *It*. Her personal success in America would have been more rewarding had she not been totally incapable of managing her finances. In 1929 she returned to England and after an unsuccessful attempt at film production resumed her novels. Her autobiography, *Romantic Adventure*, appeared in 1936. She was by now a legendary figure, thriving on admiration, and almost to the end she remained beautiful and vital. 'I am enjoying it all', she wrote from London at the height of the air raids. She died there 23 September 1943.

A portrait by P. A. de László belongs to her younger daughter, Lady Rhys-Williams; another by Henrietta Cotton to her elder daughter, Lady Davson. A portrait by J.-E. Blanche and a sketch by P. A. de László were destroyed by enemy action during the war of 1939–45 and exist only in reproduction.

[Elinor Glyn, *Romantic Adventure*, 1936; Anthony Glyn, *Elinor Glyn*, 1955; private information.]

HELEN M. PALMER

published 1959

GRANVILLE-BARKER Harley Granville

(1877–1946)

Actor, producer, dramatist, and critic, was born in Kensington 25 November 1877, the only son and elder child of Albert James Barker, who came of an old Warwickshire and Hereford family. He is spoken of as an architect, but the family was largely dependent on his wife, Mary Elisabeth Bozzi Granville, who was a well-known elocutionist and reciter of the Victorian type. She was the granddaughter of Augustus Bozzi Granville, the son of Dr. Carlo Bozzi, who in 1806 took the name Granville to commemorate his Cornish grandmother who had married an Italian, Rapazzini. There were therefore two strains of Italian blood in Harley, both on the maternal side.

There is no record of his schooling, but he grew up in an atmosphere of good speech and drama and at an early age had a thorough knowledge of Dickens and Shakespeare. A precocious child, he frequently assisted at his mother's recitals, and even deputized for her. He began his professional career in 1891 at Harrogate and in Sarah Thorne's famous stock company at Margate; his first London appearance was at the Comedy Theatre in 1892. A tour with (Sir) Phillip Ben Greet in 1895 brought him to the notice of William Poel for whom he played Richard II in 1899. An introduction to the Fabian set, with which the founders of the Stage Society were closely allied, led to his great friendship with G. B. Shaw which had a profound influence on his career and lasted until his second marriage in 1918. For the Stage Society he produced or acted in a number of first performances of plays such as *Candida*, and *Mrs. Warren's Profession*, and his own *Weather Hen* and *The Marrying of Ann Leete*. His position once established, he devoted himself to the task of raising the standard of English acting and drama, and accustoming the English actor and audience to the permanent repertory company: with the idea of a national theatre in view. With William Archer in 1904 he drew up in great detail *A Scheme and Estimates for a National Theatre* which was not made public until 1907. Meanwhile his own first great chance came when, at Archer's suggestion, he was invited to produce *Two Gentlemen of Verona* at the Royal Court Theatre in 1904. He accepted on condition that during the run he might present a set of matinées of *Candida*. These were so successful that in partnership with John E. Vedrenne, the manager of the Court Theatre, and in close association with Shaw, he embarked upon the famous Vedrenne Barker season which lasted until 1907, made Barker's name as a director and Shaw's as a dramatist, and became a landmark in the history of the British theatre. A new standard of intelligence and social criticism was brought into the theatre and in both plays and acting there was an intense regard for truth to life rather than for meretricious theatrical effect. Some 950 performances were given of 32 plays by 17 authors, including 11 of Shaw's, first plays of Galsworthy, St. John Hankin, and Mr. John Masefield, and works by Euripides (in Gilbert Murray's translations), Ibsen, Maeterlinck, and Barker. Expenses, including the actors' salaries, were kept very low but the financial stability of the enterprise was largely dependent on the success of Shaw's plays, especially *You Never Can Tell, John Bull's Other Island*, and *Man and Superman*. For the two latter Miss Lillah McCarthy joined the company in 1905 and in 1906 she and Barker were married.

The growing success of the Vedrenne-Barker partnership prompted a move in the autumn of 1907 to a larger theatre, the Savoy, but expenses increased more than receipts, Barker's new play, *Waste*, was forbidden by the censor, there were internal disputes over casting, and something of the joyful pioneering spirit had gone. The season petered out at Christmas and the new plays in preparation, Masefield's *Nan* and Galsworthy's *Strife* and others, were produced by Barker with all his care and skill but for Sunday societies or short runs under other managements. He was offered but declined control of the Millionaires' Theatre (later the Century), just completed in New York, which he found too vast for his style of work. In 1910, at the instigation of (Sir) James Barrie, Charles Frohman mounted a season of real repertory at the Duke of York's Theatre, with Barker and Dion Boucicault sharing the productions. Galsworthy's *Justice* in Barker's hands made a great sensation, and among other plays was Barker's own *The Madras House*. Although business was quite good the theatre was unsuitable for repertory, the expenses enormous, and the venture failed in three months. Barker had increased his reputation but not his finances and to recoup them he appeared for a season at the Palace Variety Theatre in a series of Schnitzler's *Anatol* duologues translated and produced by himself.

In 1911 his wife, with the help of Lord Howard de Walden, raised a small syndicate to take the Little Theatre where they produced *The Master Builder* and Shaw's *Fanny's First Play*. The latter was a great success and, transferred to the Kingsway Theatre, ran until 1912.

Plans were now maturing for building a national theatre in time for the Shakespeare tercentenary in 1916, and in preparation for this, with the backing of Lord Howard de Walden and others, Barker in 1912 mounted at the Savoy two plays by Shakespeare which set a completely new standard of production never since surpassed. Continuity of action, an apron stage, the full text spoken with great beauty and a new swiftness, an entirely new approach to the plays in intelligence, truth, and taste, a brilliant company headed by Henry Ainley and Miss Lillah McCarthy, and exquisite simple settings by Albert Rothenstein (afterwards Rutherston) and Norman Wilkinson, all contributed to Barker's achievement. He was perhaps too far in advance of his time; even the critics were startled by the violent changes from the accepted traditions, and the first play, *The Winter's Tale*, was a comparative failure. *Twelfth Night*, although almost as revolutionary, was a more familiar play and ran for a hundred nights. These two productions, with *A Midsummer Night's Dream* in 1914, have had a profound and permanent effect on the approach to Shakespeare in the theatre. Further productions proved impracticable but meanwhile in 1913 Barker achieved a great comedy success at the Kingsway Theatre with Ainley in *The Great Adventure* by Arnold Bennett which ran until after the outbreak of war. The same year (1913) saw the opening of a season at the St. James's Theatre with Shaw's *Androcles and the Lion*, followed by revivals of *Nan*, *The Doctor's Dilemma*, and plays of Ibsen and Maeterlinck. Barker was now at the height of his powers, and his productions, although costly to his backers, greatly enhanced his European reputation and marked him as the future director of the national theatre.

The war demolished all his hopes. Barker presented Hardy's *Dynasts* in an adaptation of his own with outstanding artistic success, but the theatre had turned to frivolity and the production failed completely. In 1915 he produced *Androcles and the Lion*, *The Doctor's Dilemma*, and *A Midsummer Night's Dream* in New York for an American syndicate of millionaires. A mutual attraction between Barker and the wife of Archer Huntington (one of the backers) broke his marriage, and as neither of their partners wished a divorce there ensued a period of great strain during which Barker worked first for the Red Cross in France and then enlisted, later undertaking military intelligence work. Eventually the divorces went through and in 1918 Barker married Helen Huntington (died 1950) who as Helen Gates was a poet and novelist of some distinction. Archer Huntington settled a large sum on her and Barker was able to live henceforth in luxury.

His wife insisted on almost complete severance from his work in the theatre and all his friends, however old and intimate, connected with it, and above all from Shaw.

Potentially perhaps the most remarkable theatre personality of this century Barker's career thus proved on the whole a disappointment and his influence on the theatre of this country fell far short of the hopes inspired by his brilliant start. His remaining work for the theatre was mainly professorial and literary, although almost surreptitiously he did a certain amount of directing of his own plays and translations. His last acknowledged stage production was Maeterlinck's *The Betrothal* at the Gaiety Theatre in 1921. In 1919 he took up with enthusiasm the work of the British Drama League recently founded by Geoffrey Whitworth, and was its valuable chairman for thirteen years. In 1920 he made a rather pathetic attempt to live as a country gentleman in south Devon and during this period wrote his last two plays and the first of his series of translations from the Spanish (with his wife) which introduced the Quintero brothers and Sierra to the British public. As a dramatist Barker was too meticulous a writer to be very prolific. He experimented in a number of styles and probably his best work is found in the high comedy of *The Voysey Inheritance* and *The Madras House* and in the tragedy of *Waste*. Although slow moving, the characterization is vivid and as social criticism of their time they have a cutting edge. The two plays written in retirement, *His Majesty* and *The Secret Life*, seem never to have been publicly performed and have the rarefied atmosphere of one who has detached himself from the task of satisfying an audience which has paid for its seats. His *Exemplary Theatre* (1922) shows how far his mind had travelled even then from the contemporary theatre.

In 1923 Barker undertook the part editorship of 'The Players' Shakespeare', and although the series was abandoned he continued until his death to write the prefaces he had begun for it. They will probably outlive all his other written work, for they are most valuable interpretations of the plays from the director's point of view, and as a director Barker may be regarded as the first and greatest of the moderns. As an actor he had too much critical intelligence to be really successful for, with a certain lack of common humanity, it showed vividly through his impersonations. This was valuable in detached parts such as Marchbanks and Keegan, or even John Tanner, but it marred his performance of more ordinary characters. His face lacked the true flexibility of the actor's mask and his expressive voice, probably from being overworked as a boy, had too little ground tone to carry its strong higher harmonics. Yet he was an actor to his finger-tips, and with this he combined a first-class analytical and administrative brain and an outstanding gift for leadership. As a producer he used all his varied gifts completely selflessly in the service of the dramatist to bring out and express the full emotional and intellectual content of the play. His mastery of the play before starting rehearsals inspired confidence in his actors and he had the power to stimulate and use their own imaginative ideas, blending and moulding them within the framework of the play as he saw it. His intuitive grasp, as a dramatist, of human motives, thought, and emotions, and his technical knowledge of how to express them were continually at the service of his cast with every device of witty metaphor and amusing illustration. He was a perfectionist but no dictator, criticizing to the last inch and the last rehearsal, always with good humour, every tiniest movement or vocal inflexion, until the whole play became a symphony in which every phrase, rhythm, melody, and movement reached as near perfection as he could make it.

In 1930 Barker was appointed to the Clark lectureship at Trinity College, Cambridge, and in 1937 he was Romanes lecturer at Oxford. He received honorary degrees from Edinburgh (1930), and from Oxford and Reading in 1937, in which year he became director of the British Institute in Paris where he had been living for some time. He continued to take some interest in the British theatre and in 1940 came over to take a major share of the direction of (Sir) John Gielgud's *King Lear* at the Old Vic, on condition that his name did not appear. He resigned from the British Institute in 1939 and when Paris fell he went to America where he was a visiting professor at Yale and Harvard. He returned to England in failing health in 1945 and to Paris in 1946 where he died 31 August and was buried in the cemetery of Père Lachaise. He had no children.

Of slight, wiry build, almost five feet eleven in height, until well past middle age Barker still gave an extraordinary impression of youth both in face and figure. He had a sensitive face, strong and masculine with humorous warm brown eyes, and a mouth always harder than the eyes, tending even to grimness in his later days. His thick red-brown hair was parted in the middle and thrown back. A curious feature was his very flabby handshake. The British Drama League has a bust in bronze by Clara Billing and a posthumous bust by David McFall; the National Portrait Gallery has a painting by J.-E. Blanche; a bronze by Lady Kennet is at the Shakespeare Memorial Theatre, Stratford on Avon, and a portrait statuette by the same artist is at the Garrick Club.

[Desmond MacCarthy, *The Court Theatre, 1904–7*, 1907; C. B. Purdom, *Harley Granville Barker*, with a complete catalogue of his known writings, 1955; *Who's Who in the Theatre*; private information; personal knowledge.]

Lewis Casson

published 1959

Robert Ranke

(1895–1985)

Writer and poet, was born at Wimbledon 24 July 1895, the eldest of the three sons and the third of five children of Alfred Perceval Graves, an inspector of schools, and his second wife, Elizabeth Sophie ('Amy'), daughter of Heinrich von Ranke, a medical doctor. The family ancestry included German, Danish, Irish, Scottish, and English elements. Literature of many kinds was in the boy's blood; his maternal great-uncle was the historian Leopold von Ranke; an eighteenth-century ancestor, Richard Graves, had written *The Spiritual Quixote* (1772), a novel remembered in the twentieth century; and his own father had composed the words to a popular Irish song, 'Father O'Flynn'.

Educated at various preparatory schools and Charterhouse (1907–14), Graves was about to proceed to St John's College, Oxford, when World War I broke out. Being in north Wales at the time (the family had a house at Harlech where the boy spent much, and formative, time) he reported to the nearest depot where he could be accepted for training as an officer, and since this was Wrexham he found himself commissioned, for the duration of the war, in the Royal Welch Fusiliers. After serving through some of the heaviest fighting, being twice mentioned in dispatches, and once having his death in action reported in *The Times*, he was demobilized in 1919.

In 1918 Graves married Annie Mary Pryde ('Nancy') (died 1977), daughter of (Sir) William Newzam Prior Nicholson, artist, and sister of Ben Nicholson. They had two daughters and two sons. The couple moved to Oxford in 1919, and Graves began to read English at St John's College, living in a cottage at the end of the garden of John Masefield, the poet. They stayed near Oxford till 1926, Graves first supporting his growing family by running a small grocery business and then solely by writing. He did not take an undergraduate degree because of illness but gained a B.Litt. (1925). He also became acquainted with T. E. Lawrence and heard his version of wartime events in Palestine. After spending part of a year (1926) as a lecturer at the Royal Egyptian University, he returned to England and settled to the life of a professional writer.

In 1929, parting company with Nancy, he established a household in Deyá, Majorca, that included the American poet Laura Riding, with whom he had been associated in his work since 1926. She was the daughter of Nathaniel Reichenthal, a tailor, and the former wife of Louis Gottschalk, a history teacher at Cornell University. Until the Spanish civil war uprooted them in 1936, Graves and Riding both produced a steady flow of work, some of it published by the Seizin Press, a small company they founded in England and continued in Deyá.

In 1936 they moved to London. Two years later they took a flat in Rennes, France, and in 1939 went to America. There Laura left Graves to live with Schuyler Jackson. Graves returned to England and set up house with Beryl, daughter of Sir Harry Goring Pritchard, solicitor and parliamentary agent, and wife of Alan Hodge, poet and writer; they married in 1950. They had three sons and a daughter.

The years of World War II, paradoxically, were a good period for Graves; he was productive in his country fastness at Galmpton, Devon, and happy in his second marriage (with a rich harvest of love poems to show for it); though doubtless deeply stricken by the death of his first son David, killed in Burma while serving with his father's old regiment.

Graves and his family returned to Majorca in 1946. Graves spent the rest of his life there, with excursions, notably to give the Clark lectures in Cambridge (1954) and to be professor of poetry (1961–6) at Oxford, where St John's College elected him an honorary fellow in 1971.

In the preface to his *Poems 1938–45* (1948) Graves declared: 'I write poems for poets, and satires or grotesques for wits. For people in general I write prose, and am content that they should be unaware that I do anything else.' 'People in general' did indeed know him mainly as a writer of historical novels, notably *I, Claudius* (1934, which won the Hawthornden and James Tait Black memorial prizes), *Claudius the God* (1934), *Count Belisarius* (1938), *Sergeant Lamb of the Ninth* (1940), *King Jesus* (1946), and *Homer's Daughter* (1955). His wider fame was first established, however, by the autobiography *Goodbye to All That* in 1929. This admirable book (perhaps best read in its slightly tidied-up version of 1957, which corrects the hasty syntax without blurring the honest sharp edges) stands in a perceptible relationship to the Claudius novels. The 'I' in each case is very much the product of the surrounding civilization, even while evaluating and indeed rejecting it.

As a poet Graves employs cool, restrained rhythms, often showing a fine lyrical sense of the musical possibilities of pause and stress, and a diction very close to the central core of English poetic tradition. Without actually making a count, one has the impression that his vocabulary contains very few words that do not occur in classical English poetry from Dryden to Wordsworth. His metrical and stanzaic forms, likewise, draw on a traditional, rather than an experimental vitality. The tmesic element in Graves's poetry, the element that represents a break with tradition, is sited in the subject-matter rather than the form. A large proportion of his verse, especially in the second half of his working life from about 1950 onwards, is devoted to exploring and celebrating a certain kind of relationship between the sexes, a relationship which, like the religion of matriarchal societies, makes the female the dominant principle. Graves evidently regarded this view of the sexes as determining the nature of much in his personal life and almost everything in his poetry, and he expounded it at length in *The White Goddess* (1948, revised and expanded edition 1952), a book that stands in the same relationship to his mature poetry as *A Vision* does to Yeats's.

Graves was also active as a literary critic, especially of poetry. His criticism, though always interesting, is often vitiated by a curious combativeness; at times he seems almost comically aggressive, a Mr Punch thwacking at anything in reach with a clumsily held truncheon. An early collaboration with Laura Riding, *A Survey of Modernist Poetry* (1927), seems at first an exception, since it is positively in favour of something— the 'modernist' movement. The analysis of Shakespeare's Sonnet 129 in juxtaposition with a poem by E. E. Cummings, demonstrating that 'modernist' techniques are just about equally present in both, is a superb *tour de force* of analytical criticism, to which his fellow poet doubtless contributed her share. Yet it has to be borne in mind that to advocate anything as alarming as modernism was, in the 1920s, a stick to beat the establishment. Graves particularly enjoyed an academic platform from which he could compel the learned and august to listen submissively while he assaulted their sacred cows, as can be seen from *The Crowning Privilege* (1955)—the text of his Clark lectures in Cambridge—and *Oxford Addresses on Poetry* (1961).

Graves had his share of insights, but it would seem fair comment to say that he was less the kind of critic who patiently illuminates work he admires than the kind who finds emotional release in attacking what he dislikes. He appears to have had a particular hostility to Milton, and, though never mounting a full-scale attack on that poet's art, devoted much energy to blackening his character in a novel, *Wife to Mr Milton* (1943).

Turning from Graves the writer to Graves the man (strictly speaking an impossibility, since *le style* was *l'homme même* and even the most transient of his writings always concerned something of importance in his life), one's most abiding impression is of singularity. The gigantic stature, the clipped speech (to the end his diction was that of a subaltern of 1916), the erect officer-like bearing that never seemed in conflict with the bardic majesty, the widebrimmed hats (of black felt on formal occasions, often of ragged straw in his leisure on the beach), all made a unique presence. As much as any Irish or Welsh medieval bard, Graves held that being a poet set one apart totally from the rest of mankind; and, while this did not prevent his sharing many of the best qualities of common humanity—courage, humour, cheerful hospitality, philoprogenitiveness, to name no more—it is true that one often felt in his presence a certain otherness, a wind blowing from an undefined quarter of the spirit: whether caused by the cloud of abstraction that sometimes came down over him, or by the colossal size that made him seem like a giant out of a folk tale, or the knowledge of the terrible ordeals he had endured and suffered so long ago, or most likely, a combination of all these, he was *sui generis*, and unrepeatable. He died at his home in Deyá, Majorca, 7 December 1985.

[Robert Graves, *Goodbye to All That*, 1929; Alfred Perceval Graves, *To Return to All That*, 1930; *The Times*, 9 December 1985; Richard P. Graves, *Robert Graves: the Assault Heroic*, 1986; personal knowledge.]

JOHN WAIN

published 1990

GRIEVE Christopher Murray

(1892–1978)

Poet and prose writer, who used the pseudonym Hugh MacDiarmid, was born 11 August 1892, at Langholm in Dumfriesshire, Scotland, the elder son (there were no daughters) of James Grieve, postman, and his wife, Elizabeth, daughter of Andrew Graham, farmhand, of Waterbeck. He was educated at Langholm Academy, and his first published poem appeared in the *Eskdale and Liddesdale Advertiser* while he was in his teens. During a spell as a pupil-teacher in Edinburgh, he joined the Edinburgh branches of the Independent Labour Party and the Fabian Society. After working on various newspapers in Scotland and south Wales, he joined the army in July 1915, rising through the ranks to become a sergeant. In 1916 he was posted to the RAMC in Salonika from where he sent home poems to be read and judged by one of his previous schoolmasters; he contracted malaria and in 1918 he was invalided home. In June 1918 he married Margaret Cunningham Thompson Skinner (Peggy) (died 1962), a one-time colleague on the *Fife Herald*. They were to have a son and a daughter.

The end of the war found him in an Indian hospital in Marseilles, from which he was demobilized in July 1919. His first book, *Annals of the Five Senses* (1923), largely consisted of poems written in Salonika. After the war Grieve worked as a journalist, largely on the *Montrose Review*, and became widely known as the editor of three successive anthologies of current Scottish poetry called *Northern Numbers* (1920, 1921, and 1922).

From 1920 onwards a movement was started towards the revival of Scots as a literary medium. At first Grieve resisted this, believing it to be a 'backwater', but he finally started to experiment with it, assuming the pen-name of Hugh MacDiarmid. He employed a literary Scots based largely on the speech of his native countryside, but also using and reviving words from the Scots poets and prose writers of the past. In this medium he wrote the beautiful short lyrics of *Sangschaw* (1925) and *Penny Wheep* (1926), but his most notable use of it is in his long poem *A Drunk Man Looks at the Thistle* (1926). His method is best described in his own words: 'a long poem ... split up into several sections, but the forms within the sections range from ballad measure to *vers libre*. The matter includes satire, amphigouri, lyrics, parodies of Mr. T. S. Eliot and other poets, and translations from the Russian, French and German. The whole poem is in braid Scots, ... and it has been expressly designed to show that braid Scots can be effectively applied to all manner of subjects and measures' (1925). Hand in hand with this interest in Scots went his involvement with Scottish nationalist politics. When the National Party of Scotland was formed in 1927–8, Grieve was very active in encouraging it, and he became a founder member in 1928, but was expelled in 1933. He was a Labour member of the Montrose Town Council and a JP. He moved to Liverpool and London, becoming in 1928 editor of the short-lived radio journal *Vox*.

In 1932 his first marriage ended in divorce, and in 1934 he married a Cornishwoman, Valda Trevlyn Rowlands, who had borne him a son two years previously. After a brief spell in East Lothian, in 1933 they moved to Whalsay, a small remote island in the Shetlands, where they lived until Grieve was called up for war work, first in a factory, and later in the merchant navy. Grieve joined the Communist Party of Great Britain in 1934, but four years later was expelled for 'national deviation'. The long poems written during this period, which include two 'Hymns to Lenin' (1931 and 1935), are composed in a mixture of Scots and English, but during the later part of his life his poems are largely written in English. He continued his political involvement, standing as an Independent Scottish Nationalist candidate for Kelvingrove in 1945. In *Who's Who* he listed his recreation as 'Anglophobia'. In 1957 he rejoined the Communist Party and was the communist candidate for Kinross in 1964. In 1950 he visited Russia with members of the Scottish–USSR Friendship Society, and in the same year was awarded a Civil List pension; he went to China in 1956 as a member of the delegation of the British–Chinese Friendship Society. During this time he moved to the cottage in Biggar, Lanarkshire, where he lived until his death.

In 1957 an honorary LL D was conferred upon him by the University of Edinburgh, and in the following year he was presented with the Andrew Fletcher Saltoun medal for 'service to Scotland'. He was also honorary RSA. As part of the Robert Burns bicentenary celebrations in 1959 he visited Czechoslovakia, Romania, Bulgaria, and Hungary. In 1976 he was elected president of the Poetry Society of Great Britain. His most sustained work in prose is *Lucky Poet: A Self-study in Literature and Political Ideas, Being the Autobiography of Hugh MacDiarmid (Christopher Murray Grieve)* (1943); this also includes a 'Third Hymn to Lenin'. Of his overall contribution to Scots literature, he has characteristically written: 'My job, as I see it, has never been to lay a tit's egg, but to erupt like a volcano, emitting not only flame but a lot of rubbish.' He died in hospital in Edinburgh 9 September 1978.

[Gordon Wright, *MacDiarmid, an Illustrated Biography*, 1977; Kenneth Butley, *Hugh MacDiarmid (C. M. Grieve)*, 1964; Hugh MacDiarmid, *Lucky Poet*, 1943, and *The Company I've Kept*, 1966 (autobiographies); Alan Bold (ed.), *The Letters of Hugh MacDiarmid*, 1984; *The Times*, 11 September 1978.]

JOHN WAIN

published 1986

GRIGSON Geoffrey Edward Harvey

(1905–1985)

Poet, critic, anthologist, and man of letters, was born 2 March 1905 at Pelynt, Cornwall, the seventh and last son (there were no daughters) of Canon William Shuckforth Grigson, vicar of Pelynt, and his wife, Mary Beatrice, daughter of John Simon Boldero, vicar of Amblecote, near Stourbridge, Staffordshire. At the time his father was fifty-nine years old and his mother forty-two. His childhood and adolescence, as described in his vivid, impressionistic autobiography *The Crest on the Silver* (1950), were deeply unhappy. He was sent as boarder to a preparatory school at the age of five, then to a minor public school in Leatherhead which he detested. This was succeeded by what he called a profitless sojourn at St Edmund Hall, Oxford, where he gained a third class in English in 1927. These years were marked also by grief at the death of three of his brothers during World War I, including one whom he particularly loved. Three more were to die during World War II, so that by the end of it this seventh son was the only survivor of his father's large family.

He came down from Oxford an awkward, reticent young man, loving Cornwall and the countryside, knowing little of London; yet there his talent flowered. He worked on the *Yorkshire Post*, then the *Morning Post* where he became literary editor. He founded *New Verse* (1933–9), a 'malignant egg' as he later called it, the most influential British poetry magazine of the 1930s. In *New Verse* he printed the finest poets of the W. H. Auden generation, but the magazine was almost equally known for his own criticism of his contemporaries, always unsparing and at times ferocious. He later regretted what he called such savage use of the billhook, but still employed it often, in hundreds of reviews written for the *Observer*, *Guardian*, *New Statesman*, and other papers. Some of the best and sharpest of them were gathered together in *The Contrary View* (1974) and *Blessings, Kicks and Curses* (1982).

New Verse was the beginning of a literary career which embraced art criticism, anthologies of verse and prose, guides to the countryside and its flora, and the writing of poems. He spent the war years in the BBC at Evesham and Bristol, but thereafter was a freelance, making his home at the farmhouse he had found in Wiltshire, living mostly by literary journalism, but never relaxing his standards. The results were remarkable, both in quality and variety. The finest of his essays on art are to be found in *The Harp of Aeolus* (1947), which includes appreciations of artists as diverse as George Stubbs, Francis Danby and De Chirico, and along with this book should be put *Samuel Palmer, the Visionary Years* (1947), which prompted a revised view of Palmer's genius. *The Romantics* (1943) and *Before the Romantics* (1946), two of the first among many anthologies, mark the immense scope of his reading, his endless curiosity about the relationship of man and nature, his concern with the shape and sound of language. He had a quite separate fame as author of *The Englishman's Flora* (1955), *The Shell Country Book* (1962), and other works about the English countryside.

And, last and to him by far the most important, he was a poet. His first book, *Several Observations* (1939), fulfilled his own requirements of 'taking notice, for ends not purely individual, of the universe of objects and events'. All his poems do this, whether they are lyrical, satirical, or views of scenes and people. A genuineness of feeling and observation, and a refusal of rhetorical gestures, are the hallmarks of his poetry. *Collected Poems* appeared in 1963, and a further volume covering the years up to 1980 in 1982. In the same year he published *The Private Art*, a 'Poetry Notebook' of comments and quotations that emphasized again the generosity and tough delicacy of his mind. *Grigson at Eighty*, edited by R. M. Healey, a collection of tributes from friends and admirers, appeared in the year of his death.

Both the breadth of his knowledge and interests, and the integrity with which he pursued them, made Grigson a uniquely valuable figure in twentieth-century literary Britain. In person he was tall, handsome, enthusiastic, with an attractive blend of sophistication and innocence. The fierceness of his writing was belied by a gentle, sometimes elaborately polite manner. He distrusted all official bodies dealing with the arts, and served on no committees. When, in 1972, he received the Duff Cooper memorial prize for a volume of poems, his short speech made clear his uneasiness on such large formal occasions.

Like his father Grigson was married three times. In 1929 he married Frances, daughter of Thomas Trauldin Galt, attorney, of St Louis, Missouri. They had one daughter. Frances died in 1937 and in 1938 he married Berta Emma Beatrix, daughter of Otto Kunert, an Austrian major from Salzburg. They had a son and daughter. This marriage was dissolved and he married thirdly Jane, daughter of George Shipley McIntire, CBE, town clerk of Sunderland. Jane Grigson became a celebrated cookery expert; they had one daughter. Grigson died 28 November 1985 at Broad Town Farm, his Wiltshire home, and is buried in Christ Church, Broad Town, churchyard.

[R. M. Healey (ed.), *Grigson at Eighty*, 1985; Geoffrey Grigson, *The Crest on the Silver*, 1950 (autobiography); private information; personal knowledge.]

JULIAN SYMONS

published 1990

GURNEY Ivor Bertie

(1890–1937)

Composer and poet, was born at 3 Queen Street, Gloucester, 28 August 1890, the elder son and second in the family of two boys and two girls of David Gurney, proprietor of a small tailoring business, and his wife Florence, daughter of William Lugg, house decorator. He was educated at the King's School as a chorister of Gloucester Cathedral, then as an articled pupil of the cathedral organist, (Sir) A. Herbert Brewer, and finally, on winning a composition scholarship (1911), at the Royal College of Music under Sir Charles Stanford.

Though rejected by the army in 1914 on grounds of defective eyesight, Gurney enlisted on 9 February 1915 while still a student and from 25 May 1916 served in France as a private with the 2nd/5th Gloucesters. He sustained a minor bullet wound on Good Friday 1917 and more serious gas injuries on or about 10 September 1917 during the third battle of Ypres

(Passchendaele). Invalided back to England, he spent time in various war hospitals and, after exhibiting signs of mental instability (including a suicide attempt on 19 June 1918), he was finally discharged in October 1918.

He resumed his studies at the Royal College but was unable to concentrate. He returned to Gloucester and, failing to find permanent employment, was obliged to live on a small disability pension and the charity of friends and family. Music and poetry now poured from him, but his behaviour (eccentric before the war) grew increasingly erratic. Further threats of suicide followed and in September 1922 he was diagnosed as suffering from paranoid schizophrenia and committed to Barnwood House Asylum, Gloucester. On 21 December 1922 he was transferred to the City of London Mental Hospital, Dartford, Kent, where he remained until his death.

As a composer Gurney found his voice in 1913/14 with the composition of *Five Elizabethan Songs*. Although he wrote chamber and orchestral music, songs were his true vocation. Manuscripts of more than 300 are to be found in the Gurney archive at the Gloucester city public library. Poetry was a secondary interest that grew only when conditions in the trenches made composition almost impossible. After the war he pursued both arts with equal fervour. Gurney's songs began to reach publication from 1920, but it was not until the Oxford University Press issued two volumes of twenty songs in 1938 that his true stature could be appreciated. Further collections followed in 1952, 1959, and 1979. These were made possible by the faith and industry of Gurney's friend, the musicologist Marion Scott, who had preserved his manuscripts, and the editorial expertise of the composers Gerald Finzi and Howard Ferguson. His manuscripts pose formidable ethical and aesthetic problems because so much of his work is uneven, unpolished, and sometimes incoherent.

Similar considerations afflict his poetry, of which over 1,700 items exist in the Gloucester archive. Two volumes were published during his lifetime: *Severn and Somme* (1917) and *War's Embers* (1919); and minor selections appeared in 1954 and 1973, edited by Edmund Blunden and Leonard Clark respectively. In 1982 the Oxford University Press issued a major selection of some 300 poems, edited by P. J. Kavanagh, and it is on the basis of this volume that his importance as a poet came to be recognized. Gurney's poems celebrate his love of the Gloucestershire countryside with the same unsentimental vigour as they report on the realities of trench warfare and chart his gradual descent into madness. His songs are equally forceful and direct, covering a wide range of emotional expression and empathizing with poets of every period, particularly his contemporaries, the Georgians. In both fields he was an individualist, and in both his successes mark him out as an artist of power and originality.

Gurney died from tuberculosis 26 December 1937 at the City of London Mental Hospital, Dartford, Kent. He was unmarried.

[Michael Hurd, *The Ordeal of Ivor Gurney*, 1978; R. K. R. Thornton, *Ivor Gurney: Collected Letters*, 1991.]

MICHAEL HURD

published 1993

HAMILTON Charles Harold St. John

(1876–1961)

Writer, better known as Frank Richards, was born 8 August 1876 at 15 Oak Street, Ealing, the sixth in a family of five brothers and three sisters. His birth certificate states that his father, John Hamilton, who married Marian Hannah Trinder, was a carpenter. In fact, John Hamilton was a journalist, and sometime bookseller and stationer, of unstable temperament who enjoyed confusing officialdom. He died when Charles was seven, after which the family moved house frequently. Of Charles Hamilton's early years little is known and he was reticent on the subject. He attended various church schools in the west London area and possibly private schools as well—never, he once said, a state school—and acquired a good knowledge of Latin and French, along with an enduring passion for the classics.

By his own account he received his first cheque for a short story at the age of seventeen from a 'Mr M' who cut later payments from five guineas to four pounds on finding that his contributor was a stripling. Hamilton concentrated his efforts on boys' papers, notably those of Trapps, Holmes & Co. and Pearsons, and never had difficulty in getting his work accepted. In 1907 the Amalgamated Press started a boys' paper, the *Gem*, following it in 1908 with the *Magnet*, and Hamilton turned out 'long, complete' stories for these weeklies for more than thirty years. He still found time to write elsewhere, under many pseudonyms, and maintained an annual output of one and a half million words. Once, when pressed, he wrote 18,000 words in a day. In the *Gem*, as Martin Clifford, he wrote about a school called St. Jim's, which had originally appeared in *Pluck*, and to which Tom Merry and his friends moved from Clavering College to become the 'Terrible Three' of the Shell. Hamilton's favourite came to be the *Magnet* in which, as Frank Richards, he wrote about Greyfriars School and its 'Famous Five' of the Remove, who included Harry Wharton, Frank Nugent (a self-portrait), and the 'dusky nabob' Hurree Jamset Ram Singh. Greyfriars' most famous character, however, was Billy Bunter, the Fat Owl, the prevaricating tuck-hunter for ever waiting for a postal order which never came. Bunter became a legend in the lifetime of his creator who liked to recall that an editor to whom he had outlined the character many years earlier had failed to 'see much' in him.

The outbreak of war put an end to the *Gem* in 1939 and the *Magnet* in 1940. Their circulation had been ailing under strong competition from the D. C. Thomson boys' papers. For Hamilton this was a hard blow. Although he had earned upwards of £2,500 a year, a substantial income for those days, he had spent freely and helped to sustain the casinos of Europe. As a literary prodigy he was then almost unknown; but in the post-war mood of nostalgia his talents were again in demand and Billy Bunter began to appear between hard covers. More than thirty Bunter titles were published, first by Charles Skilton (for whom Hamilton offered to write at his old rate of 30s. per thousand words) and later by Cassell. From 1952 Hamilton wrote Bunter scripts for television, the chief role being played by Gerald Campion. Bunter Christmas shows were also staged in London.

Hamilton's autobiography, published in 1952, greatly disappointed his followers, chiefly because it ignored his origins. It was written in the third person, as by Frank Richards. By now he was Frank Richards and it was under this name that his evasive entry appeared in *Who's Who*. His eyesight had deteriorated but he kept going with the aid of a heavily inked typewriter ribbon. Visitors to his bungalow at Kingsgate-on-Sea, near Broadstairs, found an old-fashioned, reserved figure in black skull-cap, dressing-gown, and trousers cycle-clipped against the cold. Belated fame did not affect him.

George Orwell and others criticized Hamilton's school stories on the grounds that they were wholly escapist, nurtured snobbishness, and represented foreigners as funny. The mentality, Orwell complained, was that of 'a rather exceptionally stupid member of the Navy League in the year 1910' (*Horizon*, March 1940). Replying, Hamilton maintained (*Horizon*, May 1940) that the aristocratic virtues were worth preserving and that foreigners *were* funny. He made no apology for excluding sex from his stories. At all times he was alert to defend his work from condescension and misrepresentation: he threatened legal action on hearing that his tales were to be discussed in a book provisionally titled *The Penny Blood*. He was aware that many parents would have preferred their children to read the *Boy's Own Paper*, but he was unashamed of giving harmless pleasure to the masses. His never-ageing characters were compounds of cheek and manliness; even the bounders had redeeming streaks. If there were 'barrings-out' at Greyfriars, the example did not infect his readers.

Hamilton was little influenced by earlier writers on school life. He simply cultivated the already flourishing market for school tales, avoiding the ferocities of the Jack Harkaway stories and the *Angst* of *Eric, or Little by Little*. A suggestion by Orwell which rankled was that, since not all the stories under his pen-names could have been written by one man, they had been couched in a style easily copied, with standardized ejaculations like 'Yarooh'. Hamilton always resented the use of 'his' pseudonyms by stand-in writers. His admirers, endlessly analysing his work in specialist magazines, claimed that they could always detect the work of other hands. Hamilton's style was curiously repetitious and strewn with classical allusions, but he rarely failed to bring his characters to vigorous life. He appears to have created at least thirty schools. As Owen Conquest he founded Rookwood with Jimmy Silver & Co. in the *Boys' Friend*; as Hilda Richards he launched Bessie Bunter of Cliff House School in the *School Friend*; and as Ralph Redway he wrote many Wild West tales. Under his *Gem* name of Martin Clifford he penned a fanciful account of Frank Richards's schooldays at a backwoods school in Canada. His editors joined in the game of laying false trails. Many of his contemporaries who wrote for the juvenile market were astonishingly prolific, but it is unlikely that anyone exceeded Hamilton's lifetime output, which had been put at the equivalent of nearly a thousand ordinary novels.

Hamilton, who never married, died at his home on Christmas Eve 1961.
[*The Autobiography of Frank Richards*, 1952; E. S. Turner, *Boys Will be Boys*, 1948, revised edn. 1957; Brian Doyle, *Who's Who of Boys' Writers*, 1964; files of *Collector's Miscellany*, *Collector's Digest*, and *Story Paper Collector* (Manitoba); private information.]

E. S. TURNER

published 1981

HARDY Thomas

(1840–1928)

Poet and novelist, was born 2 June 1840 at Higher Bockhampton, a hamlet near Stinsford in Dorset. On both sides he came of the native Dorset stock. Although his father's people no doubt originally sprang from the Jersey family of Le Hardy, they had for centuries belonged to the Frome valley: a numerous clan which had given several worthies to the county, among them Vice-Admiral Sir Thomas Masterman Hardy, Nelson's flag-captain. His mother's ancestors, mostly small-holders in the north of the county, bore Saxon names—Swetman and Childs and Hand or Hann. There was strong character on both sides; and also decided talent, although not of a kind to achieve more than local fame. Both his maternal grandmother and his mother, Jemima, daughter of George Hand, of Melbury Osmund, were notable women of vigorous and lively minds, and from them perhaps Hardy drew his keen sensitivity and his tenacious intellectual curiosity. But in depth of character—and especially in his quiet, unassuming determination, wholly unambitious in worldly affairs—he seems more to have resembled his father; who also, moreover, had one conspicuous talent which had proved heritable in the family, and which was obviously important in Hardy's early experience and must have done something to shape his genius. For his father, Thomas Hardy the elder, like his grandfather (also a Thomas Hardy), had a consuming passion for music. The Hardys, indeed, had made Stinsford parish church celebrated for the instrumental music which they contributed to the services there; and they were always ready to provide the music for secular festivities also. In his boyhood Thomas Hardy very willingly fell in with this family tradition of rural music, sacred and profane. His father, too, was not unwilling to show himself an expert dancer in the rustic style, and was profoundly attached to the manners of Dorset life as well as to the wild nature of the countryside: he liked to lie on a bank in hot weather 'with the grasshoppers leaping over him'. He was a builder by trade, and for that business his out-of-the-way house in Bockhampton was most unsuitably placed; but he refused to leave it, and the woods and heaths he inarticulately loved; neither would he let business interfere with music. That such a man was the father of the author of the Wessex novels is clearly significant. He was not, naturally, very successful in his trade; but did good work, and was always sound financially. It is of some importance to note that his son, although he had to make his own way, was never in immediate need of money, and always knew, while his father lived, that he could have assistance if required, unwilling though he was to be dependent.

Hardy was the eldest of four children—two sons and two daughters. He was the only one of them who married, and he had no children himself. The surgeon thought that he was stillborn, but the midwife roused the life in him; and he grew to healthy childhood, though of slight physique, rather dangerously precocious, and of unstable emotions, being strangely sensitive to the music of his father's indefatigable fiddle. Of his babyhood one incident, which in ancient days would have been considered ominous, may be mentioned: his mother found him one hot day asleep in his cot with a sleeping snake coiled on his breast (or, in another version, on the floor beside him). At eight years old he began his schooling in the village, but went next year as a day boy to an unusually good private school, kept by a nonconformist master, in Dorchester; there he was soon well grounded in Latin and French, to which he afterwards added some study of German on his own account. Later on he made himself fairly proficient in Greek. Of his schooldays a characteristic trait was that, while his amiable nature made him generally liked, he himself secretly disliked the familiarities of schoolboy companionship, and resented the touch of arm-in-arm affection.

Out of school, Hardy's life at home, and in rural society round about, gave him many experiences of which it would be impossible to exaggerate the importance; for his deeply retentive nature kept them vividly alive in his mind, and from them, more or less transformed, supplied many years later rich material for his art. Thus, by good fortune, as a very small boy he attended one of the last of the old-fashioned harvest-home suppers at which the full tradition of these celebrations was still unimpaired, to the inestimable advantage of *Far from the Madding Crowd*; and when we learn that some of the military were there too, it is impossible not to think of Sergeant Troy. Hardy frequently acted as the fiddler at local dance-parties, and to the wealth of experience which he gained thereby both his prose and his verse bear witness throughout; as they also do to his equally lively familiarity with church services, church music, and the habits and per-sonages of church choirs. It was the same with experiences of purely subjective importance. A capital instance is the lyric, 'To Louisa in the Lane', written shortly before his death, in which he completely resumes a shy romance of his early boyhood—an affair of childish sentimental reverie almost without any incident, but preserved intact into old age. But this vivid preserving of experience was a trait which continued long after boyhood, and is an essential characteristic of Hardy's genius. Thus the famous lines 'In Time of the Breaking of Nations' were written in 1915, but the experience which they record came to him in 1870, when the battle of Gravelotte was fought. So, too, the mummers' play of 1923, *The Famous Tragedy of the Queen of Cornwall*, releases and gives form to feelings and dreams which, ever since as a young man he had visited Tintagel with the lady whom he was to marry, he had retained for fifty years.

In 1856, when he was sixteen, Hardy was placed as a pupil with John Hicks, an ecclesiastical architect in Dorchester for whom his father had worked as a builder. He continued to study Latin and Greek; he did not read many authors, but those he read he knew well, especially Virgil; the Greek tragedians, too, strongly attracted him, and Homer. About this time he became acquainted with the Rev. William Barnes, the Dorset poet, whom he occasionally consulted in his classical studies; long afterwards

(1908) he edited a selection of Barnes's poems. Another friend and helper of this time was Horace Moule, of Queens' College, Cambridge, a good Grecian, and a miscellaneous writer: he it was who first decisively encouraged Hardy to continue his own experiments—it is impossible to say when they began—in prose and verse. A somewhat odd cause moved Hardy also to intense study of the New Testament in Greek. A fellow pupil in Hicks's office was a strong Baptist, and insisted on discussing paedobaptism, supported by two young friends from Aberdeen University, sons of the local Baptist minister, whose ready knowledge of the Greek Testament gave them an advantage which Hardy was determined to reduce. The topic of paedobaptism reappears in *A Laodicean*, along with a portrait of the minister; and the two young Scotsmen perhaps gave some suggestions for the character of Farfrae in *The Mayor of Casterbridge*.

By the time he was twenty, Hardy was proficient enough in his architecture to be employed by Hicks on the disastrous restoration of old churches then in vogue. As may be supposed, he later came to regret this; but the work which it gave him must have been of the greatest value in the unconscious education of his art. He used to speak later of the 'three strands' in his life at this time—architecture, study of the classics, and participation (musical and otherwise) in the rural society of Bockhampton. Hardy, with more book-learning, might have become a scholar; but for the man he was to become, the poet and novelist, it is difficult to imagine an education more suitable than the intertwining of these 'three strands'. However, believing that he ought to advance himself in his profession, he decided, on his friend Moule's advice, not to go on exploring Greek tragedy, but to give all his mind to architecture; and he seems to have become an expert Gothic draughtsman. In 1862, at the age of twenty-two, in accordance with his father's wish that he should by then be earning his own living, he sought work in London, with naïve prudence taking a return-ticket. The return half was not needed; he almost at once found employment with (Sir) Arthur William Blomfield, to whom Hardy's training in Gothic was a strong recommendation.

Hardy remained five years in London, and got to know the town well. He worked hard at architecture, in 1863 winning the essay prize offered by the Royal Institute of British Architects. He worked hard, too, at educating himself generally, reading systematically in ancient and modern literature, and attending evening classes for a while at King's College in order to improve himself in French. It was not long before he was writing again; and in March 1865 *Chambers's Journal* took a mildly humorous article, 'How I Built Myself a House.' But his interest at this time was almost entirely in poetry. That Walter Scott, after such a 'Homeric' performance as *Marmion*, should have taken to novels, he thought deplorable. His letters to his sister Mary mention Thackeray, Lytton, and Trollope as writers of repute, but, except for some approval of 'truthful representation of actual life' in Thackeray, without any sign of being personally interested. Meanwhile he was quite unsuccessfully trying the magazines with poems, many of which, however, he preserved and some thirty years and more afterwards published, slightly revised, in *Wessex Poems* and later volumes. The literary life of London was unknown to him; but he made a very methodical study of pictures in the National Gallery, and was impressed by the acting of Samuel Phelps in Shakespeare, by Dickens in his readings, and, as would be expected, by the oratorios at Exeter Hall. It must have been about this time that he read, with enthusiasm, *The Origin of Species*. This may have had something to do with his change from the orthodoxy of his youth; but the steady progress of his mind towards the very individual determinism of *The Dynasts* seems to have been largely the evolution of his own nature, independently of external influences.

Ill-health in London made Hardy return in 1867 to Dorchester, and to architectural practice with Hicks again. But by this time he was bent on writing; now, however, determined, for purely practical reasons, to try his hand at prose fiction. *The Poor Man and the Lady* was the result, a comprehensive satire of socialist tendency, said to resemble Defoe in style. Alexander Macmillan rejected it as being too ferocious a view of society, but expressed both his own admiration and that of John Morley, who praised the rustic part. Chapman & Hall accepted it in 1869; but their reader requested an interview. This reader was no other than George Meredith, who advised against publication, and urged on Hardy the importance of 'plot'. Hardy was completely unaware of the formidable nature of his first novel, the loss of which is very regrettable. The manuscript was destroyed, but a shortened and, apparently, much modified version of the story was published in the *New Quarterly Magazine* for July 1878, as *An Indiscretion in the Life of an Heiress*. The quality of the original work can scarcely be judged from this mildly charming novelette which, however, occasionally foreshadows, in setting and psychology, the art of his mature fiction. It was reprinted by Mrs. Hardy for private distribution in October 1934, and independently published in America, with an introduction by Professor Carl Weber, of Colby College, in 1935.

Too faithfully following Meredith's recommendation of plot, Hardy wrote *Desperate Remedies*, and submitted it in 1870 to Macmillan, who refused it. Hicks having died meanwhile, his practice was taken over by one Crickmay, of Weymouth, who sent Hardy as his deputy to make surveys for the restoration of the remote church of St. Juliot, near Boscastle in Cornwall. This expedition was the source of *A Pair of Blue Eyes*;

and it was at St. Juliot that he met his first wife, the rector's sister-in-law, Emma Lavinia, daughter of John Attersoll Gifford, a Plymouth lawyer, and niece of Edwin Hamilton Gifford, archdeacon of London.

The St. Juliot restoration was Hardy's last work of any importance in Gothic. For a couple of years more he accepted temporary architectural engagements in London and Weymouth, but, in spite of some discouragement and uncertainty at first, gave himself chiefly to fiction. *Desperate Remedies* was published anonymously in 1871 by William Tinsley, to whom Hardy had to pay £75; it received some good reviews, but was bludgeoned by the *Spectator*. Yet the sales were such that Hardy recovered £60 of his outlay. In the summer of this year, following the advice implied in Morley's criticism of *The Poor Man and the Lady*, he found his true vein and wrote *Under the Greenwood Tree*, which Tinsley bought for £30 and brought out in 1872. It was well received, and Tinsley suggested a serial for his *Magazine*. Hardy agreed, made much better terms, and wrote *A Pair of Blue Eyes*, which, when published in book form (1873), had considerable success. While he was busy with this last novel (Sir) Leslie Stephen, strongly attracted by *Under the Greenwood Tree*, wrote proposing a serial for the *Cornhill*, of which he was then editor. Still hoping to get back to poetry, and regarding prose fiction chiefly as a means of livelihood, Hardy, with no more immediate ambition than to be 'considered a good hand at a serial', sent Stephen some chapters of *Far from the Madding Crowd*. It was accepted and began to appear (anonymously) in the *Cornhill* for January 1874; and was at once recognized as something remarkable. Hardy finished the book at Bockhampton during the summer, close to the district where the scene of the story was laid, which, he said, he found a 'great advantage'. In September he and Miss Gifford were married. *Far from the Madding Crowd* was published in two volumes in November, and had great success—a fact imperfectly appreciated by Hardy himself, then living at Surbiton with his wife after a honeymoon abroad.

It might be supposed that, with the publication of this masterpiece, so richly confirming the promise of *Under the Greenwood Tree*, Hardy had found past mistake the right road for him as a novelist. But he had a curious faculty of being unaware of his own powers. His next book, *The Hand of Ethelberta* (1875), also a *Cornhill* serial, might well disconcert his admirers then, as it still does now, not so much by the difference of its subject, as by its lapse in quality, although that was doubtless due to the subject. But in 1878 *The Return of the Native* appeared; and thenceforth for close on twenty years his fiction was not only his profession (a fact which he still at times regretted), but an art of noble form, amazing wealth of substance, and profound significance. There is variety, and no doubt inequality, in the series of his novels. *The Trumpet-Major* (1880), a story in an historical setting, may, for all its charm and good-humour, be ranked below, if only just below, his highest achievements. *A Laodicean* (1881) and *Two on a Tower* (1882) show that his art was not confined to rural society, though plainly at its best there; and *The Romantic Adventures of a Milkmaid* (summer number of the *Graphic*, 1883) is a pleasant modern fairy-tale. But *The Mayor of Casterbridge* (1886) and *The Woodlanders* (1887) must be grouped with the earlier *Far from the Madding Crowd* and *The Return of the Native*, their prelude *Under the Greenwood Tree*, and with the two later novels of more extended, more epic, structure, *Tess of the D'Urbervilles* (1891) and *Jude the Obscure* (1895), as together forming one of the supreme and most individual achievements of the art of fiction in English. Between these two last came the strange experiment of *The Well-Beloved* (serially, 1892; revised and published in book form, 1897); and interspersed among the series of the novels were several collections of admirable short stories, *Wessex Tales* (1888) and *Life's Little Ironies* (1894), and two sets of tales linked together by the occasion of their telling, *A Group of Noble Dames* (1891; incomplete in Christmas number of the *Graphic*, 1890) and—a minor masterpiece—*A Few Crusted Characters* (1891). A collection of stories not hitherto published, *A Changed Man and Other Tales*, was made in 1913. All the novels except the first two had come out serially; *Tess* and *Jude* were deliberately modified to suit the delicacy of editors, while the final form of *The Mayor of Casterbridge* was a drastic revision of the more sensational serial version.

Hardy's career as a writer of prose fiction was now at an end. He had never himself required more of it than a means of modest subsistence; but now at long last he could devote himself to poetry, which he had, in fact, been writing off and on during his work as a novelist. In spite of his practical attitude to the business of novel-writing, he had made his fiction, both in its conduct and its substance (his own Wessex life, for instance), as personal an expression of his artistic genius and of his deepest convictions as poetry could well be. But with *Jude the Obscure* it seemed that he had exhausted the possibilities of the novel as a vehicle for his artistic and intellectual idiosyncrasy. He was perhaps subconsciously aware of this; if so, the feeling was doubtless confirmed by some stupid, and some malignant, abuse of *Tess* and *Jude*. That he was nettled by the outcry is certain; and some impatient remarks of his ascribe his abandonment of fiction to this strident noise of journalistic disapproval. In itself the reason seems inadequate, especially considering the immense success of both books, and the splendid praise of such men as Swinburne. The truth is that the novel had served Hardy's turn, both practically and artistically. He was now free of the profession which he had served so long, and secure, and could be without interruption what he had always wanted to be—a poet.

After living in several places—Sturminster Newton (1876), Upper Tooting (Trinity Road, near Wandsworth Common, 1878), Wimborne (1881, after a long and severe illness)—he had settled finally (1883) near Dorchester in a house, Max Gate, which he had built for himself (1885); but he made regular visits to London, attended functions, was a good clubman, and knew and frequently met most of the people worth knowing in his day. He had always been a man of large and varied culture, and throughout his life continued to read widely in all kinds of imaginative literature, and in history and philosophy. His delighted interest in his own Wessex people, needless to say, never changed.

Hardy's first task, in his new and specifically poetic career, was to collect in two volumes (*Wessex Poems*, 1898, and *Poems of Past and Present*, 1901) lyrics composed from the time when he first began seriously to write at all down to the time when he had broken with the profession of fiction. They elaborate and concentrate moods and thoughts discoverable, no doubt, in the novels, but in a remarkably original poetic style, which now is seen clearly to announce the revolutionary lyrical art of his last years. But a grand project had long been gradually taking shape in his mind, and was now ripe for execution. Hardy's imagination was full of local memories and traditions of Napoleonic times, and he had drawn on these for *The Trumpet-Major* and several poems and stories; but from quite early years the vast theme of the Napoleonic wars as a whole had presented itself to his poetic ambition. Already in 1875, as his note-books testify, he had thought of 'an Iliad of Europe from 1789 to 1815' in the form of a ballad-epic; later on the project defined itself as a 'grand drama' or chronicle-play. In 1892 he is considering 'methods for the Napoleon drama. Forces; emotions; tendencies. The characters do not act under the influence of reason'; and by 1896 (when he visited Waterloo with the poem in his mind) the drama is planned as 'three parts, five acts each'—almost in its present form. The three parts of *The Dynasts* were published in 1903, 1906, and 1908 respectively, the whole in one volume in 1910. 'The Spectacle here presented' (to quote the preface) 'in the likeness of a Drama' is, then, although dramatic in manner, epic in progress and proportion. The colossal historical theme is both enlarged and unified by the invention of a symbolic supernatural world contemplating and commenting on earthly events. By this invention Hardy was enabled to present history as epic with a success which no previous attempt at any such thing (Lucan's or Ercilla's, for instance) had ever come near: he kept the substantial accuracy of his history, but he gave it the emotional scope and imaginative reverberation of epic. Moreover, he was thereby enabled to give explicit artistic form to the 'metaphysic' implicit in his fiction and progressively becoming more and more insistent as the series of the novels advanced. *The Dynasts* is thus by far his greatest single achievement, and the fullest and most complete expression of his genius. A work of such dimensions, and so unprecedented both in content and in style, was not unnaturally somewhat coolly received at first. But it was not very long before it made its way, and in its grand exhibition of absolute determinism—the 'Immanent Will' ruthlessly and purposelessly working itself out through the welter of human affairs—has seemed to many the one modern English poem which fulfils the nature of the great epics of the past: it shapes a spectacle of large action so as to convey a significance characteristic of its time.

This was the climax of Hardy's whole career, and a noble justification of his jealously preserved poetic ambition. But in that extraordinary career nothing is more extraordinary than what followed. Soon after *The Dynasts* came (1909) *Time's Laughingstocks*, a collection of lyrics, some (previously overlooked) from very early years, some of recent composition. This inaugurates the third period of his art, the period of wholly lyrical activity, except for the mummers' play of Tristran and Iseult, *The Famous Tragedy of the Queen of Cornwall* (1923): *Satires of Circumstance* (1914), *Moments of Vision* (1917), *Late Lyrics and Earlier* (1922, including a further gathering of poems from former years), *Human Shows, Far Fantasies* (1925), and *Winter Words* (1928, published after his death). It is of course completely mistaken to regard Hardy as having turned to poetry in his last years. He had been writing poetry all his life, and if he had never written a line after he had finished his work as a novelist he would still have been a very considerable poet. But in both bulk and quality his lyrical poetry is chiefly the work of his old age, from his seventieth year until his death at eighty-seven. It is all surprisingly original in theme and manner, with a diction throughout wholly unlike any other poet's, while keeping as a rule to orthodox forms or kinds of form; and it ranges from extremely subtle subjectivity to vigorously objective balladry. From his earliest efforts in the 'sixties down to his last poems the general character of his poetic style is quite continuous; but the full expansion and most daring development of his lyrical art belongs to the third and last phase of his life.

Hardy's first wife died in 1912. In 1914 he married Florence Emily, daughter of Edward Dugdale, of Enfield (but of a Dorset family). He received the Order of Merit in 1910, and, what especially pleased him, the freedom of Dorchester in the same year. In 1909 he succeeded Meredith as president of the Society of Authors. He received honorary doctorates from the universities of Aberdeen, Cambridge, and Oxford, and was an honorary fellow of Magdalene College, Cambridge, and of Queen's College, Oxford. He died at Max Gate 11 January 1928. His ashes were buried in Westminster Abbey, but his heart was interred in the churchyard of Stinsford.

There are several portraits of Hardy in public collections: in the National Portrait Gallery, oil paintings by W. W. Ouless (1922) and R. G. Eves (1923), a pencil drawing by William Strang (1919), and a bronze bust by Sir Hamo Thornycroft (1917); in the Tate Gallery, another portrait in oils by R. G. Eves (1924); in the Fitzwilliam Museum, an oil painting by Augustus John (1923) with the pencil study that preceded it, and another pencil drawing by William Strang (1910); in the Dorset County Museum, Dorchester, an oil painting by (Sir) Hubert von Herkomer (1906), and a bronze bust by Mrs. M. R. Mitchell (1923). In the possession of Mrs. Hardy at Max Gate are two portraits earlier than any of these—viz. oil paintings by Winifred Hope Thomson (&c. 1891), and by William Strang (1893), who about the same time also did the etching published in the first edition (1894) of Lionel Johnson's book (see below).

[The sole authority for Hardy's biography is the invaluable memoir by his second wife, *The Early Life* (1928) and *The Later Years* (1930), which contain some letters and many extracts from his note-books. His literary career has been studied by Lionel Johnson, *The Art of Thomas Hardy* (1894); F. A. Hedgcock, *Thomas Hardy, penseur et artiste* (1911); Lascelles Abercrombie, *Thomas Hardy, a critical study* (1912); Harold Child, *Thomas Hardy* (1916); H. C. Duffin, *Thomas Hardy. A Study of the Wessex Novels* (1916); S. C. Chew, *Thomas Hardy, Poet and Novelist* (1921); R. E. Zachrisson, *Thomas Hardy as Man, Writer, and Philosopher* (1928); W. H. Gardner, *Some Thoughts on 'The Mayor of Casterbridge'* (1930). F. A. Hedgcock's work contains a valuable detailed bibliography of the fiction and the early poems. See also the bibliography by John Lane (revised and brought down to date 1923) appended to Lionel Johnson's book; and A. P. Webb, *A Bibliography of the Works of Thomas Hardy, 1865–1915*, 1916.]

L. ABERCROMBIE

published 1937

HARRIS John Wyndham Parkes Lucas Beynon

(1903–1969)

Writer, best known under the name of John Wyndham, was born at Knowle in Warwickshire 10 July 1903, the elder son of George Beynon Harris, a barrister-at-law of Welsh descent, and his wife, Gertrude Parkes, the daughter of a Birmingham ironmaster. The younger son, Vivian Beynon-Harris, became the author of four light novels published between 1948 and 1951. Because his parents separated when he was eight, John gained a wide experience of English preparatory schools before being sent to Bedales from 1918 to 1921.

He then tried his hand at several careers, including his father's profession of law, farming, commercial art, and advertising, but a small private income—coupled with something in his temperament—made it difficult for him to settle to anything. He began to write short stories. An early affection for the novels of H. G. Wells prompted him towards science fiction. He sold a slogan to an American science fiction magazine in 1930 and, encouraged by this minor success, wrote fiction published in American magazines like *Wonder Stories* and *Amazing Stories*, under the name of John Beynon Harris.

Honour demanded an attempt at the English market. The *Passing Show*, in its third midsummer double number for 20 July 1935, launched a new serial in nine parts, 'The Secret People', by John Beynon. Harris had gone; Beynon sounded more literary. His was an unlikely tale of a man and woman captured by pygmies under a Sahara which was being flooded to create the New Sea; it was published as a book in 1936. It was successful enough to encourage both Wyndham and the magazine to try again for, in May 1936, the *Passing Show* began serialization of 'Stowaway to Mars', published as a book (*Planet Plane*) in the same year. Both these novels were reprinted in the 1970s.

The war brought a halt to this stop-go career. Wyndham became a civil servant and worked as a censor; later, in 1943, he joined the Royal Corps of Signals, working in a cipher office with the rank of corporal, and playing his part in the Normandy landings.

After the war, Wyndham had to start again. He was a familiar figure at the Penn Club in Bedford Place, just off Russell Square in London, and knew the publisher (Sir) Robert Lusty, then a director of Michael Joseph Ltd. One day he brought Lusty a manuscript, saying: 'This is a novel I've managed to write. I don't quite know what to do with it and I thought you might advise me.' Michael Joseph published the novel in 1951, as *The Day of the Triffids*. In the same year it was serialized in five parts in *Collier's* magazine and from then on Wyndham's was a famous name—for he had shuffled through his generous supply of forenames and arrived at 'John Wyndham'. His story of the perambulating vegetable menace which takes over a Britain stricken with blindness was an immediate success. The inferior MGM film version (1963) starred Howard Keel. The novel sold as well and steadily as a Penguin book as did any by Agatha Christie.

The Kraken Wakes was published in 1953. The story is one of interstellar invaders who settle on the sea-bed and flood the land. It provides a chance for the type of mild surrealism—motor boats chugging up Oxford Street—which Wyndham enjoyed, and it brought more success. Wyndham's most powerful novel, *The Chrysalids*, was published in 1955; a puritanical post-nuclear war community in Labrador oppresses its children, who eventually discover telepathic powers and break free. A similar theme, this time with the children unsympathetically cast, emerged in *The Midwich Cuckoos* (1957), the story of a sleepy English village where all the women are astrally impregnated at the same time. The novel was filmed with notable success as *Village of the Damned* (1960), starring George Sanders. A sequel followed, *Children of the Damned* (1963), which owed less to Wyndham and more to commerce. *The Outward Urge* appeared in 1959; this time Wyndham had found a collaborator, 'Lucas Parkes'. Thus, Harris economically used up his two remaining forenames. This story depicted an English family, the Troons, venturing into space, but Wyndham was less successful on Arthur C. Clarke territory. Although *Trouble with Lichen* (1960) has its supporters, it is an indecisive attempt to tackle the debating point of 'Immortality: Is it Democratic?' *Chocky*, published in 1968—and ominously serialized in the magazine *Good Housekeeping*—was a too cosy account of a boy taken over by an interstellar something. *Web* was published posthumously in 1979.

Among Wyndham's many short stories, collected in such volumes as *Jizzle* (1954) and *The Seeds of Time* (1956), special mention must be made of the collection *Consider her Ways* (1961), a strikingly nasty glimpse of a future world where men are extinct and gigantic breed mothers perpetuate the species.

In 1963 Wyndham married Grace Isabel Wilson, a teacher and long-term member of the Penn Club. They had no children. Wyndham died 11 March 1969, in Petersfield, Hampshire.

Although the vogue for Wyndham's type of 'cosy catastrophe', as one critic termed it, may have passed, Wyndham's importance in the rebirth of British science fiction after the war of 1939–45 was second to none. His very English style ('the Trollope of science fiction', according to one reviewer), coupled with the Wellsian gift for exploring emotive ideas, brought him international success and encouraged others to strike out in the same way. Writers as diverse as John Christopher, Charles Eric Maine, J. G. Ballard, and Christopher Priest owe him much. Indeed, it can be claimed that, however hesitatingly, Wyndham established a flourishing school of writers.

[Donald H. Tuck, *The Encyclopaedia of Science Fiction and Fantasy*, vol. i, Chicago, 1974; Sir Robert Lusty, *Bound to be Read*, 1975; private information; personal knowledge.]

BRIAN W. ALDISS

published 1981

(1902–1974)

Novelist, was born 16 August 1902 at Wimbledon, the eldest of three children and the only daughter of George Heyer, MA, MBE, teacher at King's College School, Wimbledon, and his wife, Sylvia, daughter of John Watkins, Thames tugboat owner, of Blackheath. She was educated at various schools in Paris and London, and at the age of seventeen she started telling the story of what was to be her first historical novel, *The Black Moth* (1921), to one of her younger brothers, who at that time was recovering from a serious illness. Her father encouraged her to seek publication, and within the next eight years she wrote *The Great Roxhythe* (1922), *Powder and Patch* (1923), and *These Old Shades* (1926), the latter two, like *The Black Moth*, set in the Georgian period. A fifth book, which she later suppressed, was *Simon the Coldheart* (1925), set in the England of Henry IV.

In August 1925 she married George Ronald Rougier (died 1976), a mining engineer, son of Charles Joseph Rougier and Jean Cookston of York. During the next few years she followed her husband on prospecting expeditions to Tanganyika, where she wrote her next Georgian novel, *The Masqueraders* (1928), and Macedonia. In the early 1930s they finally settled in England, and Ronald Rougier, with his wife's encouragement, began to read for the bar, at the Inner Temple—he was called in 1939, eventually becoming a QC in 1959. In 1932 their only child, a son, was born, who in due course also read for the bar and also became a QC.

Between the 1930s and 1950s Georgette Heyer wrote a number of modern detective novels, based on plots and legal situations suggested to her by her husband, among which *Death in the Stocks* (1935) proved particularly popular at the time. However, it is upon her historical novels that her reputation rests, and although over the years she used the Restoration (*The Great Roxhythe*), the Elizabethan period (*Beauvallet*, 1929), and the Norman Conquest (*The Conqueror*, 1931), as background for occasional novels, as her writing developed she turned increasingly to the Regency period. Here her deep and meticulous research into the social customs, the manners and mannerisms of polite society, and the minutiae of everyday life and speech of the time allowed her to develop into one of those rare novelists who are able to create a totally convincing world of their own. Nor did she confine herself entirely to comedies of manners. What to many readers are her two finest novels, *An Infamous Army* (1937) and *The Spanish Bride* (1940), are superb accounts respectively of the Battle of

Waterloo and the last stages of the Peninsular War, where in each case a romantic plot is skilfully intertwined with a masterly account of the military history.

Georgette Heyer always vehemently denied that she herself was a romantic; her heroines are always young women of good sense and humour, able to remain level-headed through the vicissitudes that beset them. Perhaps the most memorable characteristic of the Regency novels, however, is their sparkling wit and pace, and it is this verve and the sound common sense and knowledge of human nature that lie beneath it that distinguish her books from those of her many imitators.

In her latter years Georgette Heyer's interest turned once again to the medieval world, and she did a good deal of detailed research for a trilogy on the life of John, Duke of Bedford, brother of Henry V. The stringencies of the British tax system, which required payments for past successes, forced her to lay this work aside at intervals to write other bestselling Regency romances, and at her death her work on the Duke of Bedford remained unfinished. She had, however, almost completed the first volume, *My Lord John*, and this was eventually prepared for publication by her husband, appearing in September 1975.

A professional to her fingertips, Georgette Heyer's manuscripts were always delivered on time in immaculate condition, and it was a foolhardy publisher's editor who dared question her use of the vocabulary of the period she was describing, particularly the Regency period. Finding much about the modern world distasteful, she had a lively impatience with intrusive journalists and admirers, and although her family and friends and her letters bear witness to a person of great warmth, humour, loyalty, and affection, she regarded her private life as very much her own. She confined herself to a small, select circle of friends whom she trusted, and this may have made her appear to the outside world a little aloof and detached. She had a great sense of fun, and was thrilled when after the Queen had asked her to one of her informal lunches, she was told that Her Majesty had bought a number of her latest books to give away for Christmas, and had commented that she seemed to be a formidable person. 'Me formidable?' said Georgette Heyer, completely astounded.

Her readership was enormous—her readers were among all ages and both sexes and included professional historians. She also had odd fans like the engineering tycoon who arrived on a West Indian island in his private jet airliner, and half an hour later both he and his wife were comfortably seated with a dozen Georgette Heyer novels each. He explained that the sun, the sea, and a Georgette Heyer book was his idea of a perfect holiday, though he had read them many times before.

Georgette Heyer gave pleasure to many millions of people, and her fans have remained undiminished since her death, in Guy's Hospital, 4 July 1974.

[Jane Aiken Hodge, *The Private World of Georgette Heyer*, 1984; private information; personal knowledge.]

MAX REINHARDT

published 1986

HICHENS Robert Smythe

(1864–1950)

Novelist, was born 14 November 1864 at Speldhurst, Kent, the eldest son of the Rev. Frederick Harrison Hichens, then a curate, and his wife, Abigail Elizabeth Smythe. Educated at a private school and at Clifton College, his heart was set upon becoming a musician, and he studied for several years in Clifton before proceeding to the Royal College of Music. A parallel talent for writing, however, presently proved the stronger. After achieving a number of lyrics—one of which was sung by Patti—he began to write stories and at twenty-four determined to make a career as an author. He took a year's course at a school of journalism, and contributed industriously to many newspapers. His juvenile novel, *The Coastguard's Secret*, written when he was seventeen, had been published in 1886 and well reviewed; but he was alarmed at the proposal to reprint this crude effort after he scored his first great success in 1894. This was *The Green Carnation*, published anonymously after a holiday, enforced by illness, in Egypt, a place which was always to prove fortunate and inspiring for him. London was delighted with the novel, a sparkling sophisticated satire on Oscar Wilde and his followers.

Hichens became music critic on the *World* in succession to G. B. Shaw, but eventually gave up regular journalism in order to travel abroad and write his books which had a rapidly increasing public. Edwardian society was alternately shocked, thrilled, intrigued, and dissolved in laughter. The jests of one generation seldom amuse the next; but *The Londoners* (1898) is still a very funny piece of pure fooling. Hichens kept his humour in its place, however, and did not allow it to interfere with the dramatic tension of his romances, or the horror of his essays in the macabre. Of these latter, the short story 'How Love Came to Professor Guildea' (in *Tongues of Conscience*, 1900) is acknowledged a small classic. His greatest success and

best-known novel was *The Garden of Allah* (1904) which he later dramatized. So popular was this romance of passion and conflict in the desert
that he wrote from time to time other stories with a similar setting. Egypt
and North Africa were familiar ground to him; he spent much of his time
there, riding in the desert; and otherwise preferred the Riviera or Switzerland to any permanent residence in England. He belonged to a generation of writers eminent for good workmanlike story-telling; and to the
very end his hand never faltered, although naturally there must be some
loss of power and freshness in the course of half a century. He also wrote
several plays, including *Becky Sharp* written for (Dame) Marie Tempest in
collaboration with Cosmo Gordon Lennox.

In 1947 Hichens published his memoirs, *Yesterday*, which illustrate his
confession: 'The Edwardian age through which I lived was certainly very
attractive to me.' He never married. He died in hospital at Zürich 20 July
1950.

[R. S. Hichens, *Yesterday*, 1947; *The Times*, 22 July 1950.]

M. Bellasis

published 1959

HOLTBY Winifred

(1898–1935)

Novelist, feminist, and social reformer, was born in Rudstone, Yorkshire,
23 June 1898, the younger daughter (there were no sons) of David Holtby, a
prosperous farmer, and his wife Alice Winn of the East Riding. An independent and precocious child, she was encouraged in her literary
ambitions while at Queen Margaret's School, Scarborough. She went up
to Somerville College, Oxford, in 1917, but left a year later to join the
Women's Army Auxiliary Corps, and served in France until August 1919 as
a hostel forewoman.

Returning to Somerville, she formed a close friendship with a contemporary, Vera Brittain. Holtby—tall, fair, confident, gregarious—was
Brittain's 'opposite'; but they discovered in each other complementary
experience, literary ambitions, and social ideals. They left Oxford in 1921,
with seconds in modern history, and shared a flat in London while establishing parallel careers.

Holtby's forceful, witty articles and reviews soon gained her a high
reputation as a journalist. She became a regular contributor (and from 1926

a director) of the feminist journal *Time and Tide*, and a friend of its founder and editor, Margaret Haig Thomas, Viscountess Rhondda. With Vera Brittain she became an influential feminist and member of Rhondda's Six Point Group. Both also joined the League of Nations Union, lecturing widely for it on world peace; and in 1922 they toured Europe to investigate postwar conditions. Both joined the Labour party. Both published novels in 1923 and 1924.

In 1926 Winifred Holtby visited South Africa for over five months, to speak on behalf of the League of Nations Union. Appalled by the racism she observed there, she worked energetically against it for the rest of her life, giving extensive financial support to the Black trade union movement. On her return to London, she was welcomed by Vera Brittain, who was now married, into a household soon further enlivened by two children, to whom Holtby became a beloved 'aunt'. They now had a wide circle of acquaintances, mutual or individual, many prominent as writers, feminists, and socialists.

Extremely generous and dutiful, Winifred Holtby sacrificed much of her time and energy to her friends and family (she later likened her life to 'a clear stream which has simply reflected other people's stories and problems'). Yet her literary career of less than fifteen years was notably prolific. Her first two novels—*Anderby Wold* (1923) and *The Crowded Street* (1924)—were followed by *The Land of Green Ginger* (1927), *Poor Caroline* (1931), and *Mandoa, Mandoa!* (1933). Increasingly satirical and ambitious, they are unpretentiously direct and witty in style, imaginative in using her experience, and firmly focused on social and political problems. Among the other seven books she published are a fine pioneering critical study of *Virginia Woolf* (1932); *The Astonishing Island* (1933), a satire; a feminist treatise, *Women and a Changing Civilisation* (1934); *Truth is Not Sober and Other Stories* (1934); and a collection of poems, *The Frozen Earth* (1935). A play attacking the rise of Fascism, *Take Back Your Freedom* (1939), was published posthumously, as were a further volume of short stories (1937) and two selections from her lively correspondence (1937 and 1960).

During the last four years of her life, Winifred Holtby fought gallantly against the depredations of a kidney disease. Her courage and consideration were so remarkable that even close friends did not know until near the end that she was seriously ill. Equally remarkable were the ambition and determination that pushed to completion her final novel, which is also her masterpiece, *South Riding* (published posthumously in 1936 and awarded the James Tait Black memorial prize): a rich regional study of social change and local government, it drew to some extent on her mother's experiences as the first woman alderman in the East Riding of Yorkshire.

Housman

On her deathbed in a London nursing home, Winifred Holtby was betrothed to the man she loved, Harry Pearson. She died 29 September 1935.

[Vera Brittain, *Testament of Friendship: the Story of Winifred Holtby*, 1940; Geoffrey Handley-Taylor, *Winifred Holtby: a Concise and Selected Bibliography together with some Letters*, 1955; Paul Berry and Alan Bishop (eds.), *Testament of a Generation: the Journalism of Vera Brittain and Winifred Holtby*, 1985; Vera Brittain, *Diary of the Thirties 1932–1939: Chronicle of Friendship*, ed. Alan Bishop, 1986.]

A. G. Bishop

published 1993

HOUSMAN Alfred Edward
(1859–1936)

Poet and classical scholar, was born at the Valley House, Fockbury, in the parish of Catshill, Worcestershire, 26 March 1859, the eldest child in the family of five sons and two daughters of Edward Housman, a solicitor practising in the neighbouring town of Bromsgrove, by his first wife, Sarah Jane Williams, who died in 1871. In the previous year Housman had been sent to Bromsgrove School, whence in 1877 he passed as a scholar to St. John's College, Oxford.

At Oxford Housman gained first class honours in classical moderations in 1879, but in 1881 he failed to obtain honours in *literae humaniores*. This failure, due to his neglect of philosophy and history, seriously affected his spirits. He worked at home for the civil service examination, at the same time helping his old headmaster in sixth form teaching. In 1882 he became a higher division clerk in the Patent Office, and took lodgings in Bayswater with his greatest friend, Moses John Jackson, to whom he later dedicated the first volume of his Manilius. Jackson went to India in 1887, and about the same time Housman settled in Highgate, whence in 1905 he moved to Pinner, which he did not leave until he went to Cambridge in 1911.

In the Patent Office Housman found time for classical study. At Oxford he had already worked on the text of Propertius, and had corresponded with the great Cambridge Latinist H. A. J. Munro, but his first publication was in the year of his entry into the civil service. This was a powerful paper on Horace in the *Journal of Philology*, followed next year by a note on Ovid's *Ibis*, but he printed no more until 1887, when he contributed to the first volume of the *Classical Review* an article on passages of Sophocles and Euripides. In every later year, including that of his death, he published at least one classical article or review, and the output of the years following 1887 was especially striking. It dealt with textual problems in all three Greek tragedians and in half a dozen Latin poets.

In 1889 Housman became a member of the Cambridge Philological Society, and he contributed several papers to its *Proceedings* and *Transactions*, as well as to the *American Journal of Philology*. The high quality of his work attracted such wide attention that when in 1892 the death of Alfred Goodwin, professor of Greek and Latin at University College, London, gave him the chance of entering academic life, he obtained testimonials from fifteen British scholars, and also from Basil Lanneau Gildersleeve of Baltimore and Nikolaus Wecklein of Munich. In place of Goodwin's combined chair two professorships were now established. Housman stood in the first instance for the Latin chair, but desired to be considered, if the Latin went to another candidate, for the Greek chair. He obtained his first preference, and remained until his death a professor of Latin: thenceforward his published work was almost confined to that language. It is true that between 1897 and 1910 he made several brilliant contributions to the restoration of lost works of Greek poetry then coming to light in Egyptian papyri, and that in later years he was often consulted by the editors of the *Oxyrhynchus Papyri*, and of Liddell and Scott's *Lexicon*, but almost all his other classical work was concerned after 1892 with Latin. He remained, nevertheless, as his review (published in the *Classical Review*, vol. xxxix, 1925) of the text of Sophocles of A. C. Pearson suffices to prove, one of the best Grecians in Europe.

Housman's tenure of his London chair lasted until 1911. For most of that time University College was served by a professorial staff of great distinction in many departments, but in the words which Housman used of his colleague John Arthur Platt, 'much of the teaching which he was required to give was elementary, and he seldom had pupils who possessed a native aptitude for classical studies or intended to pursue them far'.

The work which Housman published while he was in London dealt with most of the chief Latin poets from Lucilius to Juvenal. Of these Propertius and Ovid had been among his earliest interests. He now published four masterly papers on the manuscripts of Propertius, a step towards an edition which he had contemplated at least as early as 1882, but which he never produced. Of Ovid he edited the *Ibis* for vol. i of the *Corpus Poetarum Latinorum* edited by J. P. Postgate, published in 1894, and in 1897 he wrote a series of important papers on the text of the *Heroides*. His next publications concerned Manilius and Juvenal. In 1898 he printed a short paper emending without discussion some fifty passages in Book I of

Manilius and three years later a similar paper on Book V. In 1903 he published an edition of Book I which showed every sign of long preparation. It became the first story of that 'monument', to borrow his own phrase, which he resolved to build himself, and which he completed twenty-seven years later with the publication of Book V in 1930.

The preface to Book I was a challenging assertion of Housman's views on scholarship. Its ruthless wit and unanswerable severities enchanted his juniors, although they were less pleasant reading to some of his seniors and contemporaries. The Latin commentary was designed 'to treat of two matters only: what Manilius wrote, and what he meant', without including 'the illustration of his phraseology and vocabulary'; but this restriction did not exclude single notes running to over a thousand words, or pages where a line or two of text stands above fifty of small-print commentary.

The text of Manilius in Postgate's *Corpus* had already been assigned to another, but in 1903 Housman was asked to edit Juvenal for a later fascicule. He had hitherto dealt in print with little except the new lines found in 1899 in a Bodleian manuscript, and he had 'no design of publishing or composing any such work', but he accepted the offer and produced in 1905 both this *Corpus* text, with a short Latin preface, and an independent edition, provocatively aimed *editorum in usum*. This was not on the scale of his Manilius, and the notes were much briefer, but it gave fresh proof of his learning and acuteness and has remained the standard text. The English preface, about half as long as that to Manilius I, was no less brilliant in expression and even broader in range, and Juvenal's greater popularity put the book into the hands of a larger public.

Housman's next classical work, the second volume of Manilius, appeared after his election to his Cambridge chair, but in 1896, four years after his London appointment, he startled his family and friends by the publication of *A Shropshire Lad*. He later revealed some facts about the dates of these sixty-three lyrics. In the foreword to *Last Poems* (1922) he spoke of 'the continuous excitement under which in the early months of 1895 I wrote the greater part of my other book', and he stated elsewhere that his most prolific period was the first five months of that year. The definite dates of twenty of the poems are known, and of these nine are assigned, at least in their inception, to the first six months of 1895, and three more to its second half. The other eleven are earlier, the earliest being of 1890, in which year he had contributed to Alfred William Pollard's *Odes from the Greek Dramatists* three lyric translations of Aeschylus, Sophocles, and Euripides. Housman also stated that he wrote verse at the age of eight or earlier, but very little until he was thirty-five. Some early verse survives showing little of his later power, but the characteristic piece which his brother Laurence printed as number xlviii of the posthumous *More Poems* (1936) had appeared in an Oxford periodical in 1881.

There has been speculation about the 'continuous excitement' of 1895, but it is likely that Housman referred simply to an unexplained outburst of creative activity: he said in 1933, in his Leslie Stephen lecture, that he had seldom written poetry unless he was rather out of health. His English writing in his London period was not confined to verse, for he delivered in 1892, the year of his election, an admirable introductory lecture, defending classical studies, which happily survives, and at intervals he contributed papers on English and Scottish poets to the University College literary society, but he instructed his executors to destroy them.

Late in 1910 the death of J. E. B. Mayor threw open the Latin chair at Cambridge, and Housman was persuaded to stand. The election took place early in 1911: the field was strong, but Housman was successful, and Trinity College elected him into a fellowship. In May he delivered a striking inaugural lecture. His main theme was a sharp distinction between the functions of a classical scholar and those of a literary critic. He had no wish to suppress this lecture, and he often quoted from it, but unluckily he had stressed a textual point in Shelley's Lament' which he was unable to verify, and he never printed it.

The move to Cambridge was Housman's last, and, as he never married, he lived in Trinity until his death. He lectured regularly, almost always on some portion of a Latin poet, and he delivered between twenty and thirty distinct courses. Some dealt with books prescribed for textual study in part ii of the classical tripos: the poets whom he chose for himself were Lucretius, Catullus, Horace, Ovid, Lucan, and Persius.

Housman's most important classical publications after 1911 were the last four books of Manilius, which appeared in 1912, 1916, 1920, and 1930. The prefaces to the second, third, and fourth books, which lucidly explain the complex astronomical and astrological theories imperfectly expounded by the poet, contain flashes of brilliant wit, but little general criticism or discussion. In the fifth volume, however, he dealt trenchantly with the Manilian literature of the past three decades, winding up with a proud defence of his own methods and achievement.

Apart from an *editio minor* of Manilius, with short critical notes, which appeared in 1932, and a reprint of his Juvenal, with a second preface, in 1931, Housman published no more classical works, except an edition of Lucan in 1926, reprinted with corrections in the following year. This book, aimed, like the Juvenal, *editorum in usum*, is one of his best. The preface is brilliant, and the text and notes show an unerring grasp of Lucan's rhetorical modes of speech and thought. Here, as elsewhere, some of his most striking corrections are simple changes of punctuation.

In 1922 Housman published *Last Poems*, containing forty-one lyrics. He says in the foreword: 'About a quarter of this matter belongs to the April of the present year, but most of it dates between 1895 and 1910.' Some poems plainly refer to the death in action of his youngest brother Herbert in 1901. He contributed in 1927 a charming preface to J. A. Platt's posthumous *Nine Essays*. In 1932 he accepted the Leslie Stephen lecturership at Cambridge, and in 1933 delivered and printed a striking lecture, *The Name and Nature of Poetry*, which threw light on his tastes and on his own poetical creation.

At Cambridge Housman's regular habits included between luncheon and tea one or other of Cambridge's country walks, when he avoided company, but watched with a keen and subtle eye the progress of the seasons in tree and flower. He took many short holidays in England, and often went abroad. He always shunned Germany, but as a young man he went to Constantinople, and he paid a few visits to Italy, chiefly to Venice. He early formed the habit of spending three weeks or a month every summer in different parts of France.

Housman's health deteriorated in 1932, and three years later he was seriously ill. He was able, however, to visit France in the summer of 1935, and he lectured as usual in each term of that year and also in the Lent term of 1936, but in the Easter term he broke down after two lectures, and he died in a nursing home at Cambridge on 30 April.

Housman's will forbade any collection of his published classical papers, and any attempt to print what he had not published, and he extended the ban to all unprinted English prose but, happily, not to his unprinted poetry. Here, referring to his brother Laurence, he wrote: 'I permit him but do not enjoin him to select from my verse manuscript writing, and to publish, any poems which appear to him to be completed and to be not inferior to the average of my published poems; and I direct him to destroy all other poems and fragments of verse.' His brother found it possible to print forty-eight pieces, which appeared in 1936 under the title *More Poems*. A few of these scarcely deserved to be saved, but the average is high, and some may rank with his best. The same can hardly be said of the further eighteen serious poems which his brother appended to his memoir *A. E. H.* in 1937, but the light verse and parodies which accompanied them are delightful. The best text of the posthumous lyrics will be found in *The Collected Poems of A. E. Housman* (1939).

Housman was of slender build, with delicately sensitive features. His sensitiveness was indeed acute and it made him so reserved that most people found his company difficult; but he enjoyed social meetings, and his conversation, when he felt at ease, was full of wit and charm. He did not smoke, but was a connoisseur of food and wine. He had a powerful memory, which occasionally played him tricks, and decided views on most subjects. In classical scholarship his disciplined passion for truth made him ready to accept new evidence and to modify old conclusions, but in other matters he was not tolerant of opposition. In history and politics, especially, he was apt to pin his faith to a few not infallible authorities, and he often allowed his prejudices to warp his judgement. His antinomianism did not prevent him lending strong support to most established institutions, and he combined declared atheism with an hereditary attachment to the high church party. He admired Aristippus 'who was not afraid of words', and he sometimes professed a cult of ruthlessness, but his working philosophy was tinged with the Stoicism which he rejected, and he hated cruelty. He was deeply read in English literature and he had by heart an immense amount of poetry. His taste was catholic, but he had strong preferences, which are clearly shown in his Leslie Stephen lecture.

Housman was eminent in two fields, the distinctness of which he often emphasized, that of classical scholarship and that of original poetry. In the first his permanent rank was assured before his death, and it is among the highest. As he knew, he was not fully comparable to Bentley, whom he outshone in patience and intellectual honesty and closely approached in swiftness of insight and brilliant power, but whose scholarship had a sweep and range which he could not equal. To the rest of the giants we may extend what Housman said of himself matched with Porson: 'the comparison is not preposterous—he surpassed me in some qualities as I claim to surpass him in others'. Of contemporary scholars he most admired, and rated above himself, U. von Wilamowitz-Moellendorff, a lesser man than Bentley, but cast in the same titanic mould. His admiration for Wilamowitz is one of many disproofs of the belief that he was unfair to German learning. He was pitiless to pretentious incompetence, of which he found too much in the contemporary scholarship of all countries, including England; and if Germany filled most space in his onslaughts this was because nine-tenths of the work in his special fields was done by Germans.

Housman's restriction to Latin after 1892 was a loss to Greek scholarship, but the choice is intelligible. His passion for perfection came nearer being satisfied in the narrower field, and as a textual critic he even preferred to concentrate his attention on writers not of the first rank, since their ideas and means of expression were in some degree predictable. His early notes on Aeschylus, always his favourite poet, are brilliant, but not equal to his best work in Latin, and, had he ever begun to edit him, he would probably have abandoned the task from the conviction that it was less difficult than impossible. Manilius, on whom he lavished his richest gifts, was, as he knew, a poor poet with a bad subject, but his edition throws invaluable light on Latin usage and on the facts of textual transmission, and the problems of this corrupt text exercised his highest faculties.

On Housman's rank as an English poet it would be rash to attempt a verdict. When *A Shropshire Lad* appeared it struck a new note in late nineteenth-century literature. The chief sources of which he declared himself conscious were Shakespeare's songs, the Scottish Border ballads, and Heine. Other influences have been noted, especially those of the English Bible and of Matthew Arnold, and there are many delicate re-miniscences of Greek and Latin poetry, but his work remains unmistakably personal. He has been accused of monotony, and his favourite themes are not numerous, but he shows great variety in metre and a Horatian felicity of expression: every poem has phrases that no one else could have written. It is often said that *Last Poems* is inferior to *A Shropshire Lad*, but both are uneven, and some of his best work is in the later volume: one at least of the very finest ('Tell me not here') was composed in the year of its pub lication. Housman's low estimate of much of the verse of the seventeenth and eighteenth centuries angered some younger critics, and both the form and the content of his own poetry were out of fashion in the same circles before he died, but it can hardly be doubted that his best poems will always rank high, although perhaps, unlike his scholarship, not in the highest class of all. He refused almost all honours, including the Order of Merit, but accepted an honorary fellowship from his Oxford college in 1911.

There is no painted portrait of Housman, but there are several drawings: of these, two made by (Sir) William Rothenstein in 1906 are respectively in the National Portrait Gallery and at Trinity College, Cambridge. His appearance in later life is best shown in that made by Francis Dodd in 1926 for St. John's College, Oxford. Another drawing by Dodd (1936), and a plasticine medallion by Theodore Spicer-Simson (1924), are in the National Portrait Gallery.

[*The Times*, 2 May 1936; A. S. F. Gow, *A. E. Housman, A Sketch, together with a List of his Writings and Indexes to his Classical Papers*, 1936; Alfred Edward Housman Memorial Supplement to the *Bromsgrovian*, 1936; Laurence Housman, *A. E. H.*, 1937, and *The Unexpected Years*, 1937; Percy Withers, *A Buried Life*, 1940; F. T. Grant Richards, *Housman 1897–1936*, 1941; J. Carter and J. Sparrow, *A. E. Housman, An Annotated Check-List*, 1940; A. S. F. Gow, 'A. E. Housman at Oxford' in *Oxford Magazine*, 11 November 1937; R. W. Chambers, *Man's Unconquerable Mind*, 1939; private information; personal knowledge.]

D. S. ROBERTSON

published 1949

(1894–1963)

Man of letters, was born at Laleham, a house near Godalming, 26 July 1894, the third son of Leonard Huxley, an assistant master at Charterhouse and subsequently editor of the *Cornhill Magazine*, by his first wife, Julia Frances Arnold, a granddaughter of Thomas Arnold of Rugby and niece of Matthew Arnold. As a grandson of T. H. Huxley and greatgrandson of Dr Arnold, Aldous Huxley inherited both a passionate interest in science and the pursuit of truth, and his high sense of moral purpose. Mrs Humphry Ward, the novelist, was his aunt; (Sir) Julian Huxley his eldest brother.

Huxley was educated first at Prior's Field, a successful avant-garde school founded by his mother, then at Hillside, a near-by preparatory school, from which he won a scholarship to Eton in 1908. Shortly after arriving there he suffered the first of three traumatic experiences: the premature death of his mother at the age of forty-five. Huxley was wholly devoted to her, and this sudden loss when he was only fourteen came as an appalling shock and deprivation. Then, scarcely more than two years later, he contracted an infection of the eyes (*keratitis punctata*) which sent him virtually blind and obliged him to leave Eton before the end of his eighth term. He faced this calamity with extraordinary determination and courage; taught himself to read braille, to type, and to play the piano; he continued his education doggedly with a series of tutors. In the spring of 1912 his sight had improved sufficiently for him to walk alone, to read large print with the aid of a magnifying glass, and to have hopes of going to Oxford. In October 1913 he went up to Balliol. There, despite his irreparably damaged sight, he read assiduously for a degree in English literature (in which he obtained a first, in 1916, as well as winning the Stanhope prize), developed a taste for Proust and the French symbolists, but also found time to play jazz and take part in amateur theatricals. By then Huxley was immensely tall (6 feet 4½ inches), and so thin that he was accurately described as having to 'fold himself and his legs, like some gigantic grasshopper, into a chair'. But what people noticed most particularly was his unaffected charm, his extraordinarily mellifluous voice, his sense of humour, and, above all, his gentleness. In later life, many people who disagreed profoundly with some of his views and deplored his propensity for entertaining the most improbable hypotheses (a by-product of his immense intellectual curiosity) nevertheless found it impossible to quarrel with this most lovable of men. For in addition to gentleness, there was an innate modesty and a sweet reasonableness about him that disarmed contention. His first year at university was intoxicating and he took everything that Oxford had to offer. The spell was broken by the outbreak of war in August 1914, and almost simultaneously by the third of the personal tragedies which afflicted him before he came of age: the suicide of his gifted elder brother Trevenen.

It was while he was still an undergraduate that Huxley started writing poetry chiefly but also short stories, and first discovered that he had 'some kind of natural gift for it'—a gift that supported him and his family for the rest of his life. It was also while he was at Oxford that, towards the end of 1915, he was taken to Garsington, home of the pacifist member of Parliament Philip Morrell and his wife, Lady Ottoline, where he met most of the younger and more advanced writers and painters of the day. Huxley was both alarmed and fascinated by this immensely talented and varied *galère*, but after he left Oxford he spent part of the war years working on the land there (he was totally unfit for military service), and came to regard Garsington as one of the seminal factors in his education. More important, it was there that he met and became engaged to Maria Nys, the eldest daughter of a well-to-do Flemish family from Courtrai which had sought refuge in England; it was nearly three years, during which Huxley taught at Repton and Eton, before they could get married in July 1919. They set up house in Hampstead, and lived for some time in great financial stringency on Huxley's earnings as a journalist; their only child, Matthew, was born in April 1920.

The next ten years saw the emergence of Huxley as a novelist and short-story writer of marked originality, whose pungent wit, uninhibited dialogue, and frank discussion of subjects hitherto considered taboo in fiction, quickly won him a public, and a place as 'cultural hero' among the young. His first novel, *Crome Yellow* (1921), was shortly followed by *Antic Hay* (1923) and *Those Barren Leaves* (1925), all of which satirized contemporary society, through characters who challenged or flouted accepted conventions and were not always without resemblance to living people. The novels were interspersed by collections of brilliant short stories, including *Mortal Coils* (1922), *Little Mexican* (1924), and *Two or Three Graces* (1926). In addition, volumes of essays and books of travel made a regular appearance, among them *On the Margin* (1923) and *Jesting Pilate* (1926): in all a dozen books in eight years—a remarkable achievement for a man almost bereft of sight. Moreover, they made him money, and amply justified the faith his publishers had shown by offering him a three-year contract, at £500 a year, as early as 1923—an arrangement which was renewed at intervals, in varying terms, up to his death. But it was 1928, the year in which his most ambitious novel to date, *Point Counter Point*, was published, which saw him become a best-seller both in Britain and America. The years 1925 to 1937 were among the happiest in Huxley's life. With the gradual easing of his financial position, he and his wife were able to spend more time abroad, especially in Italy, where they became close friends of D. H. Lawrence, whose *Letters* Huxley edited (1932); they also visited India and the Far East, as well as Germany, Spain, the West Indies, and Mexico; in 1928 they bought a house near Paris, and later a villa at Sanary, near Toulon, which they occupied on and off from 1930 to 1937. There Huxley painted a good deal as well as wrote, entertained, and visited friends. In the intervals, regular visits were paid to London for the publication of a book or the production of a play (Huxley remained mistakenly convinced that he could become a successful dramatist), or to Italy for refreshment of his delight in Italian painting and architecture.

Early in 1937 the Huxleys began a prolonged visit to America, and by 1938 they had finally decided to remain there. It has been suggested that this was a result of the threat of war already developing in Europe, that Huxley was turning his back on the ugly prospects ahead (he was an ardent supporter of the Peace Pledge Union, for which he lectured and wrote pamphlets). Huxley himself, however, believed that the clear sunlight of California would enable him to see and read better, and he heard encouraging reports of a new American method, invented by Dr W. H. Bates, of improving the vision of partially sighted people. In this, according to his own and his wife's reports, he was not disappointed. By the middle of 1939 he was able to read and write without spectacles, and in 1942 he published his conclusions in *The Art of Seeing*. By then his writing had taken an entirely fresh turn. The 'philosophy of meaninglessness', as Huxley himself described it in *Ends and Means* (1937), which had informed all his early work and proved so potent a liberating force for his readers, no longer satisfied him. Something positive, something transcendental, something which would set mankind on the road to a fuller realization of its potential, was what he sought. He found it, he believed, in a form of mysticism derived in part from oriental philosophy, but largely from his own intuitive aspirations. 'Men and women', he wrote, 'are capable of being devils and lunatics. They are no less capable of being fully human', and for the rest of his life he devoted himself to trying to persuade them to be so. The books which followed, *The Perennial Philosophy* (1945), *Science, Liberty and Peace* (1946), *Themes and Variations* (1950), and *Brave New World Revisited* (1958), and in a sense also *Grey Eminence* (1941), spelt out the temptations which life presents in the modern world with its materialist values and dangerous technological advances, and suggested ways of overcoming them. The ways were unorthodox, and of such originality that they inevitably exposed him to accusations of abandoning reason for mumbo-jumbo. Huxley was unmoved, and later his views found powerful support among some of the best minds of the day. Similarly, the novels of that period, *After Many a Summer* (1939) which won the James Tait Black memorial prize, *Time Must Have a Stop* (1944), *Ape and Essence* (1948), and *The Genius and the Goddess* (1955), were distinguished by a combination of irony and compassion with a profound regard for humanity which lifted them on to a different plane from his earlier novels. In that context, Huxley wrote two fictional Utopias: one, *Brave New World* (1932), was a nightmarish prognostication of a future in which humanity has been destroyed by science; and the other, *Island*, published exactly thirty years later, was a picture of the good life possible for humans if only they would behave rationally. It was ironic that the former, despite its pessimism, should prove easily his most popular (and many good judges continued to think his best) novel, while the latter was clearly unsatisfactory as fiction but comprised his most sustained, imaginative, and moving account of *la condition humaine*, which for Huxley was ever 'the beast in view'.

In 1953 Huxley's interest in the therapeutic value of hypnosis was extended to other methods of releasing the human body from the domination of its ego: notably the use of mescalin and other psychedelic drugs such as LSD. His own experiments with these, and the practical use which he believed could be made of them, he described in *The Doors of Perception* (1954) and *Heaven and Hell* (1956). He was subsequently much criticized for the part he was thought to have played in encouraging young people to take these drugs, although he had warned that they must be used with caution. The year before his first experiment, his wife, Maria—his 'dragoman', as he called her for her practical good sense and tact—was seriously ill; she died from cancer early in 1955. A year later Huxley married Laura Archera, an Italian concert violinist and psychotherapist from Turin, whom he had first met some years earlier. But it was not long before Huxley himself contracted cancer of the tongue, in 1960. The disease at first yielded to radium treatment (he refused surgery because it would have impaired his speech), and the next three years were spent indefatigably writing, lecturing, and attending conferences in America and all over Europe. This was interrupted, in May 1961, by the catastrophic fire which totally destroyed his home in Los Angeles, leaving him 'a man without possessions and without a past'. Huxley accepted the disaster philosophically, describing it as 'a sign that the grim reaper was having a good look at me'. A year later the cancer returned, this time incurably. By the autumn of 1963 his condition was hopeless, although he remained stoically detached and serene to the end. He died in Los Angeles 22 November 1963. In 1971 his ashes were returned to England and buried in his parents' grave at Compton cemetery, Surrey.

An oil portrait by his uncle, John Collier (1926), is privately owned; there is an ink and wash drawing by A. Wolmark (1928) in the National Portrait Gallery, and a drawing of Huxley and the Revd H. R. L. ('Dick') Sheppard by (Sir) David Low (1938) in the Tate Gallery. (Sir) William Rothenstein drew Huxley several times and one of these (1922) is reproduced in *Twenty-Four Portraits* (2nd series, 1923).

[*Listener*, 16 October 1947; *Aldous Huxley: a Memorial Volume*, ed. Sir Julian Huxley, 1956; *Letters of Aldous Huxley*, ed. Grover Smith, 1969; Laura Archera Huxley, *This Timeless Moment*, 1969; Sybille Bedford, *Aldous Huxley: a Biography*, 2 vols., 1973–4; personal knowledge.]

IAN PARSONS

published 1981

JACOBS William Wymark

(1863–1943)

Writer, was born in Wapping, 8 September 1863, the eldest child of William Gage Jacobs by his first wife, Sophia Wymark. The boy's father was a wharfinger; and in his teens young Jacobs spent much time on Thames-side, growing familiar with the life of the neighbourhood, the habitués resident and transient, and the comings and goings of ships. The family was a large one, living on narrow and precarious means, so that W.W. (as he came to be known to his friends) regarded the times when with his brothers and sisters he ran wild in Wapping as happy interludes in a life of nagging discomfort. Almost the only other alleviations of a dreary and restricted childhood were sojourns at a cottage near Sevenoaks and visits to relations in rural East Anglia. Those fleeting delights permanently endeared country-village life to him, and produced the 'Claybury' stories which, although less popular than the vernacular reminiscences of the Night Watchman, are no less beautifully wrought, no less perfect in timing and in unobtrusive compression.

Jacobs was educated at a private school in the City, and later at Birkbeck College, where he made friends with Pett Ridge. In 1879, at the age of sixteen, he became a boy clerk in the Civil Service, formally joined as a second division clerk in the Savings Bank department in 1883, and there remained until 1899. His work became increasingly a drudgery; but memories of a boyhood of poverty caused him to cling to the safety of a dull and subordinate job until he could feel reasonably sure of earning a living by his pen.

Already in 1885 he had contributed anonymous and tentative sketches to *Blackfriars*, but not until in the early 'nineties Jerome K. Jerome accepted a number of his stories for the *Idler* and for *To-day*, not until about 1895, when he was admitted to the well-paid preserves of the *Strand Magazine*, was there any foreshadowing of the Jacobs to come. These tales—artless, almost naïve—had individuality and gave promise, although as yet experimental, of the humour and mastery of his medium which, in its matured form, was to ensure both livelihood and international repute. In 1896 appeared his first collection of stories, *Many Cargoes*, followed in 1897 by a novelette, *The Skipper's Wooing*, with, appended, a moderately successful horror story, and in 1898 by *Sea Urchins*. The next year he resigned the Civil Service and became an author by profession.

On account of his shy, low-voiced address and gentle melancholy of manner, Jacobs—slight, pale-complexioned, and of almost albino fairness—seemed a smaller man than he really was. In a crowded room he withdrew into self-effacement; but enjoying casual conversation with one or two of his own kind, he talked (as he looked) with a twinkle, and gained stature in proportion as his diffidence fell away. To listen to Jacobs chatting with Will Owen, his inspired illustrator, and with Pett Ridge, was to savour the essence of a wholly distinctive epoch of English humour which, for the time being at any rate, has ceased to exist. Pett Ridge, plump and genial, would recall the latest cockney absurdity, overheard or encountered on the top of an omnibus; Owen, ridiculously like one of the sturdy little seafarers whom he created for his friend's stories, would chuckle rosily; while W.W., hardly raising his eyes and speaking out of the corner of his mouth, would throw in a simple but deft aside, whose fun was implied and at one remove.

Jacobs wrote short stories of three kinds—describing the misadventures of sailor-men ashore; celebrating the unscrupulous ingenuities of the artful dodger of a slow-witted country village; and tales of the macabre. He also wrote half a dozen novels (they are really series of short stories woven together) of which the two best (*At Sunwich Port*, 1902, and *Dialstone Lane*, 1904) display his genius for re-rendering personalities, comic episodes, and characteristic talk without repeating them or himself. Popularity as a humorist obscured, even in his hey-dey, Jacobs's superb technique as a writer of stories. His economy of language, his perpetual understatement, his refusal himself to be the joker but the suggestion in a rapid exchange of conversation by his characters of the ludicrous catastrophes which have overtaken or are about to overtake them—these are qualities in a writer granted only to a master of his craft.

It is instructive to compare his first collection of stories with one of those published at the zenith of his powers. *Many Cargoes* contains several of the principal personages and types who were to make Jacobs famous. The Night Watchman is there; also the quick-witted beauty, sparring with, scoring off, and finally succumbing to, an unabashed and persistent lover; also rival ladies exchanging barbed civilities; also embarrassed skippers baited by their mates with allusions to redundant feminine entanglements. Yet, although the patterns of stories are dimly conceived, construction is lacking. The tales are mere anecdotes, whereas, by the time we reach *Light Freights* (1901), every moment, from the nonchalant opening to the gentle click of the closing door, is deliberately planned and faultlessly controlled.

Uncritical public favour apart, the period of Jacobs's supremacy as an artist in story-writing lasted for less than fifteen years. In *Light Freights* not only Ginger Dick, Peter Russet, and old Sam Small, but also Bob Pretty, Henery Walker, the bibulous ancient on the bench outside the 'Cauliflower', and other notabilities of Claybury made their bow. In 1902 came *The Lady of the Barge* which contained the author's master-tales of horror— *The Monkey's Paw, The Well*, and *In the Library*—deftly mixed with seafaring and bucolic absurdities. *The Monkey's Paw* was dramatized by L. N. Parker with whom Jacobs collaborated in writing *Beauty and the Barge* (1904). He wrote a number of other plays, and published several collections of stories, all on the highest level, ending with *Night Watches* (1914).

One cannot read the books which appeared after 1914 without feeling that Jacobs had begun to tire of what readers still tirelessly demanded. He never published slipshod work, and did his best to devise new variations on old themes; but the heart had gone out of him. He allowed nothing to be issued in volume form in the seventeen years before he died in London 1 September 1943. In 1900 he married Agnes Eleanor, daughter of Richard Owen Williams, bank accountant, of Leytonstone, Essex. They had two sons and three daughters. A portrait of Jacobs (1910) by C. Moore-Park was presented in 1944 by Jacobs's executors to the National Portrait Gallery where there is also a pen-and-ink drawing by H. Furniss.

[Personal knowledge.]

MICHAEL SADLEIR

published 1959

JAMES Henry

(1843–1916)

Novelist, was born at 2 Washington Place, New York, 15 April 1843. He came of a stock both Irish and Scotch, established in America from the eighteenth century. His father, Henry James, senior, was an original and remarkable writer on questions of theology. His mother's name was Mary Walsh. Henry James the younger was the second son, the elder being the distinguished philosopher William James. They received a very desultory education, at first in New York, afterwards (during two lengthy visits of the family to Europe) in London, Paris, and Geneva. Henry James entered the law school at Harvard in 1862, and lived with his parents at Cambridge, near Boston, until he finally settled in Europe in 1875. From 1865 onwards he was a regular contributor of reviews, sketches, and short stories, to several American periodicals; his life as a writer began from that year, and owed much to his acquaintance, soon a close friendship, with the novelist W. D. Howells. James's first piece of fiction long enough to be called a novel, *Watch and Ward*, appeared serially in 1871; his first volume of short stories was published in 1875, and *Roderick Hudson*, the novel which definitely marked the end of his literary apprenticeship, in 1876.

It was during the years spent in Europe as a boy that James had absorbed once for all what he afterwards called the 'European virus', the *nostalgia* for the old world which made it impossible for him to live permanently elsewhere. In 1869, and again in 1872, he came to Europe as a tourist, lingering chiefly in Rome, Florence, and Paris. These visits intensified his desire to find a fixed home on this side of the Atlantic; and when he came again, in 1875, it was with the decided intention of remaining for good. He proposed at first to settle in Paris; but after a year there he began to see that London (which he then knew very slightly) was the place where he could best feel at home, and he removed thither in 1876. He lived constantly in London, in lodgings off Piccadilly or in a flat in Kensington, for more than twenty years. In 1898 he moved to Lamb House, Rye, Sussex, where he mainly lived for the rest of his life, and where all his later novels were written. He was never married.

Henry James was thus thirty-three years old when he established himself in the country he was to make his own, and the fact is important for an understanding both of his character and his work. His youth, so far as it was European, had been almost entirely continental; his culture was French; he was a highly civilized, very critical and observant young citizen of the world. He came to England almost as a stranger, in spite of the fact that English life seemed to him in many ways barbarously insular; and he came because he was convinced that here only could an American really strike root in European soil. He accordingly proceeded with intense application to study and assimilate his chosen world—a narrow world, it may be said, for it was practically bounded by the social round of well-to-do London, but quite large enough, as he felt, to task his powers of absorption and to give him what he sought, a solid home in his expatriation. This was one side of the matter. The other concerned the exercise of his keen and unresting imagination, which found in London, and even in a small section of London, the inexhaustible material that it needed.

It is commonly said that James's work as a novelist falls into three distinct 'periods' or 'manners'; and the classification is convenient, though it may tend to obscure the unbroken steadiness with which his art was developed from book to book. In the first of these periods he was chiefly occupied with the 'international' subject, the impact of American life upon the older, richer, denser civilization of Europe; and it was not until he had been living for a good many years in England that he felt ready to drop the many possibilities of this fruitful theme and to treat a purely English subject. By that time he had written all those of his novels which were ever likely to be popular with the public at large; and though their simplicity may seem rather thin and their art ingenuous compared with his later work, books like *Roderick Hudson* (1875), *The American* (1877), *Daisy Miller* (1879), and more especially *The Portrait of a Lady* (1881), have a charm of freshness and neatness, which their author himself recognized when many years later he re-read and to some extent revised them. He had come to Europe at the right moment for the effect of the contrast which he found so pictorial, the clash of new and old, while the American in Europe (particularly the American girl) was still inexperienced and unfamiliar enough to create a 'situation', seen against the background of London or Paris or Rome. In half a dozen novels and a long series of shorter pieces James recurred to this situation, so rich in variety and so expressive of national character.

The Tragic Muse (1890) may be said to inaugurate James's second period, partly because the peculiar development of his art begins to show plainly in this book, partly because he here for the first time treated on a large scale a subject from English life, social, political, and artistic. In *The Spoils of Poynton* (1897), *What Maisie Knew* (1897), *The Awkward Age* (1899), and in several volumes of short stories, he continued to explore the field of English character, though it remained true that the England of his knowledge was confined to a comparatively small circle of London life. His sensitive appreciation of the minute distinctions, the fine shades, the all but inaudible tones, in the intercourse of very civilized people, together with his now complete mastery of his craft, began to give his work the strange and deeply individual aspect which it wore increasingly to the end. His style, matching the extreme subtlety of his perceptions and discriminations, developed an intricacy which might sometimes appear perversely obscure, though at its best it is really the simple expression of the effects he sought—suggestive, evocative effects, that gradually shape out a solid impression. (It is worth mentioning that all his later books were dictated by him to his secretary, a practice that fostered and perhaps exaggerated the natural amplitude of his style.) His fiction thus passed imperceptibly into its final phase, culminating in his three last novels, *The Wings of the Dove* (1902), *The Ambassadors* (written before *The Wings*, but not published till 1903), and *The Golden Bowl* (1904). In these books he returned once more to the 'international' theme, the contrast of American and European character, bringing the maturity of his experience and his imagination to bear on the subject which had occupied so much of his early work. After *The Golden Bowl* he wrote no more fiction, save a few short stories, till 1914, when he began to work upon two long novels, *The Ivory Tower*, and *The Sense of the Past*, both of which he left unfinished at his death. These two fragments were published posthumously in 1917, together with the extremely interesting notes which he had composed for his own guidance—a kind of leisurely rumination over the subject in hand which more than anything else reveals the working of his imagination.

For the revised and collected edition of his novels and tales, the issue of which began in 1907, James wrote a series of prefaces, partly reminiscent, mainly critical, which are of the highest importance as a summary of his view of the art of fiction. This view he had elaborated by degrees through many years of uninterrupted work; and he was certainly the first novelist in any language to explore with such thoroughness the nature and the possibilities of the craft. Even the passionate absorption in technical matters of such a writer as Flaubert seems slight and partial compared with the energy, the concentration, and the lucidity of James's thought upon the question of the portrayal of life in a novel. The form and design of a story had preoccupied him from the first; and if much of his early work was curiously thin, as though he were shy of plunging into the depths of human nature, it was largely because he would not attempt anything that he felt to be beyond his means, while he was engaged in consciously perfecting these. The most obvious influences under which he began to write were those of Hawthorne and Turgenev; but he was soon pursuing his own way in the search for a manner of presentation that should satisfy his more and more exacting criticism. It is not possible to describe in a few words the complexity of the art which reached its highest point, to the author's mind, in *The Ambassadors*; but what is perhaps most characteristic in it is the rhythmical alternation of 'drama' and 'picture' (they are James's words) in the treatment of the subject. By 'picture' he meant the rendering of life as reflected in the mind of some chosen onlooker (as the hero, Strether, in *The Ambassadors*), watching and meditating upon the scene before him; by 'drama' the placing of a scene directly before the reader, without the intervention of any reflecting, interpreting consciousness. All his later books (with one exception) are built up by the use of these contrasted methods, the old-fashioned device of 'telling' the story ('on the author's poor word of honour', as he put it) being entirely discarded. The single exception is *The Awkward Age*, in which the dramatic method alone is used, and there is no 'going behind' any of the characters, to share their thought. It may be said very roughly that he employs 'picture' for the preparation of an effect, 'drama' for its climax; the purpose throughout being to make the story *show itself* (instead of being merely narrated), to the enhancement of its force and weight. It was only when this process had been carried so far as to leave no relevant aspect of the subject in hand unillustrated and unaccounted for that he could regard the story as truly and effectually 'done'—a favourite word of his, expressing his highest praise. But, for a full understanding of the originality of his methods of criticism and creation it is necessary to study carefully the prefaces written for the collected edition.

Even the most enthusiastic admirers of James's later work have sometimes felt that the importance of his subjects was hardly equal to the immense elaboration of his treatment of them—a judgement more crudely expressed by saying that 'nothing happens' in his books, for all their densely packed extent. It is true that his central theme, baldly stated, is often a small affair, and that he seldom allows a glimpse of the fiercer passions that are the common stock-in-trade of the novelist. But this criticism implies some misunderstanding of his view of a subject—the importance of which he held to depend primarily on the value, the intelligence, and the sensibility, of the people involved. An event is nothing in itself; the question is what a fine mind will make of it; and more and more, in James's books, the characters tended to become men and women of rare and acute perception, capable of making the utmost of all their experience. A very simple theme, entrusted to a few such people, would give him more than enough for dramatic development; and if their deeper feelings remain all but hidden under the delicate surface-play of their reflections and reactions, it was because the last results and furthest implications of a thing were to him always more significant, more charged with history, than the thing itself in its nakedness could possibly be. Hence his dislike of the raw, the crude, the staring, his love of the toned and seasoned and civilized, both in literature and in life. In the immense procession of characters that he created, while it is the American girl (Daisy Miller, Isabel Archer of *The Portrait*, and many more) who predominates in his earlier books, the type nearest his mind in his later fiction is perhaps the 'poor sensitive gentleman' of stories like *The Altar of the Dead, The Great Good Place, Broken Wings*, with Strether of *The Ambassadors* at the head of them—elderly men, slightly worn and battered and blighted in the struggle of life, but profoundly versed, to use another characteristic phrase of James's, in the 'wear and tear of discrimination'.

Besides some twenty novels and nearly a hundred short stories, James published several volumes of sketches of travel and of literary criticism. He also wrote a number of plays; indeed for several years, from about 1890 to 1894, he devoted himself almost entirely to a determined attempt to win fame and fortune as a dramatist. The venture, which on the whole was certainly against the set of his genius, was not successful; very few of his plays have been acted, and none has had any lasting success on the stage. In *The American Scene* (1906) he recorded the profusion of impressions that he received from a visit to America after an absence of twenty years. Towards the end of his life he wrote two volumes (and part of a third) of reminiscences of his childhood and youth, an evocation of early days in America and Europe which shows how intense had been the activity of his imagination from his earliest years. A collection of his singularly rich and copious letters was published in 1920.

During the earlier years of his life in London, James probably seemed to those who knew him but slightly a somewhat critical onlooker, highly correct in style and manner, with a cautious reserve not easily to be penetrated. He was engaged in exploring the social world that readily opened to him; he was seen at innumerable dinner-parties and country-house visits, observantly making his way; but it was long before he felt able to lay aside the guarded prudence of a stranger and to take his ease in his acquired home. Meanwhile, among a host of acquaintances his intimate friends were few—among them may be named Burne-Jones, George du Maurier, J. R. Lowell, R. L. Stevenson; and perhaps it was only to his own family, and particularly to his brother William, to whom he was very deeply attached, that he freely confided his mind. Gradually a remarkable change took place in him; after twenty years of England he seemed at last to feel at home, and no one who met him in later days could think of him as other than the most genial, expansive, and sympathetic of friends. To a wide and ever increasing circle he became a figure uniquely impressive for the weight, the authority, the luxuriant elaboration of his mind, and lovable to the same degree for his ripe humour, his loyalty, his inexhaustible kindness—as also for something more, for a strain of odd and unexpected simplicity, that survived in him after a lifetime of ironic observation and experience. Yet those who knew him best remained conscious of something secluded and inaccessible in his genius, sufficient to itself and shared with no one.

James's published letters give a very complete picture of his habit of life, which from the time of his settlement in England varied little from year to year. The chief break was made in 1898, when Rye became his head quarters instead of Kensington; but he was never very long absent from London, and he retained a room at the Reform Club for his frequent visits. Both there and in his charming old house at Rye he was lavish in enter-tainment of his many friends; as a host his standard of hospitality was very high—so high, indeed, as to make him at times impatient of the conse-quences it entailed. He could take nothing lightly, and the burden of sociability roused him to much eloquent lamentation. Yet he soon missed it in solitude, and he was easily tempted by any congenial call; he was not less generous as a guest than as a host, and in a circle which was not exactly that of society or of the arts or of the professions, but mingled of all three, he enjoyed himself and gave enjoyment. Nothing, however, not even his occasional excursions abroad, to Paris and Italy, was ever allowed to interrupt the industrious regularity of his work. Though his health was sometimes a difficulty and always a matter of a good deal of anxiety to himself, his constitution was remarkably strong, and he never seemed to feel the need of a holiday. In his seventy-second year, at the outbreak of the European War, his zeal in his work was as keen as ever, and his im-agination teemed with material to be turned into art before it should be too late.

His portrait by J. S. Sargent, R.A., now in the National Portrait Gallery, was presented to him by a large group of friends in 1913, in commem-oration of his seventieth birthday; and in 1914 a bust of him was executed by Mr. Derwent Wood. The portly presence, the massively modelled head, the watchful eye, the mobile expression, recall him as he was in his later years (till about 1900 he wore a close beard, and Mr. William Rothenstein made and possesses a drawing showing him with a moustache and beard), and may suggest the nature and manner of his talk. This, in a sympathetic company, where he could take his time to develop a topic or a descrip-tion in his own way, was memorably opulent and picturesque. To listen to him was like watching an artist at work; the ample phrases slowly un-coiled, with much pausing and hesitating for the choice word, and out of them was gradually constructed the impression of the scene or the idea in his mind; when it was finished the listener was in possession of a characteristic product of Henry James's art. It was hardly to be called conversation, perhaps; it was too magnificent, too deliberate, for the give-and-take of a mixed gathering; but his companionable humour, his quick sensibility, his ornate and affectionate courtesy, set it further still from any appearance of formality or display. Though in any company he was certain to be the dominant, preponderant figure, his interest and his participation in the life around him were unfailing, and he seemed to have the gift of creating a special, unique relation with every one who came his way.

The shock of the War fell very heavily upon him; but he withstood it in a passionate ardour of patriotism that brought him at last, after nearly forty years of life in England, to take a step which he had never contemplated before. In July 1915 he became naturalized as a British subject. At the following new year he was awarded the order of merit: but by that time he was already lying ill and near his death. Three years before he had acquired a flat in Cheyne Walk, Chelsea, and it was there that he died on 28 February 1916. His body was cremated, and a commemorative tablet placed in Chelsea Old Church, close to his last home by the London riverside.

[Correspondence, published and unpublished; the autobiographical volumes, *A Small Boy and Others*, 1913, *Notes of a Son and Brother*, 1914, *The Middle Years*, 1917 (the dates and order of events in these books are not always to be relied on); personal knowledge. A bibliography of Henry James's works (to 1905), compiled by Le Roy Phillips, was published in America in 1906.]

PERCY LUBBOCK

published 1927

JEROME Jerome Klapka

(1859–1927)

Novelist and playwright, was born at Walsall 2 May 1859, the younger son of Jerome Clapp Jerome, a colliery proprietor and nonconformist preacher, by his wife, Marguerite Jones, elder daughter of a Swansea solicitor. The colliery business proving unsuccessful, Jerome's father left Walsall and set up as a wholesale ironmonger in the East End of London. Jerome was educated at Marylebone grammar school until, at the age of fourteen, he began to make his own way. He obtained work, first as a railway clerk, and later as a schoolmaster; then he went on the stage, and finally took to journalism. It was his experience as an actor which led to the publication in 1888 of his first book, *On the Stage and Off*. In 1889 followed *The Idle*

Thoughts of an Idle Fellow and *Three Men in a Boat*. Both these achieved considerable success; the latter has been translated into a great number of languages and, curiously enough, had an enormous circulation in Russia. The blending of farcical humour with somewhat naïve sentiment, and of pretty descriptive writing with simple philosophizing, suited the taste of the period, and brought Jerome immediate popularity.

In 1892, with Robert Barr and George Brown Burgin, Jerome founded *The Idler*, an illustrated monthly magazine which owing to its humour and originality had for some years a remarkable success. With the exception of Bret Harte, Mark Twain, and W. L. Alden the contributors were nearly all young men, notably Israel Zangwill, Eden Phillpotts, and W. W. Jacobs. Features of the magazine were the informal discussions of the 'Idlers' Club', and *The Idler* monthly teas, where the editors met their contributors—an innovation at that time regarded as imperilling the sanctity of editorship. In 1893 Jerome founded a twopenny weekly paper, *Today*, in which with characteristic vigour he constantly attacked Kaiser Wilhelm II and warned his readers to beware of his over-weening ambition. Jerome's connexion with this publication was ended in 1897 by a costly lawsuit.

After producing several volumes of tales and sketches, Jerome published in 1900 *Three Men on the Bummel*, a humorous account of a tour in Germany, and in 1902 *Paul Kelver*, a long autobiographical novel which he himself thought his best work.

Jerome had always been anxious to write for the stage, and an early play of his, *Barbara*, was accepted by Sir Charles Hawtrey and produced at the Globe Theatre in London 19 June 1886. It was not, however, until 1908 that he won fame as a dramatist by *The Passing of the Third Floor Back*, produced at the St. James's Theatre with Sir Johnston Forbes-Robertson playing the chief part. This has several times been revived. His other plays include *Miss Hobbs* (1899), *Fanny and the Servant Problem* (1908), *The Master of Mrs. Chilvers* (1911), on the woman suffrage problem, and *The Great Gamble*, a study of German life produced shortly before the outbreak of war in 1914. He wrote many other novels, plays, and sketches, and in 1926 published a volume of reminiscences, entitled *My Life and Times*.

Jerome, who was a good rider and oarsman, served during the European War as driver of a French motor ambulance on the Western front. During the last years of his life he lived at Belsize Park. In 1927, although in failing health, he decided to make a long motoring tour through England; he was taken ill, and died in Northampton general hospital 14 June 1927. His body was cremated, and his ashes subsequently buried in the churchyard of Ewelme, Oxfordshire. A tablet to his memory has been placed on the house at Walsall where he was born.

Jerome married in 1888 Georgina Henrietta Stanley, daughter of Lieutenant Nesza, of the Spanish army. They had one daughter.

[*The Times*, 15 June 1927; J. K. Jerome, *My Life and Times*, 1926; Alfred Moss, *Jerome K. Jerome: his Life and Work*, 1929.]

G. B. BURGIN

published 1937

JOHNS William Earl

(1893–1968)

Writer, journalist, and creator of the children's popular fiction character 'Biggles', was born 5 February 1893 at Hertford, the eldest son of Richard William Eastman Johns, a tailor, and his wife, Elizabeth Earl. He was educated at Bengeo School and Hertford Grammar School, also attending evening classes at the local art school.

After leaving school he completed indentures with a firm of surveyors. Taking a job in Norfolk, he fulfilled an ambition to become a soldier by enlisting as a part-time private with the Norfolk Yeomanry. He was called up for active service on the outbreak of World War I. In the autumn of 1914 he married Maud Penelope Hunt, daughter of a Norfolk clergyman, and their only son was born in March 1916.

Johns served with the Yeomanry at Gallipoli and then with the Machine-Gun Corps in the Salonika campaign, transferring to the Royal Flying Corps in 1917. He was commissioned as second lieutenant on 26 September, training as a pilot. After several postings as a flying instructor, he joined No. 55 Squadron at Azelot, France, in August 1918, flying DH4 bombers on long-range raids into the Rhineland.

On 16 September the squadron raided Mannheim. Johns's aircraft was damaged by anti-aircraft fire and, as he returned to base, he found himself fighting a battle with Fokker DVIIs of Ernst Udet's famous Jadgstaffel. Johns's observer was killed and Johns, wounded, crashed and was captured. At Strasburg he was tried and condemned to death for 'war crimes', accused of indiscriminate bombing of civilian targets, but saved by the possibility of an armistice. He spent the rest of the war in prisoner-of-war camps, attempting two escapes.

He remained in the Royal Air Force until 1927, being promoted to flying officer in 1920. He flew in RAF displays and was on the organizing committee of the Hendon air display.

In 1923 it was Johns who, as recruiting officer, admitted T. E. Lawrence into the RAF as 'Ross'; he wanted to reject him for giving a name that was obviously false, but accepted him under orders. Later, Johns exploded the myth that Lawrence's identity in the RAF was ever a secret; from the first day, one officer warned another that 'aircraftman second class Ross' dined with Cabinet ministers.

By 1923 Johns had left his first wife and met Doris May Leigh. In 1924 they had set up home in Newcastle. On leaving the RAF Johns became an aviation illustrator (sharing a studio with the illustrator Howard Leigh, Doris's brother) and then tried his hand at journalism. In 1932 he became founder-editor of the monthly *Popular Flying*. It was in this magazine that he first introduced 'Biggles', the archetypal RFC pilot. The first collection of these stories appeared as *The Camels are Coming* (1932). By the time of his death, Johns had written ninety-six 'Biggles' books and his airman had been consecutively a World War I 'ace', a freelance adventurer, a World War II squadron-leader, and, finally, an 'air-detective' at Scotland Yard.

Johns's output was prodigious. In the 1930s he wrote regularly for the *Modern Boy, Pearson's Magazine*, and *My Garden*, as well as editing *Popular Flying*. In April 1938 he also edited a weekly, *Flying*. In 1939, owing to his criticism of government air defence policy, he was dismissed from his editorships. At the outbreak of war he lectured to the Air Training Corps (in whose foundation he had been involved) and wrote for the *ATC Gazette*. He also wrote specialized aviation books for the Air Ministry and Ministry of Information. Johns's 'Biggles' stories had an immense impact on recruitment to the RAF.

'Worrals of the WAAF', the female counterpart of 'Biggles', was created by Johns at the request of the Air Ministry to promote the Women's Auxiliary Air Force, and a similar demand from the War Office for a soldier hero was met by the creation of 'Gimlet'—a commando.

After ten years in Scotland, where Johns indulged in his favourite pastimes of shooting and fishing, he and Doris Johns moved to Park House, Hampton Court, in the mid 1950s. When he died at Park House 21 June 1968, he had published 169 titles: 104 under 'Biggles'; 11 under 'Worrals', 10 under 'Gimlet', 10 science-fiction adventures, 5 'Steeley' novels, 8 miscellaneous juvenile titles, 11 adult thrillers, and 6 non-fiction titles. His works were translated into fourteen languages, issued in braille, serialized in newspapers and magazines in Britain, Australia, and Europe, broadcast on radio in Britain, Australia, and South Africa, televised by Granada TV, turned into strip cartoons, and issued as cassette recordings. After Enid Blyton, Johns was the most prolific and popular children's writer of the time.

In his later years, and after his death, Johns came under attack from children's librarians and others who accused him of racialism, outmoded concepts, and stereotype characters. Although some of his books reflect the prejudices of his times, a reading of his works reveals his tremendous, almost puckish, sense of humour, and his habit of making fun of his own supposed prejudices. The critic Stanley Reynolds summed up the secret of Johns's success: 'The appeal is that "Biggles" is a flier and Captain Johns writes wonderously about flying . . . The writing is so vivid that it sticks in your mind and years after you remember it.'

Popular in Service circles and the book world, Johns, with his short bulky figure and his well-groomed grey hair and ready smile, was greeted enthusiastically by his wide range of friends. A craftsman, he always delivered his work on time and to the exact length required.

[RAF officers' records, Ministry of Defence; W. E. Johns, articles in *Popular Flying*, June 1933, June 1935, and June 1936; Kriegsarchiv, Bayerisches Haupstaatarchiv, Munich; Alan Morris, *First of Many—The Story of the Independent Force, RAF*, 1968, *The Times*, 22 June 1968; *Guardian*, 6 January 1979.]

PETER BERRESFORD ELLIS
PIERS WILLIAMS

published 1981

JOHNSON Pamela Hansford

(1912–1981)

Lady Snow

Novelist, dramatist, and critic, was born 29 May 1912 in London, the elder child (the younger daughter died as a baby) of Reginald Kenneth Johnson, a colonial administrator in the Gold Coast, and his wife, Amy Clotilda, daughter of C. E. Howson, actor and treasurer to Sir Henry Irving for twenty-five years. She was educated at Clapham County Secondary School, leaving at the age of sixteen to learn shorthand and typing. Her father had died five years earlier leaving only debts and there was no money for further education. She never regretted this deprivation, claiming that 'a course in Eng. Lit. has rotted many a promising writer' and finding in *Texts and Pretexts* (1933) by Aldous Huxley the key to her own 'higher education' in both English and French literature.

For five years she worked in a bank, writing (and occasionally publishing) verse, essays, and short stories in her spare time. In 1934 she won the *Sunday Referee*'s annual poetry prize—a subsidy for a book of her poems. She met and fell in love with Dylan Thomas who won the prize the following year. They contemplated marriage but decided amicably to go their separate ways. Her diaries for the two years of their friendship and his letters to her are now in the library of the University of New York at Buffalo.

She had an immediate success, both critical and commercial, with her first novel, *This Bed Thy Centre* (1935), although it was widely considered to be shocking. For a while she was disowned by her late father's family and was subjected to a shoal of anonymous letters. But, reassured and encouraged by Cyril Connolly and others, she abandoned the bank in favour of full-time writing. She went on to publish thirty-one novels; seven plays; a book of memoirs, *Important To Me* (1974); an appraisal of contemporary 'permissiveness' in the light of the infamous Moors murder case, *On Iniquity* (1967); and six Proust reconstructions (1958), the radio plays in which she placed Proust's characters in different settings and situations. These were commissioned by the BBC Third Programme and were repeated frequently during the 1950s. The tapes have now been erased.

After the great promise of her first novel it seemed that she had lost both her way and her touch. She wrote five undistinguished novels in four years and it was not until 1940 that she regained her true form with *Too Dear for my Possessing*. She was invited to review regularly for the *Sunday Times* and became well-known as a demanding but generous-minded and constructive critic.

She married in 1936 Gordon Neil (Stewart), an Australian journalist, and they had a son, Andrew, in 1941, and a daughter, Lindsay, in 1944. The marriage came to an end in 1949.

She was married again in 1950 to the writer Charles Percy (later Lord) Snow. Their considerable talents were complementary, their tastes and interests largely coincided, and they made a formidable and influential literary partnership. They travelled widely in the United States and in the Soviet Union and her books were published with success in both countries, leading to translations in many European languages.

She wrote ten of her best and best-known novels between 1950 and 1978 including *Catherine Carter* (1952), her only novel with a theatrical setting; *The Unspeakable Skipton* (1959), a satirical comedy based on the character of Frederic Rolfe, Baron Corvo, and generally accepted as her masterpiece; *The Humbler Creation* (1959) about an unfashionable London parish, and *The Honours Board* (1970) set in the enclosed world of the teaching staff of a boys' preparatory school. Her last novel *A Bonfire* (1981) was published two months before her death.

Her work was popular in the best sense: she had a large 'library' following as well as attracting the respect and admiration of the literary pundits of the day. She was generous with help to young writers and was a warm-hearted and entertaining friend and companion. She was a fellow of the Royal Society of Literature and was appointed CBE in 1975. She had four American honorary degrees. A sufferer for thirty years from migraine she helped to found the Migraine Trust in 1969.

She had a second son, Philip, in 1952 by her second husband, C. P. Snow. She died 18 June 1981 in the London Clinic after a series of strokes.

[Pamela Hansford Johnson, *Important To Me*, 1974; Isabel Quigly, *Pamela Hansford Johnson* in Writers and their Work, no. 203, 1968; personal knowledge.]

ALAN MACLEAN

published 1990

JONES David

(1895–1974)

Painter, poet, and essayist, was born 1 November 1895 in Brockley, Kent, the younger son and youngest of three children of James Jones, printer, from Holywell, Flintshire, and his wife, Alice Ann, former governess, daughter of Ebenezer Bradshaw, a mast and block maker of Rotherhithe, Surrey. His father's father was a master plasterer from Ysceifiog, his mother's mother Italian. His father worked on the *Flintshire Observer* until 1883 and knew some Welsh songs; David learnt what Welsh he knew later. He was baptized Walter, which name he discarded. His earliest animal drawings, some of which survive, date from 1902 or 1903. From 1910 to 1914 he attended Camberwell School of Art under A. S. Hartrick (who had known Van Gogh and Gauguin) and others.

After trying to join the Artists' Rifles and some new Welsh cavalry, he enlisted in the Welch Fusiliers, 2 January 1915, serving as a private soldier until December 1918, in a London unit of Lloyd George's 'Welsh army'. He was wounded in the leg on the night of 11 July 1916 in the attack on Mametz Wood on the Somme. He returned to action in October but by chance avoided the Passchendaele offensive. He left France with severe trench fever in February 1918. On demobilization he wished at first to rejoin, but accepted a grant and some parental help to work (1919–21) at Westminster School of Art. He already spoke at that time of Post-Impressionist theory fitting in with Catholic sacramental theology, and in

1921 became a Roman Catholic and went to work under A. Eric R. Gill, then at Ditchling in Sussex, and from August 1924 at Capel-y-ffin in the Black Mountains near the Welsh border. Jones was brought up at home on Bunyan and Milton, but with strong touches of inherited Catholic feelings; he had been deeply moved by a mass just behind the front line glimpsed through a barn wall. He had liked the businesslike atmosphere. His first job was to paint the lettering of the war memorial at New College, Oxford.

In 1924 he got engaged to Gill's daughter, Petra. His close friend René Hague was in love with her sister, Joan, and married her, but Jones had little money and no prospects; Petra broke off the engagement in 1927 to marry someone else, and Jones never did marry, though he was not homosexual and had *amitiés amoureuses*, mostly conducted on the telephone as he grew older. He visited the Gills at Pigotts in Buckinghamshire often until 1933, but he was too devoted to his work and usually too poor not to live alone. His closest friends loved him intensely; they included Tom Burns, Harman Grisewood, Douglas Cleverdon, Jim Ede, Father M. C. D'Arcy, and Helen Sutherland, his greatest patron. He spent time in the twenties on Caldey Island, in Bristol, at Brockley with his parents, in Berkshire with Robert Gibbings of the Golden Cockerel Press, and in France. In 1928 Ben Nicholson had him elected to the Seven and Five Society, where he exhibited with Henry Moore, Christopher Wood, (Dame) Barbara Hepworth and John Piper. The same year he began *In Parenthesis* (1937), which has its climax at Mametz in World War I. This book won the 1938 Hawthornden prize.

The delicacy and freshness of his colours, and the purity and power of his forms as a painter, let alone the strength and grace of his engraving work and his occasional wooden sculpture, would be enough to win him a high place among the artists of his generation and in a tradition that goes back to William Blake, whose nature and genius with many differences David Jones recalls. His work as a poet, in *In Parenthesis, The Anathemata* (1952), and *The Sleeping Lord* (1974), was almost more impressive, and in the lettering and the texts of his 'inscriptions', words painted on paper, he devised a new and moving art. In his severest engravings he was warm, in painting of solemn beauty lyrical and humorous. His visions of nature were as fresh as Ysceifiog, his poetry as thrilling and abundant as the Thames at Rotherhithe. He greatly admired the Cornish fisherman painter, Alfred Wallis.

His intellectual insights were profound and complex. They were based on a restless and never-ending meditation of the art of painting, of theology for which he had a brilliant flair, of the nature of technology, of heroic legends, prehistoric archaeology, and the history of the British Isles. He admired James Joyce, T. S. Eliot, Baron Friedrich Von Hügel, Christopher Dawson, and Père de la Taille; at least for a few years in the late thirties he flirted heavily with Oswald Spengler's *Decline of the West* and unseriously with Adolf Hitler's *Mein Kampf*, although he was innocent of the faintest trace of fascism; he simply loved mankind, and hated what everyone hates about modern times. In London in the blitz he wrote a lot of poetry, painted some of his finest mythical paintings, and began his great 'inscriptions'. His 'Aphrodite in Aulis' (1941) is the goddess and lover of dying soldiers both German and English. His work was grossly interrupted by eye trouble from 1930 onwards, by a severe breakdown in 1932 with chronic insomnia, and then by a worse attack in 1947. He bore all this with an uncomplaining goodness he seemed to have learnt in the trenches.

In 1934 Jones was taken to Cairo and Jerusalem by Tom Burns. It was there he conceived the equivalence of British and Roman soldiers, and of his central statement, *The Anathemata*. In the later thirties he lived mostly at Sidmouth. After the 1947 breakdown he lived in fine rooms on the hill at Harrow, later in a little hotel in the town, and in the end in Calvary Nursing Home, Harrow, where he was looked after by the nuns. Among the new friends of his last years were Nancy Sandars, archaeologist, and Philip Lowry, silversmith.

Jones had a boyish gaiety and a charmingly wide smile. His conversation was full of humour and inventive parody; his sympathy and the range of his interest were extraordinarily wide. The fulcrum of his morality was the decency of the infantrymen of 1914. Under stress he would drop his shopping, lose his papers, or find himself smoking two cigarettes, one in each hand. His notes became long writings, and his letters, annotated in several colours, tumbled effortlessly from sheet to sheet and subject to subject like the dialogues of Plato. He concentrated on a friend, on a subject of conversation, on a detail of any kind, historical or technical or visual or intellectual, with uncommon intensity. His eyes twinkled and glittered deeply.

His first retrospective exhibition at the National Museum of Wales and the Tate Gallery was in 1954–5, his second (posthumously) in 1981. He was appointed CBE in 1955 and CH in 1974. He won many prizes and awards, and received an honorary D.Litt. from the University of Wales in 1960. He died at the Calvary Nursing Home, Harrow, 28 October 1974, after some years of increasing illness.

[René Hague (ed.), *Dai Greatcoat, a Self-Portrait of David Jones in his Letters*, 1980; Paul Hills in Tate Gallery catalogue, 1981; David Jones, *The Roman Quarry*, with foreword by Harman Grisewood and notes by René Hague, 1981; Colin Hughes, *David Jones, The Man who was in the Field*, 1979; private information.]

PETER LEVI

published 1986

JOYCE James Augustine

(1882–1941)

Poet, novelist, and playwright, was born in Dublin 2 February 1882, the eldest son of John Stanislaus Joyce, a member of an old Cork family and a well-known Dublin figure. A fine singer, a wit, and a jovial companion, he figures prominently in Joyce's first novel and also in certain episodes of *Ulysses*. His personality made a deep impression on young Joyce and the verbal audacity of *Ulysses* no less than the boisterous humour of *Finnegans Wake* certainly owes much to this early influence. 'Hundreds of pages and scores of characters in my books', wrote Joyce in a private letter, 'come from him.' Joyce's mother, a brilliant pianist, was Mary Jane, daughter of John Murray, an agent for wines, of Longford. In 1893 Joyce entered Belvedere College, Dublin, a Jesuit school, where his natural taste for literature was fostered by an exceptionally able English master and he was also given a good grounding in French and Italian. He went on to University College, Dublin, where, while specializing in languages, he sharpened his wits on the works of St. Thomas Aquinas and Aristotle, the influence of both of whom is apparent throughout his work. Joyce's first work was published in the *Fortnightly Review* in April 1900. It was an essay entitled 'Ibsen's New Drama'—a remarkable achievement for an eighteen-year-old undergraduate.

After graduating in 1902 Joyce left Dublin. Following a brief stay in London where he had a friendly reception from W. B. Yeats and Arthur Symons, he crossed to Paris, devoting himself to enlarging his knowledge of life and literature. He lived on loans and small sums of money sent by his family and friends and came near to destitution. The next year the illness and death of his mother caused him to return to Dublin where in 1904 he met Nora Joseph Barnacle. Together they left Ireland, and after a short stay in Zürich Joyce taught English for a time in the Berlitz school, first in Pola and then in Trieste. He found great difficulty in supporting himself and his family (he had one son and one daughter), and tried many methods of increasing his income, including writing articles in Italian for the *Piccolo della Sera*, and starting the Volta cinema theatre in Dublin. In 1912 he paid his last visit to Dublin with a view to securing the publication of his book of short stories, *Dubliners*. Failing in this, he returned to Trieste.

Joyce spent the greater part of the war of 1914–18 in Zürich, where he soon found himself in financial straits. His literary abilities were beginning to be recognized and the prime minister, Asquith (at the suggestion of (Sir)

Edmund Gosse, W. B. Yeats, George Moore, and (Sir) Edward Marsh), granted Joyce £100 from the privy purse. In 1918 Mrs. Harold McCormick (daughter of J. D. Rockefeller) provided him with a monthly allowance of a thousand Swiss francs which continued until the autumn of 1919. Meanwhile in 1917 Miss Harriet Shaw Weaver (editor of the *Egoist* magazine) added an allowance of half this amount. Subsequently on two occasions she settled on Joyce substantial capital sums, the income from which ensured his monetary independence.

In 1920 Joyce moved to Paris, his home for the next nineteen years. Throughout his life he had trouble with his eyes and during his later years he underwent many operations for cataract. His method of literary composition, which entailed the fitting together mosaic-wise of thousands of brief entries jotted down in the big notebooks he always carried in his pockets, put a great strain on his sight, but he could count on the aid of his many friends for the deciphering of these sometimes almost illegible notes, and his powerful memory enabled him always to indicate the page and often even the line where each fragment was to be inserted.

Joyce's first published book, *Chamber Music* (1907), was a set of lyrical poems composed in early youth. They have a delicate precision which owes something to the French poets of the late nineteenth century, and much to the Elizabethans. His next published work was *Dubliners* (1914), a collection of *nouvelles* somewhat in the manner of Flaubert, whose style and methods Joyce most admired. In 1916 Joyce's first full-length work, *A Portrait of the Artist as a Young Man*, was published in the United States and sheets were imported into England for publication in the following year. An autobiographical novel (the condensed version of a much longer work, *Stephen Hero*, a fragment of which was published after Joyce's death, in 1944), the *Portrait* described with exactitude the formative years of the writer's life and the theory of aesthetics he had built up from his wide reading. It served as a prelude to *Ulysses* (1922), the major work on which Joyce spent seven years and which brought him world-wide fame. Owing to the strong language used in certain passages, *Ulysses* could not be published in Great Britain or the United States and it was produced by Miss Sylvia Beach, owner of a well-known Anglo-American bookshop, Shakespeare and Company, in Paris. A growing understanding of the true nature of *Ulysses* (in no sense a pornographic work) gradually paved the way to a removal of the ban. A New York publishing firm instigated a test case and after a long and careful hearing it was decided that *Ulysses* might be published in the United States. It appeared in 1934 and in Great Britain two years later.

It is easy to understand the influence which *Ulysses* exercised on writers of the period between the wars. This influence was chiefly concerned with problems of style and technique, notably in the use as a means of narrative of the so-called *monologue intérieur*, which purports to be an exact transcript of the 'stream of consciousness' in the mind of a character. The structure of *Ulysses* (which is a modern approximation to the Odyssey) is highly elaborate; each of its eighteen interlocking episodes has its own style, symbol, Homeric references, associated colour and technique, and the whole action takes place within twenty-four hours. Thus, despite its air of romantic turbulence, *Ulysses*, the record of a Dublin day (16 June 1904), has an internal logic, structural harmony, and almost scientific precision of language entitling it to be regarded as, in a sense, a 'classic' of its age.

During the next seventeen years Joyce was engaged on what he himself regarded as his magnum opus, *Finnegans Wake* (1939). The strangeness of the language, recalling the 'portmanteau words' invented by Lewis Carroll, and the extreme complexity of its structure gained for it a mixed reception, and no final verdict on this work, despite many expository articles, had been pronounced ten years after its appearance. It has been aptly described as a *divertissement philologique*. But it is also a mine of rich, earthy humour, interspersed with passages of much verbal beauty. The central idea, as in *Ulysses*, is that of recurrence; the history of the world, the rise and fall of civilizations, is condensed into a Dublin Night's Dream. For his purposes Joyce created a language of his own, compounded of a vast number of languages dead and living, and based less on philological affinities than on sounds. None of the new terms used is a 'nonsense word'; each is tightly packed with allusions, the greater part being basically English. Joyce also wrote one play, *Exiles* (1918), somewhat in the Ibsen manner, and a second volume of poems, *Pomes Penyeach* (Paris, 1927).

Joyce had an agreeable presence and a quiet distinction which came as a surprise to some of those visiting the author of *Ulysses* for the first time. In conversation he used none of those ribald turns of speech which gave offence to many readers of that work, and he tacitly discouraged such remarks in his entourage. He was very fond of music and himself possessed a fine tenor voice. His mind was at once encyclopaedic and synthetic and he rejected no scrap of knowledge on the score of its triviality. While it seems unlikely that *Finnegans Wake* will have the influence of *Ulysses*, it may well hold its place as the most remarkable book of its period, a treasury of curious scholarship and word-lore.

In 1940 Joyce migrated to Zürich where he died 13 January 1941. His wife (they were married in 1931) died in 1951. There are two portraits of Joyce by J.-E. Blanche, in the National Portrait Galleries of London and Dublin; another by Patrick Tuohy is owned by the family and one by Frank Budgen is privately owned. There are also drawings by Augustus John, Wyndham Lewis, Sean O'Sullivan, Brancusi, and others.

[Herbert Gorman, *James Joyce*, 1941; L. A. G. Strong, *The Sacred River*, 1949; Alan Parker, *James Joyce: A Bibliography*, Boston, 1948; J. J. Slocum and Herbert Cahoon, *A Bibliography of James Joyce, 1882–1941*, 1953; *Letters of James Joyce*, edited by Stuart Gilbert, 1957; personal knowledge.]

STUART GILBERT

[Stanislaus Joyce, *My Brother's Keeper*, edited by Richard Ellmann, 1958.]

published 1959

KEYES Sidney Arthur Kilworth

(1922–1943)

Poet, was born 27 May 1922 in Dartford, Kent, the only child of Captain Reginald Keyes of the Queen's Own Royal West Kent Regiment, and his second wife Edith, daughter of the Revd Arthur Blackburn, rector of St Paul's, Bradford. Because his mother died from peritonitis when he was only six weeks old, Keyes was brought up in Dartford by his paternal grandparents, and his grandfather, Sidney Kilworth Keyes, a wealthy farmer, dominated his childhood. On the death of his grandfather in 1938 Keyes was inspired to write his first serious poem 'Elegy'. Keyes's childhood was lonely and isolated. Because he was frail it was thought unwise to allow him to mix with other children or to spend time out of doors, and in consequence he became an avid reader. Being attracted to books dealing with history and legend he soon created an imaginary world of his own, and birds and reptiles provided him with companionship until at the age of nine he was eventually sent to a preparatory school in Dartford. When he was eleven he attended Dartford Grammar School, and three years later he went to Tonbridge School, where his main interests continued to centre on literature and the natural world. By the time he left Tonbridge in July 1940 Keyes had written more than seventy poems, discovered in a manuscript book shortly after the war; many are inevitably juvenilia, but 'Nefertiti', written when he was seventeen, marks an advance towards maturity, and his poem 'The Buzzard', the last to be written at Tonbridge, is probably his most accomplished schoolboy work.

On entering Queen's College, Oxford, with a history scholarship in October 1940, Keyes embarked on a fruitful friendship with the future winner of the Queen's gold medal for poetry, John Heath-Stubbs. Heath-Stubbs, whose own disturbed childhood had been marred by insensitivity to his progressive blindness, instinctively responded to the darker images of Keyes's own imagination. He understood very well Keyes's desire to investigate through poetry the subjects of pain and death, and his feeling of being in far closer communion with William Blake, William Wordsworth, and Johann Schiller than with any living contemporaries. In particular, Keyes had come to identify with the Romantic movement, and it was Heath-Stubbs who was able to broaden Keyes's base by tracing for him the origins of Romanticism in primitive legends through the medieval to the Augustan poets. It was Heath-Stubbs, too, who helped to perfect Keyes's poetic technique, which had tended to trail behind the complexity and variety of his ideas.

Keyes became editor of *Cherwell*. In 1941, with Michael Meyer, he edited *Eight Oxford Poets*. He was awarded a first class in part i of the history examination (1941). He had been writing on average a poem a week, and by the end of 1941 he had enough poems to form a first volume, *The Iron Laurel*, but he withheld publication until 1942 in order to include 'The Foreign Gate', a long poem in which, for the first time in his work, Death appears as a real presence. Keyes joined up in April 1942 and in September that year he was commissioned in his father's old regiment. He sailed for Algiers in March 1943 and during the last days of the Tunisian campaign he saw a mere fortnight's active service. He was killed near Sidi Abdulla 30 April 1943. The military historian, James Lucas, who served in Tunisia as Keyes's runner, remembered him as 'a gallant Christian gentleman who sacrificed himself for the men under his command'. He was twenty when he died.

A second, posthumous, collection of Sidney Keyes's poems, *The Cruel Solstice*, was published in 1943 and won the Hawthornden prize. His collected poems were edited in 1945 by Michael Meyer, who has recalled that, although Sidney Keyes was inclined to be taciturn in a large gathering or among strangers, to his friends he was witty and delightful company. Notwithstanding his extreme youth, his output was prodigious and far-ranging, and, with Keith Douglas and Alun Lewis, he must be regarded as one of the outstanding poets of World War II, so much of his work having been inspired, before his brief sortie into battle, by an internal preparation for death.

[John Guenther, *Sidney Keyes: a Biographical Inquiry*, 1967.]

MICHAEL DE-LA-NOY

published 1993

KOESTLER Arthur
(1905–1983)

Writer, was born 5 September 1905 in Budapest, the son of Henrik Koestler, talented eccentric and usually prosperous Jewish businessman, and his wife, Adela Jeiteles Hitzig, of an old Prague-Viennese Jewish family. She considered Hungarians barbarians, refusing to speak their language. Koestler admired his self-taught father and disliked his snobbish mother who treated him unkindly, was shamed by his sensational political adventures, belittled his literary successes, and whom he hated meeting even when she was old. Educated originally in Budapest and then in the Vienna Polytechnic High School and University, where the family finally settled after the Hungarian communist revolution in 1919, he read engineering which stimulated his lifelong passion for science. When twenty-one he went to Palestine and became Middle East correspondent of Ullstein, the great newspaper chain, soon moving to Paris and then to Berlin where in 1930 he became science editor of their *Vossische Zeitung* and foreign editor of their evening paper thus developing his knowledge both of science and politics.

Alert to the Hitler menace he joined the Communist Party as the best prospect of defeating Nazism and hence was courteously dismissed by the alarmed Ullstein in 1931. Financed by the Communist International to write a book on the first five-year plan he travelled widely in Russia, but the book, completed in 1934, was rejected by Soviet censorship as insufficiently adulatory. Back in Paris among anti-Nazi exiles he began his first novel *The Gladiators* (1939) showing that Spartacus was doomed because he would not apply 'the law of detours' requiring leaders to be 'pitiless for the sake of pity' in executing dissidents. He returned to the theme in *Darkness at Noon* (1940) in which the old Bolshevik Rubashov followed the 'law of detours' but was also doomed.

In 1936 he went to Franco's Seville headquarters to report for the Liberal *News Chronicle*. Denounced as a communist he escaped and returned in 1937 to report from the Republican side. Captured by Franco's troops he was imprisoned in Malaga and Seville from February to June, daily awaiting execution (*Spanish Testament*, 1937), an experience which made him disapprove of capital punishment against which he campaigned prominently during the post-war years in England. The vigorous activities of his first wife, Dorothy Asher, induced the British government to intervene to save him. He had married her in 1935; they had no children and were divorced in 1950. She came from Zurich.

In 1938 he left the Communist Party, in revulsion from Stalin's mass arrests and show trials and from the communist duplicity and incompetence he had seen in Russia and Republican Spain. His internment as a political suspect in a French concentration camp, from which he was released in 1940, gave him further writing material (*Scum of the Earth*, 1941). After joining the French Foreign Legion under a false name to avoid the Gestapo he escaped to England. Although his first language was Hungarian, he wrote in German until 1940 and thereafter in English. Put in the Pioneer Corps (1941–2), his latent love for England, despite his anglophile father forcing him to wear an Eton suit in Budapest when he was thirteen, blossomed. He became a British citizen in 1948. Such curiosities as compulsory tea breaks in the midst of war and the distinction between saloon and public bars fascinated him. Sexually hyperactive, which he thought normal for a Continental male, he was delighted by his successes with a series of pretty, upper-class Englishwomen, not least because they were upper-class. One liaison led to marriage in 1950 to Mamaine (died 1954), daughter of Eric Morton Paget, country gentleman. They had no children and were divorced in 1953. He treated her abominably, believing women's role to be that of a willing servant with the ability to please of a delicately nurtured, skilful courtesan. Possibly because of his mother's indifference he needed the unstinting love of women, 'but to write about them bores me'.

As well as the unattached, friends' wives or girl friends were fair game. He thought Bertrand (Earl) Russell petty to refuse to address a meeting organized by Koestler to protest against Russian suppression of the 1956 Hungarian revolution because Koestler was a co-respondent in Russell's divorce from Peter Spence.

Intolerant of disagreement, arrogantly certain of his genius, frequently and irrationally angry with friends, Koestler's questing charm and boyish curiosity made him deeply loved and liked by the many men and women he chose to please. A whole-hearted evening drinker with a lively humour he made parties rollick till the small hours. To be with him was to be aware of a considerable intellect brilliantly deployed in proselytizing the causes he believed mankind must adopt. The most important and seminal of these was his exposure by fiction and fact of the aridity and inevitably concomitant horrors of communism and its hopelessness as a better alternative to free societies based on capitalism. He shocked many gullible idealists into reality.

That is likely to be his greatest memorial though he would have preferred it to have been his scientific writings, particularly those relating to parapsychology, or telepathy, which he regarded as his most significant work, insisting that as nuclear particles can communicate with each other faster than light there must be a scientific basis for the belief that human minds can do the same. Among such books were *The Sleepwalkers* (1959), *The Act of Creation* (1964), and *The Case of the Midwife Toad* (1971). In his will he left over £500,000 to endow a chair of parapsychology, which was later founded at Edinburgh University. An atheist, his hope that there might be some vague continuation after death possibly lay behind his parapsychological enquiries. He was generous to persecuted writers and provided annual cultural prizes to prisoners in British jails for whose barren lives he had sympathy and understanding. He was appointed CBE in 1972 and C.Lit. in 1974. He had honorary degrees from Queen's University, Kingston, Ontario (LLD, 1968), and Leeds (D.Litt., 1977).

Koestler's third wife was Cynthia Jefferies, née Paterson, the daughter of a South African surgeon. She was twenty-two years younger than himself. He employed her in 1948 first intermittently and then permanently as secretary. There was the customary seduction and the starstruck, naïve South African girl became a willing slave in a harem which changed frequently even while Koestler was married to Mamaine. When her breakaway attempt ended in a failed marriage she was adoringly grateful to be put condescendingly on the strength again and eventually to marry him in 1965, not complaining at his unrestrained unfaithfulness. As his Parkinson's disease advanced over seven years culminating in terminal leukaemia, he became so dependent on her doglike devotion that there was a near reversal of roles. Their suicide with an overdose of barbiturates and alcohol on the night of 1 March 1983, in their London flat, was joint because she could not live without him. Both were adherents of Exit, the voluntary euthanasia group. Although his wives bore him no children he had a daughter.

[Arthur Koestler, *Spanish Testament*, 1937, *Arrow in the Blue*, 1952, and *The Invisible Writing*, 1954 (autobiographies); Iain Hamilton, *Koestler*, 1982; George Mikes, *Arthur Koestler*, 1983; Brian Inglis, *Arthur Koestler and Parapsychology*, 1984; Arthur and Cynthia Koestler, *Stranger on the Square*, 1984; Mamaine Koestler, *Living with Koestler*, 1985; Arthur Koestler's contribution in *The God That Failed* (ed. Richard H. Crossman), 1949; personal knowledge.]

WOODROW WYATT

published 1990

(1922–1985)

Poet, was born in Coventry 9 August 1922, the only son and younger child of Sydney Larkin, treasurer of Coventry, who was originally from Lichfield, and his wife, Eva Emily Day, of Epping. He was educated at King Henry VIII School, Coventry (1930–40), and St John's College, Oxford, where he obtained a first class degree in English language and literature in 1943. Bad eyesight caused him to be rejected for military service, and after leaving Oxford he took up library work, becoming in turn librarian of Wellington, Shropshire (December 1943–July 1946), assistant librarian, University of Leicester (September 1946–September 1950), sub-librarian of the Queen's University of Belfast (October 1950–March 1955), and finally taking charge of the Brynmor Jones Library, University of Hull, for the rest of his life.

Larkin, while always courteous and pleasant to meet, was solitary by nature; he never married and had no objection to his own company; it was said that the character in literature he most resembled was Badger in Kenneth Grahame's *The Wind in the Willows*. A bachelor, he found his substitute for family life in the devotion of a chosen circle of friends, who appreciated his dry wit and his capacity for deep though undemonstrative affection. His character was stable and his attitude to others considerate, so that having established a friendship he rarely abandoned it. Most of the friends he made in his twenties were still attached to him in his sixties, and his long-standing friend and confidante Monica Jones, to whom he dedicated his first major collection *The Less Deceived* (1956), was with him at the time of his death thirty years later.

Larkin was a highly professional librarian, notably conscientious in his work, and an active member of the Standing Conference of National and University Libraries. In the limited time this left him he did not undertake lecture tours, very rarely broadcast or gave interviews, and produced (compared with most authors) very little ancillary writing; though his lifelong interest in jazz led him to review jazz records for the *Daily Telegraph*, 1961–71. Some of the reviews were collected in *All What Jazz* (1970). In his forties he discovered a facility for book reviewing, of which he had previously done very little, and a collection of his reviews, *Required Writing* (1983) reveals him as an excellent critic; though perhaps 'reveal' is not the right word, for a decade earlier he had done much to influence contemporary attitudes to poetry with his majestic and in some quarters highly controversial *Oxford Book of Twentieth-Century English Verse* (1973), prepared with the utmost care during his tenure of a visiting fellowship at All Souls College in 1970–1. He spent much time working on behalf of his fellow writers, as a member of the literature panel of the Arts Council, helping to set up and then guide its National Manuscript Collection of Contemporary Writers in conjunction with the British Museum, and serving as chairman for several years of the Poetry Book Society. He was chairman of the Booker prize judges in 1977. To this Dictionary he contributed the notice of Barbara Pym.

Larkin's early ambition was to contribute both to the novel and to poetry. His first novel *Jill* (1946), published by a small press (which paid him with only a cup of tea) and not widely reviewed, did little to establish him, though its merits were recognized when it was reprinted in 1964 and 1975; but the second, *A Girl in Winter* (1947), attracted the attention of discerning readers, and the only reason he did not write more novels was that he found he could not, though he tried for some five years before giving up and working entirely in poetry, an art he loved but did not regard as necessarily 'higher' than fiction. The poet, he said, made a memorable statement *about* a thing, the novelist demonstrated that thing as it was in actuality. 'The poet tells you that old age is horrible, the novelist shows you a lot of old people in a room'. Why the second became impossible to him, and the first remained strikingly possible, it is useless to speculate.

As a poet, Larkin's early work, written when he was about twenty, already shows a fine ear and an unmistakable gift; but the breakthrough to an individual, and perfectly achieved, manner came some ten years later, in the poems collected in *The Less Deceived*. From that point on, his work did not change much in style or subject matter throughout the thirty years still to come, in which he produced two volumes, *The Whitsun Weddings* (1964) and *High Windows* (1974), plus a few poems still uncollected at his death. There were surprises, but then there had been surprises from the start, for Larkin's range was much more varied than a brief description of his work could hope to convey. He was restlessly alive to the possibilities of form, and never seemed constricted by tightly organized forms like the sonnet, the couplet, or the closely rhymed stanza, nor flaccid when he moulded his statement into free verse. It is instructive to pick out any one individual poem of Larkin's and then look through his work for another that seems to be saying much the same thing in much the same manner. As a rule one finds that there is no such animal. Most poets repeat themselves; he did not, and this should qualify the frequently repeated judgement that his output was 'small'.

Both in prose and verse, Larkin's themes were those of quotidian life: work, relationships, the earth and its seasons, routines, holidays, illnesses. He worked directly from life and felt no need of historical or mythological references, any more than he needed the cryptic verbal compressions that were mandatory in the 'modern' poetry of his youth. Where 'modern' poetry put its subtleties and complexities on the surface as a kind of protective matting, to keep the reader from getting into the poem too quickly, Larkin always provides a clear surface—one feels confident of knowing what the poem is 'about' at the very first reading—and plants his subtleties deep down, so that the reader becomes gradually aware of them with longer acquaintance. The poems thus grow in the mind until they become treasured possessions; this would perhaps account for the sudden explosion of feeling in the country at large when Larkin unexpectedly died at the Nuffield Hospital, Hull, 2 December 1985 (he had been known to be ill but thought to be recovering), and the extraordinary number who crowded into Westminster Abbey for his memorial service on St Valentine's Day 1986.

Philip Larkin was an honorary D.Litt. of the universities of Belfast, 1969; Leicester, 1970; Warwick, 1973; St Andrews, 1974; Sussex, 1974; and Oxford, 1984. He won the Queen's gold medal for poetry (1965), the Loines award for poetry (1974), the A. C. Benson silver medal, RSL (1975), the Shakespeare prize, FVS Foundation of Hamburg (1976), and the Coventry award of merit (1978). In 1983 *Required Writing* won the W. H. Smith literary award. In 1975 he was appointed CBE and a foreign honorary member of the American Academy of Arts and Sciences. St John's College made him an honorary fellow in 1973, and in 1985 he was made a Companion of Honour.

[Personal knowledge. See also Anthony Thwaite (ed.), *Larkin at Sixty*, 1982.]

JOHN WAIN

published 1990

LAWRENCE David Herbert

(1885–1930)

Poet, novelist, and essayist, born 11 September 1885 at Eastwood, near Nottingham, was the fourth child and third son of John Arthur Lawrence, a coal-miner, by his wife, Lydia Beardsall. As a child Lawrence had pneumonia, and became susceptible to consumption. Later in life he contracted the disease, and eventually died of it. Life as a collier was therefore out of the question. At the age of thirteen, however, he won a scholarship at Nottingham high school, and, after a short period as a clerk, went to the

British school at Eastwood as a pupil teacher. At the age of eighteen he entered Nottingham University College, matriculated, and two years later took his teacher's certificate, and was appointed to the Davidson Road School, Croydon. This education was made possible by the self-sacrifice of his mother, to whom he was passionately devoted; and it is possible that her example influenced his literary pursuits, since she had been a school teacher, had a taste for reading, and had written poetry. Mr. Ford Madox Hueffer, at that time editor of *The English Review*, encouraged Lawrence to write, published contributions by him, and introduced him to his first publisher. Lawrence was also assisted by the friendship and advice of Mr. Edward Garnett. After the publication of his novel, *The White Peacock*, in 1911, Lawrence resigned his post (receiving very honourable certificates from his superiors), and determined to live by his writing.

The circumstances of his early life made a deep impression on Lawrence's sensitive nature. The conditions of life in a mining community filled him with bitter hatred of industrialism and machinery, because he believed that men were degraded by them. Fortunately, he was able to escape to the open country on long walks, and the poet in him awoke as he responded to the rhythm of natural life with a passionate sensibility which is apparent throughout his writings. He felt the universe as a living thing, a mystic inspiration ('Not me, not me, but the wind which blows through me'), and his life might be explained as the passionate and fruitless quest for a society where men 'lived breast to breast with the cosmos'. His human sympathies were no less vivid, stimulated by contact with miners and farm people and by his profound filial love for his mother. From them Lawrence learned to value quality of feelings more than intellectual distinction, sensibility more than agreeable manners, vitality more than success.

After *The White Peacock*, Lawrence wrote *The Trespasser* (1912) and one of the most widely read of all his books, *Sons and Lovers* (1913), which appeared soon after his first book of poems, *Love Poems and Others* (1913). Meanwhile he had gone abroad for the first time, to Germany in May 1912. There he lived in a small cottage in the Isar valley; then he moved into Austria, and went on foot over the Brenner Pass to Lake Garda, where he stayed (at Gargnano) until April 1913. After a brief return to Germany and thence to England, he lived at Lerici, in Italy, from September 1913 until June 1914. In July 1914 he was married in England to Frieda von Richthofen, after her divorce from her first husband, Professor Ernest Weekley. She was the daughter of Baron von Richthofen, military governor of Metz. It is entirely erroneous to suppose that Lawrence either practised or countenanced 'free love'. He placed the sanctity of marriage in the reality of the human relationship and not in its social or legal aspect. For the poetry of this period, see his *Amores* (published 1916) and *Look, We Have Come Through* (published 1917).

Like most people who achieve anything, Lawrence had gambled on the future, by abandoning teaching and by assuming the responsibilities of marriage. It was not so imprudent as might be thought. In 1914 he had already won a certain reputation as an author, and was welcomed in London by distinguished members of his own profession as well as by people in society. And he was in no danger of being spoiled by success. He was a man of frugal, even austere habits, to which he owed the preservation of his always delicate health. To spare his lungs, he never smoked; he drank little, and lived on the plainest food, which he frequently prepared himself; all his tastes were simple. He was indifferent to material success and to all the usual rewards; but he did ardently desire a sympathetic response to his writings and was convinced that what he had to say was of value to mankind. Here he was defeated by the disarray and hectic psychology of the years of the European War.

During the early part of the War, Lawrence lived in or near London, and in December 1914 he published a volume of short stories, *The Prussian Officer*. The topical title was not his. Active service was impossible for a man so fragile, even if his views had allowed him to serve willingly; but though he could not be a conscientious objector, and was twice rejected for service, he held that the War was wholly evil. Something of this attitude is expressed in the latter part of *The Rainbow*, a novel which he published in 1915, though the war there denounced is the Boer War. This book, perhaps the most profound and poetical of Lawrence's novels, was the subject of a prosecution, and was condemned as indecent. The blow to Lawrence was far more staggering than is generally realized. It involved him in pecuniary difficulties which he did not escape for years; it marked him with a disgrace which he felt keenly, and believed to be undeserved; it was a severe rebuff to his idealistic beliefs. All this was mingled with acute suffering over the continuance of the War and its destructiveness.

Lawrence's chief desire now was to leave England, and he applied for passports for himself and his wife to America. Lack of money for the passage frustrated his project, and he retired to a small cottage at Zennor, Cornwall, where he worked on *Women in Love* (privately printed in New York, 1920; published in London, 1921). For reasons unknown to him, he and his wife (who was cousin to the well-known German airman, von Richthofen) were ordered to leave Zennor in October 1917, and not to enter any prohibited area. He went first to London; then lived in small cottages, at Hermitage near Newbury, and at Middleton-by-Wirksworth in Derbyshire. His sufferings during this period are related in two long chapters, headed 'The Nightmare', in his Australian novel, *Kangaroo* (1923).

Towards the end of 1919 Lawrence scraped together a few pounds and left England, to which he never returned except on very brief visits. While resentment at the treatment he had received may have had something to do with this, the chief motive of his exile was despair at the hostile attitude displayed in England towards himself and his writings. For the remainder of his life he was a wanderer, and only the main outline of his pilgrimage can or need be traced here. He went first to Florence (see the Florentine chapters in *Aaron's Rod*, 1922), then to Picinisco in the Abruzzi (see the latter part of *The Lost Girl*, 1920). He fled from the intense cold of the Abruzzi to Capri, liked and disliked it, and then settled for a time at Fontana Vecchia, near Taormina, where he remained until February 1922, except for short excursions. In *Sea and Sardinia* (1921) he produced the second of his remarkable travel books—the first was *Twilight in Italy* (1916), describing a walking tour through Switzerland to Italy—and accomplished the feat of making an interesting book out of the impressions and experiences of a few days.

The chronology of Lawrence's writings cannot at present be precisely determined; what is certain is that the order of composition does not correspond with the dates of publication. Among the books published at this time may be mentioned *Psychoanalysis and the Unconscious* (New York, 1921), *Fantasia of the Unconscious* (1922), and the short stories entitled *England, My England* (New York, 1922). Traces of his life in Sicily will be found in his beautifully written introduction to *Memoirs of the Foreign Legion* by 'M. M.' (London, 1924) and in the poems, *Birds, Beasts and Flowers* (1923). *Studies in Classical American Literature* was issued in America in the same year (1923).

Early in 1922 Lawrence left Sicily for America, by way of Ceylon and of Australia, where he stayed for a time. He reached San Francisco in September 1922, travelled in the United States and in Mexico, and settled on a small mountain ranch near Taos, New Mexico. Between December 1923 and March 1924 he paid a flying visit to England and the Continent, returning to Taos, from which he moved in October 1924 to Oaxaca, Mexico. Experiences there are recorded in his novel *The Plumed Serpent* (1926) and in *Mornings in Mexico* (1927). In 1925 he was seriously ill with malaria, and nearly died; this may have been the basis of his imaginative story, 'The Man Who Died', published in 1929 under the title *The Escaped Cock*. His illness compelled him to leave Mexico in October 1925. He lived at Spotorno, Italy, until March 1926, and then settled at the Villa Mirenda, Scandicci, near Florence. There he wrote *Lady Chatterley's Lover* (Florence, 1928) and remained until May 1928. No fewer than three manuscript versions of this novel are extant, showing the pains which he took over its composition; yet in many ways it is one of the least satisfactory of his books.

Lawrence's last years were agitated by the police prosecution of *Lady Chatterley's Lover*, the confiscation of the original manuscript of his poems, *Pansies* (1929), police action over an exhibition of his pictures held in London in 1928, and the suppression of the book containing facsimile reproductions of these paintings. It is an ironical fact that far more attention was drawn to Lawrence by these unfortunate scandals than by the excellence of his other and very varied productions; while his private edition of *Lady Chatterley's Lover* brought him more substantial earnings than any of his previous books. While living near Florence Lawrence had more than once been seriously ill and near death, yet he had found energy to visit Etruscan towns, and produced the unfinished *Sketches of Etruscan Places*, published posthumously. After leaving Florence, he lived at Bandol, near Toulon, and visited Spain. Early in 1930 his condition became so serious that he was moved to a clinic at Vence, where he died on 2 March 1930. His grave there is marked by a mosaic of the risen phoenix, which he had long before chosen as his emblem. His literary activity continued to the very end, and an unfinished poem was written only a few days before he died. Among the posthumous books the most important are: the *Letters* (1932); *Apocalypse* (Florence, 1931), a statement of his attitude to life; and *Last Poems* (Florence, 1932), which contains, among pieces of slighter interest, the poignant record of his feelings and thoughts as he faced the reality and certainty of death. His spiritual loneliness was complete.

Since his death Lawrence's reputation has grown with astonishing swiftness, and, though opinion is far from unanimous, he is now widely recognized in many countries as one of the most original and gifted English writers of his age. The misunderstanding which original genius often meets with from contemporaries is gradually being cleared away, and his reputation cannot but gain by closer and more serious study of his books.

[*Letters of D. H. Lawrence*, edited by Aldous Huxley, with photographs, 1932; Ada Lawrence (sister), *Young Lorenzo*, with photographs, 1932; *Bibliography of the Writings of D. H. Lawrence*, Philadelphia, 1925; private information; personal knowledge.]

R. ALDINGTON

published 1937

LEAVIS Frank Raymond
(1895–1978)

Literary critic, editor, teacher, and educationist, was born 14 July 1895 in Cambridge, the second child of three and elder son of Harry Leavis, who sold pianos and musical instruments, and his wife, Kate Sarah Moore. Except for the years of his service in World War I, Leavis lived in Cambridge throughout his life. His boyhood home was affectionate and cultivated, with much music and with readings from Shakespeare and Dickens. Educated at the Perse School, he gained a history scholarship to Emmanuel College, switching to the English tripos for his part ii in which he obtained a first class in 1921. Between school and university, however, lay the horrifying 'great hiatus' (as he later described it) of his years on the western front, serving with the Friends' Ambulance Unit as a stretcher-bearer; and this experience permanently impaired his digestion and left him with insomnia. It was partly in order to exhaust himself into sleep that he took up long-distance running; he continued to run till he was an old man and his academic career was to reveal a good deal of the wiry, relentless tenacity of the long-distance runner.

As an undergraduate, and later while researching for his doctorate (which he received in 1924) into the relationship of journalism to literature, he was a good deal influenced by I. A. Richards and Mansfield Forbes. The latter, more than anyone else, had brought 'Cambridge English' into being and Leavis retained the strongest admiration for him. In 1927 he was appointed a probationary faculty lecturer in English; he was already known for having stimulated students to take an interest in writers like James Joyce, T. S. Eliot, and D. H. Lawrence, none of them acceptable at that time in academic circles. His first major book, *New Bearings in English Poetry* (1932), was to be a similar revaluation of poetry in the modern world, in which he argued that G. M. Hopkins, W. B. Yeats, Eliot, and Ezra Pound were the most significant and creative writers. Reflecting on this period forty years later, he remarked that 'We didn't need Nietzsche to tell us to live dangerously; there is no other way of living', and in 1931 both his probationary lectureship and his fellowship at Emmanuel were terminated. However, he declined to leave Cambridge, and the offer of the new directorship of studies in English at Downing College (1932) provided him with a modest livelihood. He was not appointed to a lectureship in the English faculty until 1936 (when he was over forty) and then only part-time; not until 1954 was he invited to join the English faculty board, and only in 1959, at the age of sixty-four, was he appointed reader. He was to retain for the rest of his life, even when success and wide recognition had come to him, including appointment as CH in 1978, an embittered sense of having been the victim of 'obloquy, slander and worldly disadvantage'. Undoubtedly this sharpened his formidable wit and led him into uncompromising animosities, although with students and friends he was a gentle person of great courtesy, humour, and charm.

In 1929 Leavis married Queenie Dorothy Roth (1906–1981). She was the daughter of Morris Roth, master draper and hosier, and his wife, Jenny Davis. Educated at the Latymer School, she went as Carlisle scholar to Girton College, Cambridge, and took first class honours in the English tripos in 1928. An outstanding research student, she was now working for her Ph.D. (1932) on the theme that was to be published in the same year as *Fiction and the Reading Public*. This 'socio-literary study', in Leavis's own words, was 'a wholly original kind of research ... into the old working-class culture of which the processes of civilization were eliminating the traces', and it extended historically, and with great verve, the central theme of Leavis's *Mass Civilization and Minority Culture* (1930). In that year Queenie Leavis became the first woman to be awarded the Amy Mary Preston Reid scholarship by the university. In 1933, they and Denys Thompson, a schoolmaster, wrote *Culture and Environment* and this early critique of mass culture, which offered itself as an 'education against the environment', had a seminal influence on teachers and students. This concern with what Leavis later castigated as 'the hubris of a technologico-positivist or Benthamite enlightenment', allied to his own profound anti-reductionism, made him a strong anti-Marxist. He made this the theme of such noted forays as his calculatedly destructive dismissal of C. P. (later Lord) Snow in his Richmond lecture of 1962, and of the many closely and trenchantly argued essays which he gathered together in *For Continuity* (1933) and in *Nor Shall My Sword* (1972), with its revealing sub-title 'Pluralism, Compassion and Social Hope'. But he also pursued this theme in much of his specifically literary criticism, having coined the concept that it is 'the great novelists [who] give us our social history'; thus his first essay on Dickens, in 1948, was on *Hard Times*, that bitter denunciation of an inhuman utilitarianism, to be followed by the full-scale study, *Dickens the Novelist* (1970), which he and his wife wrote jointly and which was the peak of their work as literary critics. And the same preoccupation formed a major strand in his studies of George Eliot (1945 and 1946) and of D. H. Lawrence (1930, 1955, 1976), who became for Leavis the major, life-enhancing writer of this century.

Leavis's twenty or so books were nearly all created out of essays originally written for *Scrutiny*. It was this quarterly, which he and his wife helped to launch in 1932 and which they kept in being for twenty-one

years, which eventually established their reputation. It was an achievement of singular timeliness and total devotion. It provided a constant, even
an unremitting, incentive to write; and it became, in Leavis's mind, a
vitalizing 'centre' of standards, of literary studies and discussions. *Scrutiny*
gained a considerable reputation for its critical rigour; for its detailed
textual 'revaluations' of a very wide range of writers and themes; for its
pioneering analyses of 'novels as dramatic poems', particularly Leavis's
essays on George Eliot, Henry James, and Joseph Conrad which made up
the major part of his influential book, *The Great Tradition* (1948); and for its
comparable articles on music, education, mass society, and the cultural
establishment. It has been said that *Scrutiny* educated a generation of
future teachers of English teachers. But finally in 1953 the Leavises gave up
the struggle. It had become impossible to keep together a team of regular
contributors, and above all Queenie Leavis, who had carried the sub-
editorial burden, had been fighting for very many years a battle against
cancer. Her many articles, especially the series, 'A Critical Theory of Jane
Austen's Writings' (1941–2), and her penetrating and high-spirited reviewing had been a distinctive feature of *Scrutiny*. The total run of *Scrutiny*
was republished in 1963 by the Cambridge University Press. If *Scrutiny* had
been one source of education, the Downing English school was a second.
Until his retirement in 1962, Downing was the centre of Leavis's teaching.
He was a compelling and devoted teacher: genial, often racy, attentive to
individual students, possessing an immediate command of a vast body of
literature in many languages, and with a marvellous sensitivity for the
distinctive movement and texture of a passage of poetry or prose. And his
reading of poetry, in his oddly nasal, high-pitched voice, was a triumph of
sincerity and meaning. He dedicated *Revaluation* (1936), the book in which
he established the non-Spenserian–Miltonic–Tennysonian 'tradition and
development in English poetry' as he saw it, to 'those with whom I have
discussed literature as a "teacher": if I have learned anything about the
methods of profitable discussion, I have learned it in collaboration with
them'.

In 1962, at the age of sixty-seven, Leavis retired from his university
readership and was appointed to honorary fellowship at Downing, which
however he resigned in 1964 because he felt the college was turning its
back on the English policies he had established. This rupture preoccupied
him emotionally till the end of his life. However, he continued teaching for
many more years. In 1964 he was Chichele lecturer at Oxford; in 1965 he
became visiting (later honorary visiting) professor at the University of
York; in 1968 he and his wife made their first lecturing visit to the USA, out
of which came *Lectures in America* (1969). In 1967 he delivered the Clark
lectures at Cambridge on the theme *English Literature in our Time and the*

University (published in 1969) in which he took up the major preoccupation of an earlier book, *Education and the University* (1943): the university's task is to be 'a focus of humane consciousness, a centre where . . . intelligence, bringing to bear a mature sense of values, should apply itself to the problems of civilization': this was to be achieved pre-eminently through an English school which 'trains, in a way no other discipline can, intelligence and sensibility together'. For Leavis, to read seriously is to discriminate, and in the last resort such judgements, closely linked to the words on the page, are liable to be moral judgements. It was in these exacting terms that he understood and practised the discipline of literary criticism. Finally, in 1969 he was visiting professor at the University of Wales, and in 1970 Churchill visiting professor at Bristol University.

Leavis's lectures during these years, if often still laced with polemic, were intricately argued. His style remained sinewy, urgent, authoritative, as he grappled with the central concepts that had formed the burden of his life's thinking: 'life is growth and growth change' and 'the nature of livingness in human life is manifest in language, [which] embodies values, constatations, distinctions, promptings, recognitions of potentiality'. The titles of his last books, during what proved an astonishingly productive decade, testified to his indestructible sense of urgency and hope: *Nor Shall My Sword* (1972), *The Living Principle* (1975), and *Thought, Words and Creativity* (1976).

Leavis died in Cambridge 14 April 1978. Now a familiar and influential figure, he had been awarded honorary doctorates at Leeds, York, Queen's University (Belfast), Delhi, and Aberdeen. Yet he would probably not have found it easy to accept the tributes and the expressions of admiration that quickly proliferated in obituaries, articles, and books. *The Times* (18 April 1978) best summed up the man in words at once judicious and intimate: 'A certain Spartan frugality and fine intensity of living marked him with a mixture of vitality and asceticism . . . above all the flame-like nimbleness of his speech and glance compelled attention. . . . His influence extended far beyond the boundaries of the subjects to which he confined himself.'

In her remaining years, Queenie Leavis lectured widely and edited and wrote with energy on the Brontës, George Eliot, and Herman Melville. Her last lecture, for the Cheltenham Festival of 1980, was on 'The Englishness of the English Novel', and it was of a remarkable scope and sympathy. She died in Cambridge 17 March 1981, being survived by their two sons and a daughter. F. R. and Q. D. Leavis dedicated their book *Dickens the Novelist* to each other, as proof 'of forty years and more of . . . devotion to the fostering of that true respect for creative writing, creative minds and . . . the English tradition, without which literary criticism can have no validity and no life'.

[D. F. McKenzie and M.-P. Allum, *F. R. Leavis: A Check-List 1924–1964*, 1966; William Baker, 'F. R. Leavis, 1965–1979, and Q. D. Leavis, 1922–1979: A Bibliography of writings By and About Them', in *Bulletin of Bibliography*, vol. 37, iv, 1980; *The Times*, 18 April 1978; Ronald Hayman, *Leavis*, 1976; William Walsh, *F. R. Leavis*, 1980; Denys Thompson (ed.), *The Leavises*, 1984; private information; personal knowledge.]

BORIS FORD

published 1986

LLOYD Richard Dafydd Vivian Llewellyn

(1906–1983)

Novelist and dramatist under the name of Richard Llewellyn, was born between 8 and 10 December 1906 at St David's, Pembrokeshire, the son of William Llewellyn Lloyd, hotelier, and Sarah Anne. His birth was not registered.

Llewellyn's scattered autobiographical sketches are not always consistent, but it is clear that his father's peripatetic career led to frequent changes of school in south Wales, London, and elsewhere. At sixteen he entered the hotel trade, briefly as a dishwasher in Claridge's and then in Italy. In 1926 he enlisted in the army and served in India and Hong Kong, returning to Britain in 1931 to a period of near destitution before being taken on as a film reporter by *Cinema Express* and cobbling together a career as bit-player, assistant director, production manager, and scriptwriter. A play, 'Poison Pen', had a successful run in London in 1937 and this emboldened him to take time off to complete his first novel, of which a draft had been written during his army days in India. The publication in October 1939 of *How Green was my Valley* (originally entitled 'Slag') brought him instant celebrity and an assured income. The twenty-one translations include versions in Hindi, Japanese, and Turkish as well as two in German. The setting was his paternal grandfather's village of Gilfach Goch and, though Llewellyn later referred somewhat vaguely to a period underground and to an escape from a serious roof fall, it is safer to conclude that the novel was based on stories he had picked up there on holiday. The simple virtues of an idealized community, buttressed by the stereotypes of imagined Welshness, are portrayed against the stresses of industrialization, and the novel created an indelible mythology of the mining valleys, reinforced by the 1941 film directed by John Ford.

Llewellyn's subsequent novels are notable for their variety of backgrounds. *None but the Lonely Heart* (1943, expanded in 1970) grew from his difficult years in London in the early 1930s; *A Few Flowers for Shiner* (1950) was set in Italy, visited again as a captain in the Welsh Guards between 1941 and 1946. He soon established a pattern of going to live in a country in which he would then place a novel: Kenya and the culture of the Masai in *A Man in a Mirror* (1964); Israel, which he much admired, for *Bride of Israel, my Love* (1973) and *A Hill of Many Dreams* (1974). Other countries in which he lived included France, India, Switzerland, Brazil, Chile, Paraguay, Uruguay, Argentina, and Ireland.

Two novels of life among the Welsh of Patagonia, *Up, Into the Singing Mountain* (1963) and *Down where the Moon is Small* (1966) followed the fortunes of Huw Morgan from *How Green*. Then a visit to Wales in 1973 kindled a patriotic fervour that produced *Green, Green My Valley Now* (1975), involving Huw Morgan, somewhat implausibly, on the fringes of revolutionary activity. He wrote several other novels, bringing the total to twenty-three with four stage plays.

Llewellyn's novels are rich in character and incident, with high emotional impact and ingenious stylistic devices creating atmosphere and suggesting national diversity. There is much background detail, not all of it convincing, and he was not slow to supplement observation with copious injections from his imagination. If he did, indeed, speak eight languages the novels reveal a tenuous enough grasp—including his boyhood Welsh. The fictions are often garish and artificial and his apparent grasp of contemporary cultural clashes is frequently coloured by sentiment. Yet he created in *How Green was my Valley* a picture or a dream that appeared to bring the values and culture of a whole community to new life. In person he was military with a dash of Hollywood, his manner somewhat brusque, his opinions generally illiberal or naïve. He was profoundly indifferent to most contemporary literature.

He married in 1952 Nona Theresa Sonsteby, of Chicago. This marriage was dissolved in 1968, and in 1974 he married a publisher's editor from New York, Susan Frances, daughter of Heinrich Heimann, patent attorney and mechanical engineer. Llewellyn died of a heart attack in Dublin 30 November 1983.

[Stanley J. Kunitz (ed.), *Twentieth Century Authors*, 1950; Alan Road, *Observer* colour supplement, 20 April 1975; Mick Felton in *British Novelists 1930–59* (ed. Bernard Oldsey), 1983 = *Dictionary of Literary Biography*, vol. xv; *The Times*, 1 December 1983; private information.]

GLYN TEGAI HUGHES

published 1990

Clarence Malcolm

(1909–1957)

Author, was born at Liscard, Cheshire, 28 July 1909, the youngest son of Arthur Osborne Lowry, cotton broker, by his wife, Evelyn Boden, both Methodist teetotallers.

He was educated at Caldicote preparatory school, Hitchin, and the Leys School, Cambridge. He won the Junior Public Schools Golf Championship, played the ukelele, wrote jazz music and poems. Before going up to St. Catharine's College, Cambridge, he persuaded his father to send him to sea as 'the quickest way out of Liverpool'. A voyage to the China Seas (May–October 1927) provided material for his first novel *Ultramarine*. There followed a year at the English School in Bonn and a visit to the poet Conrad Aiken in Cambridge, Massachusetts, before he went to St. Catharine's. Aiken and Nordahl Grieg the novelist whom he visited in Norway as an undergraduate became his lifelong literary fathers. He left Cambridge in 1932 with an undistinguished third class in the English tripos and a fabulous reputation as a writer and drinker of enormous capacity.

Recognizing both, his father throughout his lifetime made an allowance, generous enough, he hoped, to allow him to write and insufficient for him to drink himself to death.

In 1933, after many rewritings and a characteristic loss of the manuscript, Lowry published *Ultramarine*, distinguished from other 'before the mast' novels by its subjectivity and symbolic undertones.

In December 1933 Lowry married, in Paris, a young New York writer, Jan Gabrial, whom Aiken had introduced in the hope that she would solve Lowry's alcoholic problem. The marriage was turbulent and in 1935 Lowry went to New York ahead of her, seeking new material for his autobiographical myth. After an alcoholic fugue, he was given brief treatment in Bellevue Hospital. Out of this experience he wrote *Lunar Caustic*, a novella frequently revised, but only posthumously published: in *Paris Review* (No. 29) in 1963 and in book form in 1968.

Joined by Jan, Lowry drifted first to Los Angeles, then to Mexico, where they rented a villa in Cuernavaca in 1936. Attracted by the Mexican awareness of death, Lowry wrote a short story about the roadside death of an Indian. This became the central episode of *Under the Volcano*. But before this was published much had to happen.

After a period of sobriety, Lowry started drinking again. When his wife left him and went to Los Angeles in December 1937 he plunged into the alcoholic abyss, seeking there his literary subject. He was gaoled in Oaxaca and in July 1938 deported. He followed Jan to Los Angeles but she refused to see him and demanded a divorce. He met Margerie Bonner, another American aspirant writer, and after his divorce married her in December 1940 in Canada where he lived, with intermissions, until 1954.

Working for the most part in a seashore shack at Dollarton, British Columbia, Lowry wrote and rewrote *Under the Volcano*, descriptive of the Day of the Dead in Mexico, 1938, the last day in the life of the drunken consul Geoffrey Firmin and his wife Yvonne. Lowry was aided by Margerie, a simple life, and wartime scarcity of hard liquor and by June 1945 the fourth and final version was finished and dispatched.

In the summer of 1944 the Dollarton shack burnt down and the Lowrys tried to rebuild it themselves. It was not completed by the winter of 1945 and in December Lowry took his second wife to Mexico to show her places and people described in *Under the Volcano*, hoping incidentally to find material for a new novel. Although their visit was cut short by the Mexican authorities, he found material for two novels, never finished. *Dark as the Grave Wherein my Friend is Laid*, edited by Professor Douglas Day and Margerie Bonner Lowry from Lowry's notes and drafts, appeared in 1968. *La Mordida* awaited similar editing.

While in Mexico in 1946 Lowry learnt of the acceptance of *Under the Volcano* by Reynal and Hitchcock in the United States and of the interest of Jonathan Cape provided the book was drastically revised. In rebuttal of Cape's arguments, Lowry wrote an astonishing 15,000-word letter explaining the plan and purpose of his masterpiece 'so designed, counterdesigned and interwelded that it could be read an indefinite number of times and still not have yielded all its meanings or its drama or its poetry'. No author has ever written so brilliant a defence and exposition of his work. The achievement is the more astonishing since Lowry was drinking heavily throughout and at one point attempted suicide.

A work of genius, *Under the Volcano* has glaring faults. Lowry partially distributed elements of his personality and experience among the main male characters, but the wife Yvonne begins as Jan Gabrial and ends as Margerie Bonner without ever attaining substance. Its success after publication in 1947 was immediate in the United States and Canada, not long delayed in France, but slower in Great Britain. American students of Eng. Lit. found it a treasury of Ph.D. theses, as rich in literary allusions and cross-references as *Ulysses*, if not *Finnegans Wake*. Lovers of literature cherish it for the robustness of its humour, the beauty of its description, the resonance of its imagery, the intricacy of its mosaic pattern, the preservation of sanity within insanity, and the Faustian sense of the spiritual damnation in attempting through alcohol to take a short cut to mystical illumination.

Lowry intended all his work to be part of a vast corpus called *The Voyage That Never Ends*, of which *Under the Volcano* was the central novel. Perhaps for that reason the work on the rest never ended in the lifetime which was cut short, after several attempted suicides, by his death 'by misadventure', 27 June 1957, at Ripe, Sussex, where he and his wife had been living since 1955. *Hear Us O Lord From Heaven Thy Dwelling Place*, a collection of short stories and occasional pieces (1962), *Selected Poems* (1962), *Lunar Caustic*, and *Dark as the Grave*, like the undergraduate novel *Ultramarine*, are all unmistakably by the author of *Under the Volcano*. But though they have individual passages of beauty, wit, power, and strangeness, their main importance is that they provide the foothills by which the more easily to scale the eminence of Lowry's masterpiece. Leaving aside the as yet unpublished *La Mordida*, the most important aid to *Under the Volcano* (apart from the letter to Cape printed in *The Selected Letters*, 1967), is *Dark as the Grave* which rehearses, though with deliberate changes of fact, the events which went towards the composition of *Under the Volcano*. The second Mexican excursion was a deliberate reliving of the first, in the conscious hope of finding a happier end and the unconscious desire by venturing once more into Hell to discover a self-fulfilment (or self-annihilation) which had not been found in the Paradise of Dollarton.

[*The Selected Letters of Malcolm Lowry*, ed. Harvey Breit and Margerie Bonner Lowry, 1967; 'Portrait of Malcolm Lowry', especially Professor Douglas Day, B.B.C. Third Programme, 1967; Conrad Knickerbocker, 'Malcolm Lowry in England', *Paris Review*, No. 38, 1966 (an untrustworthy source); personal knowledge.]

ARTHUR CALDER-MARSHALL

published 1971

LUBBOCK Percy

(1879–1965)

Author, fourth son of Frederic Lubbock, merchant banker, and his wife, Catherine, daughter of John Gurney, of Earlham Hall, Norfolk, was born in London 4 June 1879. He was the grandson of Sir J. W. Lubbock and nephew of Sir John Lubbock (later first Baron Avebury). He was educated at Eton, in the house of A. C. Benson, and as a scholar at King's College, Cambridge. In 1901 he was placed in the first class of the classical tripos. As an undergraduate he eschewed games but the love of birds and flowers and rural landscape, which remained with him throughout life, prompted long expeditions into the East Anglian countryside.

In 1906 he resigned from an uncongenial post in the Board of Education after his election as Pepys librarian at Magdalene College, Cambridge, on the recommendation of A. C. Benson, then a fellow. For two years he enjoyed a semi-academic life with rooms in college, but in 1908 he resigned in order to devote himself entirely to literature and writing. (He had already published, in 1906, *Elizabeth Barrett Browning in her Letters*.) One fruit of his term as librarian was the publication, in 1909, of *Samuel Pepys*, which, although to some extent superseded by later more elaborate studies, deserves to hold its place in Pepysian biography as a concise and clearly written introduction to the *Diary*.

Between 1908 and 1914 Lubbock contributed regularly to *The Times Literary Supplement*, writing several main articles which he was urged in vain to republish as a volume. It was during this period that he first met Henry James, the author who was to have so strong an influence on Lubbock's concept of literature and indeed on his literary style. James died in 1916, and in the following year Lubbock saw through the press and wrote a short general preface for three of James's unfinished works—*The Ivory Tower, The Sense of the Past*, and *The Middle Years*. In 1920 he edited, in two volumes, a selection of James's *Letters*; and he contributed the notice of James to this Dictionary.

The Craft of Fiction, Lubbock's main critical work, was first published in 1921 and has been many times reprinted, both in this country and abroad. (A new edition appeared a few years before his death.) The author confined his theme to a consideration of the technical aspect of the novel: 'how it is made is the only question I shall ask'. He fulfilled his object by a series of analyses, or rather dissections, of certain novels (including those by Tolstoy, Flaubert, Henry James, and Thackeray), setting forth his views and theories in straightforward terms, free from jargon. This critical study of the form and design of the novel has proved of enduring value not only for its insight and freshness of outlook but, incidentally, as pointing the way to an appreciation of the art of reading.

Earlham, Lubbock's best-known work, was first published in October 1922. It describes in detail the background of a late Victorian childhood spent during the holidays in an old Norfolk house which for generations had been the home of the Gurneys. Each room of the house, the garden and beyond, members of the family, past and present, all are affectionately described in tranquil and measured prose. The book appeared at a time when readers could at least put behind them, or at least temporarily forget, the horrors of war, and so lose themselves in these memories of a serene vanished world. It at once became something of a bestseller.

In 1923 Lubbock showed another facet of his craft as writer. *Roman Pictures* is a social comedy, seen through the mind of a young English tourist in Rome at the turn of the century. Naïve the narrator may appear to be, but he observes his characters—natives, visitors, and exiles—with an ironical yet good-humoured detachment which impliedly points the contrast between them and the splendour of the architectural background to which they are largely indifferent.

Lubbock's only novel, *The Region Cloud*, appeared in 1925. It attracted little attention, perhaps justifiably, for the underlying theme, the affectation of genius, is too concentrated, and there is throughout a certain diffuseness of thought and expression. The central character, Channon, was inspired by a chance encounter Lubbock had in Toledo, in 1906, with (Sir) Hubert von Herkomer, the Victorian painter.

In *Shades of Eton* (1929) Lubbock limited his survey to the time he was there during the 1890s, a studious imaginative boy who did not quite fit into the conventional pattern of the period. It gave scope to his skill in portraying character, particularly of those masters who, weathered by Eton, had taken the rank of monuments by the Gothic richness of their mouldings. Of these may be instanced Frank Tarver, the handsome and patriarchal French master, whose teaching, with a splendid disregard of the phrases one may require at Boulogne, recalled 'the spacious days of the Grand Tour, of the English gentleman rolling across the Continent in his travelling chaise'.

Lubbock on several occasions published 'sketches from memory' of his friends: of *George Calderon*, for example, in 1921, and of *Mary Cholmondeley* (1928), whose 'outspoken' novels, exposing the frailties of clergy and county, were once on the shelves of many country-house libraries. Mention, too, should be made of his selection (1926) from a vast quarry of notebooks, of the *Diary* kept between 1897 and 1925 by A. C. Benson, with an introduction and connecting narrative of Benson's life. Finally, in 1947 was published what proved to be his last work, *Portrait of Edith Wharton*, American writer and discerning admirer of Henry James.

In 1926 Lubbock married Lady Sybil Marjorie Scott (died 1943), younger daughter of the fifth Earl of Desart, widow of W. C. Cutting of New York and of Geoffrey Scott, and mother of the author, Iris Origo. They lived in Italy, first in the Villa Medici in Fiesole, then in a house, Gli Scafari, designed for them at Lerici on the Gulf of Spezia.

In appearance Lubbock was tall and in later years bulky. His sight had been failing for some time and at the end he was almost totally blind.

He was not unhappy, living amid beautiful surroundings, solaced by the music that most delighted him, that of Wagner, Brahms, Schubert, enjoying and contributing to good conversation, and read to by young friends. He died at Lerici 2 August 1965.

(Sir) Edmund Gosse, writing in 1923, regarded Lubbock as one of the best prose writers of his time. His works, although relatively few, were diverse, and each was a careful and sincere piece of prose, attuned to its purpose, quiet, efficient, and well-mannered. His literary style could be complex, even involved, but it was never affected or obscure. Before the end of his life he had the satisfaction of knowing that there was a revival of his reputation, especially as a critic, a recognition reflected in his appointment, in 1952, to CBE.

[*The Times*, 3 August 1965; private information.]

D. PEPYS-WHITELEY

published 1981

MACHEN Arthur Llewelyn Jones-

(1863–1947)

Author and essayist, was born 3 March 1863 in Caerleon-on-Usk, Monmouthshire, the only child of the Revd John Edward Jones, rector of Llanddewi Fach, and his wife Janet Robina Machen, whose maiden name was adopted by the family in order to please her Scottish relations. He was educated at Hereford Cathedral School. The splendours of the landscape surrounding Llanddewi rectory, his boyhood home near Caerleon, and his passion for romantic literature inspired him to begin writing. *Eleusinia* (1881), a mystical poem, was his début in print. The mystery and wonder it expressed characterized all his later creations.

His father's penury prevented Machen attending university, and his attempt to pursue a medical career proved short-lived when he failed the preliminary examination of the Royal College of Surgeons in 1880. In 1881 he moved to London in an unsuccessful endeavour to enter journalism. Living in poverty, he wrote while variously employed as a tutor, publishers' clerk, and cataloguer of occult books. His early works included *The Anatomy of Tobacco* (1884), translations of *The Heptameron* (1886) and Casanova's *Memoirs* (1894), and *The Chronicle of Clemendy* (1888).

In the next decade he composed his most notable work. *The Great God Pan* (1894) and *The Three Impostors* (1895), his early ventures into the macabre, appeared in the Bodley Head's 'Keynotes' series. *The Hill of*

Dreams, one of the period's most remarkable and decadent novels, was completed in 1897 but remained unpublished for ten years.

After his wife's death in 1899 Machen briefly sought solace in the occult fraternity, the Order of the Golden Dawn, but ultimately found its teachings sterile. He joined the Shakespeare repertory company of (Sir) Frank Benson as an actor in 1901, and subsequently toured with several theatrical companies. He resumed writing between stage engagements. His literary theories were trenchantly expressed in *Hieroglyphics* (1902), and his supernatural tales collected in *The House of Souls* (1906).

From 1910 to 1921 Machen worked as a reporter for the *Evening News*. Although he detested journalism his Johnsonian manner and compelling character established him as one of Fleet Street's most charismatic figures. The *Evening News* carried several of his wonder stories, and the appearance in September 1914 of his wartime fantasy 'The Bowmen' brought him to public attention. The tale of phantom archers from Agincourt aiding British troops was widely accepted as factual, and by the summer of 1915 the legend of the 'Angels of Mons' had swept the country.

In the 1920s, after the British literary establishment had neglected him for forty years, Machen attracted a coterie of admirers in the United States. Writers such as Vincent Starrett and Carl Van Vechten, extolling the lyrical power of his prose, proclaimed him a mystagogue of the secrets of life and art in the tradition of Edgar Allan Poe and Nathaniel Hawthorne. Machen's reminiscences, *Far Off Things* (1922) and *Things Near and Far* (1923), movingly recaptured his youth in Monmouthshire and his struggles as a writer during the *fin de siècle*, and revealed the depth of his dedication to literature.

By the end of the 1920s, as the vogue for his books diminished, Machen encountered renewed financial hardship. He and his family moved to Amersham, Buckinghamshire, where he produced essays, reviews, innumerable letters, and a final crop of stories. In old age he maintained a relish for life in defiance of tribulations and failing health, and his geniality and goodness made him the centre of a circle of faithful friends and admirers.

In 1887 he married Amelia, daughter of Frederick Metcalfe Hogg, gentleman, of Worthing, Sussex. She died of cancer in 1899, after several years of illness. In 1903 he married Dorothie Purefoy Hudleston, one of the actresses in Benson's company, the daughter of Colonel Josiah Hudleston, formerly of the Indian Army. They had one son and one daughter. Machen died in St Joseph's Nursing Home, Beaconsfield, Buckinghamshire, 15 December 1947.

[Aidan Reynolds and William Charlton, *Arthur Machen*, 1963; Wesley D. Sweetser, *Arthur Machen*, 1964.]

ROGER DOBSON

published 1993

MACKINTOSH Elizabeth

(1896–1952)

Author and dramatist under the pseudonyms of 'Josephine Tey' and 'Gordon Daviot', was born in Inverness 25 July 1896, the eldest of the three daughters (there were no sons) of Colin Mackintosh, fruiterer, and his wife Josephine Horne. She was educated at Inverness Royal Academy and the Anstey Physical Training College in Erdington, Birmingham (her thriller, *Miss Pym Disposes*, 1946, was to be set in such a college). She taught briefly in schools in Liverpool, Oban, and Eastbourne, and for a longer period in Tunbridge Wells, but eventually returned to Inverness to keep house for her invalid father, whom she outlived by only two years.

Her first detective novel, *The Man in the Queue*, a highly accomplished piece of work for a novice hand, was published in 1929 under the pseudonym of Gordon Daviot—the name by which she preferred to be known, in both public and private—though for her seven other works in this genre she took the name Josephine Tey. She was to refer to them wryly as her 'yearly knitting', but they are classics of their kind, deftly constructed with strong characterization and a meticulous prose style. Five of them feature as their main character Inspector Alan Grant, a gentleman police officer in the style often favoured by women writers, 'not coarse like a bobby' and with independent means 'to smooth and embroider life'. It is Grant who, in her most original story, *The Daughter of Time* (1951), satisfies himself by reading and reason while immobilized in hospital that the infamous Richard III of Shakespeare, school history books, and folk memory is a Tudor fabrication. Her case for the defence is notably restrained, unlike her treatment of the same subject in *Dickon*, a play published posthumously in 1953. *The Franchise Affair* (1948), a story of two women wrongly accused of kidnapping, and based on an eighteenth-century *cause célèbre*, was another popular work, later to be made into a film.

Her plays, while well crafted and with shrewdly observed characters, lack the pace and tension of her thrillers. Her most successful was *Richard of Bordeaux*, inspired, it was said, by seeing (Sir) John Gielgud in *Richard II*. First performed in 1932, it was enthusiastically received and ran for a year. Later plays fell below this promise. *The Laughing Woman* (1934), about the sculptor Henri Gaudier, was a failure. It was followed in the same year by the rather more successful *Queen of Scots*. But *The Stars Bow Down*, with its biblical theme of Joseph and his brethren, though published in 1939 had to wait ten years before it was performed at the Malvern festival. *The Little Dry Thorn*, another biblical play based on the story of Abraham and Sarah, published posthumously in *Plays* (1953), received its first public perform-ance in Glasgow in 1946.

In these and her historical plays the author made a point of making her characters speak in modern idiom. 'They have some of the romantic glamour of the old historical drama, without the pseudo-period dialogue and fustian sentiment,' said John Gielgud in his preface, speaking of her also as an elusive character, deeply reserved, 'proud without being ar-rogant, and obstinate, though not conceited'. During the last year of her life, when she knew herself to be mortally ill, she resolutely avoided seeing anyone she knew. Her last work, *The Privateer* (1952), was a romantic novel based on the life of the buccaneer Henry Morgan. Among her other works are a number of short plays written for broadcasting and a biography, *Claverhouse* (1937). Her main interests were the cinema and horse-racing; she drew upon her knowledge of the latter in *Brat Farrar* (1949), a novel featuring a false claimant to an estate. She died in Streatham, London, 13 February 1952.

[*The Times*, 15 February 1952; *Inverness Courier*, 15 February 1952; private in-formation.]

GILLIAN AVERY

published 1993

MACNEICE (Frederick) Louis

(1907–1963)

Writer, was born in Belfast 12 September 1907, the youngest of three children of the Revd John Frederick MacNeice, then rector of Holy Trinity, Belfast, by his wife, Elizabeth Margaret, daughter of Martin Clesham, of Galway. Originally a Galway man, Louis MacNeice's father was from 1908 to 1931 rector of Carrickfergus; in those early years his mother was often ill, his father preoccupied and remote: 'My mother was comfort and my father was somewhat alarm.' His only brother, William, was a mongol and MacNeice was much dependent for company on his sister, Caroline Elizabeth, who was later to marry (Sir) John Nicholson, third baronet. The death of their mother in 1914 was a severe blow, which threw a sombre shadow over MacNeice's adult recollections of childhood, imparting to much of his poetry a poignant sense of the impermanence of men and things. The children were looked after by a cook and a governess until 1917, when their father brought home a new wife, Georgina Beatrice, second daughter of Thomas Greer, of Sea Park, county Antrim, and Carrickfergus; she brought 'much comfort and benevolence' into their lives. MacNeice's father became bishop of Cashel and Waterford in 1931, bishop of Down and Connor and Dromore in 1935, and died in 1942. In later life MacNeice came to appreciate him, as well as the family background of Galway, Dublin, and Connemara which acted as a counterpoise to that element of stern Ulster reticence which he did not always find it easy to accept in his own character.

When MacNeice was ten, he was sent to Sherborne preparatory school—at that time a happy place, and he was happy in it. In the autumn of 1921 he went with an entrance scholarship to Marlborough, where he enjoyed rugby and running on the Downs, and specialized in the classics. (Sir) John Betjeman, Bernard Spencer, John Hilton, Graham Shepard, and Anthony Blunt were among his contemporaries; they remained lifelong friends. MacNeice matured rapidly and even precociously in an aesthetic and intellectual ambience, wrote a great deal of verse, and developed a persona which took pride in an opposition to science as well as religion, a contempt for politics, and a scepticism of all values except the aesthetic.

In 1926 he won a postmastership to Merton College, but Oxford was at first disappointing; he found much of the work arid, and his Marlborough friends were in other colleges. But he continued to write—chiefly poems and stories of satire and fantasy—and in time became friendly with other poets, notably W. H. Auden, Stephen Spender, and Clere Parsons. He took a first in classical honour moderations in 1928, and eagerly devoured the philosophy prescribed for 'Greats', ranging beyond it in quest of a system to replace a world founded on the religion he had lost, with one founded on reason. But his obsession with the logic of poetry ran counter to any other logic, and his quest did not find a solution either then or later, although it was to be a continuing drive which underlay all his poetry. His Oxford studies did, however, give him a firm intellectual foundation, and in spite of emotional strains, his last year there—1930—was a year of successes. He got a first in *literae humaniores*, edited *Oxford Poetry* with

Stephen Spender, published his first book of poems, *Blind Fireworks*, and, on the security of a lecturership in classics at the university of Birmingham, he married Giovanna Marie Thérèse Babette ('Mariette') Ezra, step-daughter of (Sir) John Beazley.

Industrial Birmingham and its university were a rude shock after the youthful snobberies and 'preciousness' of the Oxford aesthetes; MacNeice had to revise his ideas of how and what to teach, and he confronted the problems inevitable to a man who honestly wants to fulfil his obligations, whether to his employers or to his wife, yet who at a deep level regards his creative writing as more important than anything else. According to his posthumous autobiography, *The Strings Are False* (1965), he and his wife at first withdrew from these problems into a 'hothouse' of their private world, in which he wrote a novel, *Roundabout Way* (1932), under the pseudonym Louis Malone. The book he soon came to see as a fake, and it was not a success. But he was unable to shut off the outside world, and at Christmas 1933 he wrote *Eclogue for Christmas* with 'a kind of cold-blooded passion' which surprised him. His son Daniel was born in 1934, and about this time MacNeice also began to take more interest in the life of Birmingham and the university, where there was then a remarkably able group of people; he became a lasting friend of the head of his department, Professor E. R. Dodds, his lifelong mentor who became professor of Greek at Oxford; of Ernest Stahl, a lecturer in German and later Taylor professor at Oxford; and of John Waterhouse, a lecturer in English. And among the students he came to know R. D. Smith, with whom he was later to be associated at the BBC, and Walter Allen. MacNeice was also becoming known as a poet through his contributions to *New Verse* and other periodicals and his second volume of *Poems* (1935), and he was at work, with Dodds's encouragement, on his translation of Aeschylus' *Agamemnon* (1936), which is of permanent value.

Looking grimly at the outside world in 1933 he had wanted to 'smash the aquarium'; instead, in 1935 his own golden bowl was broken when his wife abruptly left him. He had to turn his mind to domestic problems, and reconcile himself to the fact of rejection. His autobiography dissimulated the grief and concentrated on the gain of freedom: 'I suddenly realized I was under no more obligation to be respectable.' But freedom and loneliness made him restless, and at Easter 1936 he and Anthony Blunt visited Spain. His Birmingham years may have made him more conscious of social and political injustice, but he does seem to have seen only the pictures of Spain and not the whole picture, with its intimations of turmoil to come. On his return, he felt he could not endure the reminders of his broken marriage, and in the summer of 1936 he accepted a post as lecturer in Greek at Bedford College, London. He then went to Iceland with W. H.

Auden, a journey about which they subsequently wrote *Letters from Iceland* (1937).

MacNeice discharged his university duties in London punctiliously, although living the literary life and moving gradually away from 'the old gang who were just literary' towards 'the new gang who were all Left'. The Group Theatre produced his *Agamemnon* in 1936, which was well received, and, less successfully, his *Out of the Picture* in 1937. His life at this period was 'a whirl of narcotic engagements'—parties, private views, and political meetings and arguments. But, although he was left-wing in his sympathies, he was never himself formally committed to the revolutionary Left, and he found the Communist Party unacceptable; nor can the whirl have been too narcotic, for in the single year 1938 he published another book of poems, *The Earth Compels*; two prose works written to commission, *I Crossed the Minch*, and *Zoo*; and a critical book, *Modern Poetry*, which exhibited a close study of metrics and a keen eye and ear, drew upon a wide range in the classics and English, and showed a great balance of judgement. And in August he began a long poem, *Autumn Journal* (1939), which it took him the rest of the year to finish. This poem is a long lyric meditation on the preceding years, with revocations of childhood, sharp glimpses of the contemporary scene, sombre autumnal premonitions of national catastrophe, and a rejection at times overt of contemporary political nostrums.

He paid a second visit to Spain early in 1939 and found it much changed; Barcelona was on the eve of collapse and Franco's cause triumphing. This, and the outbreak of war with Germany, brought his dilemmas to a head: he had also been in the United States that spring, and now, loitering in Ireland, he decided to take leave of absence from Bedford College, and go back to America to try to find a woman he had met earlier, and see if events might make up his mind for him. His visit was a success, and he enjoyed lecturing at Cornell, but by July 1940 it had become clear to him that if he stayed there he would be 'missing history'. In the event he was forced to stay on, due to peritonitis, and he did not get back to England until December. He was rejected for active service because of bad eyesight, and joined the BBC Features Department in May 1941. There, under Laurence Gilliam, MacNeice applied his mind to the principles and techniques of his new medium and to exploiting it to creative ends. His mastery was apparent in such programmes as the series 'The Stones Cry Out', 'Alexander Nevsky', and 'Christopher Columbus'. He adapted his old love of the stage to radio drama, and produced at least two memorable contributions: *He Had a Date* (1944), an elegy for his friend Graham Shepard who had been killed on convoy duty; and *The Dark Tower* (1946), a synthesis of two favourite themes, the morality quest and the parable.

During the war years he also produced three more books of poetry, *The Last Ditch* (1940), *Plant and Phantom* (1941), and *Springboard* (1944), and another critical work, *The Poetry of W. B. Yeats* (1941). In 1942 he made a fresh start in family life by marrying Hedli Anderson, the actress and singer; his son Daniel rejoined him from Ireland, and in 1943 his daughter Corinna was born.

The Features Department provided him with security and employment which he found useful, satisfying, and compatible with his vocation as poet. It was natural to continue in this work after the war, more especially as Gilliam had recruited other stimulating colleagues, many of them also poets—W. R. Rodgers, Rayner Heppenstall, Terence Tiller, and, on occasion, Dylan Thomas. Rodgers and Thomas in particular became his close friends, as did Francis (Jack) Dillon, the producer. MacNeice was proud of his skill in this medium and took pleasure in the company and technique of the teams with which he worked. The BBC of those years, and Gilliam particularly, knew how to get loyalty and dedicated work out of the intractable race of poets, and drove them with relaxed reins. MacNeice was given leave to visit Ireland in 1945—an Antaean and necessary return to his origins; his curiosity about the wider world was also given scope and he had many assignments abroad—to Rome, to India and Pakistan (in 1947 and again in 1955), to the United States (1953), to the Gold Coast, and to South Africa.

In 1949, to mark the Goethe bicentenary, the BBC produced his version of *Faust*—a major undertaking on which he worked in collaboration with his old friend Ernest Stahl. He had published another collection of poems, *Holes in the Sky* (1948), and the following year *Collected Poems 1925–1948*. From January to September 1950 he was on leave from the BBC as director of the British Institute in Athens, and he stayed on until the following March as assistant representative. Again, he led the double life: conscientious in discharging his duties, while writing—in spite of the rueful 'This middle stretch of life is bad for poets'—the poems published in 1952 as *Ten Burnt Offerings*. Back in London, MacNeice was beginning to be strongly conscious of time slipping away, and in elegiac mood he began *Autumn Sequel* (1954), a complement and reprise of *Autumn Journal*; he was in the midst of writing this when Dylan Thomas died, in November 1953, and grief for that death strongly marked the mood of the poem. He published no more until *Visitations* in 1957—the year in which he received an honorary doctorate from the Queen's University, Belfast. In 1958 he was appointed CBE.

But some desperate discontent was working in him, and a desire for renewal. In 1960 he and his second wife separated, and in 1961 he gave up full-time employment in the BBC to be freer for his own work. He felt himself to be in a fresh creative phase of which *Solstices* (1961) was the first harvest; he delivered the Clark lectures in 1963 (published as *Varieties of Parable* in 1965), and he went to Yorkshire that summer to make a programme, *Persons from Porlock*, which involved recording underground. He insisted on going down with engineers to see that the sound effects were right and caught a severe chill. By the time his sister discovered how ill he was and made him go into hospital it was too late; he died of virus pneumonia in London 3 September 1963.

Before his death MacNeice had been assembling the poems for *The Burning Perch* (1963). Of this he wrote, 'I was taken aback by the high proportion of sombre pieces, ranging from bleak observations to thumbnail nightmares ... All I can say is that I did not set out to write this kind of poem: they happened.' It was a central tenet of his critical theory that the poet cannot be completely sure of what he has to say until he has said it, and that he works towards his meaning by a 'dialectic of purification'. And in a sense what gives MacNeice's poetry its excitement is the tension between his mastery of words and technique, and the uncertainty for which he was trying to find a resolution. It was fortunate for him as a poet that he did not find it, for perplexity over the irreconcilables in life was the yeast that fermented his best work. Any comprehensive theoretical solution would have been sterilizing.

Even so, his escape from the frigidities of his classical education had been narrow, as he realized in *Modern Poetry*: 'Marriage at least made me recognize the existence of other people in their own right and not as vicars of my godhead.' And it was in Birmingham that he learnt to respect the ordinary man, and came to form his own conception of what a poet should be: '... able-bodied, fond of talking, a reader of the newspapers, capable of pity and laughter, informed in economics, appreciative of women, involved in personal relationships, actively interested in politics, susceptible to physical impressions.' But this description omits the qualities which made MacNeice special as a poet: the capacious mind with full memory; the dazzling skill with metaphor and image and symbol; the control of verbal technique—'the sharp contemporary tang of his scholar-poet's idiom', ranging from lyric to acute observation, even slapstick; the basic seriousness, the search for a belief which could explain without destroying the delight of 'the drunkenness of things being various'. The absence of a firm and forming conviction meant that he was open to experience but often passive in his acceptance of it, however creatively he might give back the experience in poetry. He was himself aware of this: 'But the things that happen to one often seem better than the things one chooses. Even in writing poetry ... the few poems or passages which I find wear well have something of accident about them ...' And in the same passage of his autobiography he expressed the feeling that what makes life worth living is the surrenders to the feelings and sensation which the given moment may present.

As poet and critic, and as man—humanist and stoic—MacNeice was all of a piece. Once he had found himself and his deepest themes he developed as a tree develops, the years adding rings and ruggedness to the trunk and density of branch and foliage, but the basic shape not changing. As the tree, rooted where it stands, must accept and surrender to the winds and seasons, so MacNeice stoically and passively accepted whatever life brought him next. And in the end it was that passiveness, the stoical confidence in his power to survive, which brought about his death.

A portrait by Nancy Coldstream (Mrs Spender) remained in the possession of the artist. From a death-mask in the possession of Hedli MacNeice, their daughter Corinna has made drawings.

[Louis MacNeice, *The Strings are False*, 1965; private information; personal knowledge.]

D. M. DAVIN

published 1981

(1900–1984)

Writer, was born 11 October 1900 in Clapham, the eldest of three children (the middle one a boy) of Robert Mannin, a postal sorter, and his wife, Edith Gray, a farmer's daughter. Robert Mannin was a Londoner, with Irish ancestry, who, from his youth, spent much of his earnings on books. Ethel was educated at the local council school, and left at fifteen to become a stenographer in the London advertising agency of Charles F. Higham. Two years later she was appointed associate editor of the *Pelican*, a theatrical and sporting periodical. In 1919 she married John Alexander Porteous (died 1956), a Scotsman, thirteen years her senior, who worked as a copy-writer at Higham's, and later became general manager. He was the son of William Porteous, who had a grocery business. Their only child, a daughter, was born within a year.

By then, Ethel Mannin was already selling articles to women's magazines, and had embarked on her career as a compulsive writer of novels, travel books, children's stories, and volumes of autobiography. Her first novel, *Martha* (1923), was runner-up in a competition for first novels. Her first success came with *Sounding Brass* (1925) in which she satirized the world of advertising, using her intimate knowledge of its practices. This she thought to be her best novel, but, such was her prolific output, that she could not hope to maintain the same standard in all her later novels.

During the next fifty years she published nearly one hundred books, but, as she herself admitted in *Brief Voices* (1959), she had 'only a limited talent' and was well aware of her limitations.

In her first autobiographical volume *Confessions and Impressions* (1930), she set out to shock an older generation since, to use her own words, she was 'angry with the existing social system, angry with the humbug of conventional morality, angry with the anti-life attitude of orthodox religion and the futility of orthodox education'. In 1930 she also published *Children of the Earth*, a novel with a Channel Islands background, and from then onwards she deliberately set out to produce one novel and one non-fiction book every year.

In 1929 she had been able to buy Oak Cottage, Wimbledon, a house to which she had been attracted since as a young girl she had walked across Wimbledon Common. She lived there for nearly forty years and there she entertained her many friends, including (Sir) Allen Lane, Christina Foyle, and (Dame) Daphne du Maurier. As her second husband, Reginald Reynolds, wrote in his autobiography *My Life and Crimes* (1956) she also gave hospitality to numbers of visitors from overseas for whose causes she worked tirelessly, 'from Spanish anarchists to Arabs'.

Her interests were in the main the theatre, cinema, ballet, and the best-selling novels of the period such as *The Green Hat* (1924) by Michael Arlen. She admitted quite honestly that she was not attracted by the more esoteric works such as those of Virginia Woolf, published in that decade.

She held certain opinions very strongly. She was a confirmed pacifist from the time of the Spanish civil war; she was fiercely anti-Zionist; and she regarded monarchy as an anachronism. In 1933 she joined the Independent Labour Party but in later life became disenchanted with the policies of the left, and particularly with those of the USSR.

Her marriage to John Porteous broke down (they were divorced in 1938), though she continued to maintain amicable relations with him, and when he died she hastened to Devon to be with her daughter at his funeral. In *Brief Voices* she wrote: 'That we were able to be friends for the last fifteen years of his life was absolution for me for the wrong I had done him in my youth.' In 1938 she married Reginald Reynolds (died 1958), with whom she had been friendly since meeting him at an ILP dance in 1935. The son of Bryant Reynolds, market gardener, of Sanderstead, he was a Quaker, a pacifist, and a friend of Mahatma Gandhi. He and his wife were both great travellers, but they never travelled together.

However, she and her daughter frequently travelled abroad together and spent many happy weeks walking and climbing in the Lake District and boating in Connemara. Whatever she did and wherever she went Ethel Mannin described in her travel books and novels. In 1934 she published *Men Are Unwise*, a novel about mountaineering; her *Connemara Journal* (1948) is the story of her cottage in that corner of Ireland near Mannin Bay; and her novel *Late Have I Loved Thee* (1948) is also set in Ireland. Her early visits to the Continent are described in such books as *Bavarian Story* (1950) and *German Journey* (1948). After her visit to India she published *Jungle Journey* (1950) and a novel *At Sundown, the Tiger ...* (1951); Morocco is described in *Moroccan Mosaic* (1953) and Burma in *Land of the Crested Lion* (1955) and a novel *The Living Lotus* (1956).

Ethel Mannin's father died in 1949. When she was a young girl he had encouraged her to write and they had always been very close. In *This Was a Man* (1952) she paid tribute to him in a little memoir which she herself believed to be 'perhaps the best thing I have written'.

She had a distinctive hairstyle; her hair, parted in the middle, was brushed smoothly aside from her broad forehead. In *Sunset over Dartmoor, a Final Chapter of Autobiography* (1977) she describes how she decided to leave Oak Cottage and retire to Overhill, a bungalow which her daughter Jean Faulks had found for her at Shaldon, overlooking the Teign estuary. She found old age hard to bear. In looking back on her career as an author she said, 'I did not write to any pattern, merely accepting and using material as it came to hand', and of her early work she admitted: 'I had too much too soon; too much facile success, too much money, too much unassimilated experience.' She realized that her books might have been of higher quality had she been prepared to restrict herself to a lower output. In July 1984 she was hurt in a fall at her home and was taken to Teignmouth hospital where she died 5 December 1984.

[*The Times*, 8 December 1984; Ethel Mannin, *Confessions and Impressions*, 1930, *Privileged Spectator*, 1939, *Brief Voices*, 1959, *Young in the Twenties*, 1971, *Stories from my Life*, 1973, and *Sunset over Dartmoor*, 1977 (autobiographies); information from Jean Faulks (daughter).]

H. F. Oxbury

published 1990

MASEFIELD John Edward

(1878–1967)

Poet laureate, was born at The Knapp, Ledbury, Herefordshire, 1 June 1878, the son of George Edward Masefield, solicitor, and his wife, Caroline Louisa Parker. He was left an orphan at a very early age, and was brought up by relatives. His childhood on a late Victorian farm was followed by education at the King's School, Warwick, and in the *Conway* where he began to learn, from the age of thirteen, the seamanship which informs much of his most authentic writing. He crossed the Atlantic and for several years worked in a carpet mill in Yonkers, New York, and travelled around in America doing menial jobs. Yet Masefield found time to read widely in the English poets, and Chaucer, Shelley, and Keats, in a foreign land at the impressionable age of seventeen, served to stimulate his love and reverence for England and its countryside. He also developed a passionate sympathy with the unfortunate, the persecuted, and the weak, which enabled him in the fullness of time to write his narrative masterpiece *Reynard the Fox*.

By 1897 he had made his way back to England, where he first attracted attention with *Salt Water Ballads* (1902); in his next volumes, *Ballads* (1903, revised and enlarged 1910), and *Ballads and Poems* (1910), there was a surer touch, and the 'Dirty British coaster with a salt-caked smoke stack ...' betokened a new and rousing voice in English poetry which owed as much to Rudyard Kipling as to Masefield's own sea-going experience: he was never ashamed to admit the influence of other writers. He had by then settled in London and he began to contribute, with the help and encouragement of friends, to the *Outlook*, the *Academy*, and the *Speaker*, and in 1907 he began to work on the *Manchester Guardian*.

The Everlasting Mercy (1911), Masefield's first major poem, was a shock to the literary world. Significantly it is a narrative, redolent of life as he knew it, a mixture of beauty and ugliness and couched, in places, in the language of the tap-room. This form was especially his, and in *Dauber* (1913) he tells, again as a poetic story, of the conflict facing the artist set amongst philistines and frustrated in his artistic ambition. Here was a man who had sailed before the mast writing a narrative poem about a life at sea he knew and understood.

The zenith of Masefield's achievement as a poet came in 1919 with the publication of *Reynard the Fox*. No English poet since Chaucer had called up the vision of the English countryside so effectively as he did there, with his powers of honest and accurate observation and his mastery of metrical pattern and pace. In this, as in many other poems, he drew upon his childhood at Ledbury for that real experience of rural life and the natural world which was a mainspring of vitality in much of his best work.

However, Masefield was not simply a poet. Over the years he wrote naval histories, and edited selections of the works of various poets and dramatists, some in collaboration with his wife. Many critics judged his *William Shakespeare* (1911) to be a work of scholarship, or at least of such imaginative power as to make it appear that he had entered into Shakespeare's very thought processes: his warm humanity and capacity for feeling for other people made his judgements appeal to all but the most desiccated of scholars.

As a novelist Masefield showed that he could tell a tale in prose as compellingly as in poetry, and with the same lucid clarity which effaced any sense of the author intervening between reader and events or characters. In *Lost Endeavour* (1910) there is hardly a false note: the force of his imagination makes it more than just a racy story for boys, although it is certainly that too. It is a variation on a theme close to the heart of all his work: that hope and idealism and energy can never be completely frustrated or overcome by mundane human considerations. In *The Bird of Dawning* (1933) the elements are the same: on one level it is a parable about sustained bravery and tenacity on the old China clippers, on another, a gripping tale told by a man with a blazing imagination.

As a playwright, Masefield was less convincing. He came nearest to success in the rather uneven *The Tragedy of Nan* (Royalty, with Lillah McCarthy, 1908); the theme was another favourite of his—that human problems come nearest to solution in a state of nature. Next he embarked on a historical play, *The Tragedy of Pompey the Great* (Stage Society, Aldwych, 1910), in which an uncharacteristic torrent of words often fogs the main issues. Although Masefield was devoted to the theatre, and did much to promote poetry reading and amateur dramatics (stimulated by his friends W. B. Yeats and Gilbert Murray), both in the little theatre in his garden at Boars Hill, Oxford, and elsewhere, nevertheless his plays lack the sense of reality which imbues his poetry and much of his prose. One thing which he did well, however, was religious drama with such plays as *Good Friday* (1916), *The Trial of Jesus* (1925), and *The Coming of Christ* (1928).

He was also a great entertainer of children, and his perennially youthful heart never lost the sense of surprise and wonder which could be seen in his eyes. There are few more enchanting children's books than *The Box of Delights* (1935), or *The Midnight Folk* (1927), written for children of all ages, for anyone willing to fly on the wings of imagination to magic lands where witches and strange animals abound.

Masefield

As poet laureate, a post to which he was appointed in 1930 when Ramsay MacDonald was prime minister, Masefield felt bound to do what he thought was expected of him, and dutifully produced occasional pieces for thirty-seven years. He took his responsibilities in this capacity very seriously, and the Order of Merit which he received in 1935 was warmly acclaimed. For many years he was a popular visitor to the United States and in Europe, where he gave numerous lectures and lecture-tours as laureate. It was significant that in 1940 he should have been stirred so deeply by the miracle of Dunkirk that he wrote one of his finest short prose works on this subject—*The Nine Days Wonder* (1941). All that had gone before, including his own distinguished service in the Red Cross in France and the Dardanelles during the war of 1914–18, prepared him for this work: it was the proud and loving Englishman who spoke, the man who believed that the spirit of goodness would, in the end, prevail. His life had always been modestly dedicated to helping the weak against the strong, the fox against the hounds; his innate courtesy was appreciated by all who knew him, and his sensitivity and integrity were never questioned by contemporary poets. More, perhaps, of his work appeared in print than a more self-conscious writer or a less courageous man would have permitted, but the reward for chancing his arm so often was, on occasion, to produce a work which no other man of his age could match. Masefield was awarded honorary degrees by the universities of Oxford, Liverpool, and St. Andrews; he was appointed C.Lit. in 1961. He was president of the Society of Authors from 1937, and of the National Book League in 1944–9. He died at his home near Abingdon 12 May 1967.

He married in 1903 Constance (died 1960), daughter of Nicholas de la Cherois Crommelin, of Cushendun, county Antrim; they had a son who died in action in 1942 and a daughter, Judith, who illustrated some of his books. Portraits of Masefield by William Strang and Henry Lamb hang in the National Portrait Gallery; Sir William Rothenstein drew him twice: one drawing is reproduced in *Twenty-Four Portraits* (1st series, 1920), and the other is in the Fitzwilliam Museum, Cambridge. There are also portraits of him by Sir John Lavery, John Mansbridge, and Norma Bull.

[John Masefield, *So Long to Learn*, 1952, his poems, and other works; *The Times* 13 May 1967; W. J. Entwhistle and E. Gillett, *The Literature of England, A.D. 500–1960*, 4th edn., 1962; Constance Babington Smith, *John Masefield: A Life*, 1978; personal knowledge.]

D. R. W. Silk

published 1981

(1869–1928)

Poet, the eldest daughter of Frederick Mew, an architect, by his wife, Anne, daughter of Henry Edward Kendall, an architect well known in the middle of the nineteenth century, was born in Doughty Street, London, 15 November 1869. She was educated privately, and later attended lectures at University College, London. She passed almost the whole of her life in Bloomsbury, and lived for over thirty years at 9 Gordon Street. In 1923 she was awarded a civil list pension of £75. Shortly afterwards her much loved sister and companion, Anne Mew, was smitten with a mortal illness of which she died in 1927. From this blow Charlotte Mew was unable to rally, and she died by her own hand in a nursing home in London 24 March 1928.

Early in her life Charlotte Mew showed an unusual talent for writing verse and prose, and from her twentieth to her thirtieth year she was a regular contributor to *Temple Bar*. She published one excellent story, 'Passed', in the *Yellow Book*, July 1894. Her poems, stories, essays, and studies appeared in periodicals from time to time, mainly in *The Nation*, *The New Statesman*, *The Englishwoman*, and *The Chap-book*. Her work was admired by her contemporaries, notably by Thomas Hardy, who greatly valued it and considered her to be the best woman poet of her day.

Although Charlotte Mew continued to write throughout her life, only two small books of her verse have been published—*The Farmer's Bride* (1915) and *The Rambling Sailor*, which appeared posthumously in 1929. Her fastidious self-criticism prevented her even from preserving anything that did not conform to the standard which she had set for herself. The appearance of her first book brought her immediate recognition. The title poem exhibits to the full her peculiar powers of condensation and her dramatic and psychological insight. She had a particularly individual manner and mode of expression. Her verse is characterized by a tense fine-drawn rhythm which varies according to the emotion of the poem. It is clear, concise, and remarkably direct. Her passionate insistence on facing the truth is particularly evident in *Madeleine in Church*; her uncanny power of arousing in her readers the same emotion as had inspired her own poem makes *In Nunhead Cemetery* almost too piercing; and *Sea Love* is a notable example of lyrical condensation.

[*The Times*, 29 March 1928; personal knowledge.]

A. MONRO

published 1937

(1882–1956)

Author, was born 18 January 1882 at Henley House in Kilburn. He was the youngest of a family of three sons, a fact which seems to have suggested to him as he grew up the romantic approach to life of a fairy-tale. His father, John Vine Milne, a Scotsman of Aberdonian descent, had married, at Buxton, Sarah Maria, daughter of Peter Heginbotham, a manufacturer. Both parents at the time conducted private schools. While the mother is remembered chiefly as an embodiment of all the domestic virtues, his father was an educational enthusiast, hero and mentor to his sons. H. G. Wells was for a time a science master at Henley House and remained always a family friend.

A. A. Milne obtained a Westminster scholarship at the age of eleven, an unprecedented achievement, and proceeded to Trinity College, Cambridge, where he disappointed his tutor by accepting the editorship of the *Granta* and preferring journalism to the mathematical tripos, in which he gained a third class (1903). It was not only his ambition to write, but to write exactly as he pleased, and returning to London he became in 1906, after various less successful ventures, assistant editor of *Punch* under (Sir) Owen Seaman. In this capacity he showed a remarkable gift for light and witty dialogue and a sense of dramatic form, which soon attracted the attention and admiration of a large circle of readers.

The war interrupted his literary career. He served as a signalling officer in the Royal Warwickshire Regiment in England and overseas, but he was able in 1917 to stage his first fantasy, *Wurzel-Flummery*, which was followed in 1920 by the far more considerable comedy, *Mr. Pim Passes By*.

Leaving the staff of *Punch* in 1919, Milne thereafter devoted the greater part of his time to stage comedy. Clearly the success of Sir J. M. Barrie was a guiding influence: the paradoxical situation, the mingling of much laughter with a little pathos, and, if need be, the fairy wand. But Milne had a fancy and a style which were all his own, and if his dream world was not so wistful as Barrie's, it was whimsical enough and his characters could sustain ingenious and airy conversations which never failed to amuse.

His first successes were followed by a long series of plays in which the attempt to create genuine characters became more marked. The most notable of these were *The Truth About Blayds* (1921), the story of a poetical imposter, which provided an excellent part, as the unmarried daughter, for (Dame) Irene Vanbrugh; *The Dover Road* (1922), a light-hearted homily on divorce, in which Henry Ainley appeared; and *The Great Broxopp* (1923), in which the role of a romantic advertising agent was assumed by Edmund Gwenn. Later came *To Have the Honour* (1924); *The Fourth Wall* (1928), a cleverly contrived murder mystery; *Michael and Mary* (1930); and *Other People's Lives* (1932). *Toad of Toad Hall*, his dramatization of *The Wind in the Willows* by Kenneth Grahame, was first staged in 1929.

Milne also wrote *The Red House Mystery*, a detective story (1922); two novels: *Two People* (1931) and *Chloe Marr* (1946); and many essays in various moods, some of them an expression of his serious views on world politics and peace. But he had found a new and wider public as early as 1924 when he published *When We Were Very Young*, a series of verses for children dedicated to his son, Christopher Robin, who was born in 1920. *Now We Are Six* followed in 1927. In the same genre, but in prose, he produced *Winnie-the-Pooh* (1926) and *The House at Pooh Corner* (1928), which bring to life the unforgettable character of a child's nursery toys, a thought suggested to him by his wife. On both sides of the Atlantic and in other languages, including Japanese and Bulgarian, these enchanting stories with their attractive illustrations by E. H. Shepard acquired a popularity which seemed almost likely to rival an earlier Wonderland.

Milne married in 1913 Dorothy (Daphne), daughter of Martin de Sélincourt, a City merchant. He died at his home at Hartfield, Sussex, 31 January 1956. The National Portrait Gallery has a drawing by Powys Evans.

[*The Times*, 1 February 1956; A. A. Milne, *It's Too Late Now*, 1939; private information; personal knowledge.]

E. V. KNOX

published 1971

MITFORD Nancy Freeman-

(1904–1973)

Novelist and biographer, was born at 1 Graham Street (now Terrace), Chelsea, 28 November 1904, the eldest child in the family of six daughters and one son of David Bertram Ogilvy Freeman-Mitford, the second Baron Redesdale, and his wife, Sydney, daughter of Thomas Gibson Bowles, MP. In different ways her grandfathers were remarkable men: the first Baron Redesdale being a diplomat, oriental traveller (author of *Tales of Old Japan*, 1871), horticulturist, and intimate friend of King Edward VII, whereas Gibson Bowles, the creator of *Vanity Fair*, was a brilliant *enfant terrible* back-bencher. Through her Redesdale grandmother, Lady Clementine Ogilvy,

Nancy had the blood of the Stanleys in her veins. She was to edit two volumes of their correspondence, *The Ladies of Alderley* (1938), of whom one was her great-grandmother, and *The Stanleys of Alderley* (1939). She was also directly descended from William Mitford the historian. With these antecedents it is hardly surprising that, in spite of a conventional up-bringing, the six sisters and one brother Thomas David (killed in action in Burma, 1945), all endowed with striking good looks and gifts, have emerged in different degrees of fame and notoriety as a legendary family.

After her father succeeded to the Redesdale title and estates in 1916 Nancy Mitford's childhood was spent in the Cotswolds—at Batsford Park (sold in 1919), Asthall Manor (sold 1927), and Swinbrook Manor, a rather cumbersome house designed by her father. Her education was sketchy. Her father would not hear of her being sent to an ordinary boarding-school, deeming education of his daughters quite unnecessary, if not reprehensible. All her life Nancy Mitford deplored her lack of academic education, which she held against her parents. Yet she became an early and avid reader of biographies, memoirs, and letters which she found in the library her father had inherited but never himself looked at. For he was, in spite of natural intelligence and humour, a professed low-brow, whom Nancy Mitford caricatured mercilessly but affectionately as the blustering 'Uncle Matthew' of her novels. Indeed he was the source of most of her family jokes.

After a short spell at a finishing school at Hatherop Castle, Glouces-tershire, and then as an art student at the Slade School under Henry Tonks (where she did not excel) she was sent, heavily chaperoned, to Paris. The French way of life immediately captivated her. After a first taste she was obliged to return to England in order to 'come out'. For three seasons she flung herself into London balls and country house parties where she was extremely popular. She soon met a group of Bohemian contemporaries— Evelyn Waugh, Robert Byron, Brian Howard, Mark Ogilvie-Grant, John Sutro, Christopher Sykes, and (Sir) Harold Acton, to name a few. They were fascinated by her intelligence, vivacity, wit, and beauty. On the fringe of these clever, sophisticated, provocative, and bright young people was James Alexander (Hamish) St. Clair-Erskine, a beguiling younger son of Lord Rosslyn, but improvident, impecunious, and five years her junior. For five unsatisfactory years they were engaged.

Not until she was twenty-four was Nancy Mitford able to break away from her family. In 1928 she took a room in the London flat of Evelyn Waugh and his first wife (Evelyn Gardner), then a close friend. But when the Waughs' marriage collapsed Nancy's sympathies were transferred to the 'he-Evelyn'. She soon took to writing, precariously supporting herself by articles for *Vogue* and *Harper's Magazine*. In 1931 her first novel, *Highland*

Fling, was published. *Christmas Pudding* (1932), in which Hamish Erskine and (Sir) John Betjeman were thinly disguised, and *Wigs on the Green* (1935) followed.

In 1933 she married Peter Murray Rennell Rodd (died 1968), a younger son of the first Baron Rennell; he was handsome and intelligent, with a certain panache. But he was impecunious, with no regular job. Moreover he was from the start unfaithful and neglectful. The marriage was not happy although his wife would never brook any criticism of him by her friends. When she could no longer tolerate his escapades she left him and at his request agreed to a divorce in 1958. There were no children. In 1939 she followed him to Perpignan where he was working in a camp for Spanish refugee victims of Franco's regime. The experience made her violently anti-fascist and turned her into a socialist.

On the outbreak of war in 1939 she became an ARP driver. Then once again she worked for evacuees, this time from Nazi-invaded countries. In 1940 her fourth novel, *Pigeon Pie*, a skit about the phoney war, was published. In March 1942 she became employed as an assistant in Heywood Hill's Curzon Street Bookshop. She helped make this shop into a favourite wartime rendezvous of intellectuals who were drawn by her astonishing knowledge of the books she sold, her cheerfulness and vaunted enjoyment of the war. On her retirement in 1946 she was made a partner of the firm.

Almost overnight her state of poverty and insecurity was turned to affluence by the publication of her fifth novel, *The Pursuit of Love* (1945). It was a wild success and sold over a million copies. The theme was a consequence and the reflection of the most important crisis of her life, namely her meeting and falling deeply in love with Gaston Palewski, a member of the Free French forces, a gallant and cultivated follower of General de Gaulle, who was to become one of his closest advisers and future ministers. The 'Colonel', as he was known to her friends, aroused in Nancy a latent capacity for hero-worship and a total dedication to France and all things French. Henceforth the 'Colonel' was transmuted into the idealized characters of her future books, whether the Duc de Sauveterre in *The Pursuit of Love*, or Louis XV in *Madame de Pompadour* (1954). When the war was over Nancy went straight to Paris. In 1947 she rented the ground floor of an old 'hotel' in the rue Monsieur where she lived with her faithful maid, Marie, until obliged to move to a house in the rue d'Artois, Versailles, in 1967.

Until she was forty Nancy Mitford was not a public figure. Her excitement and pleasure in her sudden popularity and comparative riches were endearing. With *Love in a Cold Climate* (1949) and *The Blessing* (1951), the most accomplished of her novels having for theme fashionable French society, she had changed from amateur to professional status. Her writing was now compact, terse, and simple. Her plots were subtle, satirical, and humorous. In Parisian circles she was in great demand because of her renown, elegance (beautiful clothes from Dior), sparkling wit, and mischievous fun. Yet for all her extolling of France and the French and her disparagement (occasionally tiresome) of England and the English, her most intimate friends were her own countrymen.

In the 1950s she turned to biography, of which *Madame de Pompadour* was her first and most lively. She was an industrious researcher who soaked herself in the court life of Louis XV's reign. In spite of an air of self-confidence she went in much anxiety and fear of reviewers. However, their reception of the book was generally rapturous. It was followed by *Voltaire in Love* (1957), the profusely illustrated *The Sun King* (1966), a life of Louis XIV on whom and whose satellites she also became a specialist, and *Frederick the Great* (1970), whose battles she revelled in. During her biographical phase she wrote one more novel, *Don't Tell Alfred* (1960), a story centred on the British embassy, which she frequented during the ambassadorships of her friends the Duff Coopers and Gladwyn Jebbs.

Her one attempt at drama was a translation of André Roussin's farce, *The Little Hut*. In 1950 it appeared in the provinces and London where it was highly acclaimed. Her contribution, more serious than comical, to *Noblesse Oblige* (1956) on correct upper-class usage of words brought her prominently into the limelight as arbiter of social conduct. Of all her books *The Water Beetle* (1962), a collection of fourteen short essays, perhaps shows her to greatest advantage as a writer. In these succinct, perceptive, evocative, and extremely funny stories and anecdotes she shared her private jokes and prejudices with her readers. They are the nearest approach to the as yet unpublished correspondence with her family and friends. She took her writing extremely seriously and mastered an unmistakably individual style, which at first was marred by too frequent lapses into the exclusive jargon of her class and generation. For she was essentially a child of the twenties. Yet with all her sophistication she remained fastidious, abstemious, and seemingly spinsterish. She was a marvellous guest, staying for weeks on end with friends, whom she entertained during the intervals of her reading and writing.

She was much photographed by (Sir) Cecil Beaton. She was painted as a young woman by William Acton and in middle age by Mogens Tvede (1947), seated at her writing-table in the rue Monsieur. She was slim and vivacious. She had dark brown hair and delicately moulded features. Her dancing blue-green eyes and downward-sloping brows were vibrantly expressive of her moods which alternated from insatiable curiosity to mockery and merriment.

In January 1969 she was stricken with agonizing pains which persisted, with intermittent periods of relief, until her death 30 June 1973 at no. 4 rue d'Artois, Versailles. She bore these cruel sufferings with almost super-human courage and cheerfulness. In 1972 she was awarded the Légion d'Honneur, which gave her inordinate pleasure, and appointed CBE, of which she remarked, 'I've never heard of the CBE but of course I'm delighted to have it . . . I hear it ranks above a knight's widow, oh, good.'

[Harold Acton, *Nancy Mitford, a Memoir*, 1975; Selina Hastings, *Nancy Mitford*, 1985; private information; personal knowledge.]

JAMES LEES-MILNE

published 1986

MOORE George Augustus

(1852–1933)

Novelist, was born at Moore Hall, Ballyglass, on the shores of Lough Carra, co. Mayo, 24 February 1852. His family, which had good but not indisputable assurance of descent from the author of *Utopia*, was certainly old and distinguished, a Captain George Moore, of Ballina, having been 'vice-admiral of Connaught' under William III. The novelist's great-grandfather made a fortune at the end of the eighteenth century and built Moore Hall, which was burned by republicans in 1923. His son George, who had a tendency towards literature, married Louisa Browne, grand-daughter of John Browne, first Earl of Altamont, thus linking the Moores with the marquessate of Sligo. Louisa having been brought up by nuns, her eldest son, George Henry Moore, was educated at Oscott College, Birmingham, and in 1851 added to the family's Roman Catholic connexions by marrying Mary, eldest daughter of Maurice Blake, of Ballinafad, co. Mayo. Their eldest son, the novelist, although sent to Oscott in his turn, never took kindly to the Roman Church and, in later life, emphatically repudiated it.

Moore's childhood and early youth, spent chiefly in Ireland, provided him with little education of the kind which he could assimilate, but the countryside, the tenants, the servants, and the racing stables yielded to his curious and observant mind a rich store of memories. His father died in 1870, and in 1873, as soon as Moore was of age, he set out for Paris, determined to paint. Finding that he had not talent enough, and having the courage to admit defeat, he put away his brush for ever and began to write. The growing embarrassment of his estate recalled him from France, and by early 1880 he was struggling in London to earn a living by his pen. Little had been visibly accomplished during his years in Paris, but he had been admitted to the society of great artists, had absorbed the influences of impressionism in painting and of naturalism in literature, and was bursting with what were then, in England, aesthetically revolutionary ideas. What he lacked was discipline, which he was temperamentally incapable of accepting from others, and this, with an industry that never failed him, he now began to apply to himself.

Moore's first novel, *A Modern Lover*, appeared in 1883. It had, as a story, originality and boldness, but the treatment was crude, the writing incorrect. It succeeded in drawing attention to itself, but scarcely prepared Moore's acquaintances, who appear still to have regarded him as slightly ridiculous, for the firmness and intelligence of *A Mummer's Wife* (1885), which, owing something to Zola and in its principal female character even more to Emma Bovary, has good claim to be considered the first realistic novel in English since Defoe. But it was not a masterpiece; the writing was still flawed; Moore was still serving his long apprenticeship. Although *A Drama in Muslin* (1886) and *Confessions of a Young Man* (1888) added to his reputation, and two volumes of essays established him as a challenging critic, the nine years following *A Mummer's Wife* were marked by the failure of four novels excluded by him from his collected works, and *Esther Waters*, his earliest book unquestionably of the first rank, did not appear until 1894.

There followed another doubtful period of nine years. In *Evelyn Innes* (1898) and *Sister Teresa* (1901) there was a garishness, produced by a social phase in the artist's life, which caused him afterwards to reject them from the canon. At the turn of the century Moore appears to have been conscious of his art having run into a barren patch and of a need to seek new pastures. This and the influence of an old friend, Edward Martyn, and of W. B. Yeats led to his leaving England in 1901 and settling in Dublin, hot with the notion of becoming a leader of an Irish renaissance. Politics, clericalism, and Yeats cooled his enthusiasm for this idealistic project and he returned to London after ten years; but his Dublin period served his purpose. It released him, at any rate for a time, from the rich and fashionable, and took him back to his native country and the deep perceptions of childhood. A volume of Irish stories, *The Untilled Field* (1903), and a short novel, *The Lake* (1905), were the foundation of his later style, and the three great volumes of autobiography, *Hail and Farewell: Ave, Salve*, and *Vale*, published in 1911, 1912, and 1914, had their root in Ireland.

From 1911 until the end of his life Moore lived at 121 Ebury Street. He seldom read for the pleasure of reading or lived for the pleasure of living; for him literature and life existed chiefly for what he could wring from them for his own books. Although impressionable for a time by any person or any aspect of art that seemed likely to serve as steel to his flint, he was of an almost ferocious independence. As a man he was unique. He could be on occasions tempestuously intolerant, and yet he commanded an elaborate and charming courtesy. No one to him was anonymous. He would learn about football from footmen, and, with an easy familiarity that belonged to the eighteenth century, was interested in his servants' personal lives; and yet, if a housemaid was clumsy, he could, with eighteenth-century directness, throw his boots at her. A corresponding candour and intimacy mark his autobiographical writing. It is unlike any other because what he chiefly cared for in it was to tell a story that should conform to his aesthetic principles of story-telling, and because, having this single purpose, he treated himself and his friends with a ruthless impartiality of grace, ridicule, insight, and indiscretion. The same approach to criticism gave to his writing in this kind—even to the mature *Avowals* (1919) and *Conversations in Ebury Street* (1924)—a mingled freshness and rashness, an air of proceeding newly minted from a wilful but fearless mind. Moore was never 'safe', seldom sure of himself for long even when writing, and, after his work was published, always eager to improve it. Certain ideas came up for treatment again and again. One, the idea of celibacy, may be watched in the volumes of short stories, *Celibates* (1895), *In Single Strictness* (1922), and *Celibate Lives* (1927). Another, the life of St. Paul and the death of Jesus, may be traced from 1911 onward through several versions of his play *The Apostle* to its culmination in *The Brook Kerith* (1916). This novel stands, together with *Héloïse and Abélard* (1921), at the peak of Moore's achievement in fiction, although good critics have given almost as high a place to *A Story-Teller's Holiday* (1918). But this brilliant treatment of old Celtic legends has neither the depth nor the lovely elegance of the two epics; nor has *Aphrodite in Aulis* (1930) their strength.

It is likely that Moore will be remembered best for three achievements: for *Esther Waters*, which has more warmth and compassion than any other work of his; for *Hail and Farewell* because no other book resembles it; and for the structural firmness and supple narrative of *The Brook Kerith* and *Héloïse and Abélard*. In these two books he accomplished the purpose of his later life—to escape from the rubbed jargon and journalistic subjects of ordinary novels, to treat in prose an epic theme, and to discover a language and a rhythm, beautiful and dignified, which should yet preserve the illusion of a story melodiously spoken. Landor, Pater, and Balzac were his masters, and, when he wrote *The Lake* and *The Untilled Field*, Turgenev. Such masters and such single-mindedness were unlikely to make him popular in England between the wars of 1914 and 1939. He sought lucidity and 'the melodic line' at a time when that quest was little valued, and fashionable criticism was therefore inclined to overstress his limitations. Of these, the chief were a lack of mystical intuition and an impatience of metaphysics. By gigantic labour he did much to overcome them, and of this *The Brook Kerith* is honourable proof. When he had a subject that avoided, or enabled him to overcome, these faults, he was unrivalled, and his translation of *The Pastoral Loves of Daphnis and Chloë* (1924) which could not tempt him to them, is, as prose, of rare beauty. In *Esther Waters*, the first realistic masterpiece in the language, and in *Héloïse and Abélard*, he twice did what none other had done in the English romantic medium, and it is improbable that these services will be forgotten.

In his middle life Moore was regarded by many as a shocking or scandalous writer, for he made no concessions to Victorian prejudice. In his later years controversy died down; the school of sociological criticism then fashionable passed him by in silence. To a great mass of novel readers he was unknown even by name, and he received no honour from the universities or from the state. Nevertheless, on his eightieth birthday (1932), a memorial was addressed to him in which a group of distinguished men hailed him as 'a master of English literature', and, so long as he lived, he had, after Hardy's death, a strong claim to be considered the chief novelist of his day, Kipling's greatness being different in kind. He died, unmarried, in London 21 January 1933.

There is a drawing of Moore as a young man by Edouard Manet; an oil-painting by Richard Sickert is in the Tate Gallery; and a pastel ('The Red Dressing-Gown') by Henry Tonks is in the National Portrait Gallery. He also figures in the groups 'Hommage à Manet' (1909) by Sir William Orpen in the Manchester Corporation Art Gallery and 'Saturday Evening at the Vale' by Tonks in the Tate Gallery.

[*The Times*, 23 January 1936; G. A. Moore, *Hail and Farewell*, 1911–1914; Joseph Hone, *The Life of George Moore* (with bibliography), 1936; Charles Morgan, *Epitaph on George Moore*, 1935; personal knowledge.]

CHARLES MORGAN

published 1949

(1894–1958)

Novelist, critic, and playwright, was born at Bromley, Kent, 22 January 1894, the younger son of (Sir) Charles Langbridge Morgan, civil engineer, president of the Institution of Civil Engineers in 1923–4, and his wife, Mary, daughter of William Watkins. Both parents were of Welsh origin: their forebears had migrated to Australia to take part in the construction of railways, whence Charles Morgan senior returned to make his career in England.

Charles Morgan, youngest of his four children, entered the Royal Navy in 1907 and served in the Atlantic Fleet and China station. Although he was always proud of his naval training, it proved a false start for an acutely sensitive boy already ambitious to become a writer. The ill treatment which he and his fellow midshipmen suffered in the *Good Hope* became the theme of his first novel *The Gunroom* (1919). In 1913, encouraged by (Commander) Christopher Arnold-Forster whom he encountered in the *Monmouth* and who became a lifelong friend, Morgan resigned from the navy. He was entered at Brasenose College, Oxford, but with the outbreak of war in 1914 immediately rejoined the Service and took part in the disastrous Antwerp expedition with the Naval Brigade of the R.N.V.R. After the fall of Antwerp, part of the Naval Brigade crossed the frontier into Holland, where Morgan remained interned until 1917. This period was of the greatest importance in his development as a writer, since he had the good fortune to be put on parole and to live almost as a guest of the de Pallandt family on their estate of Rosendaal in Guelderland. There he received an education in the culture and languages of Europe, acquired especially an enduring love of French thought, and learned to believe that literature has no frontiers. Later, in *The Fountain* (1932), he used the background of Rosendaal Castle (but not the family of Baron de Pallandt) for one of his most successful novels. Meanwhile in Holland he had written *The Gunroom*, and rewritten it after a German mine had sunk the ship in which he was returning to England, with all his baggage, including the manuscript of his novel.

The year 1919 brought Morgan to the long-desired goal of Oxford, where he read history and became president of the Oxford University Dramatic Society. A meeting with A. B. Walkley, dramatic critic of *The Times*, led to his joining the paper's editorial staff in 1921, and on Walkley's death in 1926 he succeeded him as principal dramatic critic, a post which he held until 1939.

A second novel, *My Name is Legion*, was published in 1925. Morgan later regarded his first two books as juvenilia; not until 1929 did he achieve an accomplished mastery of the novelist's craft with *Portrait in a Mirror*, which brought him recognition and the Femina Vie Heureuse prize (1930). Turgenev's influence is apparent in the form of the book. On the nature of inspiration, where the artist's joy is described as receptive rather than creative, there is a debt to Keats and a key to much of Morgan's thought. *The Fountain* (1932), winner of the following year's Hawthornden prize, to the author's surprise was an immediate best-seller in England, on the Continent, and in America. The amalgam of a passionate love story, set in 1915, with echoes of the poetry and quietism of seventeenth-century mystics, told with great lucidity, technical skill, and beauty of diction, proved to the taste of critics and public alike.

Epitaph on George Moore (1935), a brilliant essay in place of the full biography which Moore had wished Morgan to undertake, was followed by *Sparkenbroke* in 1936. It is the longest and most inward-looking of his novels, set partly in Italy, with the triple theme of 'art, love, and death'. Two years later, Morgan turned playwright with *The Flashing Stream*, produced in London, September 1938, with (Sir) Godfrey Tearle and Margaret Rawlings in the leading parts. The play prospered, but the author considered it 'a swerve' from his novels and returned gladly to *The Voyage* (1940), a story warm with his love of France, placed in the country of the Charente and the Paris music-halls, which won the James Tait Black memorial prize.

During the war of 1939–45 Morgan served with the Admiralty, with an interval for a lecture tour in the United States on behalf of the Institute of International Education. A short novel, *The Empty Room*, appeared in 1941. The following year, while still working for naval intelligence, he began a series of weekly articles for *The Times Literary Supplement* under the title of 'Menander's Mirror', republished in the two volumes of *Reflections in a Mirror* (1944–6). Their purpose—a reconsidering of values in life and literature—showed the range of his ideas and his quality as an essayist.

Among Frenchmen exiled in England in these years, and with Resistance workers abroad, the name of Charles Morgan was potent. Articles from his pen circulated secretly through Occupied France. For Morgan the permanence of French genius was freedom of thought. Regimentation of ideas, in his opinion, as shown constantly in his writing, was the greatest danger threatening humanity. When the liberation of Paris came in August 1944, he was among the first English civilians to enter the city. A month later an 'Ode to France' from his pen was read aloud at the re-opening of the Comédie Française.

This passionate belief in a man's right to think for himself can be found in the next novel, *The Judge's Story* (1947), a conflict between good and evil which reflects Morgan's innate puritanism. A lecture tour of French universities in the following year became a triumphal journey among delighted students. France was the partial scene of his next book, *The River Line* (1949), later turned into a play (1952). It is a tale of enemy occupation: the study of a spiritually minded man against a background of movement and violence.

At this period Morgan was obsessed by a sombre vision of the human lot if science were allowed to outstrip man's moral nature. In another book of essays, *Liberties of the Mind* (1951), he predicted the overthrow of human personality, threatened by possessive control and 'barren materialism'. The same grave warning was the theme of his last play, *The Burning Glass*, produced in 1953; yet in the preface to the printed edition he wrote, 'To doubt that there is a way out is to acquiesce in chaos and to doubt God's mercy.' For some years Morgan had been working on an immense novel dealing with this same problem. It was never finished, but for a time he abandoned it and wrote a youthful love story, *A Breeze of Morning* (1951), which returned happily to the spirit of his master, Turgenev, and to his own *Portrait in a Mirror*. The last of his novels, *Challenge to Venus*, with an Italian setting, was published in 1957.

Charles Morgan was a romantic, a philosophic idealist, and something of a mystic. The strong appeal which he made to his English public in the thirties and early forties had ebbed by the time he reached middle age, so that he grew isolated from the young intellectuals of the day, not then concerned with Morgan's attentiveness to an inner world, his message of renewal, or the loftiness of his standards. The highest integrity, with extreme care and polish, marked everything he touched, from the urbane essays of his ripe years to the smallest piece of anonymous dramatic criticism. His books were translated into nineteen languages, and readers on the Continent continued to hold him in the greatest esteem as a novelist.

Although good-looking and distinguished in appearance, Morgan was often suspected of being cold and aloof. He was neither, being a man of deep friendships, a kind, witty, and even gay companion. His presidency of International P.E.N. from 1953 to 1956 was a notable success. He received many honours, including honorary degrees at Scottish and French universities and was an officer of the Legion of Honour. Nothing gave him keener pleasure than when, in 1949, he was made a member of the Institute of France, to which no other English novelist, except Rudyard Kipling, had been elected.

In 1923 Morgan married the novelist, Hilda Vaughan, daughter of Hugh Vaughan Vaughan of Builth, Breconshire, a solicitor, descended from the family of Henry Vaughan, the seventeenth-century poet. They had one son and a daughter who married the seventh Marquess of Anglesey in 1948. Morgan died in London 6 February 1958.

A drawing of Morgan by Augustus John is in the National Portrait Gallery. There are other portraits in the possession of the family.

[Personal knowledge; private information, and the editing of Charles Morgan's letters published in 1967.]

EILUNED LEWIS

published 1971

MUIR Edwin

(1887–1959)

Writer, was born at the Folly in Deerness on the Orkney mainland 15 May 1887, the youngest of the six children of James Muir, farmer, and his wife, Elizabeth, daughter of Edwin Cormack. Two years later the family moved to the Bu, a hundred-acre farm on the small island of Wyre, where there was a strong sense of community among its few families. The child had also a sense of a larger unity—between the human community and the animals and the natural surroundings. In the home the arts were a natural part of life, and the evenings were filled with story-telling and singing. When he was eight the family moved to Garth, another hundred-acre farm, four miles from Kirkwall on the mainland. He went irregularly to the grammar school and began to read avidly. The farm did not prosper and when he was fourteen the family moved to Glasgow—a sudden transition from a pre-industrial community into the modern world. Within five years his father and mother and, after slow painful illnesses, two of his brothers were dead. Muir worked as office-boy and clerk in Glasgow and Greenock. As a boy he had experienced two emotional conversions at revivalist meetings, but his early religious faith was undermined by what he saw in the slums and by the deaths of his brothers, and was replaced by faith in socialism and later in Nietzscheanism, two philosophies which he desperately tried to reconcile. He was a member of the Clarion Scouts, of the Independent Labour Party, and of the Guild Socialist movement. From 1913 he contributed to the *New Age* propagandist verses of little merit and later aphorisms in the manner of Nietzsche which were collected in *We Moderns* (1918). He volunteered for the army but was rejected as physically unfit.

In 1919 he married Wilhelmina (Willa) Johnstone, daughter of Peter Anderson, draper, of Montrose, Angus, left Glasgow for London, and became assistant to A. R. Orage on the *New Age*. The unhappiness of the Glasgow years had brought him close to nervous breakdown and he underwent a course of psychoanalysis. This, and more congenial work, but especially his wife helped him in the quiet years which followed, in Prague, Germany, Italy, and Austria (1921–4), to recover inner peace; his imagination woke, and he began to write poetry.

In Buckinghamshire (1924–5), France (1925–7), Surrey (1927–8), Sussex (1928–32), Hampstead (1932–5), and St. Andrews (1935–42), Muir made his living by voluminous work as critic and, with his wife, translator; wrote three novels, a life of John Knox (1929), and *Scottish Journey* (1935), and gradually improved in skill as a poet. With his wife, a better linguist who did most of the work, he produced some forty volumes of translations, mostly from German, making the works of Kafka and of Hermann Broch available to English readers, as well as Feuchtwanger's *Jew Süss*. His criticism is contained in about a thousand reviews; in numerous articles (some collected in *Latitudes* (1924), *Transition* (1926), and *Essays on Literature and Society* (1949)); in broadcast talks; and in *The Structure of the Novel* (1928), *Scott and Scotland* (1936), *The Present Age* (1939), and *The Estate of Poetry* (1962); it is marked by scrupulous fairness and independence of judgement. T. S. Eliot thought his 'the best criticism of our time'. Fiction was not his *métier*, but his novels are of interest for their poetic quality. His finest prose work is *An Autobiography* (1954) in which visionary radiance is combined with the realism to be expected in a farmer's child. His mature prose reflects his character—quiet, lucid, witty without striving after effect. But his poetry is his great achievement.

Coming to poetry late, Muir went on maturing to the end, and wrote his best poems when over fifty. He used traditional metres and made no startling innovations in technique, being concerned only to convey his vision clearly and honestly. Beneath the story of his life he saw the fable of man—Eden, the Fall, the journey through the labyrinth of time. He made much use of his dreams and of myths, for in them the fable is most clearly seen; but in his later poems he was able to relate a widening range of temporal experiences—the war, the Communist victory in Prague, fears of atomic war, his marriage—to his perception of an underlying timeless reality. He experienced to the full the doubts and fears characteristic of his century, and his honest facing of them makes the more impressive his vision of 'boundless union and freedom'. He came to see the Incarnation as the answer to the problems of time and eternity, necessity and freedom; but his poetry embodied vision rather than belief. Immortality was to him a state of being, something immediately experienced. His apparently simple words carry a great weight of meaning. His poems are mostly short; but they are not fragments—all are related to his central vision of the mystery of our common humanity. His collected poems were published in 1960.

From 1942 to 1945 Muir worked for the British Council in Edinburgh and was then director of its Institutes in Prague (1945–8) and Rome (1949–50), and warden of Newbattle Abbey, an adult education college near Edinburgh (1950–55). After a year as Charles Eliot Norton professor at Harvard (1955–6), he settled at Swaffham Prior near Cambridge. He was appointed C.B.E. in 1953 and received honorary degrees from Prague (1947), Edinburgh (1947), Rennes (1949), Leeds (1955), and Cambridge (1958). He died in Cambridge 3 January 1959. He had one son. Willa Muir died in 1970.

Muir was a man of complete integrity; gentle, unassuming, and vulnerable, but with firm tenacity of purpose; sometimes abstracted, but strongly affectionate and quick in sympathy. He spoke in a soft lilting voice and sang almost in tune.

In a picture by Stanley Cursiter in the Glasgow City Art Gallery, Muir is portrayed with O. H. Mavor, Eric Linklater, and Neil Gunn. There is a bust by Marek Szwarc owned by the Saltire Society, Edinburgh.

[Edwin Muir, *An Autobiography*, 1954; P. H. Butter, *Edwin Muir: Man and Poet*, 1966; Willa Muir, *Belonging: a Memoir*, 1968; personal knowledge.]

P. H. BUTTER

published 1971

MURRY John Middleton

(1889–1957)

Author, was born at Peckham, London, 6 August 1889, the elder of two sons of John Murry, a clerk in the Inland Revenue Department, and his wife, Emily Wheeler. Murry's father had taught himself to read and write and had begun as a boy messenger; the family was poor and it was through scholarships that Murry obtained his education at Christ's Hospital and Brasenose College, Oxford, where he obtained a first class in honour moderations (1910) and a second in *literae humaniores* (1912). He wrote for the *Westminster Gazette* (1912–13), then for the *Times Literary Supplement*, and worked in the political intelligence department of the War Office from 1916, being appointed chief censor in 1919 and O.B.E. in 1920. In *Between Two Worlds* (1935) he has described his early life up to and including his marriage in 1918 to Katherine Mansfield with whom he had lived since 1912. His second marriage (1924) was to Violet, daughter of Charles le Maistre, general secretary of the International Electrotechnical Commission. After her death in 1931 he married Elizabeth Ada, daughter of Joseph Cockbayne, farmer; and on her death in 1954, fourthly, Mary, daughter of Henry Gilbert Gamble, architect, with whom he had lived since 1941.

Murry had been forced to overwork as a child and for the greater part of his life he worked, at first from financial necessity and later, perhaps, partly from habit, at abnormally high pressure. It is therefore all the more remarkable that so much of his prodigious output of both literary and social criticism should be of value. When he was appointed editor of the *Athenaeum* in 1919, at the age of thirty, he was a key figure, and perhaps then the leading figure, of the post-war literary generation which included T. S. Eliot, Aldous Huxley, and D. H. Lawrence with whom his relations were particularly intimate and stormy. Murry's literary popularity was short-lived and he came to be described by a friendly critic as 'the best-hated man of letters in the country'. Although it had been brilliantly successful intellectually, the *Athenaeum* had lost money and in 1921 it was merged with the *Nation*, when Murry resigned, mainly on account of Katherine Mansfield's serious illness. After her death in 1923 Murry founded the *Adelphi*, which he controlled until 1948. At first it was a sensational success, but the success was of a kind to alienate some of his most discriminating readers. Although this was partly due to their own impercipience, it is nevertheless true that in the *Adelphi* Murry did at times exhibit an emotionalism which was the flaw in the element of mysticism which had been latent in his work from the beginning and became more manifest after Katherine Mansfield's death. At its best this mystical element was responsible for the extraordinary penetration of Murry's criticism, which is evident in his first critical study, *Dostoevsky* (1916), and in all his more important works. It was, however, completely at odds with the prevailing literary trends.

For many years after Katherine Mansfield's death, Murry lived a strenuous and tormented life which was divided into what appeared to be three almost water-tight compartments: first, his literary work, which included books on Keats, D. H. Lawrence, Blake, and Shakespeare; second, his political and social activities, which included lecturing and the organization of a farm community, but which also produced books on his religious thought, on Communism, and on pacifism; third, his home life, which was almost continuously painful. His second wife, by whom he had a son and a daughter, died, like his first, of consumption. There were also a son and a daughter of his third marriage which was unhappy; it was only with his fourth wife that he at last achieved a life of peaceful happiness. With his *Jonathan Swift* (1954), *Unprofessional Essays* (1956), and *Love, Freedom and Society* (1957) he began to regain some of his former reputation as a literary critic. Yet *Love, Freedom and Society*, which was based upon a comparative study of Albert Schweitzer and D. H. Lawrence, was in reality a masterly synthesis of his own literary, religious, and social thought, and its favourable reception might suggest that readers were beginning to catch up with Murry's method. In the long run, however, he will probably be best remembered for his studies of Shakespeare, Keats, and D. H. Lawrence, and perhaps even more for his adherence, in an age of academic sterility, to the humane tradition of culture. In the words of his biographer, F. A. Lea, he owed 'his unique understanding of the Romantics and his total neglect by the academics to the persistence of his quest for "the good life"—a quest that carried him, as it did Coleridge and Arnold, ever farther away from literature in the direction of philosophy and sociology' (*A Defence of Philosophy*, 1962).

Murry died at Bury St. Edmunds, Suffolk, 13 March 1957. There is an interesting drawing of him in his youth in (Sir) William Rothenstein's *Twenty-Four Portraits* (2nd series, 1923).

[J. M. Murry, *Between Two Worlds*, 1935, and other works, *passim*; F. A. Lea, *Life of John Middleton Murry*, 1959; private information; personal knowledge.]

RICHARD REES

published 1971

MURRY Kathleen

(1888–1923)

Writer under the pseudonym of Katherine Mansfield, was born at Wellington, New Zealand, 14 October 1888, the third daughter of (Sir) Harold Beauchamp, banker and company director, by his first wife, Annie Burnell, daughter of Joseph Dyer, secretary of a provident society. Her early childhood was passed for the most part at Karori, a village near Wellington. Her first story was published at the age of nine. In 1903 she was taken to England, and was a resident student for three years at Queen's College, Harley Street, London, where she edited the college magazine. In 1906 she returned unwillingly to New Zealand, but came back to England two years later on a modest allowance from her father. She married in

London in 1909 George Bowden, from whom she parted soon after. In 1910 and 1911 she contributed regularly to a weekly paper, *The New Age*, and in 1911 published, under the pseudonym of 'Katherine Mansfield', her first collection of short stories, *In a German Pension*, based on experiences which she underwent in Woerishofen in Bavaria.

In 1911 Katherine Mansfield met John Middleton Murry, the critic, eldest son of John Murry, of the Inland Revenue Department. They lived together from April 1912 until their marriage in 1918. From 1911 to 1913 she published short stories and poems in *Rhythm* and *The Blue Review*, two periodicals of which Mr. Murry was associate editor. In 1915 she compiled and edited, with the help of Mr. Murry and D. H. Lawrence, a magazine called *The Signature*.

Nervous strain due to the European War, a physical constitution weakened by operations and recurrent pleurisy, and the loss of her only brother, Leslie Heron Beauchamp, who was killed in France in 1915, led Katherine Mansfield to withdraw herself for a time into memories of her childhood, and she now sought to frame these memories in collections of short stories. *Prelude* was published in 1918 and *Je ne parle pas français* printed privately in 1919. Katherine Mansfield was divorced from George Bowden in 1918 and married John Middleton Murry in London in the May of that year. In April 1919 her husband was appointed editor of the *Athenaeum*, and she began to review current novels in its pages. These reviews were collected and published as *Novels and Novelists* in 1930.

Bliss, a volume of short stories, published in 1920, established Katherine Mansfield's reputation. Another volume, *The Garden Party* (1922), was the last of her books to be published in her lifetime. In December 1917 she had been found to be consumptive, and thereafter her life was marked by chronic illness. She travelled from place to place in Italy, Switzerland, and the south of France, returning infrequently to England. Her letters and journals describe her physical and spiritual conflict in poignant detail. She now came to feel that her attitude to life had been unduly rebellious, and she sought, during the days that remained to her, to renew and compose her spiritual life. With this object in view she entered on 17 October 1922 the Gurdjieff Institute, near Fontainebleau, which aimed at achieving physical, mental, and spiritual health by esoteric methods. She died there of pulmonary haemorrhage 9 January 1923, and was buried in the communal cemetery at Avon, near Fontainebleau.

The Doves' Nest (1923) and *Something Childish* (1924) are posthumous collections of Katherine Mansfield's stories. Her *Poems* were collected in 1923, her *Journal* edited in 1927, and her *Letters* published in 1928. *The Aloe*, an early draft of *Prelude*, appeared in 1930.

As a short story writer Katherine Mansfield is closely akin to Tchehov. Their sensitiveness of perception is similar, their grasp of significant detail, their sense of quiet pattern, and their insistence on the poetic quality of simple homely familiarities. Katherine Mansfield broke completely with the older tradition of English tale-telling. Her influence on her own generation, which has been great, has served to render it conscious of the possibility of the short story as an art form presenting life at an arrested moment. Her *Journal* and her *Letters* belong to the permanent literature of self-revelation. They record with integrity the sensitive response of her generation to the War, and to the difficult years of transition after it, when youth, after a shattering experience, was endeavouring to formulate new values. Her *Poems* show promise rather than achievement.

[Ruth Elvish Mantz, *The Critical Bibliography of Katherine Mansfield*, 1931; Ruth Elvish Mantz and J. Middleton Murry, *The Life of Katherine Mansfield*, 1933; Katherine Mansfield, *Journal*, 1927, and *Letters*, 2 vols., 1928; *Letters of D. H. Lawrence*, ed. Aldous Huxley, 1932; private information.]

E. O'BRIEN

published 1937

NAIPAUL Shivadhar Srinivasa (Shiva)
(1945–1985)

Writer, was born 25 February 1945 at a kinsman's house in Woodbrook, a quarter of Port-of-Spain, but was soon taken to Nepaul Street in the neighbouring quarter of St James, where he grew up. He was the sixth of the seven children, two of them sons, of Seepersad Naipaul, journalist, and his wife Droapatie Capildeo; his elder brother by more than twelve years was the novelist V. S. Naipaul. The family belonged to the Indian community which had originally migrated to Trinidad as indentured labourers in the nineteenth century.

Family life was close and essentially feminine after the death of his father when Shiva was seven and his brother's departure to England. Naipaul himself wrote that he enjoyed the company of women and was 'responsive to the tidal motions of their moods—their curious gaieties and darknesses; and without consciously intending it, I see that they have had a major role in my fiction'. He was educated at Queen's Royal and St Mary's Colleges in Port-of-Spain whence he won an Island scholarship to Oxford. It was a release. Naipaul later wrote that he never revisited Port-of-Spain without a sense of panic 'that, having arrived there, I may never be able to get out again'.

He sailed to England in 1964 and went up to University College, Oxford, where he read psychology, philosophy, and physiology before changing capriciously to Chinese; he took a third class in 1968. Naipaul was a striking figure at Oxford—he wore long black boots and long black hair in those days—with an affectionate and bibulous circle of friends. As an undergraduate he met Virginia Margaret, daughter of Douglas Stuart, a BBC journalist. 'Jenny' was to be his helpmeet for eighteen years. They were married in Oxford 17 June 1967 and their son Tarun was born in 1973.

Before he left university, Naipaul had begun a novel. It was continued in a bedsitter off Ladbroke Grove in London, first of several modest accommodations before he found a flat in Warrington Crescent in 1975. The result was *Fireflies*, published in 1970 and recognized as a work of very high talent. It was set in Indian Port-of-Spain and told the story of Ram Lutchman, his long-suffering wife, and their two sons; told it in limpid prose, with a crystal ear for dialogue, with electric comedy, but also with deep feeling for the struggle of human beings to come to terms with life and one another. The book won three awards, the John Llewellyn Rhys memorial prize, the Jock Campbell *New Statesman* award, and the Winifred Holtby memorial prize of the Royal Society of Literature. It was followed in 1973 by *The Chip-Chip Gatherers*, also set in Trinidad, tragi-comic again though palpably more sombre in tone. It was enthusiastically received and won the Whitbread award.

The enthusiasts were perplexed that no novel followed for ten years. During those years Naipaul travelled and wrote a good deal of outstanding journalism, much of it collected in *Beyond the Dragon's Mouth* (1984), an anthology of articles and short stories. He also published two works of non-fiction. *North of South* (1978) was a bleak account of a journey through Kenya, Tanzania, and Zambia. It was too bleak for those *bien pensants* who wanted to see only the best and the most hopeful in independent Africa. Naipaul was in fact a painfully honest observer, reacting with savage indignation to this 'hopeless, doomed continent . . . swaddled in lies—the lies of an aborted European civilisation; the lies of liberation. Nothing but lies.'

He had a specific advantage over the *bien pensants* as a non-European quite free from 'white liberal' hang-ups of colonial and racial guilt. This advantage was put to further use. In 1979–80 the Naipauls spent more than a year intermittently in San Francisco and Connecticut as he worked on a bleaker subject still. *Black and White* (1980) recounted the background to a ghastly story, the mass suicide at a jungle camp in Guyana by the deluded followers of a Californian heresiarch called Jim Jones. If *North of South* had been called 'anti-African', the unflinchingly sharp-eyed *Black and White* was called 'anti-American'; again unjustly: it was another cry of rage at folly and cruelty. Naipaul's third novel appeared at last in 1983. He had evidently had some block or inhibition, but at the same time *A Hot Country* is a tribute to his fastidiousness and perfectionism, which were always as much a blessing to his readers as they were a trial to his publishers and editors: he was a writer who could spend a morning working on one sentence, to delete it in the afternoon. Direct and intense, his style is now pared down to a minimum. Maybe for that reason the book was under-rated at the time.

In 1984 Naipaul visited Australia to write a book about the country. His work in progress on that book was included in his posthumous collection *An Unfinished Journey* (1986). He had just moved to an airy flat in Belsize Park Gardens where in a small work-room he wrote in longhand standing at an old-fashioned lectern.

Naipaul was above medium height but stooping and thickly built. He was bear-like in looks and also in manner. Prickly, acutely sensitive, difficult at times, he provoked hostility without trying; or perhaps without trying much. Some found him arrogant or truculent, and by his own hilarious account his visit to Australia ended in a succession of socially disastrous evenings. Others relished his company. A group of friends, a number of them writers associated with the *Spectator* where his wife was the editor's secretary, regarded him with amused affection and awed respect. Sardonic and world-weary, over a long wine-fuelled lunch or a long whisky-fuelled evening he was the most engaging and rewarding of companions.

He celebrated his fortieth birthday at home in February 1985. He had always been afraid of death. In that sense alone it came to him mercifully six months later when he was struck by a thrombosis at his flat on 13 August 1985 and died instantly. He was cremated by Hindu rites at Golders Green crematorium.

[Shiva Naipaul, *Beyond the Dragon's Mouth*, 1984, and *An Unfinished Journey*, 1986; private information; personal knowledge.]

GEOFFREY WHEATCROFT

published 1990

Nevil Shute

(1899–1960)

Novelist under the name of Nevil Shute and aeronautical engineer, was born in Ealing 17 January 1899, the younger son of a Cornishman, Arthur Hamilton Norway, who became an assistant secretary of the General Post Office, and his wife, Mary Louisa Gadsden. At the age of eleven Norway played truant from his first preparatory school in Hammersmith, spending days among the model aircraft at the Science Museum examining wing control on the Blériot and trying to puzzle out how the engine of the Antoinette ran without a carburettor. On being detected in these precocious studies he was sent to the Dragon School, Oxford, and thence to Shrewsbury. He was on holiday in Dublin, where his father was then secretary to the Post Office in Ireland, at the time of the Easter rising of 1916 and acted as a stretcher-bearer, winning commendation for gallant conduct. He passed into the Royal Military Academy with the aim of being commissioned into the Royal Flying Corps; but a bad stammer led to his being failed at his final medical examination and returned to civil life. The last few months of the war (in which his brother had been killed) were spent on home service as a private in the Suffolk Regiment.

In 1919 Norway went up to Balliol College, Oxford, where he took third class honours in engineering science in 1922 and rowed in the college second eight. During the vacations he worked, unpaid, for the Aircraft Manufacturing Company at Hendon, then for (Sir) Geoffrey de Havilland's own firm, which he joined as an employee on coming down from Oxford. He now fulfilled his thwarted wartime ambition of learning to fly and gained experience as a test observer. During the evenings he diligently wrote novels and short stories, unperturbed by rejection slips from publishers.

In 1924 Norway took the post of chief calculator to the Airship Guarantee Company, a subsidiary of Vickers, Ltd., to work on the construction of the R.100. In 1929 he became deputy chief engineer under (Sir) Barnes Wallis and in the following year he flew to and from Canada in the R.100. He had a passionate belief in the future of airships but his hopes foundered in the crash of its government rival, the R.101, wrecked with the loss of Lord Thomson, the minister of aviation, and most of those on board. He had watched with mounting horror what he regarded as the criminal inefficiency with which the R.101 was being constructed. His experience in this phase of his career left a lasting bitterness; it bred in him almost pathological distrust of politicians and civil servants.

Recognizing that airship development was a lost cause, he founded in 1931 Airspeed, Ltd., aeroplane constructors, in an old garage and remained joint managing-director until 1938. The pioneering atmosphere of aircraft construction in those years suited his temperament. He revelled in individual enterprise and doing things by improvisation on a financial shoestring. When the business grew and was becoming one of humdrum routine, producing aircraft to government orders, he decided to get out of the rut and live by writing. He had by 1938 enjoyed some success as a novelist and had sold the film rights of *Lonely Road* (1932) and *Ruined City* (1938).

On the outbreak of war in 1939 Norway joined the Royal Naval Volunteer Reserve as a sub-lieutenant in the miscellaneous weapons department. Rising to lieutenant-commander he found experimenting with secret weapons a job after his own heart. But his growing celebrity as a writer caused him to be in the Normandy landings on 6 June 1944, for the Ministry of Information, and to be sent to Burma as a correspondent in 1945. He entered Rangoon with the 15th Corps from Arakan. Soon after demobilization in 1945 he emigrated to Australia and made his home in Langwarrin, Victoria. High taxation and what he felt to be the decadence of Britain, with the spirit of personal independence and freedom dying, led him to leave the old country.

His output of novels, which began with *Marazan* (1926), continued to the end. Writing under his Christian names, Nevil Shute, he had an unaffectedly popular touch which made him a best-seller throughout the Commonwealth and the United States. The secret of his success lay in the skill with which he combined loving familiarity with technicalities and a straightforward sense of human relationships and values. He conveyed to the readers his own zest for making and flying aircraft. The hazards and rewards of backroom boys have never been more sympathetically portrayed nor with closer inside knowledge. His natural gift for creating briskly moving plots did not extend to the delineation of character in anything more than conventional terms. He retained to the last the outlook of a decent, average public-school boy of his generation. Although he lived into the James Bond era he never made the slightest concessions to the fast-growing appetite in the mass fiction market for sadism and violence.

No Highway (1948), dealing with the drama of structural fatigue in aircraft, set in human terms of those responsible for a competitive passenger service, gave full scope to both sides of his talent. Machines and men and women share in shaping the drama. *A Town Like Alice* (1950), describing the grim Odyssey of white women and children in Japanese-occupied Malaya, captured the cinema audiences as completely as it did the reading public. *Round the Bend* (1951) was thought by Norway himself to be his most enduring book. It told of the aircraft engineer of mixed eastern and western stock who taught his men to worship God through work conscientiously and prayerfully performed and came to be regarded as divine by people of many creeds. *On the Beach* (1957) expressed Norway's sensitive appreciation of the frightful possibilities of global warfare and annihilation by radio-active dust.

Other novels, several of them filmed, were *What Happened to the Corbetts* (1939), *An Old Captivity* (1940), *Landfall* (1940), *Pied Piper* (1942), *Pastoral* (1944), *In the Wet* (1953), and *Requiem for a Wren* (1955).

In *Slide Rule* (1954), sub-titled 'the autobiography of an engineer', he told, candidly and racily, of his life up to 1938 when he left the aircraft industry.

The stammer, which was as much a stimulus as a handicap, did not prevent Norway from being good company, always welcome at social gatherings of his many friends. An enthusiastic yachtsman and fisherman as well as an air pilot, he delighted in outdoor life, and his gaiety was not dimmed by the heart attacks from which he suffered.

In 1931 Norway married Frances Mary Heaton, by whom he had two daughters. He died in Melbourne 12 January 1960.

[Norway's own writings; personal knowledge.]

A. P. Ryan

published 1971

O'CASEY Sean

(1880–1964)

Irish dramatist and author, was born in Dublin of Protestant parents 30 March 1880, the youngest of the five surviving children of Michael and Susanna Casey. His real name was John Casey, but he subsequently Gaelicized his name to Sean O'Cathasaigh and still later changed the surname to O'Casey. His father, who worked as a clerk for the Irish Church Mission, died when John was six; two brothers and a sister who were already approaching adulthood went their several ways. O'Casey with his mother and the remaining brother, who was able to provide but little financial support, lived in the poverty and squalor of tenement life.

O'Casey

O'Casey himself suffered from a painful eye disease which prevented any formal education; but by the age of fourteen he had taught himself to read. From then onwards he read voraciously. His inborn feeling for the splendour of language had been nourished from an early age by reading from the Bible. His bent for the theatre quickly showed itself: two authors in whose work he took special delight were, at their different levels, masters of stagecraft—Shakespeare and Dion Boucicault.

But self-education, though it may be intense and profound, is almost of necessity narrow—especially when it starts late and from illiteracy. Not for many years was O'Casey able to make use of his hard-earned culture to improve his way of life. Until he was thirty he worked as a casual labourer, often unemployed and further handicapped by poor health. Even when he did escape from drudgery, it was into the fervid atmosphere of Irish politics rather than the comparatively calm world of Irish literature. He was in turn a member of the Gaelic League, the Irish Republican Brotherhood, Jim Larkin's union, the Irish Citizen Army, and the Irish Socialist Party. But he was too independent to remain long in any movement. After 1916 he turned seriously to writing plays. Although the first three which he submitted to the Abbey Theatre were rejected, he received encouragement from Lady Gregory and W. B. Yeats. Not until he was forty-three was his first play staged; but it was quickly followed by others which made it clear that he was a writer of genius.

Genius was a word which came easily to commentators on O'Casey's command of language, once his career was fully launched. His prose had about it an amplitude and a poetic colour which set it apart from and above the drab realism which was the aim of most of his contemporaries; and while many faults of craftsmanship were laid to his charge as his career continued the special magic of his style was never, or very seldom, questioned.

This special quality was seen at its finest in his early plays about the Irish troubles produced at the Abbey Theatre, all written from his own personal experience, and in the six volumes of his magnificent autobiography (1939–54). But even in his least successful plays he showed this quality. He was still unmistakably a genius, but one who had somehow lost his way to the heights.

O'Casey's three Dublin plays established him as a great writer but destroyed him as a dramatist. While the first of them, *The Shadow of a Gunman* (1923), was packing the Abbey Theatre he was still working as a day labourer, mixing cement. After the success of his masterpiece, *Juno and the Paycock* (1924), he turned professional. But his next play *The Plough and the Stars* (1926), of which the setting was Dublin during the Easter rising of 1916 and the main characters non-combatants, gave great offence. When he was awarded the Hawthornden prize in 1926 for *Juno* he was invited to London and he determined to retreat to an exile in England which was to endure for the rest of his life.

An exile indeed it was, and continued to be. O'Casey never understood England, nor she O'Casey. Even the welcome which his Dublin plays received in London was based on a misapprehension. English audiences of the time had little patience with any dramatic dialogue which was not realistic, and they took O'Casey's lyric prose to be the authentic speech of Irish slum dwellers. Consequently when he turned later to more obvious fantasy the English public, expecting more realism, lost interest in his work.

O'Casey in his turn contributed strongly to this misunderstanding. After a perfunctory glance at the London theatre he decided that its aims were too trivial to be worth his attention. A man more worldly wise or less self-assured might have realized that London had much to teach him, both in the way of broader culture and a greater experience of stagecraft; but O'Casey, who had a theory that an artist should develop naturally along his own lines, saw no need for this. As a result, his lack of education remained always in his way.

For example, he had the idea, in itself brilliantly original and destined to be valuable in the hands of later generations, of using different styles of writing in the same play. But because he was not skilled in the various techniques he employed, such a play was foredoomed to failure. His anti-war play, *The Silver Tassie*, with its symbolic second act, was a case in point. Its rejection by the Abbey Theatre in 1928 gave rise to a public dispute between the author and Yeats. Produced in London at the Apollo (1929) it was praised by the critics for its originality, but it did not draw the public. *Within the Gates* (Royalty, 1934), written with a similar disregard of realism, was found incomprehensible by critics and public alike. It gave ample evidence of O'Casey's inability to adapt himself to his new surroundings. It was set in Hyde Park and the characters included a kind of chorus of down-and-outs. Yet there was not a hint of a London atmosphere in the whole composition. It was not surprising that this was the last of his plays to command an important production as a matter of course.

After that he had to fight a losing battle to obtain production of any kind at all, although *Red Roses for Me* was favourably received by the critics when it was produced at the Embassy in 1946. In 1938 O'Casey settled in Devon where he continued to write busily but it was as an increasingly frustrated, disappointed, and embittered man with his mind's eye always on the Ireland which had rejected, and continued to reject, him. For the Dublin International Theatre Festival of 1958 he was invited to provide a new play. But difficulties were made about its production and O'Casey withdrew the play (*The Drums of Father Ned*) and went on to withdraw all his plays from production in Dublin.

In 1927 O'Casey married Eileen Reynolds, an actress (as Eileen Carey) of Irish Roman Catholic parentage. They had two sons, the younger of whom died in 1957, and one daughter. O'Casey died in Torquay 18 September 1964.

The National Portrait Gallery has a drawing by Powys Evans.

[*The Times*, 21 September 1964; O'Casey's autobiography; David Krause, *Sean O'Casey, The Man and his Work*, 1960; Eileen O'Casey, *Sean*, 1971; private information; personal knowledge.]

W. A. DARLINGTON

published 1981

ORCZY Emma Magdalena Rosalia Marie Josepha Barbara

(1865–1947)

Baroness Orczy

Novelist, was born 23 September 1865 at Tarna-Örs, Hungary. She was named Emma (or Emmuska) after her mother, Countess Wass. Her father, Baron Felix Orczy, a talented amateur musician, came of an ancient landowning family. On taking over the property of Tisza-Abád he attempted to introduce modern farming methods, but when the peasants, distrustful of innovation, burnt his crops and buildings, he abandoned agriculture for a musical career. The family moved first to Budapest, then to Brussels, where Emma was a pupil at the Visitation convent, afterwards attending another convent school in Paris. When she was fifteen the family settled in London where she met many musical celebrities. Having no musical talent herself she studied painting at the West London School of Art and at Heatherley's, and whilst still a student had three pictures hung in the Academy. At Heatherley's she met (Henry George) Montague (Maclean) Barstow, a black-and-white artist and illustrator, son of a clergyman, the late Rev. Michael William Barstow. Their marriage took place in 1894 and their only child, a son, was born in 1899.

With her husband, Baroness Orczy wrote and illustrated some volumes of children's stories, but her career as a writer really began with a short story, 'Juliette', published in August 1899 in the *Royal Magazine*. Her first novel, *The Emperor's Candlesticks*, appeared the same year. It was a failure, but she had considerable success with a series of crime stories in the *Royal Magazine*, entitled 'The Old Man in the Corner'. In 1902 she wrote *The Scarlet Pimpernel*, a novel of the French revolution. The manuscript was rejected by at least twelve publishers, but a dramatic version, written in collaboration with her husband, was accepted for production with Fred Terry and Julia Neilson in the leading parts. Produced in Nottingham in the autumn of 1903, the play did not appear in London until 1905, when, after an unpromising start, it achieved phenomenal popularity. Until Terry's death in 1933 it was regularly revived in London and the provinces, whilst translations appeared abroad in French, German, Spanish, and Italian. The first London production coincided with the publication of the novel, which proved an immense and immediate success. Its hero, Sir Percy Blakeney, the indolent British aristocrat who, as the mysterious Scarlet Pimpernel, rescued victims from the guillotine, quickly became and remained to successive generations one of the best-known characters in popular fiction.

Baroness Orczy was henceforth a prolific writer, producing two and sometimes three books in a year. Several of them were filmed, including *The Scarlet Pimpernel*, played by Leslie Howard. With the exception of an autobiography, a biography of the Duchesse de Berri, and the early crime stories, all are historical romances. The emphasis is definitely on romance rather than history, but a real gift for narrative and for simple characterization distinguish the unsophisticated, swift-moving stories with which she delighted a huge public.

In 1906 Baroness Orczy inherited the property of Tarna-Örs, but she continued to live in England until the end of the war of 1914–18, when she and her husband settled in Monte Carlo. There they were obliged to remain throughout the war of 1939–45, Montague Barstow dying in 1943. Baroness Orczy herself died in London 12 November 1947.

[Baroness Orczy, *Links in the Chain of Life*, 1947; *The Times*, 13 November 1947; private information.]

GEORGINA BATTISCOMBE

published 1959

Playwright, was born in Leicester 1 January 1933, the eldest child in the family of two sons and two daughters of William Orton, gardener, and his wife, Elsie, machinist and charwoman. He was educated at Marriots Road Primary School; and after failing his eleven-plus examination took a secretarial course at Clark's College, Leicester. Bored by a series of office jobs, Orton became interested in amateur dramatics and in 1951 won a scholarship to RADA. Puckish and handsome, Orton did well enough at RADA to earn his diploma in 1953. But he did not enjoy it: 'I completely lost my confidence and my virginity. I was lost. I didn't have a very good time because I found that in the very first term that I wasn't learning anything.'

After a four-month stint at the Ipswich Repertory Company, Orton became disenchanted with acting. Too young and inadequate a performer to get major roles, he was also too ambitious and full of fun for the arid grind he discovered was the regimen of the repertory actor. Returning to London, he set his sights on a literary career. He was ill equipped for this task. The idea of writing was suggested by Kenneth Leith Halliwell (1926–67) whom Orton met at RADA and with whom he lived until his death. Halliwell was seven years Orton's senior and much better educated. He set about to transform Orton into his intellectual equal and constant companion. Orton was especially influenced by the writings of Ronald Firbank whom Halliwell also imitated. Together, between 1953 and 1962, they wrote a series of novels, none of which deserved to be published. The books included *The Silver Bucket* (1953), *The Mechanical Womb* (1955), *The Last Days of Sodom* (1955), and *The Boy Hairdresser* (1956). They lived a hermetic existence first at 161 West End Lane in West Hampstead, moving in 1959 to another bedsitter in Islington at 25 Noel Road. For a time they existed on Halliwell's small inheritance; but when that ran out they worked at odd jobs six months at a time to subsidize their writing.

By 1957 Orton had begun to write novels and plays on his own. He had no luck; but he had begun to identify in himself a great appetite for anarchy. 'Cleanse my heart, give the ability to rage correctly', prays Gombold, Orton's spokesman in *The Vision of Gombold Proval* (1961)— posthumously published as *Head to Toe* (1971). In the novel, Orton dreamed of a cauterizing verbal power which would create a 'seismic disturbance'. In his writing Orton had not found the right tone or target for his rage. But

in public pranks he found another way of satisfying his hunger for vin-
dictive triumph, and one in which the verbal and visual power of his plays
were first planted. Under the pseudonym of Edna Welthorpe, he assumed
a suburban attitude and wrote letters to a variety of institutions which
goaded them into idiotic correspondence. (In later years, Edna Welthorpe
would damn and praise Orton's plays in the letters columns of newspapers
to stir up controversy.) In 1959 Orton also began to deface public library
books by writing false blurbs in the jacket sleeves and pasting outrageous
images on book jackets. The cut-up images were well done: concise, irreverent, and very funny. Orton admitted later that he was 'enraged that
there were so many rubbishy novels and rubbishy books' in libraries. His
prank was intended to shock. He and Halliwell would return the tampered
books to the shelves and wait to see if they got a response. In 1962, they
did. They were arrested and sent to prison for six months. Prison brought
a saving detachment to Orton's writing and clarified his view of life. 'Before
prison, I had been vaguely conscious of something rotten somewhere:
prison crystallized this', Orton said.

In 1963, after a decade of total literary failure, Orton completed a radio
play, *The Ruffian on the Stair*, which was accepted by the BBC and
broadcast on 31 August 1964. Between 1964 and 1967 when he died, Joe
Orton became a playwright of international reputation. His output was
small but his impact was large. By 1967 the term 'Ortonesque' had worked
its way into the English vocabulary, a shorthand adjective for scenes of
macabre outrageousness. Orton wrote three first-class full-length plays:
Entertaining Mr. Sloane (1963, produced in 1964), which (Sir) Terence
Rattigan called the best first play he had ever seen; *Loot* (presented in 1965);
and the posthumously produced *What the Butler Saw* (1967, produced in
1969). Orton wrote four one-act plays: *The Ruffian on the Stair* (1965,
produced in 1966), *The Good and Faithful Servant* (1964, produced in 1967),
The Erpingham Camp (1965, produced in 1966), and *Funeral Games* (1966,
presented in 1968). Films were made of *Sloane* (1969) and *Loot* (1970), which
also won the *Evening Standard* award for the best play of the year (1966).
Orton wrote one original, but unproduced, film script, *Up Against It* (1967).

Orton's plays often scandalized audiences, but his wit made the outrage
scintillating. He found people 'profoundly bad and irresistibly funny'. He
was the first contemporary English playwright to transfer into art the
clown's rambunctious sexual rapacity from the stage to the page. He aspired to corrupt an audience with pleasure. Orton's laughter bore out
Nietzsche's dictum that 'he who writes in blood and aphorisms does not
want to be read, he wants to be learned by heart'. Orton brought the
epigram back to modern theatre to illuminate a violent world. 'It's life that
defeats the Christian Church, she's always been well-equipped to deal with

death' (*The Erpingham Camp*). 'All classes are criminal today. We live in an age of equality' (*Funeral Games*).

Orton searched for a way to marry terror and elation and found it in farce. In his hands, farce became a paradigm of the tumult of consciousness as well as of society. Orton fed his characters into farce's fun machine and made them bleed. He found a way of making laughter at once astonishing and serious. A voluptuary of fiasco, Orton's career ended as sensationally as it began. On 9 August 1967 he and Halliwell were found dead in their Islington flat. Halliwell, disturbed by the contrast between Orton's success and his own failure and by Orton's homosexual promiscuity, had battered in his friend's head with a hammer and taken his own life with an overdose of sleeping pills. Orton's death—laced as it was with the irony of his own fascination with the grotesque—had special public interest. No playwright in living memory had met a more gruesome end. It was a great loss to world drama. *The Times* obituary called Orton 'one of the sharpest stylists of the British new wave ... a consummate dialogue artist and a natural anarch'.

[John Lahr, *Prick Up Your Ears: The Biography of Joe Orton*, 1978; Orton's private diaries; *The Times*, 10 August 1967; private information.]

JOHN LAHR

published 1981

PEAKE Mervyn Laurence

(1911–1968)

Artist and author, was born at Kuling, China, 9 July 1911, the younger son of Ernest Cromwell Peake, MD, Congregational missionary doctor, of Tientsin, by his wife, Amanda Elizabeth Powell. Peake was educated at Tientsin Grammar School, Eltham College, Kent, and the Royal Academy Schools where he won the Hacker prize (1931). After finishing at the Academy Schools he spent two years in an 'artists' colony' of friends on the island of Sark; on the strength of his work he was offered a position at the Westminster School of Art in 1935, where he taught life drawing until 1939. There, too, he met Maeve, youngest of the six children of Owen Eugene Gilmore, MD, FRCS; they married in 1937, and had two sons and a daughter. During the war Peake served in England in the Royal Artillery, being later transferred to the Royal Engineers, but was invalided out in 1943 after a nervous breakdown. For the next two years he was attached to the Ministry of Information, and it was not until just after the end of the war that he was appointed war artist with the rank of captain. In 1946 he returned to Sark with his family, where they spent three serenely happy years; but a retainer from his publisher and a few commissions could not continue to meet the needs of a growing family, and in 1949 they came back to England where Peake secured a part-time teaching post at the Central School of Art, Holborn; this, together with commissioned paintings and illustrations for books, and to a lesser extent his writing, formed the often uneven ground on which he supported his family. From 1957, after the failure of his first and only West End play, *The Wit to Woo*, which was to have solved all their financial problems, he became increasingly incapacitated by what was eventually diagnosed as a form of Parkinson's disease, and by 1960 he was obliged to give up teaching.

After his death in 1968 Peake became best known for his three 'Titus' novels, *Titus Groan* (1946), *Gormenghast* (1950), and *Titus Alone* (1959), which describe the growth of Titus, the seventy-seventh Earl of Groan, in his ancestral home Gormenghast castle, his rebellion against Gormenghast and his restrictive duties, and his attempt to find a new identity for himself in another land. Although showing the influence of Dickens, Lewis Carroll, and Kafka, these books defy ready classification. The term 'fantasy' is perhaps the least inadequate, although Peake's work has nothing of the lightweight or evasive commonly implied by the word: but it is fantasy in being the creation of a fully realized 'other' world, ontologically separate from our own. The strength of *Titus Groan* is the thoroughness with which it is imagined, and the dialectical play throughout of the static, unchanging nature of the castle against the dynamic of the enemies within it. In Gormenghast Peake found the perfect literary expression for his interests as an artist: the slow, heavily descriptive method of the style and the delight in the individualities of people and objects are paralleled in the unmoving character of the castle, the obsessive preoccupation with minutiae which epitomizes the ritual laws which govern it, and the eccentric personalities it produces. Gormenghast castle is the natural home of Peake's imagination, a home to which he was irresistibly drawn, even while as a man and an artist he wished to escape it and explore new worlds. The undertow of Gormenghast drains the life from the portrayal of Titus's rebellion, and the imaginative unity and power of *Titus Groan* is increasingly lost in the succeeding volumes. Yet, considered as a whole, the 'Titus' books remain a massive achievement.

During his lifetime, Peake was known more as an artist, particularly as an illustrator of books. The finest examples are his work for the editions of Lewis Carroll's *The Hunting of the Snark* (1941) and the *Alice* books (1946 and 1954); Coleridge's *The Rime of the Ancient Mariner* (1943); the Grimm brothers' *Household Tales* (1946); and R. L. Stevenson's *Dr. Jekyll and Mr. Hyde* (1948) and *Treasure Island* (1949). Peake also illustrated much of his own work; and his children's books, *Captain Slaughterboard Drops Anchor* (1939) and *Letters from a Lost Uncle from Polar Regions* (1948), are composed round his brilliant drawings. In collections of his individual sketches, *The Craft of the Lead Pencil* (1946) and *The Drawings of Mervyn Peake* (1949), Peake also outlined his views on art as at once intensively subjective and objective. The primary concern of Peake's drawings is with the human figure, rather than with landscape: of Gormenghast he has left us scarcely a pictorial trace. One of the most frequent and powerful of his effects is the portrayal of the frail verticality of his figures struggling against a dense and crushing atmosphere, or else bent or deformed by it: this is also his vision of the lives of the personages of Gormenghast, and of those who rebel against the castle. Later publications, such as his *Writings and Drawings* (1974) and his *Drawings* (1974), showed a return of interest in Peake the artist.

Peake was also recognized in his own day as a poet. Poetry was for him the most moving form of human expression. Much of his poetry for adults appeared in his *Shapes and Sounds* (1941), *The Glassblowers* (1950), *The Rhyme of the Flying Bomb* (1962), and *A Reverie of Bone* (1967). For *The Glassblowers* (and *Gormenghast*) he was awarded the W. H. Heinemann Foundation prize of £100 and an honorary fellowship of the Royal Society of Literature (1951). He is at his best when an experience and its significance for him are fused, as for instance in 'The Glassblowers' or the frightening 'Heads Float About Me', rather than when he reflects on or self-consciously tries to proportion his feelings to his experience. A recurrent motif in his poetry is the idea of a face or body as a building or city, and vice versa: this transference is also seen in the interrelations of Gormenghast and its inhabitants. Peake also wrote children's and nonsense poetry (the latter often in the vein of Lewis Carroll). His poetic impulse is as divided between the serious and the comic as is his *Gormenghast*: Peake would have written more good poetry, as he did the prose of *Titus Groan*, had he fused both sides of his nature in the making of it.

Tall, thin, dark, and haggard, Peake was a romantic figure, whose passionate and intense nature exhausted him: he lived always on 'this desperate edge of now', and wrote to pour himself forth, to empty himself of all his 'golden gall'. In some ways shy and reserved, he was innocently open and generous to all who asked his help. He was enormously sensitive to human suffering, and a visit to Belsen in 1945 (commissioned by the *Leader* to sketch what he saw) left him emotionally scarred. In character he was gentle, gracious, unworldly, and unpractical. He lived in many ways outside convention, wearing strange clothes and behaving in a gently whimsical fashion which puzzled the ordinary. He did not care for 'arrangements' in life: he would gather materials for drawings simply by walking the streets of central London and stopping interesting subjects for on-the-spot sketches; and he would write in the midst of his family circle. It was in part Peake's very proximity to and delight in life which produced his fantasy, and his sense of the individual his art of exaggeration: 'Anything,' he once said, 'seen without prejudice, is enormous.'

Peake died at Burcot, Berkshire, 17 November 1968. Several portraits done by his widow, Maeve Gilmore, remained in her possession. A Mervyn Peake Society was formed in 1975.

[Maeve Gilmore, *A World Away: A Memoir of Mervyn Peake*, 1970, and *Peake's Progress*, 1979; John Watney, *Mervyn Peake*, 1976; private information; personal knowledge.]

C. N. MANLOVE

published 1981

PLATH Sylvia

(1932–1963)

Poet, was born 27 October 1932 in Boston, Massachusetts, the older child and only daughter of Dr Otto Emil Plath, entomologist and teacher, and his wife Aurelia Schober. Both parents were Americans of Germanic extraction. She was partly brought up by her maternal grandparents, Otto Plath suffering much illness; and he died in 1940, just after Sylvia's eighth birthday. Her father's death was the great wound not just of her childhood but of the rest of her life. She determined to excel, at Bradford Senior High School in Wellesley, Massachusetts, and at Smith College, and she did so. At Smith, which she entered in 1950, she was a prize pupil. She had been writing poems since her childhood, and at university was busy with poems, stories, editing the *Smith Review*, keeping up a high academic standard, and leading a full social life. She began to publish her poems in such places as *Harper's*, and won a guest post on the magazine *Mademoiselle*.

But she was already under stress, in her ambitions and her wish to please her mother with her success. She attempted suicide in 1953, after undergoing electroconvulsive therapy. Nevertheless, during her final year at Smith she took entrance examinations for Oxford and Cambridge, in the hope of doing further work in England. She graduated from Smith *summa cum laude*, was awarded a Fulbright grant to study at Newnham College, Cambridge, and arrived there in October 1955. She threw herself into the literary and social life of Cambridge. Tall, pretty, vivacious, with an eager and obvious appetite for every kind of experience, she fell in and out of love, as she had at school and college. She wrote and published in student magazines and in national magazines on both sides of the Atlantic. Early in 1956, at a Cambridge party to launch a student magazine, *St Botolph's*, she met one of the contributors, the poet (later poet laureate) Ted Hughes, a recent graduate. The next day she wrote in her journal: 'And I screamed in myself, thinking: oh, to give myself crashing, fighting, to you.'

Sylvia Plath and Edward James ('Ted') Hughes were married in London on 16 June 1956. He was the son of William Henry Hughes, carpenter and later shopkeeper. After she completed her degree course, they moved to the United States, where she took up an appointment as an instructor in English at Smith College. All this time she was writing prolifically, but she had not yet developed an individual voice. Instead she produced intelligent and efficient pastiches drawn from a variety of models—W. B. Yeats, Dylan Thomas, John Crowe Ransom, Robert Lowell, Theodore Roethke. Ted Hughes himself dates 'the first real breakthrough in her writing' to the autumn of 1959, shortly before their return to England. But her first book of poems, *The Colossus*, published in Britain in 1960, was put together too early to represent much of this new phase.

Between *The Colossus* and the end of her life less than three years later, Sylvia Plath wrote the poems (well over a hundred were written during this period) by which she is chiefly remembered. Some are concerned with pregnancy, birth, and infancy: a daughter, Frieda, was born in April 1960, and a son, Nicholas, in January 1962. Some have a vivid and excited sense of life and renewal. But a great deal of the poems' subject matter is justly described by Philip Larkin in a review of the *Collected Poems*: 'It was, variously, neurosis, insanity, disease, death, horror, terror.' What gives the work excitement and, indeed, transcendence, is the verbal and rhythmical energy, the sometimes almost comic audacity (as in 'Daddy' and 'Lady Lazarus'), and in other poems a dream-like remoteness and impersonality, as if these were messages from another planet.

In September 1962 Sylvia Plath separated from her husband and moved with the two small children to a flat in London. Early in 1963 she published a novel, *The Bell Jar*, under the pseudonym 'Victoria Lucas'. On 11 February 1963 she gassed herself in the flat.

Much work, both verse and prose, was published after her death, and her posthumous fame can in particular be dated from the appearance of her volume of poems, *Ariel*, in 1965. The *Collected Poems*, edited and with an introduction by Ted Hughes, was published in 1981.

[Frances McCullough (ed.), *The Journals of Sylvia Plath*, 1982; Anne Stevenson, *Bitter Fame: a Life of Sylvia Plath*, 1989; personal knowledge.]

ANTHONY THWAITE

published 1993

PLOMER William Charles Franklyn

(1903–1973)

Writer, was born 10 December 1903 at Pietersburg, Transvaal, the eldest of the three sons, the second of whom died in 1908 (there were no daughters), of Charles Campbell Plomer, then an official in the Department of Native Affairs, and his wife Edythe Mary, daughter of Edward Waite-Browne, farmer. William Plomer's English ancestry was a source of pride and research throughout a life to which a start in South Africa had imparted a feeling of rootlessness, which he balanced with the keen social and literary observation of an outsider. He was educated first at St. John's College, Johannesburg, then spent three disagreeable years at a preparatory school in Kent before a brief but very happy period at Rugby (1917–18) which was brought to an end by rapidly deteriorating eyesight. His vision stabilized soon after his return to South Africa, where he worked as an apprentice farmer on the Basutoland border and later with his parents at a native trading station in Zululand.

Plomer's keen aesthetic response to the scenery and native people encountered on his return to South Africa was combined with an increasing awareness of the injustices of colour prejudice there. His literary reading was intense, and his writing (encouraged by correspondence with Harold Monro of the Poetry Bookshop) developed remarkably in the isolation of his lonely country postings. His literary solitude was ended by his encounter with the unpredictable but still liberal-minded Roy Campbell, with whom and (Sir) Laurens van der Post he edited the short-lived but influential English magazine *Voorslag*, which rapidly proved to be the mental 'whiplash' of its Afrikaans title. Plomer's novel *Turbott Wolfe*, published in 1926, gave even greater offence; ferocious and passionate, dealing with love and marriage between black and white, it was well calculated to provoke South African racial sensitivities. More measured in

265

tone is Plomer's 'Ula Masondo', a long story from the same fertile period, in which an African confronts industrial society.

Local outrage was predictable enough. Plomer soon took the opportunity to travel, initially as a journalist, to Japan. He was not to return to Africa for thirty years, a visit in 1956 proving a tense and depressing experience for him. The three years he spent in Japan, mainly in teaching work, were aesthetically stimulating and productive of several close friendships; Plomer's sympathetic responses showed themselves in poetry and short stories, and in the novel *Sado* (1931) with its quietly voiced homosexual overtones.

In 1929 he moved to London to pursue a literary career, characteristically choosing the transience and anonymity of lodgings in Bayswater; too diffident and independent to belong to a group, he was nevertheless on the fringes of 'Bloomsbury' and friendly individually with Virginia Woolf and E. M. Forster. His friendships remained compartmentalized but each mattered much to him; closest among them between the wars was that with Anthony Butts, with whom he collaborated in the whimsical *Curious Relations* (by 'William D'Arfey', 1945).

In addition to productive work in poetry and fiction, and as a reviewer, Plomer succeeded Edward Garnett as literary consultant to the firm of Jonathan Cape, proving a discerning and discreet adviser. Amongst his particular successes was the recognition of the quality of the unpublished diaries of (Robert) Francis Kilvert (1840–79), of which he produced a three-volume edition (1938–40) which established their obscure clerical author as a noteworthy Victorian writer. The 'James Bond' novels of Ian Fleming were another valuable property he brought to the firm.

Plomer had encountered Fleming during war service in the Admiralty, as a temporary civilian officer (1940–5) in the Naval Intelligence Division, providing current affairs briefings for naval staff. During the war he contributed (as 'Robert Pagan') a series of topical essays to *Penguin New Writing*. Although he published little fiction after 1934, his poetical output continued, wartime conditions stimulating his wryly humorous ballads with violent themes, and he wrote much other verse in which the muted emotional force secures a penetration that poignant observation and metrical skill might otherwise have concealed. His *Collected Poems*, incorporating several smaller volumes, appeared in 1960, and was amplified in 1973.

His post-war work included a collaboration with Benjamin (later Lord) Britten, as librettist first of *Gloriana* (1953), the coronation-tide opera, and then more fruitfully in using his oriental experience to introduce Britten to the Noh plays, resulting in the fusion of Japanese theatre and European music in the three 'church operas' (1964–8). His autobiography *At Home* (1958) continued *Double Lives* published fifteen years before; neither volume is deeply self-revealing; he was working on a revision at the time of his death.

Latterly he lived quietly at Rustington (1953–66) and from 1966 at Hassocks, in Sussex. Although decorously reticent about sexual matters, he was of definite homosexual disposition, and shared the last thirty years of his life with a devoted friend, a German refugee, Charles Erdman. Plomer died at Hassocks, 21 September 1973.

His extensive correspondence and papers were presented by his literary executor to the library of Durham University, of which he was an honorary D.Litt. (1959). He was awarded the Queen's gold medal for poetry in 1963, and was appointed CBE in 1968.

[*The Times*, 22 and 28 September and 8 November 1973; *London Magazine*, December 1973; William Plomer, *Autobiography* (with postscript by Simon Nowell-Smith), 1975; Michael Herbert, 'William Plomer', B.Litt. thesis, Oxford, 1976, with full bibliography.]

ALAN BELL

published 1986

POTTER (Helen) Beatrix

(1866–1943)

Writer and illustrator of children's books, was born in South Kensington 28 July 1866, the elder child and only daughter of Rupert Potter, a well-to-do barrister who had never practised, by his wife, Helen, daughter of John Leech, of Dukinfield, Cheshire. Sir H. E. Roscoe was her uncle. Both her parents, who came of north-country dissenting stock, had inherited Lancashire cotton fortunes. Beatrix did not go to school, and had no friends. Excessively reserved and shy, she became much attached to one of her governesses, Miss Hammond, who encouraged her childish talent for drawing and introduced her to the study of natural history in the nearby museum. The happiest periods in a childhood singularly dull, repressed, and conventional, were the summer holidays, when the Potters rented large furnished houses, first in Scotland and later in the Lakes. It was here that Beatrix had her first experience of the countryside, and she responded to it with passion. She studied and drew hedgerow flowers and animals, and when she found them dissected dead mice, birds, hedgehogs, squirrels, and foxes.

Beatrix Potter's sturdy nature, which had had so little human contact or encouragement, turned towards animals with a feeling which was as strong as it was unsentimental. Pet rabbits were smuggled into the London nursery where they passed long, sophisticated lives. She kept mice, bats, frogs, snails, and a tame hedgehog, and pursued her quiet occupation of studying and drawing them.

This amusement was a purely private one until she was twenty-seven (still living in South Kensington with her authoritative parents) when she began writing letters to beguile the convalescence of the child of a former governess. In these and in other letters, illustrated with little drawings of great humour and spirit, she told anecdotes of her pets, Peter Rabbit and Benjamin Bunny, and made up adventures for her tame hedgehog, Mrs. Tiggy-Winkle. They gave such pleasure that Beatrix Potter decided to turn the story of Peter Rabbit into a book; but she failed to find a publisher, and in 1900 had it privately printed, following it in 1902 with another private publication, *The Tailor of Gloucester*. In the meantime there had begun an association, both professional and personal, with Frederick Warne & Co. which was to last her lifetime. During the next thirty years they published no fewer than twenty-four of her highly original little books for young children. Nineteen of them had appeared by 1913, including the tales of Peter Rabbit, Jemima Puddle-Duck, Mrs. Tiggy-Winkle, Squirrel Nutkin and Mr. Jeremy Fisher, which are perhaps the best known.

Against her parents' strenuous opposition Beatrix Potter became engaged, at the age of thirty-nine, to Norman Warne, son of the publisher; but he died a few months later, and she made this the occasion of a partial and tacit escape from her parents. With the earnings from her books she had bought a small mixed farm at Sawrey in the Lancashire corner of the Lake District, and from this time spent an increasing proportion of her time there, producing books for her own pleasure and learning to be a farmer. The books of this period are full of exquisite water-colour paintings of Sawrey and Hawkshead, and of that north-country farming life of her ancestors to which she reverted with satisfaction in middle-age.

In 1913, at the age of forty-seven, again acting against the wishes of her parents, she married William Heelis, solicitor, of Ambleside, and in the thirty years of happy married life which followed developed the shrewd, caustic north-country side of her character. Her creative period was finished, and she put her full energies into hill-sheep farming, becoming a successful breeder and landowner; at the time of her death at Sawrey, 22 December 1943, she was president-elect of the Herdwick Association. Her books, unique in the humour and poetic truth of their stories and in the beauty of their water-colour illustrations, were soon established as nursery classics and were translated into many languages. American enthusiasm for her work persuaded her, in old age, to attempt to revive her unique creative gift and to produce one or two stories for the American public. These attempts, however, were not successful; the stories were unexpectedly prolix, and her eye-sight was no longer equal to good drawing. *The Fairy Caravan*, a collection of tales put together for American readers in 1929, was eventually published in England in 1952, but could add nothing to her reputation.

Beatrix Potter's extensive farm property in the Lake District was bequeathed to the National Trust, which still maintains her first little farmhouse, Hill Top, Sawrey, in the same condition as when she lived in it. Twenty-two of her illustrations for *The Tailor of Gloucester* may be seen in the Tate Gallery. A portrait of Beatrix Potter by Delmar Banner is in the National Portrait Gallery.

[Margaret Lane, *The Tale of Beatrix Potter*, 1946; L. Linder and W. A. Herring, *The Art of Beatrix Potter*, 1955; private information.]

MARGARET LANE

published 1959

POWYS John Cowper

(1872–1963)

Novelist and miscellaneous writer, was born 8 October 1872 at Shirley, Derbyshire, eldest of the eleven children of the vicar, the Revd Charles Francis Powys, and his wife, Mary Cowper, daughter of the Revd William Cowper Johnson, rector of Yaxham, Norfolk, through whom Powys inherited the blood of the poets Cowper and Donne. Through both parents he came of a long line of country parsons; the Powys family was anciently of Welsh origin, connected in England with the barony of Lilford. When John was seven his father took a curacy at Dorchester, Dorset, and in 1885 became vicar of Montacute, Somerset, so that the conditioning environment on John and his two brothers, Theodore Francis and Llewelyn, was the West Country with which their names as writers are identified. John was educated at Sherborne School and Corpus Christi College, Cambridge, where he obtained a second in the historical tripos of 1894. He drifted first into lecturing at girls' schools in the Brighton area; then from 1898 to 1909 lectured for the Oxford University Extension Delegacy. Initially he had no wide ambition to be a writer, but in 1896 and 1899 he issued small collections of poems. In 1896 he married Margaret Alice Lyon (died 1947), sister of his Cambridge friend T. H. Lyon; they had one son, Littleton Alfred, who entered first the Anglican, and afterwards the Roman Catholic, priesthood and died in 1954.

In 1905 John Cowper Powys made his first lecture tour in the United States where after 1909 until 1934 he spent the greater part of each year. He drew large audiences by his remarkable eloquence and became a potent force in popular American culture; his standing may be measured by the fact that he was called as an expert defence witness at the court cases arising from publication of *The 'Genius'* by Theodore Dreiser (1915) and *Ulysses* by James Joyce (1922).

In 1915 he published his first novel, *Wood and Stone*, in New York, and thereafter while continuing his profession as lecturer he wrote regularly; and after retiring and returning permanently to Britain he wrote and published steadily until the end of his life, gaining rather than diminishing in power and imagination as time passed. Recognition came slowly, and what may be termed 'official recognition' hardly at all; in 1958 he received the plaque of the Hamburg Free Academy of Arts for outstanding services to literature and philosophy, and in 1962 an honorary D.Litt. from the university of Wales; otherwise he was ignored by those responsible for conferring honours and making awards.

The early novels, *Wood and Stone*, *Rodmoor* (New York, 1916), and *Ducdame* (1925), received little notice, but *Wolf Solent* (1929) was at once recognized by discerning critics as an important work and the reputation thus established was consolidated by *A Glastonbury Romance* (New York, 1932, London, 1933) although it remained narrow compared with the celebrity of Joyce and Lawrence. *Weymouth Sands* (New York, 1934, published in England as *Jobber Skald*, 1935) and *Maiden Castle* (New York, 1936, London, 1937) had contemporary settings, but with *Owen Glendower* (New York, 1940, London, 1942) Powys began a series of historical novels which included *Porius* (1951), *Atlantis* (1954), *The Brazen Head* (1956), and the related prose retelling of the *Iliad*, *Homer and the Aether* (1959).

Parallel with his novels Powys wrote a series of philosophical essays for the guidance of the 'common man' exposed to the stresses and frustrations of modern urban life: *The Meaning of Culture* (New York, 1929, London, 1930), *A Philosophy of Solitude* (1933), *The Art of Happiness* (1935), *The Art of Growing Old* (1944), and others. His lifelong study of the world's great writers was reflected in *The Pleasures of Literature* (1938), *Dostoievsky* (1947, dated 1946), *Rabelais* (1948), and several collections of essays; but he also appreciated contemporary developments and his *Letters to Louis Wilkinson* (1958) are scattered with perceptive judgements on such writers as Henry Miller, (Sir) Angus Wilson, and Arthur Koestler.

It is by half a dozen novels and an astonishing masterpiece, his *Auto-biography* (1934), that Powys will be longest remembered. Introducing a new edition (1967), J. B. Priestley called it 'one of the greatest autobiographies in the English language', seeing its greatness in its subjectivity. Here is no chronicle of events, no parade of famous names, almost nothing of how the author's books came to be written. Instead, we see a man as he saw himself, without reticences, without shame, without regrets, without excuses: a self-portrait unique in English and hardly paralleled elsewhere: the warts certainly displayed, but taken for granted, not underlined; and the humanity, the humility, and the genius unconsciously revealed.

The earlier novels present a minutely observed panorama of the West Country, remembered from the author's boyhood: for most of them were written in America and the terrain was deliberately and lovingly evoked—Dorchester, Montacute, Sherborne, Weymouth. The major historical novels are set in Wales, Powys's home for his last twenty-eight years, and the evocation here is imaginative for he creates a landscape studded with fortresses and peoples it with warriors, magicians, priests, and serfs. Essentially, all his novels—indeed, most of his writings—are concerned with human relationships, often devious, tortured, and hopeless, but enduring. Wolf Solent, John Crow, Dud No Man, his principal heroes, seem figures arising from himself; but his extraordinary insight into the feelings of women is displayed in a notable group of characters, and a further group of eccentrics and madmen is conceived with the compassion of a Dostoevsky. His faculty of endowing the inanimate with personality produced splendid passages, particularly in *Atlantis* and certain poems like 'The Old Pier Post'. At times his prose is uneven but it reaches and sustains heights of majesty and eloquence denied to more consistent lesser writers.

All members of this remarkable family were striking in appearance and personality, and John Cowper's magnificent head is powerfully seen in Augustus John's frontispiece drawing in *Letters to Louis Wilkinson*, and in Ivan Opfer's frontispiece to the 1934 English edition of the *Autobiography*. The portrait by his sister Gertrude Powys is in the National Museum of Wales.

After retiring, Powys lived at Corwen, and later at Blaenau Ffestiniog, Merioneth, where he died 17 June 1963; his ashes were scattered on the Chesil beach, near Abbotsbury.

[J. C. Powys, *Autobiography*, 1967, *Letters to Louis Wilkinson*, 1958; Louis Marlow, *Welsh Ambassadors: Powys Lives & Letters*, 1936; Derek Langridge, *John Cowper Powys: a Record of Achievement*, 1966; Kenneth Hopkins, *The Powys Brothers*, 1967; personal knowledge.]

KENNETH HOPKINS

published 1981

PRIESTLEY John Boynton

(1894–1984)

Novelist, playwright, and essayist, was born 13 September 1894 at 34 Mannheim Road, Toller Lane, Bradford, the only child of Jonathan Priestley, schoolmaster and Baptist layman, and his wife, Emma Holt, who died when John was an infant. He was brought up by a stepmother, Amy Fletcher, 'who defied tradition by being always kind, gentle, loving'. He had one stepsister. He attended Belle Vue Grammar School, Bradford, but left at sixteen by his own choice, and worked as a junior clerk at the wool firm of Helm & Co. When G. B. Shaw later praised Stalin's Russia 'because you meet no ladies and gentlemen there', Priestley retorted: 'I spent the first twenty years of my life without meeting these ladies and gentlemen.' But he made the most of Bradford's two theatres, two music-halls, flourishing arts club, and vigorous musical life, as well as the Bradford Manner, 'a mixture of grumbling, irony and dry wit'. He sported Bohemian dress, including a jacket 'in a light chrome green', enjoyed an attic study, where he produced poetry and articles, had them typed by a professional, 'a saucy, dark lass' who was 'paid in kisses, for I had no money', and got a few printed in the local Labour weekly, the *Bradford Pioneer*, and even in *London Opinion*.

Priestley later portrayed his Bradford life as idyllic, asserting 'I belong at heart to the pre-1914 North Country', but at the time he was bored by it and when war came promptly enlisted in the Duke of Wellington's Regiment. He had two long spells in the Flanders front line, was wounded twice, commissioned in the Devon Regiment in 1918, and demobilized the following March. He always refused to be unduly impressed by any event, however momentous, and put his war experiences quietly behind him, never collecting his medals and declining to write about the war, except briefly in *Margin Released* (1962). But it left its mark. Half a century later, when a young guest told him she never ate bread at meals, he snorted: 'I can see *you* never served in the trenches.'

With an ex-serviceman's grant he went to Trinity Hall, Cambridge, where he refused to be enchanted by the atmosphere, let alone to acquire what he termed 'a private income accent', but did a vast amount of reading, laying the foundation for his later *tour de force, Literature and Western Man* (1960). He obtained a second class in English (1920) and a second in division I of part ii of the history tripos (1921). He also produced there his first volume of essays, *Brief Diversions* (1922), which brought him the patronage of (Sir) J. C. Squire at the *London Mercury*, reviewing from

Robert Lynd at the *Daily News*, and a job as reader for the Bodley Head. For the rest of the decade he led the life of a London literary journalist, producing reviews, articles, and books, including two novels, workmanlike biographies of George Meredith and Thomas Love Peacock for Macmillan's English Men of Letters series, and a little volume, *The English Comic Characters* (1925), which became a particular favourite of actors. Such work gave him a living but no leisure and in 1928 (Sir) Hugh Walpole, always eager to assist new talent, collaborated with him in a novel, *Farthing Hall* (1929), so that the advance Walpole's fame commanded would give Priestley the time to write the major picaresque story he was plotting.

The Good Companions was begun in January 1928 and its 250,000 words finished in March 1929. Heinemann's, who had daringly printed 10,000 copies, brought it out in July and by the end of August it had sold 7,500. Thereafter it gathered pace and, to the accompaniment of the Wall Street collapse, became one of the biggest sellers of the century. By Christmas the publishers were delivering 5,000 copies a day by van to the London bookshops. Priestley, typically, did not allow his head to be turned and privately pooh-poohed the merits of his warm-hearted tale of a travelling theatrical troupe. He thought his next novel, *Angel Pavement* (1930), set in London, much better. But *The Good Companions*, besides being twice filmed (1932 and 1956), was put on the stage in 1931, where it brought out the talents of the young (Sir) John Gielgud and opened up a new career for Priestley as a dramatist.

While not a natural novelist, always having difficulty with the narrative flow, Priestley was stimulated by any kind of technical challenge and the stage offered plenty. He dismissed his first West End play, *Dangerous Corner* (1932) as 'merely an ingenious box of tricks'. But James Agate, then the leading critic, called it 'a piece of sustained ingenuity of the highest technical accomplishment' and it began a decade of theatrical success. In 1937 three Priestley plays opened within a few weeks and for several years his earnings from the theatre alone exceeded £30,000. His were not, like Shaw's, literary plays, at their best when read, but solid pieces of theatrical machinery, dependent on stagecraft and timing, offering rich opportunity for actors. Priestley never turned success into formula: all his plays are different, many of them experimental. *Eden End* (1934) evokes pre-1914 nostalgia, *Time and the Conways* (1937) deals with the theories of J. W. Dunne, *I have Been Here Before* (1937) explores the philosophy of P. D. Ouspensky, *Music at Night* (1937) examines the psychological impact of sounds, *Johnson Over Jordan* (1939) probes life after death, and *When We Are Married* (1938) is mordant Yorkshire comedy.

Priestley's desire never to repeat himself was strength and weakness. 'I am too restless', he told Agate in 1935, 'too impatient, too prolific in ideas. I am one of the hit-or-miss school of artists.' He wrote quickly—his novel *The Doomsday Men* (1938) took only nineteen days—but whatever he did had to be new and this disappointed admirers anxious to typecast him as the provider of provincial warmth. He took a close interest in new media, producing screenplays, studying pre-war TV, and writing for the BBC, including a novel, *Let the People Sing* (1939), the first instalment of which was broadcast the day war was declared. Priestley had the instincts of an actor, and indeed would act whenever opportunity offered, though his face, which he described as 'a glowering pudding', limited his range. His voice was another matter: it combined unmistakable northern values with mesmeric clarity, 'rumbling but resonant, a voice from which it is difficult to escape', he wrote. In spring 1940, with Hitler triumphant, the BBC had the inspired idea of getting Priestley to broadcast brief 'Postscripts' after the main news bulletin on Sundays at 9 p.m., starting on 5 June and running till 20 October. Throughout that historic summer, his talks, combining light-hearted pleasure in things English with sombre confidence in final victory, and delivered with exceptional skill, formed the perfect counterpoint to the sonorous defiance of (Sir) Winston Churchill's broadcasts. They made him an international figure. Indeed they excited, he believed, Churchill's jealousy and when the BBC, in its mysterious way, dropped him, he thought the prime minister responsible, though it was more probably Conservative Central Office.

Priestley never belonged to a party, but he described his father as 'the man socialists have in mind when they write about socialism' and his own ideas were usually radical. His novels, like Emile Zola's, were often journalistic in choice of subject, taking a topical theme, and such wartime stories as *Black-out in Gretley* (1942) and *Three Men in New Suits* (1945) seemed to place him on the Left. Along with the *Daily Mirror* and the Left Book Club he was credited with the size of Labour's 1945 victory and in 1950 he even made an official Labour election broadcast. He contributed regular essays on current trends to the *New Statesman*, later collected as *Thoughts in the Wilderness* (1957), *The Moments* (1966), and *Outcries and Asides* (1974). But Priestley was incapable of acting in concert with a political group, or indeed any organization which valued 'sound men' (a favourite term of disapproval). He resigned in disgust from the British committee to Unesco and from the boards of both the National Theatre and the *New Statesman*. He contributed to the latter a remarkable article in 1957 which led directly to the Campaign for Nuclear Disarmament. But at a private meeting to plan it, an objection by Denis Healey MP, 'we must be realistic', evoked a characteristic Priestley explosion: 'All my life I have heard politicians tell us to be realistic and the result of all this realism has been two world wars and the prospect of a third.' He was briefly associated with the Aldermaston marches but left the movement when it became an arena for left-wing faction. 'Commitment' was a posture he despised.

Priestley liked to think of himself as a lazy man but there were very few days in his long life when he did not write something, usually in the morning. His output was prodigious in size and variety. In the 1940s he wrote two of his most striking plays, *An Inspector Calls* (1947) and *The Linden Tree* (1948); his post-war novels included *Lost Empires* (1965) and his own favourite, *The Image Men* (2 vols., 1968 and 1969), a sustained attack on the phenomenon he called Admass. He travelled constantly, and both painted (in gouache) and wrote about what he saw. *English Journey* (1934), recording light and shade during the Slump, was constantly revived and imitated, and became a classic; there is fine descriptive writing in his autobiographical works, *Midnight on the Desert* (1937) and *Rain upon Godshill* (1939), while *Trumpets over the Sea* (1968) records an American tour with the London Symphony Orchestra. In 1969–72 he produced a historical trilogy dealing with the period 1815–1910: *The Prince of Pleasure, The Edwardians*, and *Victoria's Heyday*. Above all, there were scores of essays, long and short, relaxed and serious. He always wrote clear, unaffected, pure English, but it is his essays which best display his literary skills.

Priestley never claimed genius, another word he despised, merely 'a hell of a lot of talent'. He fought a lifelong battle with the critical establishment: 'I was outside the fashionable literary movement even before I began.' He believed himself to be undervalued after 1945, having been overvalued before it, and often pointed out that his plays were more highly regarded abroad than in Britain. In fact from the 1970s onward they were revived with increasing frequency and success. His work brought substantial material rewards. While making a decisive shot at croquet (a game he relished), he once startled a guest by listing to him the formidable aggregate sums he had paid in income tax and surtax. In 1933 he bought Billingham Manor and estate, where a roof-top study gave him a panoramic view over the Isle of Wight; after the war he moved to an ample Regency house near Stratford-upon-Avon. There, in its splendid library, its bookshelves hiding a bar where he mixed formidable martinis, he would receive a constant stream of guests and interviewers, or switch on monumental gusts of stereophonic music and, when he thought no one was watching, conduct it. He turned down a knighthood and two offers of a peerage but accepted the OM in 1977 and a clutch of honorary degrees, 'as a chance to dress up'. He was never the 'Jolly Jack' of his popular image; rather, a shrewd, thoughtful, subtle, and sceptical seer, a great craftsman who put a good deal into life, and a discriminating hedonist who got a lot out of it. In old age he became a little deaf and forgetful but stayed fit and industrious almost to the end, pleased to have got excellent value from his annuities.

In 1919 Priestley married Emily ('Pat'), daughter of Eli Tempest, insurance agent. She died in 1925 after a long distressing illness, leaving him with two daughters. In 1926 he married Mary ('Jane'), the former wife of Dominic Bevan Wyndham Lewis, author, and daughter of David Holland, marine surveyor, of Cardiff. She already had a daughter, who was brought up in the Priestley household, and she and Priestley had a son and two daughters. The marriage ended in 1952 and, after a contested divorce which left him with an abiding dislike of lawyers, especially judges, in 1952 he married the archaeologist Jacquetta Hawkes, daughter of Sir Frederick Gowland Hopkins, biochemist, and former wife of Professor (Charles Francis) Christopher Hawkes, archaeologist, by whom she had one son. Priestley died at his home, Kissing Tree House, Alveston, 14 August 1984.

[John Braine, *J. B. Priestley*, 1978; Susan Cooper, *J. B. Priestley*, 1970; private information; personal knowledge.]

PAUL JOHNSON

published 1990

PYM Barbara Mary Crampton

(1913–1980)

Novelist, was born 2 June 1913 at Oswestry in Shropshire, the elder daughter of Frederick Crampton Pym, solicitor, of Oswestry, and his wife, Irena Spenser Thomas. She was educated at Liverpool College, Huyton (later Huyton College, Liverpool) and St. Hilda's College, Oxford (1931–4), gaining second class honours in English language and literature. After leaving Oxford she lived mostly at home until war began in 1939; in 1938 she went to Poland to teach English to a family in Katowice, but returned owing to the international situation. When hostilities broke out, she undertook voluntary work in the Oswestry area, then in October 1941 became a postal censor in Bristol. From 1943 to 1946 she served with the Women's Royal Naval Service, attaining the rank of third officer and being posted to Naples. On demobilization she joined the International African Institute in London, first as a research assistant, then from 1958 until she retired in 1974 as editorial secretary and assistant editor of *Africa*, under the director, Daryll Forde.

Barbara Pym started writing at school, and it is remarkable that her first novel *Some Tame Gazelle* (1950), an amused vision of herself and her sister as fiftyish spinsters, was begun on leaving Oxford in 1934 and rejected by Jonathan Cape, who were to publish it fourteen years later. It was quickly followed by *Excellent Women* (1952), *Jane and Prudence* (1953), *Less Than Angels* (1955), *A Glass of Blessings* (1958), and *No Fond Return of Love* (1961). They were warmly received by discerning critics, and enjoyed by a faithful band of readers, but their unsensational subject matter and deceptively mild irony did not match the spirit of the times, and her publisher saw fit to refuse subsequent submissions. Although she continued to write, a depressing period of rejection followed, and when she retired her career as a novelist seemed long over. In 1977, however, the *Times Literary Supplement* published a symposium on the most over- and underrated writers of the century, and two contributors nominated Barbara Pym in the latter category. As she was the only living writer to be named twice, strong interest in her work was aroused, and a new novel, *Quartet in Autumn*, was published that year by Macmillan, the firm it had reached at the time. *The Sweet Dove Died* (in fact written earlier) followed in 1978, and *A Few Green Leaves* and *Crampton Hodnet* appeared posthumously in 1980 and 1985 respectively. While retaining many characteristics of her earlier work, her later themes were more sombre, and reflected changed fashions of society.

In her last three years Barbara Pym enjoyed many of the rewards of successful authorship: her novels were reprinted in Britain and America, and paperback editions planned; she was interviewed by press and radio, and a BBC television programme 'Tea with Miss Pym' charmingly evoked her life in the Finstock cottage (near Oxford) to which she had retired with her sister and their cats. She would probably have accepted her own description of 'most Englishwomen' ('not pretty but quite a pleasant face'), but the programme suggested the gracefulness she retained through life (she was rather tall) and the gentle watchfulness of her conversation. She frequently holidayed abroad, but took great pleasure in domesticities such as gardening and jam-making, and was always an active churchwoman. *Quartet in Autumn* was short-listed for the Booker prize in 1977, and she was elected a fellow of the Royal Society of Literature in 1979. She sustained her celebrity with unassuming pleasure, but occasionally showed that she had not ceased to regret her fifteen years of unjustified neglect.

In 1971 she had been operated on for cancer; in early 1979 a recurrence of this malady did not respond to treatment, a fact she reported unemotionally to her friends. In the constant care of her sister she completed her final novel, but did not live to see the proofs, dying in the Churchill Hospital in Oxford 11 January 1980. She was buried at Holy Trinity,

Finstock, where T. S. Eliot had been baptized into the Church of England in 1927. Reviewing her last book, a younger novelist, A. N. Wilson, wrote, 'Why have all her novels survived so well, when others, more daring, or more recent, already seem jaded or unrealistic?' The answer lies not only in their alertness of eye and ear and unsleeping sense of the ridiculous, but in their continual awareness of life's small poignancies and the need for courage in meeting them, expressed in a style exactly suited to her material and for which she never had to strive.

[Barbara Pym, *A Very Private Eye, an Autobiography in Letters and Diaries*, 1984; private information; personal knowledge.]

PHILIP LARKIN

published 1986

QUILLER-COUCH Sir Arthur Thomas ('Q')
(1863–1944)

Cornishman, man of letters, and professor of English literature, was born at Bodmin 21 November 1863, the eldest child of Thomas Quiller Couch, a medical practitioner, by his wife, Mary, daughter of Elias Ford, yeoman, of Abbots Kerswell, near Newton Abbot, Devon, and a grandson of Jonathan Couch, the doctor-naturalist, and Jane Quiller, both of Polperro, where the Quillers and the Couches had been settled for generations.

After attending Newton Abbot and Clifton colleges Quiller-Couch entered the university of Oxford as a classical scholar of Trinity College in 1882. While there, he wrote for the *Oxford Magazine*, his best contributions being parodies of English poets. It was in the *Magazine* that he first used the pseudonym 'Q', by which he came to be well known. He obtained a first class in classical moderations (1884) and a second class in *literae humaniores* (1886). He stayed a fifth year at Trinity as lecturer in classics and in 1887 left Oxford to take up journalism in London. His first novel—*Dead Man's Rock*, a romance in the style of Robert Louis Stevenson—was published in the same year and was followed by *The Astonishing History of Troy Town* (1888).

In London Quiller-Couch worked partly as a free-lance but chiefly for the firm of Cassell, of whose Liberal weekly, the *Speaker*, he became assistant editor at its foundation in 1890. He contributed literary causeries to it frequently and a short story every week. He was also contributing to other periodicals and writing novels, working very long hours to support his widowed mother and his two brothers and to pay off some family debts for which he was not responsible. Moreover, he married in 1889 Louisa Amelia (died 1948), second daughter of John Hicks, of Fowey, the small Cornish port which had won his affection in boyhood; they had one son, who survived the war but died on active service in 1919, and one daughter. Overwork led to ill health; and this, coupled with an atavistic desire to live by the sea, brought Q's journalistic career to an end in 1892, when he left London and settled at Fowey in a house called The Haven on the harbour-side. Here he was able to gratify a lifelong passion for the sea and yachting and encourage a similar one among his friends of the younger generation.

Except that he continued to write for the *Speaker* until 1899, Q earned his living entirely as a free-lance writer throughout his first twenty years at Fowey. It was during this period that most of his fiction was written, but he produced numerous other works, including several anthologies. The most important of these was *The Oxford Book of English Verse* (1900), of which nearly half a million copies were sold in his lifetime. His services to literature, to the Cornwall education committee, and to Liberalism in the county brought him a knighthood in 1910, and in 1912 the Liberal Government appointed him King Edward VII professor of English literature in the university of Cambridge. He was also elected a fellow of Jesus College, where he spent the rest of his life during term, returning to Fowey as soon as he could for each vacation.

Q was already so well known when he arrived at Cambridge that the audience at his inaugural lecture overflowed the largest lecture-room available. He proved to be a first-class lecturer, and his lectures were prepared and delivered with the thoroughness that characterized everything which he did. They were works of art, so stimulating and entertaining that attendance at them was long a fashionable pursuit. They presented literature 'with convincing enthusiasm and creative understanding, as something for hearty, rational, disciplined enjoyment by normal human beings' (George Sampson). When they appeared in print, under such titles as *On the Art of Writing* (1916) and *On the Art of Reading* (1920), they were as attractive as when they were delivered, for everything that Q wrote was stamped with his charming and courtly personality. He knew nothing about the history of the language, and for him the Middle Ages hardly existed; but, even if he went too far, he freed English studies at Cambridge from overemphasis on the philological side and from the domination of such terms as 'tendencies', 'influences', 'revivals', and 're-volts'. Above all, he brought to his chair the skill of a practised writer who encouraged his pupils to write. 'Literature', he insisted, 'is not a mere science, to be studied; but an art, to be practised.' Aided by his colleagues, particularly H. M. Chadwick and Dr. Hugh Fraser Stewart, he succeeded in getting an independent honours school of English literature firmly established in the university (1917), and long before he died he had the satisfaction of seeing large numbers of undergraduates reading for the English tripos.

Q was as popular a figure in the university as in Cornwall, and was celebrated for his hospitality, his conversation, his humour, his kindness of heart, and the care he took in choosing and wearing his picturesque clothing. During his later years many honours came to him: he was elected an honorary fellow of Trinity College, Oxford (1926), received honorary degrees from the universities of Bristol (1912), Aberdeen (1927), and Edinburgh (1930), was made a freeman of Bodmin, Fowey, and Truro, and in 1937–8 was mayor of Fowey, which, disguised as 'Troy', had been the scene of many of his novels and short stories. On his eightieth birthday in 1943 he was saluted as the doyen of English men of letters. He died at Fowey 12 May 1944 and was buried there. There are two portraits of him, by Sir William Nicholson at Jesus College, and by Henry Lamb in the art gallery at Truro. A granite monolith was erected at Fowey as a memorial to him, and a mural tablet placed in Truro Cathedral.

Q was essentially a romantic writer and was as versatile as he was prolific. He produced over sixty substantial volumes and numerous shorter works. He was a successful writer of novels, short stories, literary criticism, serious verse, light verse, and children's books, and conspicuous as an anthologist and a stylist. His chief contribution to letters was his style— neat, colourful, apparently effortless, accurate without being pedantic, and distinguished by a clarity and conciseness that were natural to him and were reinforced by his early classical training.

[Q, *Memories and Opinions*, 1944; F. Brittain, *Arthur Quiller-Couch*, 1947 (bibliography); *The Times*, 13 May 1944; personal knowledge.]

F. Brittain

published 1959

RADCLYFFE-HALL Marguerite Antonia

(1880–1943)

Novelist and poet under the name Radclyffe Hall, was born 12 August 1880 at Sunny Lawn, West Cliff, Bournemouth, the younger daughter (there were no sons) of Mary Jane Sager (née Diehl), an American widow, and Radclyffe Radclyffe-Hall, who was educated at Eton and Oxford but never pursued a career. Following her sister's death in early infancy, her parents' divorce when she was three years old, and her mother's remarriage, Marguerite was brought up at the Earls Court residence of her mother and her mother's third husband, Albert Visetti, a professor of singing at the Royal College of Music in London. Although she came from a financially privileged background, her education was superficial, governesses being followed by day-schools, a brief interlude at King's College, London, where she possibly read Latin, continental history, mathematics, and elementary science for two terms, and a year in Dresden.

Between 1906 and 1936 she published five volumes of poetry, seven novels, and a number of short stories. Her poems, of which the best known was 'The Blind Ploughman', were very popular at the time, and many of them were set to music and performed at public concerts all over Britain. They are collected in the volumes *'Twixt Earth and Stars* (1906), *A Sheaf of Verses* (1908), *Poems of the Past and Present* (1910), *Songs of Three Counties* (1913), and *The Forgotten Island* (1915). Her main literary talents, however, lay with prose, which is borne out by her novels *The Forge* (1924), *The Unlit Lamp* (1924), *A Saturday Life* (1925), *Adam's Breed* (1926), *The Well of Loneliness* (1928), *The Master of the House* (1932), *The Sixth Beatitude* (1936), and her volume of short stories, *Miss Ogilvy Finds Herself* (1934). *Adam's Breed* and *The Well of Loneliness* won her international fame, albeit in very different ways. In addition to winning its author the gold medal of the Eichelbergher humane award, *Adam's Breed* was awarded the Femina Vie Heureuse prize and the James Tait Black memorial prize. *The Well of Loneliness*, a courageous and serious novel about lesbianism, was prosecuted under the Obscene Publications Act of 1857, condemned as an obscene libel, and was not republished in Britain until 1949.

Radclyffe Hall described herself as a 'congenital invert', called herself 'John', the name Radclyffe Hall being reserved for her publications, and was strikingly masculine in appearance. She shared her private life exclusively with women, notably with Mabel Veronica Batten, under whose influence she converted to Catholicism, and later with the sculptor Una Vincenzo, Lady Troubridge. Radclyffe Hall and Lady Troubridge, who shared a number of homes in London and in Rye, Sussex, travelled extensively and associated with many well-known artists and writers of their time, among them Colette, Romaine Brooks, and Natalie Clifford Barney. Radclyffe Hall was a member of the Society for Psychical Research, the PEN Club, the Writers' Club, and the Women Writers' Club, and a fellow of the Zoological Society.

After the banning of *The Well of Loneliness* Radclyffe Hall was denied the recognition she deserved for her mastery of the narrative technique of interior monologue and as a writer who dealt with a great variety of themes, such as World War I, materialism, Catholicism, and the suppression of women by patriarchal society. She died 7 October 1943 at 502 Hood House, Dolphin Square, London. She was unmarried.

[Una Troubridge, *The Life of Radclyffe Hall*, 1961; Michael Baker, *Our Three Selves, a Life of Radclyffe Hall*, 1985; Lovat Dickson, *Radclyffe Hall at the Well of Loneliness*, 1975; Richard Ormrod, *Una Troubridge*, 1984; Sylvia Bruce, 'Biographical Notes on Radclyffe Hall' (unpublished MSS); archives of King's College, London.]

ELISABETH BRINK

published 1993

RANSOME Arthur Michell

(1884–1967)

Journalist and author, was born in Leeds, 18 January 1884, the eldest in the family of two sons and two daughters of Cyril Ransome, professor of history, who died when Arthur was thirteen, and his wife, Edith, daughter of Edward Baker Boulton, who had been a sheep farmer in Australia. He was educated at the Old College, Windermere, and Rugby, but he was a reluctant pupil. Doggedly determined from early adolescence that he was going to be a writer, he spent two unprofitable terms at Yorkshire College, Leeds (later to become Leeds University), reading science before he threw in his hand and left for London where he found a job for eight shillings a week at Grant Richards, the publishers. He was then seventeen.

His bohemian life in London, with a brief period in Paris, lasted for some twelve years. He scratched a living by writing stories and articles, some of which appeared in book form; he reviewed and ghosted. His literary friends included Edward Thomas, Lascelles Abercrombie, Gordon Bottomley, Robert Lynd and his wife Sylvia, and Cecil Chesterton, brother of G. K. Chesterton. There were also actors and artists with whom he would celebrate the sale of an article or a picture by a flagon of Australian burgundy and a meal of macaroni cheese. Many of these met at the studio 'evenings' of Pamela Colman Smith—'Pixie'; he later said that it was from her telling of Negro folk-stories that he learnt so much of the art of narration. He was very poor but nevertheless avidly buying books, and he later attributed his chronic stomach troubles to the meagre and erratic meals of that period.

If there was time for a brief holiday and he could scrape together the fare, he found himself hurrying 'through the big grey archway at Euston that was the gate to the enchanted North' on his way to the Lake District where, before his father had died, his family had spent summer months so happy that the rest of his life seemed an anticlimax. Here he passed much of his time with the family of W. G. Collingwood, adopted as an honorary nephew by the parents, and camping and boating with the children, one of whom was Robin Collingwood. Later, the four children of Dora, the oldest daughter (later Altounyan), were to identify themselves as the Walker children in his books. He hoped to marry Barbara, the second daughter, but this never came about, and it was to escape the unhappy marriage that he did make, to Ivy Constance, daughter of George Graves Walker, in 1909, that he went to Russia in 1913.

The winter of 1912–13 had been one of continual nightmare. A book commissioned by Martin Secker on Oscar Wilde had landed Ransome in a suit for libel issued by Lord Alfred Douglas, and though judgment was given against Douglas in April 1913 it was a scarring experience. Meanwhile, seeing Russian folklore as the material for a new book of folk stories retold in a simple vernacular style, he decided to visit Russia itself. Arriving there in 1913, he taught himself Russian, collected folklore, and busied himself with writing a guide to St. Petersburg commissioned by an English firm. After the outbreak of war (which prevented the guide from being published), he supported himself as a newspaper correspondent for the *Daily News*. In 1916 was published *Old Peter's Russian Tales*, the result of Ransome's investigations into Russian folklore. It had considerable success and was reprinted several times. Paying regular brief visits to England, he stayed in Russia until 1919, becoming friendly with Lenin and other Bolshevik leaders, especially Karl Radek, and making himself unpopular with the British Foreign Office by his opposition to foreign intervention in Russian affairs. For a time in 1918 a British mission in Moscow was headed by (Sir) Robert Bruce Lockhart, of whom Ransome said '. . . [he] was soon on better terms with Trotsky than I was'. In *Six Weeks in Russia in 1919* (1919) he gave a picture of Moscow in those days of starvation and high hopes, and in *The Crisis in Russia* (1921) he defended the Russian revolution and pleaded for a more balanced view of its aims.

By that time he was living in Estonia with Evgenia, daughter of Peter Shelepin (she had been Trotsky's secretary), whom he was to marry in 1924 when his first marriage had been dissolved. His long association with C. P. Scott and the *Manchester Guardian* started in 1919, and such time as he could spare from his newspaper reports he spent in the fishing and sailing that all his life were an absorbing passion. In the *Racundra*, a thirty-ton ketch, built to his specifications at Riga, he cruised round the Baltic in 1922. The log of this holiday was published in *'Racundra's' First Cruise* (1923).

At the end of 1924 Scott sent him as correspondent to Egypt and then in 1925–6 to China, but he was growing increasingly weary of political journalism and longing to settle to his own writing. In March 1929 he began to write *Swallows and Amazons*, an account of four children and their holiday camping and sailing in the Lakes, an evocation of the supreme happiness of his own boyhood holidays. Published in 1930, it was slow to sell. Jonathan Cape, the publisher, had received it politely but was more interested in his fishing essays, *Rod and Line* (1929). Nevertheless he persisted, following it up with a further account of the Walker children and their allies the Blacketts sailing Lake Windermere and exploring the fells—*Swallowdale* (1931). But only with his third story, *Peter Duck* (1932), did he soar into the popularity that made his nine other books for children best-sellers. (It was in *Peter Duck* that he first attempted his own illustrations, a practice he was to continue.). *Winter Holiday* (1933) recalled a winter he had spent on the Lakes when he was at preparatory school. There were books such as *Coot Club* (1934) about bird-watching and sailing on the Norfolk Broads, near which he lived for a time from 1935 on the river Orwell, in Suffolk. For *Pigeon Post* (1936) he received the Library Association's first Carnegie medal for the best children's book of the year. He became an honorary D.Litt. of Leeds University in 1952 and was appointed CBE in 1953. He published his last book, *Mainly about Fishing*, in 1959.

Bald, vastly moustached as he became in later life, habitually dressed in a fisherman's sagging tweeds and a thimble of a tweed hat, he still contrived to retain much of the appearance of the round, rosy, bright-eyed schoolboy that can be seen in the early photographs. With it went a boyish charm of manner with its mingling of enthusiasm and fierce indignation; a deftness of fingers—especially where tying flies was concerned—and a stimulating ability to say something new and unexpected about almost any subject.

He died 3 June 1967 at Cheadle Royal Hospital, Manchester. His second wife died in 1975. He had one daughter by his first marriage. There is a portrait by John Gilroy, 1958, in the Garrick Club.

[*The Times*, 6 June 1967; Hugh Shelley, *Arthur Ransome*, 1960; *The Autobiography of Arthur Ransome*, ed. Sir Rupert Hart-Davis, 1967.]

GILLIAN AVERY

published 1981

(1911–1977)

Playwright, was born in Cornwall Gardens, Kensington, 10 June 1911, the second of two children, both sons, born to (William) Frank (Arthur) Rattigan and his wife, Vera Houston. His father, Frank, was the son of Sir William Rattigan, at one time chief justice of the Punjab and, later, MP for North-East Lanark. Frank's career was less distinguished than his father's had been. He resigned from the Diplomatic Service in 1922 after a disagreement with the foreign secretary, the Marquess Curzon of Kedleston, over the best approach to the Chanak crisis. (Frank, who was assistant high commissioner at Constantinople, favoured intervention on behalf of Greece.) Thereafter the finances of the family were never soundly based.

Vera was seventeen when she married. She outlived her husband who, by all accounts, had a lifelong attachment to 'fluffy blondes' (his second son's expression) which may have steered that impressionable boy, not only into the arms of his mother but also, in true Freudian style, down less conventional emotional paths in later life. One of his mother's Houston relatives had, in 1863, given a public lecture, later published (Arthur Houston, 'The English Drama. Its Past History and Probable Future' in *The Afternoon Lectures on English Literature*, 1863), in which may be read the following prophetic passage: 'The highest type of dramatic composition is that which supplies us with studies of character, skilfully worked out, in a plot not deficient in probability, and by means of incidents not wanting in interest.' No truer definition of the future products of his relative, as yet unborn, is ever likely to be penned.

In 1920 Rattigan went to Sandroyd, a preparatory school near Cobham in Surrey. For one summer holiday his mother took a cottage, in which the bookshelves held nothing but plays, from a drama critic, Hugh Griffiths. Rattigan read them all and, as he said in later years, that holiday determined his career. In 1925 he won a scholarship to Harrow, thus relieving his now hard-up father from the onus of financing him. He wrote a one-act play in French, which the French master marked two out of ten, conceding that the 'theatre sense was first class'. He also wrote an article, in the *Harrovian*, on modern drama, in which he discussed 'the ceaseless conflict between Entertainment and Instruction'. Broadly speaking, the position he adopted in that article foreshadowed the stance he took, forty years on, in his battle with the New Guard drama critics, during which, in his own words, 'I had no chance with anything. They didn't give me reasons for it. They just said, "It must be bad".'

At Harrow he played cricket for the school and took the Bourchier history prize. In 1930, having won a minor scholarship to Trinity College, he went up to Oxford. By now he was a fair-haired, charming youth, with one foot on the playing-fields, the other firmly planted in the Oxford University Dramatic Society. His father, whose ambition was that he should be a diplomat, sent him to France in his first long vacation. Rattigan came home with the idea for his first successful play already in his mind.

In 1932 he and a friend, Philip Heimann, collaborated in the writing of *First Episode*, produced in 1933 at the Q Theatre and transferred to the Comedy in 1934. This play, though adolescent in conception and, indeed, in plot—the scene was set in Oxford—earned mild praise from the reviewers (not excluding James Agate, of the *Sunday Times*). At once, the fledgling dramatist left Oxford with his father's grudging blessing and a small allowance from the same source.

In November 1936 the play he had conceived in France, *French Without Tears*, came on at the Criterion. From curtain-fall until the day of his death, forty-one years later, in the same month, Rattigan was famous and his name a household word. Unhappily, the path Rattigan trod, as an outstanding British dramatist, was not invariably strewn with roses. None the less, for more than twenty years in London and New York, his touch was golden. Audiences felt not only confidence but also fulfilment in his company.

French Without Tears, his greatest comedy success (in spite of Agate's strong aversion to it) was succeeded by another triumph. With *Flare Path* (1942), based on his RAF experience, he proved himself to be a good all-rounder, capable of writing with uncanny skill on any theme that took his fancy. He reverted to light comedy, in 1943, with *While the Sun Shines*; then—his war service concluded—he again took up more serious themes—*The Winslow Boy* (1946), *The Browning Version* (1948), *The Deep Blue Sea* (1952), and *Separate Tables* (1954). His screen-plays, too, were equally successful. Many of them were produced by Anatole de Grunwald and directed by Anthony Asquith, with both of whom he worked in total harmony.

In later life the quality of Rattigan's plays fell somewhat short of what it had been at its zenith. It was never less than adequate, however, and did not merit the hostile criticism it received. His obituary in *The Times* (1 December 1977) states: 'Rattigan's opponents, at an hour of theatrical rebellion, took every chance to belittle a probing storyteller.' Kenneth Tynan called him 'the Formosa of the British Theatre', asserting that he had betrayed the revolution (the New Wave) by staying with the Old Guard. None the less, although the argument around which this sad controversy raged was sterile from the start, it needled Rattigan beyond endurance and—unwisely—to the point of fighting back, thus provoking the New Wave with his constant references to his middle-class 'Aunt Edna'—a fictitious figure he invented—whose tastes, so he said, deserved as much attention as the avant-garde.

Rattigan was a homosexual and never married. He received a knighthood in 1971, having been appointed CBE in 1958. He came to England from Bermuda, for his last play *Cause Célèbre* (1977), aware that he was dying. '*Cause Célèbre*', wrote Bernard Levin, in the *Sunday Times*, 'betrays no sign of failing powers.' Its author died, back in Bermuda, 30 November 1977. *The Times* described him as an 'enduring influence in the English theatre'. Sir Harold Hobson, in the *Sunday Times*, wrote that 'he had the greatest natural talent for the stage of any man in this century'.

In a memoir for the *Sunday Telegraph* William Douglas-Home said: 'Consider *Separate Tables*. Here, most notably, in all the goings-on concerning an unhappy army officer, the many gifts bestowed on Rattigan by providence are on parade, his humour, his integrity—above all, his compassion. There is not one character who does not speak true. There is not one sentiment expressed which is not grounded in humanity, not one line that, in any way, diminishes the dignity of man. And, as for the compassion, that most Christian of all Christian virtues, it is there in such full measure that no member of the audience, unless his heart be made of stone, will go into the street at curtain-fall, without a lift in spirit and a fuller understanding of mankind as his companion. That is Rattigan's achievement and his triumph. That, so long as theatres exist and players strut their hour upon the stage and speak the dialogue he wrote for them, is his eternal monument.'

[Michael Darlow and Gillian Hodson, *Terence Rattigan. The Man and his Work*, 1979; personal knowledge.]

WILLIAM DOUGLAS-HOME

published 1986

READ Sir Herbert Edward

(1893–1968)

Writer on art, critic, and poet, was born 4 December 1893, the eldest of the three sons of Herbert Read, of Muscoates Grange, Kirbymoorside, in the North Riding of Yorkshire, and his wife, Eliza Strickland. Of farming stock, he was always proud of his peasant origins, and gave a memorable account of them in *The Innocent Eye*, a fragment of autobiography (1933). They were also the inspiration of *Moon's Farm*, a poem written for the radio in 1951. When he left his birthplace to go to the Crossley and Porter Endowed School for orphans in Halifax, he wrote that 'no wild animal from the pampas imprisoned in a cage could have felt so hopelessly thwarted'. After employment as a clerk in the Leeds Savings Bank at the age of sixteen, he entered Leeds University, and felt the literary influence of Blake and Tennyson. At the same time he came under the spell of Nietzsche. On the outbreak of war in 1914 he was commissioned into the Green Howards, and rose to the rank of captain, winning both the MC and the DSO—the type of 'resolute soldier' who organized his men for battle as he would afterwards try to organize the world for peace. His distinguished military record, which included a mention in dispatches, lent an added authority to his pacifism.

He had also, like Guillaume Apollinaire, fought 'on the frontiers of culture'. There was a certain discrepancy between a man so traditional in his way of life, so concerned to create a 'cell of good living' for himself and his family, and the tireless apostle of the avant-garde in literature and art. He was an early pioneer of the modern movement, where his friendship with T. S. Eliot and T. E. Hulme, Ben Nicholson, (Dame) Barbara Hepworth, and Henry Moore, counted for much. Read's imagination was essentially visual. This set him apart from a poet like W. B. Yeats for whom poetry was always, in some degree, incantation, and ranked him with the Imagists who held that only free verse could guarantee to the picture its sharp outline, and to the emotion its unblurred significance. Read's output of verse was not large, but at its best—that is to say, at its most direct and concrete, and at its least explanatory—it had a moving honesty, precision, and power.

Herbert Read was aware of the two forces which shaped his life and gave it a creative tension. As he wrote in *Moon's Farm*: 'the instinctive voice that flows like water from a spring or blood from a wound and the intellectual voice that blares like a fanfare from some centre in the brain.' It was this second voice which, as time went on, was more generally heard. His public appointments registered an increasing interest in the visual arts. After a short period at the Treasury (1919–22), he became an assistant keeper at the Victoria and Albert Museum (1922–31), and Watson Gordon professor of fine art in the university of Edinburgh (1931–3). From 1933 to 1939 he edited the *Burlington Magazine*. In these years he published *Art Now* (1933), *Art and Industry* (1934), and *Art and Society* (1937), all of which were many times reprinted. Only the outbreak of war prevented the establishment of a Museum of Modern Art in London of which he would have been the first director—for his championship of the Surrealist Exhibition

(1936) had marked him out as the principal theorist of non-figurative painting and sculpture, where the intention—as Paul Klee had put it—was 'not to reflect the visible, but to make visible'. In 1947 he founded, with Roland Penrose, the Institute of Contemporary Arts—not as yet another place for study or exhibition, but as 'an adult play-centre ... a source of vitality and daring experiment'.

Through all these activities, and the numerous publications which accompanied them, Read became an international authority and indeed something of a sage. It was not a role to which he ever pretended, for he was a man of conspicuous modesty, and quite capable himself of resting in uncertainty about the essential matters of life and death. His somewhat uncritical welcoming of the new experiment often reflected his dissatisfaction with the old one. But he believed, profoundly, in the dialectic of tradition and innovation, of anarchy and order, which alone could preserve society from sclerosis. This was the meaning of his single novel, *The Green Child* (1935). His anarchism was philosophical, not political, although he was generally found subscribing to any protest on behalf of personal freedom, and he sat down with the others in Trafalgar Square while Bertrand (Earl) Russell was warning the world against the imminent threat of self-destruction. This nonconformity did not prevent the offer and acceptance of a knighthood in 1953. His anarchist friends were dismayed, but it was observed that the Queen had never dubbed a knight to whom the epithet of 'gentle' was more perfectly applicable.

Read's poetry was the classical expression of a romantic temperament, and his literary criticism emphasized his sympathy with romanticism. His Clark lectures on Wordsworth (1930) showed how a passionate love affair and a passionate political *parti-pris* had simultaneously inspired so much of Wordsworth's greatest poetry, and how its incandescence grew faint when the first had cooled and the second had been betrayed. *In Defence of Shelley* (1936) rescued the poet from the denigrations of T. S. Eliot, with whom Read remained on terms of the closest friendship, although Eliot had quoted Read's opposition of 'character' and 'personality' as an example of 'modern heresy'. Read's philosophy might not unfairly be described as 'aesthetic materialism', but the purpose of his preaching in one book after another was to link the good life with the good artefact. *Education Through Art* (1943) indicated how this might be done.

In 1950 Read returned to his Yorkshire roots at Stonegrave, only a few miles from his birthplace. A beautiful stone house was filled with pictures illustrating the achievement of the school whose prophet he had become. For some years he was a director of Routledge & Kegan Paul, and this, among other things, brought him to London for a few days every alternate week. And these years saw the publication of his Concise Histories of

Modern Painting (1959) and of *Modern Sculpture* (1964). Much of his time, however, was spent abroad, as a speaker at international congresses. He was not at all a voluble person, but it was remarked that 'when Read does at last open his mouth, you know there's nothing more to be said'. In the last years of his life the poet and the peasant, the philosopher and the paterfamilias, seemed to have realized their separate vocations in a serene and unified way of living. He was twice married: first, in 1919, to Evelyn May Roff, by whom he had one son; and, after the dissolution of the marriage in 1936, to Margaret Ludwig, by whom he had three sons and a daughter. He died at Stonegrave 12 June 1968.

The National Portrait Gallery has a portrait by P. Heron given by Dame Barbara Hepworth and Henry Moore.

[Private information; personal knowledge.]

ROBERT SPEAIGHT

published 1981

RICHARDSON Dorothy Miller

(1873–1957)

Novelist, journalist, and translator, was born 17 May 1873 in Abingdon, Berkshire, the third of four daughters (there were no sons) of Charles Richardson, grocer and tradesman, of Abingdon, and his wife Mary Miller, daughter of Edward Taylor, manufacturer, of East Coker, Somerset. She attended schools in Abingdon and Worthing, where the family settled in 1880. In 1883 the Richardsons moved to Putney. There Dorothy was educated first by a governess and then in the intellectually stimulating environment of Southborough House, which provided the only formal education she valued in retrospect.

Charles Richardson's aspirations to rise socially and live the life of an intellectual gentleman, combined with his unwise investments, led the family into bankruptcy. Dorothy thus had to start earning her own living when she was seventeen. In 1891 she taught at a finishing school in Hanover for six months and, after her return to England, at a school in Finsbury Park. Finding teaching too confining, she gave up a post as a governess in 1895. Her parents, who had been forced to sell their house in London, had moved to Chiswick in 1893. Mary Richardson, who suffered from depressions, committed suicide in November 1895 during a stay in Hastings with her daughter Dorothy.

In 1896 Dorothy Richardson moved to Bloomsbury, earning a meagre living as an assistant to a Harley Street dentist. In London she showed an interest in various political, feminist, philosophical, and religious avant-garde movements of her time. She was a close friend of H. G. Wells, with whom she also had a brief affair, and who, amongst others, encouraged her to write. Having suffered a breakdown, she gave up her job in 1907 and spent some time in Sussex. There she felt attracted to Quakerism, which became the topic of her first two books, published in 1914. From 1907 Richardson devoted herself to a journalistic career, publishing periodical articles on topics which ranged from literature and politics to dentistry, as well as reviews, sketches, short stories, and poems. She began to write fiction in 1912 while staying in Cornwall with friends. Eleven books of her best-known work, *Pilgrimage*, were published between 1915 and 1938; the first collected edition of all thirteen volumes of this novel appeared posthumously in 1967.

Pilgrimage provides an impressionistic account of the central character Miriam Henderson, which is modelled on the author's own migratory life between 1891 and 1915. Plunging into Miriam's multi-layered conscious-ness, Richardson narrates everything through the mind of her heroine, thereby frequently sacrificing form and selectivity, which she considered to be characteristics of male writing. Due to her innovatory use of the stream-of-consciousness technique, she has often been juxtaposed with James Joyce and A. Virginia Woolf, who claimed that Richardson had invented 'the psychological sentence of the feminine gender'.

In 1917 Dorothy Richardson married the consumptive artist Alan Odle, fifteen years her junior, whom she looked after until his death in 1948, spending half the year in London and half in Cornwall. He was the son of Samuel Odle, bank clerk. There were no children of the marriage. Dorothy Richardson died in a nursing home in Beckenham, Kent, 17 June 1957.

[John Cowper Powys, *Dorothy M. Richardson*, 1931; John Rosenberg, *Dorothy Richardson: the Genius they Forgot*, 1973; Gloria G. Fromm, *Dorothy Richardson: a Biography*, 1977; obituaries in *The Times* and *Manchester Guardian*, 18 June 1957.]

SUSANNE P. STARK

published 1993

(1892–1962)

Writer and gardener, was born at Knole near Sevenoaks 9 March 1892. Generally known as Vita, she was the only child of Lionel Sackville-West and his wife, Victoria Sackville-West, who were first cousins; her father later (1908) became third Baron Sackville. Knole, the background of her life from infancy until marriage, was one of the largest houses in England, a Tudor palace built round seven courtyards within a 1,000-acre park, and her romantic love of her aristocratic home, combined with her disappointment that as a female she could not inherit it, did much to form both her personal character and her professional career.

Though Vita Sackville-West loved her father, she was always critical of her charming but eccentric half-Spanish mother, and was essentially a lonely child. Educated at Knole by governesses until she was thirteen, she spent long days of solitude immersed in the private pleasures of literature and the country; she later went to a day-school in London. She was a prodigious reader and compulsive writer, having written eight novels (one in French) and five plays by the age of eighteen, all on historical themes, and many poems. Developing alongside a joy in books was a deep love of country pursuits and the fertile farmland of Kent. In her teens, she also discovered the pleasures of travel, visiting France and Italy on numerous occasions (she spoke both languages fluently), and once touring Russia, Poland, and Austria with her mother and her mother's lifelong friend, the immensely rich Sir John Murray Scott. In 1913 she also travelled in Spain.

Her security of background was threatened by two sensational lawsuits: when she was eighteen her father's right to the inheritance of Knole was challenged in the courts in 1910, unsuccessfully; in 1913 Sir John Murray Scott died, leaving her mother a large bequest, and his relatives contested the will. Vita Sackville-West, at twenty-one, tall, handsome, and strong-featured, was called as a witness, and her clear evidence and truthful manner were largely decisive; the jury decided for the Sackvilles.

In 1913 she married (Sir) Harold Nicolson, son of Sir Arthur Nicolson (later Lord Carnock), permanent under-secretary at the Foreign Office, in the chapel at Knole, having chosen him from several suitors. Not rich, he was, however, already third secretary at the British embassy at Constantinople, where they lived for a short time after their marriage. In 1914 he was recalled, and they returned to Knole where their first son, Lionel Benedict was born in August. Two months later they moved to London and in 1915 bought a country house, Long Barn, a few miles from Knole, which they kept until 1930 as a main home for herself and a base for her husband whose work was in London or *en poste* abroad.

During these years she developed as a writer from a childish amateur to a prolific professional, successful in the widely different fields of poetry, the novel, and biography. Most important of her books in this period were *Knole and the Sackvilles* (1922), a history of her home and ancestors; *The Land* (1926), a long poem in the manner of the *Georgics* which won her the Hawthornden prize in 1927; and *The Edwardians* (1930), a novel based on Knole, the Sackvilles, and Edwardian society at its extravagant peak. It was an instant best-seller, and though perhaps over-intense, it will hold its place as a period piece, a record of the sumptuous standard of living in a great house where the servants were numbered in hundreds, before the war of 1914–18. She also published some admirable essays and short travel books, of which *Twelve Days* (1928), a book about an expedition in the mountains of Persia, shows a perceptive eye for landscape and wild flowers.

Vita Sackville-West's personal life between 1914 and 1930 was always emotional and sometimes stormy, for she never attempted to rein in her powerful instincts for romance. In 1915 a son was born dead. In 1917 a third son, Nigel, was born in London. For three years, from 1918 to 1921, she had a passionate love affair with a woman, Violet Trefusis, with whom she went off on several occasions, but she returned eventually to Long Barn and resumed her marriage with a husband who was both understanding and forgiving. There were many bonds as well as affection which held them together: one was a shared love of literature; another was the beautiful garden which they were making at Long Barn. Yet another was their social life at week-ends, when they entertained many visitors from London, particularly the literary élite of Bloomsbury, and, though neither took naturally to parenthood, they enjoyed seeing their children at convenient times.

In 1925 Nicolson was posted to Persia, and his wife decided not to accompany him, for she hated diplomatic life, preferring her writing and her garden. However, they wrote to each other every day, a habit they continued all their lives, and she travelled to Persia twice to visit him. Although their marriage was unconventional in every way, for each was basically homosexual, it had become extremely happy; physical relationship had lapsed, but each needed the other to advise, amuse, sustain, and understand. Her most significant relationship during this period, apart from her marriage, was with Virginia Woolf, whose extravagant fantasy, *Orlando* (1928), was an open love-letter to her.

In 1929 her husband resigned from the Foreign Office and returned to England to become a journalist, and in 1930 the Nicolsons moved house, giving up Long Barn and buying a ruined Elizabethan mansion, Sissinghurst Castle, also in the weald of Kent, which they planned to restore and where they dreamed of making a great garden from the existing wilderness. The ruined buildings, with the adjacent farm and 500 acres of land, cost £12,000. Vita Sackville-West was thirty-eight, Nicolson forty-three. Their youth was behind them, his career was at a crossroads, and their finances were precarious, but they looked forward eagerly to the new adventure.

From 1930 until the outbreak of war, she worked continuously at her writing and her new garden. In 1930 she wrote a lyric poem of high quality called *Sissinghurst* which appeared the following year; in 1931 she also published a novel, *All Passion Spent*, and another, *Family History*, in 1932; in 1936 a biography, *Saint Joan of Arc*, and in 1937 a life of her Spanish grandmother, *Pepita*. At the same time she and her husband were planning and planting what many consider her finest memorial, the garden at Sissinghurst, a seven-acre garden consisting of linked enclosures formal in shape, but planted with romantic profusion, with an abundance of scented flowers and old roses.

She became more solitary at Sissinghurst than at Long Barn and rarely went to London, where Nicolson spent his week. However, they travelled frequently to France, Italy, and other countries and in 1933 they went on a lecture tour of the United States. Virginia Woolf remained her closest friend and she was deeply distressed by her suicide in 1941.

During the war Vita Sackville-West kept Sissinghurst going and joined the Kent committee of the Women's Land Army, and she wrote prolifically; her most important books were *The Eagle and the Dove: St. Teresa of Avila, St. Thérèse of Lisieux* (1943) and *The Garden*, begun in 1942 and published in 1946, a long poem in the manner of *The Land*. Both these poems, whether successful or not in their entirety, contain lyric passages of unquestionable beauty. In 1948 she was appointed CH for her services to literature. In 1959 she published *Daughter of France*, a biography of La Grande Mademoiselle, Duchesse de Montpensier, and in 1961 *No Signposts in the Sea*, her last novel. By now acknowledged as one of the finest gardeners in England, she wrote a gardening column for the *Observer* from 1946 to 1961, selections from which have been reprinted many times in book form. The intelligence and lucidity which characterized all her writing were as notable in a short gardening article as in a full-scale biography.

By 1950 the garden at Sissinghurst had reached its zenith, and in 1955 she was awarded a gold Veitch memorial medal by the Royal Horticultural Society. The garden was opened to the public every day in summer and in 1961 it was visited by more than 13,000 people, a figure which multiplied after her death when Sissinghurst passed to the National Trust.

In 1961 Vita Sackville-West became gravely ill with cancer, and she died at Sissinghurst 2 June 1962. A portrait of her at the age of twenty-seven by William Strang is in the Glasgow Art Gallery; a painting by P. A. de László (1910) and drawings by (Sir) William Rothenstein (1925) are at Sissinghurst.

[Her own writings; Sir Harold Nicolson's *Diaries and Letters*, ed. Nigel Nicolson, 3 vols., 1966–8; Nigel Nicolson, *Portrait of a Marriage*, 1973; Michael Stevens, *V. Sackville-West*, 1973; Anne Scott-James, *Sissinghurst: The Making of a Garden*, 1975; private information.]

ANNE SCOTT-JAMES

published 1981

SADLEIR Michael Thomas Harvey

(1888–1957)

Writer and publisher, was born in Oxford 25 December 1888, the only child of (Sir) Michael Ernest Sadler. He adopted an early variant of the family name, Sadleir, as a *nom de plume* to distinguish himself from his father, whom he called 'my best and wisest friend' and whose biography (1949) he wrote with affectionate understanding. Sadleir was educated at Rugby and Balliol College, Oxford, where he took second class honours in history in 1912 and won the Stanhope prize for an essay on Sheridan. In the same year he entered the publishing firm of Constable, of which he became a director in 1920 and chairman in 1954. He served in the war trade intelligence department (1915–18), was a member of the British delegation to the peace conference in 1919, and for a brief period in the following year of the secretariat of the League of Nations.

Sadleir was an all-round man of letters who notably distinguished himself in each department of his activity; he may be described, however, as the most accomplished book-collector of his time. His achievement as a collector not only laid the foundation of his success as a novelist and biographer, but also affected his policy as a publisher. He began to collect books as an undergraduate, specializing for some years in first editions of contemporary poets and novelists, of certain authors of the nineties, and of the French symbolists and decadents. About 1918 he reverted to an early enthusiasm for the novels of Anthony Trollope which led him, in turn, to form an unrivalled collection of Victorian fiction of the three-decker period. This was developed into a sort of bibliographical museum illustrating the history of the novel during the nineteenth century, including cheap editions, among them the famous 'yellow backs', and a variety of material on Victorian night-life. He also collected the Gothic romances of the period of about 1780 to 1820, and this collection found its way in due course to Charlottesville, Virginia, just as his Trollopes eventually went to Princeton, and his great collection of nineteenth-century fiction, over 10,000 volumes, to the university of California at Los Angeles.

The first work which showed that Sadleir was destined to revolutionize the bibliographical approach to books of the machine-printed and edition-bound era was his *Excursions in Victorian Bibliography* (1922); this was followed by two books which pioneered the revival of interest in Trollope's novels: the admirable *Trollope: A Commentary* (1927), which has become the standard biography, and the masterly *Trollope: A Bibliography* (1928). His *Evolution of Publishers' Binding Styles, 1770–1900* (1930) was another fertile and influential book. Sadleir's study of Victorian author–publisher relationships, distribution methods, and reading habits culminated in his two-volume *XIX Century Fiction: A Bibliographical Record* (1951). He was Sandars reader in bibliography at Cambridge University, 1937, and president of the Bibliographical Society, 1944–6.

In his introduction to *XIX Century Fiction* Sadleir confessed: 'I have never undertaken the intensive collection of any author or movement without the intention of ultimately writing the material collected into biography, bibliography or fiction.' Sadleir's avowed practice, most strikingly exemplified in the case of Trollope, was continued in biography with *Bulwer: A Panorama* (1931), later renamed *Bulwer and His Wife, 1803–1836*, and its successor *Blessington–d'Orsay: A Masquerade* (1933). Both these books were sparkling original studies in the morals and taste of the early nineteenth century. As a biographer Sadleir combined a fluent and graceful style with an unusually discriminating sense of period.

While Sadleir's narrative gift imparted zest to his serious historical writing, his work as a novelist brought him popular fame. In his novels his understanding of period was markedly stronger than his imaginative impulse. *Privilege* (1921) chronicled the collapse of the old order which was accelerated by the war of 1914–18, and *The Noblest Frailty* (1925) had as its theme the decay in the ruling stock of mid-Victorian times. Meanwhile *Desolate Splendour* (1923) had emphasized Sadleir's weakness for melodrama and his absorption in the seamy side of nineteenth-century life, which he investigated with a sociological passion worthy of Henry Mayhew. He returned to fiction in 1937 with *These Foolish Things*, described by himself as 'a first-person experiment in emotional intimacy'. *Fanny by*

Gaslight (1940), his most successful novel, sold 150,000 copies at its original price in five years, was made into a film, and was widely translated. Both this novel and *Forlorn Sunset* (1947) depicted the vicious underworld of the London of the 1870s in authentic detail, but while the scrupulous finish of *Fanny by Gaslight* enabled Sadleir to carry off the element of artificial melodrama so often found in his plots, *Forlorn Sunset*, no less highly coloured, proved a more rambling and consequently less convincing book.

Although he spent much of his life in London, Sadleir lived for many years in Gloucestershire and latterly at Oakley Green near Windsor. Tall, distinguished in appearance, alert in movement, he was by nature retiring but, overcoming his shyness, could dispense hospitality with great personal charm. It was not only through his own writings that he influenced the literary life and taste of his time. When his advice was sought, no trouble was too much for him, and many were the authors who benefited from his encouragement and enthusiasm, not least those whose nineteenth-century studies were published by his firm. The rare combination in his work of original research and creative exposition made Sadleir a figure of unique authority in his chosen sphere.

Sadleir married in 1914 Edith, daughter of Albert Darell Tupper-Carey, canon of the Church of England. They had one daughter and two sons, of whom the elder was killed in action while serving with the Royal Navy during the war of 1939–45. Sadleir died in London 13 December 1957.

[*The Times*, 16 and 20 December 1957; private information; personal knowledge.]

DEREK HUDSON

published 1971

SASSOON Siegfried Loraine

(1886–1967)

Poet and prose-writer, was born 8 September 1886 at Weirleigh, near Paddock Wood in Kent, the second of the three sons of Alfred Ezra Sassoon and his wife, Georgina Theresa, daughter of Thomas and Mary Thornycroft, sculptors, and sister of Sir J. I. and Sir W. H. Thornycroft. He was educated at Marlborough College and Clare College, Cambridge, of which he was later an honorary fellow. His father left home when Siegfried was seven and died in 1895, so that the boys were entirely brought up by their mother and her talented family.

He left Cambridge without taking a degree and lived as a country gentleman, hunting, playing cricket, collecting books, and writing poems, of which he privately printed nine pamphlets between 1906 and 1912. These early verses, on the strength of which he was encouraged by (Sir) Edmund Gosse, (Sir) Edward Marsh, and Robert Ross, are graceful, often imitative, full of poetical intent, but without body. He was always 'waiting for the spark from heaven to fall', and when it fell it was shrapnel, for the war of 1914–18 turned him from a versifier into a poet.

He enlisted as a trooper in the Sussex Yeomanry, and in 1915 was commissioned in the Royal Welch Fusiliers and posted to France. He soon became well known for his bravery and was nicknamed 'Mad Jack'. He was awarded the MC for bringing back a wounded lance-corporal under heavy fire, and later unsuccessfully recommended for the VC for capturing a German trench single-handed.

He was wounded in April 1917 and convalescing in England he felt impelled to write a violent attack on the conduct of the war ('I am making this statement as an act of wilful defiance of military authority, because I believe that the war is being deliberately prolonged by those who have the power to end it . . .'). This he contrived to have read out in the House of Commons, but instead of the expected court-martial, the under-secretary for war declared him to be suffering from shell shock, and he was sent to the Craiglockhart War Hospital, near Edinburgh. During his three months there he made two important friendships: with the young poet Wilfred Owen, whom he encouraged and helped, and with the psychologist and anthropologist W. H. R. Rivers, who became a loved and revered father-figure to him. Eventually he decided to fight again and early in 1918 was posted to Palestine. In May he rejoined his old battalion in France, and in July was wounded again, this time in the head. So finished his military service.

Meanwhile in *The Old Huntsman* (1917) and *Counter-Attack* (1918) his savagely realistic and compassionate war-poems had established his stature as a fully fledged poet, and despite all his later prose and verse, and his growing aversion to the label, it was mainly as a war-poet that he was regarded for the rest of his life.

In 1919 he was briefly involved in Labour politics and was the first literary editor of the reborn *Daily Herald*. This uncongenial task brought him into contact with the younger poet Edmund Blunden, who became a lifelong friend. In 1920 he read his poems on a lecture tour in the United States. Thereafter he lived in London, hunted for a few seasons in

Gloucestershire, and brought out volumes of poetry—*Selected Poems* (1925), *Satirical Poems* (1926), and *The Heart's Journey* (1927)—which greatly increased his reputation and represent his full flowering as a poet.

Then he turned to prose, and in 1928 published *Memoirs of a Fox-Hunting Man*, anonymously, though his name appeared in the second impression. This lightly fictionalized autobiography of his early years in Kent, in which he figures as the narrator George Sherston, was an immediate success, was awarded the Hawthornden and James Tait Black memorial prizes, and was quickly accepted as a classic of its kind—an elegy for a way of life which had gone for ever. He continued the story in *Memoirs of an Infantry Officer* (1930) and *Sherston's Progress* (1936), and the three books appeared in one volume as *The Complete Memoirs of George Sherston* (1937).

In 1933 Sassoon married Hester, daughter of the late Sir Stephen Herbert Gatty, chief justice of Gibraltar (1895–1905), and they settled at Heytesbury House, near Warminster in Wiltshire, where Sassoon spent the rest of his life. Their son was born in 1936, and, although the marriage ended in sadness and separation, at Heytesbury Sassoon continued to find the beauty and the solitude that his writing needed, and he became steadily less inclined to leave home for any reason.

Once established there he began to write his factual autobiography, beginning with *The Old Century and Seven More Years* (1938), his favourite among his books, dedicated to his loved and admired friend (Sir) Max Beerbohm, and continuing with *The Weald of Youth* (1942) and *Siegfried's Journey* (1945), which carried his story up to 1920. In 1948 he published a critical biography of George Meredith, and all the time he was writing poetry, published in private or public editions, which culminated in the *Collected Poems* of 1947 (enlarged edition 1961).

In 1957 he was received into the Roman Catholic Church, and the comfort and joy with which his religion filled his last years was celebrated in a spiritual anthology of his poetry, *The Path to Peace* (1960), printed and published by his dear friends, the nuns of Stanbrook Abbey.

Sassoon was strikingly distinguished in appearance, his large bold features expressed the courage and sensitivity of his nature, and he retained his slimness and agility into old age, playing cricket well into his seventies. A dedicated artist, he hated publicity but craved the right sort of recognition. He was appointed CBE in 1951, and was pleased by the award of the Queen's medal for poetry in 1957 and by his honorary D.Litt. at Oxford in 1965, but pretended that such honours were merely a nuisance. A natural recluse, he yet much enjoyed the company of chosen friends, many of them greatly his juniors, and was a witty and lively talker. He loved books and pictures and music, was a brilliant letter-writer, and kept copious diaries.

Sassoon died at Heytesbury 1 September 1967, and was buried in Mells churchyard near his friend Monsignor Ronald Knox. A portrait by Glyn Philpot is in the Fitzwilliam Museum, Cambridge.

[Sassoon's own writings; private information; personal knowledge.]

RUPERT HART-DAVIS

published 1981

SAVAGE Ethel Mary

(1881–1939)

Better known as Miss Ethel M. Dell, novelist, was born at Streatham 2 August 1881, the younger daughter of John Vincent Dell, who was on the staff of the Equitable Life Assurance Company, by his wife, Irene Parrott. She was educated at a private school in Streatham and spent most of her early life at Knockholt, near Sevenoaks. The family moved to Ashford, Middlesex, where the father and mother died, and subsequently the two Misses Dell settled in Guildford. In 1922 the younger married Lieutenant-Colonel Gerald Tahourdin Savage, Royal Army Service Corps, who survived her. She died in a nursing home at Hereford 17 September 1939.

Ethel Dell showed a facility for writing as a child, and throughout her youth she contributed to various fiction magazines of the more elementary sort. She had a huge success with her first novel, *The Way of an Eagle* (1912), and there was hardly one of her subsequent thirty-four works of fiction (of which the last is dated 1939) which was not enormously popular. Her naturally retiring disposition was rendered doubly so by her nation-wide reputation; and she insisted on living a withdrawn, unpublicized life, motoring in the country and enjoying her garden and her dogs. Physically she was a handsome woman, rather above the average in height. Casual acquaintances have spoken of her unusual charm and simplicity of manner. She was generous to a fault with the large income brought in by her books.

As a popular novelist, Ethel Dell belongs to the class of Charles Garvice, Mrs. Florence Barclay, and Miss Edith Maude Hull: that is to say, her public was an ingenuous and uncritical one, which asked only for a well-sustained, romantic narrative, with dangers averted, innocence un-smirched, and characters recognizable from the first for what they proved to be. All of these she provided. She could tell with speed and deftness a story which was always wholesome, frequently dramatic, and certain of a happy ending. Her heroes (often short of stature and rather plain) are whipcord or tempered steel. Her heroines are proud, unhappy, and inclined to be fierce before marriage, although when at last they yield to their faithful lovers' pleas they become utterly submissive. Her villains are unmistakable 'Sir Jaspers', in whatsoever guise they appear. There is a curious strain of almost sadism in a number of the books: possibly her writing-self sought to redress the balance of her other self's timidity and gentleness. The children are rough and ill mannered; young women are subjected to tyrannies and insolence; male characters, otherwise commendable, take pleasure in being rude to ladies.

Miss Dell's work is free from the mawkishness of Garvice and Mrs. Barclay. Also it is noticeable that her characters are all more or less of the same social class. She rises above the *Peg's Paper* formula of duke and dairymaid, and also above the pure and lovely woman whose radiant influence transforms an unconvincing sinner into an intolerable saint. Indeed her plots have the liveliness, and promise something of the fevered tension, of a Cynthia Stockley novel. But the promise is unfulfilled. Passion is under ultimate control, and, however black things may look, deviation from the path of propriety is checked in time. This insistence on virtue in circumstances only explicable in terms of frailty makes her stories unreal. *The Hundredth Chance* (1917) is a good specimen of her qualities and her defects.

[*The Times*, 19 September 1939; private information.]

MICHAEL SADLEIR

published 1949

SAYERS Dorothy Leigh

(1893–1957)

Writer, was born in Oxford 13 June 1893, the only child of the Rev. Henry Sayers, headmaster of Christ Church Choir School and later rector of Bluntisham in Huntingdonshire. Her mother, Helen Mary Leigh, was a great-niece of Percival Leigh, one of the earliest members of the staff of *Punch*. She was educated at the Godolphin School, Salisbury, and went as a Gilchrist scholar to Somerville College, Oxford, where in 1915 she took first class honours in modern languages. After teaching for a year at Hull

High School she became an advertiser's copy-writer with S. H. Benson, Ltd., an employment which she retained until 1931.

Her earliest publications were in verse: *Op. 1* (1916) and *Catholic Tales* (1918). Shortly after 1920 she appears to have formed a plan for earning a livelihood by writing detective stories, and she proceeded, characteristically, to master the mechanics of the craft by making a close analytical study of the best models. It was a period at which the 'classical' mystery story had already become an established genre and was understood to be the favourite reading of intelligent and cultivated persons. Dorothy Sayers foresaw the success which might attend upon a more specific appeal to such readers whose approval would establish a reputation; and since the books need not be difficult—except in the teasing sense—a wider public might quickly be educated up to them. There were already many ingenious writers, but most of them either wrote in a pedestrian style, with little concern for anything except a puzzle, or rashly incorporated out of traditional fiction elements over which they had no command. Dorothy Sayers was not always to know in advance what she could bring off. But her academic training enabled her to learn quickly. She mastered the art of giving a pleasant literary flavour to her stories while at the same time keeping within her own imaginative range.

Perhaps no writer of detective novels has yet succeeded in fusing the attractions of the kind with the values of serious fiction. But no writer since Wilkie Collins has come nearer to it than Dorothy Sayers. That her mysteries all fall within little more than a decade, and that in the remaining twenty years of her life she chose to contribute only to entirely different fields, must suggest that it was with impatience that she came finally to realize the necessary limits of the twentieth-century version of the sensation novel. But although she was to write other things with success, her detective stories are likely to constitute her best memorial. As with Sir Arthur Conan Doyle before her, she remains the prisoner of her own felicity in a literary form of which she came to speak without much respect.

Whose Body? (1923), the first fruit of her study, introduced Lord Peter Wimsey, a private detective equipped with learned and artistic interests, nonchalant manners, an insatiable interest in crime, and a reliable man-servant named Bunter. These attributes in themselves would not have taken him out of the ruck; but Dorothy Sayers developed extraordinary skill in contriving for him the illusion of penetrating intelligence and outstanding powers of logical inference. Within nine years he had appeared in eight further books: *Clouds of Witness* (1926); *Unnatural Death* (1927); *Lord Peter Views the Body* (1928); *The Unpleasantness at the Bellona Club* (1928); *Strong Poison* (1930); *The Documents in the Case* (with Robert Eustace,

1930); *The Five Red Herrings* (1931); and *Have his Carcase* (1932). The constant but varied excellence of these was the product of a mind always on the alert for seminal ideas.

Monsignor Ronald Knox, himself a writer of detective novels, told a story illustrating this. A group of writers was discussing a proposed collaboration in a play for broadcasting, and one was in favour of beginning with a river of blood flowing from under a curtain and surrounding a group of intent bridge players. Another declared that blood would not behave in such a way, 'unless it were from a haemophiliac', and the idea was abandoned. Dorothy Sayers did not contribute to the discussion at this point, but was observed to make an entry in a notebook. From this she evolved one of her cleverest novels.

In her last few years as a mystery writer she made some interesting attempts to extend her range. In *Murder Must Advertise* (1933), *The Nine Tailors* (1934), and *Gaudy Night* (1935) she allowed increased scope to her powers as an atmospheric writer and a writer of social comedy. And there was another development. In *Strong Poison* Lord Peter had cleared of a charge of murder, and fallen in love with, a woman writer of detective stories. The relationship was continued in *Gaudy Night* and again in *Busman's Honeymoon* (1937), which was sub-titled 'A love story with detective interruptions'. Dorothy Sayers rang down the curtain on Lord Peter at this point (literally so, since *Busman's Honeymoon* was successfully dramatized in collaboration with M. St. Clare Byrne). It seems probable that the writer had come to share with her readers a sense that her hero was getting a little out of hand. She had provided him with an entry for *Who's Who* and with ancestors whose histories and iconography she elaborated in the course of private literary diversions among her friends. Although she was not without pronouncedly masculine characteristics her temperament was essentially feminine; loving Lord Peter, she contrived for him these little gifts of Tudor portraiture and sixteenth-century manuscripts.

The death of the detective novelist was the birth of the Christian apologist. With *The Zeal of Thy House* (1937) and *The Devil to Pay* (1939), plays written for the Canterbury Festival, she established a second reputation which was subsequently much extended by a radio drama, *The Man Born to be King* (broadcast at monthly intervals between December 1941 and October 1942), and by several similar pieces. From 1940 onwards she published a number of volumes containing studies, essays, and speeches on critical, theological, and political topics. She had already shown an interest in the problems of verse translation by producing *Tristan in Brittany* in 1929; in 1949 she published a translation of Dante's *Inferno* and in 1955 of the *Purgatorio*, each with a commentary. She was at work upon the

Paradiso at the time of her death, which took place at Witham, Essex, 17 December 1957.

In 1926 Dorothy Sayers married Captain Oswald Atherton Fleming, well known as a war correspondent, who died in 1950. She had no children, but adopted a son. In 1950 she received an honorary D.Litt. from Durham University.

[Private information; personal knowledge.]

J. I. M. STEWART

published 1971

SCOTT	Paul Mark

(1920–1978)

Writer, was born in Palmer's Green, London, 25 March 1920, the younger son (there were no daughters) of Thomas Scott, a commercial artist, and his wife Frances Mark. He was educated at Winchmore Hill Collegiate School and entered accountancy training. He joined the army in 1940, serving in intelligence until he was posted to India where he was commissioned in 1943. He travelled extensively in India, Burma, and Malaya before returning to Britain at the end of the war with the rank of captain.

Demobilized in 1946, Scott joined the Falcon Press, a new publishing house founded by Captain Peter Baker MC (later Conservative MP for South Norfolk), in whose wartime Resurgam Younger Poets series Scott's poem 'I, Gerontius' had appeared in 1941. Associated with the Falcon Press was the Grey Walls Press, founded and directed by the writer Charles Wrey Gardiner (1901–81), who was also editor of *Poetry Quarterly*. Scott was company secretary of these two firms and during his four years there among his colleagues were the writers Muriel Spark, Seán Jennett, and Roland Gant. In 1950 Scott joined the literary agency Pearn, Pollinger & Higham and later became a director of David Higham Associates.

After having been rejected by seventeen publishers, Scott's first novel *Johnnie Sahib* was published in 1952 by Eyre & Spottiswoode who awarded it their Literary Fellowship prize. In it Scott made use of his experiences as an air supply officer in India to examine the questions of command and loyalty in a small military unit. His second novel, *The Alien Sky* (1953), was also set in India and is to some extent an exercise in the study of India at independence that was a major part of the theme of his principal work completed twenty years later. *A Male Child* (1956) was a novel set in

London but *The Mark of the Warrior* (1958) saw a return to the jungle warfare of 1942 Burma and the interplay of action and emotion among soldiers at war.

After ten years as a literary agent Scott left David Higham Associates in 1960, the year in which *The Chinese Love Pavilion* was published, a novel in which India exerts its fascination on both those who have served the British interest there for generations and on new wartime visitors in uniform. *The Birds of Paradise* (1962) continued Scott's progress towards *The Raj Quartet* and here the birds of the novel's title are dead and stuffed, hanging in a large cage in an Indian prince's gardens and haunting the memory of a man since he first saw them in childhood and returns to see them again in middle age when he and his friends, the British in India, and the princely states have like them become tattered and decayed by time.

In both *The Bender* (1963) and *The Corrída at San Felíu* (1964) Scott temporarily abandoned India as a background and seemed to take a deep creative breath to embark on his greatest work. He also experimented with some of his preoccupations as an artist—setting down a complicated choreography in a series of time levels, initiating the search for identity and meaning in society and the interplay between life's reality and artistic creation. *The Bender* is set in London in the early 1960s and while humorous and satirical it exudes a never specific unease. *The Corrída* is a kind of Chinese puzzle of fragments, about a writer who is killed in a car crash and leaves his efforts to release himself from a writing block in the form of short stories, two openings of a novel, and a novella. Yet both these novels, pauses in the margin of his main work though they seem to be, contain or imply statements that were to recur in his later work.

In 1964 Scott returned to India to revisit wartime friends and, in his own words, to 'recharge batteries'. The revival of memories and his experience of post-partition India inspired the conception of *The Jewel in the Crown* (1966) which Scott said might be the first novel of a trilogy but which, in fact, was the beginning of what came to be known as *The Raj Quartet* with the subsequent publication of *The Day of the Scorpion* (1968), *The Towers of Silence* (1971), and *A Division of the Spoils* (1975), the four novels being gathered into one volume called *The Raj Quartet* in 1976.

Apart from two further visits to India, in 1969 and 1972, Paul Scott, during the decade he was writing his *Quartet*, led an almost cloistered life, working in an upstairs room overlooking his garden and some Hampstead Garden Suburb woodland. Apart from working on his novels he wrote book reviews for *Country Life, The Times,* and the *Times Literary Supplement.* Although he was a most amusing companion, with a gift for mimicry, he kept away from cliques and what he considered to be the 'literary establishment'. On one of his rare excursions into the London literary scene he gave a talk entitled 'India: a post-Forsterian View' to the Royal Society of Literature of which he was a fellow. It was published in *Essays by Divers Hands* (Royal Society of Literature, 1970).

Recognition of Scott as a major novelist came slowly. Reviewers noted the imaginative inventiveness and the mastery of technique but were cautious about forecasting 'where it would all end'. In fact the rape of the English girl Daphne Manners in the Bibighar Gardens with which *The Jewel in the Crown* begins symbolizes, but never portentously, the relationship between India and the British: love and hate, the duality of emotion, inter-racial tension and mutual attraction, the pull of disparate loyalties, national pride, and aspirations in individuals and nations—this is what Paul Scott wrote about with such persuasive skill.

In 1976 and 1977 Paul Scott was visiting professor at the University of Tulsa, Oklahoma. Just before his second visit his last novel, *Staying On* (1977), was published. Taking two minor characters from his *Raj Quartet* who chose to stay on in India rather than to return to England Scott wrote both a pendant to the *Quartet* and a valedictory masterpiece about the relationship between a retired colonel, his wife, and their Indian landlords and servants. While recovering from surgery for cancer in Tulsa he was awarded the Booker prize for fiction in November 1977. Scott returned to England in the following month and died of cancer in the Middlesex Hospital, London, 1 March 1978.

The Granada television film of *Staying On*, starring Celia Johnson and Trevor Howard, had its first showing in December 1980 and Granada went on to film *The Raj Quartet* (under the title of *The Jewel in the Crown*) in 1982. These television plays were not Scott's first excursion into drama. He had a play, *Pillars of Salt*, published in 1948, his first novel *Johnnie Sahib* was adapted for BBC radio and television as *Lines of Communication* in 1953, and in 1955 his play *Sahibs and Memsahibs* was produced by the BBC.

In 1941 Scott married Nancy Edith, daughter of Francis Percival Avery, a Conservative political agent. She is the author of novels under the name Elizabeth Avery. There were two daughters of the marriage, one of whom illustrated Scott's story *After the Funeral*, which was produced in a limited edition of 200 copies, with a personal view of the author by Roland Gant (Whittington Press, 1979).

[Patrick Swinden, *Paul Scott—Images of India*, 1980; K. Bhaskara Rao, *Paul Scott* (Twayne English Authors No. 285), 1980; personal knowledge.]

ROLAND GANT

published 1986

SNOW Charles Percy

(1905–1980)

Baron Snow

Author and publicist, was born in Leicester 15 October 1905, the second of four sons of William Edward Snow and his wife, Ada Sophia Robinson. His father was a clerk in a shoe factory and a church organist, an FRCO. From a local elementary school Snow entered Alderman Newton's grammar school, Leicester, with a scholarship, and then studied science at the local university college (later Leicester University). He gained a first class degree in chemistry, followed by an M.Sc. (1928) in physics there, both London University external degrees, and proceeded, again by scholarship, to do postgraduate research at the Cavendish Laboratory in Cambridge. He became a fellow of Christ's College in 1930, the same year in which he gained a Ph.D. He was tutor of the college from 1935 to 1945 and was later a frequent visitor and honorary fellow. He had been a fairly good cricketer at school, and, at Cambridge, he enjoyed watching cricket at Fenner's with other bachelor dons such as G. H. Hardy to whom he dedicated *The Masters*; later, he became a member of the MCC.

Snow's research in infra-red spectroscopy failed, since it was built upon an intuition that careful experimental results did not confirm; in consequence he was not subsequently taken entirely seriously as a scientist. But he remained dedicated to science, with both a reasoned sympathy and a boyish enthusiasm for great scientists. His years at Cambridge coincided with a golden age of Cambridge physics, and he was starry-eyed about the achievements of the brilliant men whom he knew, and whom he thought (correctly) that the world in general and cultivated society in particular neither understood nor appreciated. It became his mission to explain their achievement. He read widely, increasingly in the body of European literature, and in the Cambridge English studies of Sir Arthur Quiller-Couch and Basil Willey: he adopted a posture of a cultured (and left-wing) serious interest in literature and the arts, which was deeply opposed as dilettantism by the growing body of professional scholars of English literature, especially the school represented by F. R. Leavis, university reader in English, with whom he later had a celebrated controversy. Snow published *Death under Sail* in 1932 and a second novel, *The Search*, in 1934, and in 1940 began what was to be a series, taking its title from the first book, *Strangers and Brothers*. It was this series that made his name.

Snow had three careers. He was a scientific administrator. He was a novelist and critic. He was a public man, much in demand to lecture, broadcast, and pontificate. Each career fed on the others. Though the *Strangers and Brothers* sequence was not directly autobiographical, each novel drew upon Snow's own experience, in *The Masters* (1951) of a Cambridge combination room, in *The Corridors of Power* (1964) of the relation between senior civil servants and politicians, in *The New Men* (1954) of the early attempts to develop a nuclear weapon. In form the novels harked back to the Victorian writers. Like Trollope, with well-described characters, scenes firmly set, and a strong plot, he deliberately avoided the lessons of Henry James and even more of James Joyce. The hero, Lewis Eliot, an academic lawyer, was an idealized version of the author himself made more sensitive, given to more suffering, and more respected.

In 1939 Snow joined a group organized by the Royal Society to deploy British scientific manpower; by 1942 he was director of technical personnel at the Ministry of Labour, under Ernest Bevin; and from 1945 until his retirement in 1960 he was a Civil Service commissioner in charge of recruiting scientists to government service. He was also a director of English Electric, a company designing and building nuclear power stations. He was appointed CBE in 1943, knighted in 1957, and became a life peer in 1964, joining (Sir) Harold Wilson's first government as parliamentary secretary of the newly created Ministry of Technology, which was intended to bring the benefit of technological revolution to a backward nation. Both the Ministry and Snow failed, and he left the government in 1966. As a backbencher Snow became a popular member of the House of Lords, with his ungainly figure and heavy jowled features, frequently seen in its bar and dining-room, exchanging gossip with other heavyweights.

It was this full public life, and his own chequered emotional life till his marriage, that provided the scenes and personalities of his novels. He married, on 15 October 1950, the novelist Pamela Hansford Johnson (died 1981), by whom he had a much-loved son, Philip, who to Snow's joy became a scholar of Eton. She was the daughter of R. Kenneth Johnson and had been married previously to Gordon Stewart, by whom she had a son and a daughter. Snow's novels deal much with the unhappy private and inner lives of his characters, in dissonance with their active and often successful public lives; he was an acute observer both of public and private stress. The books are most gripping when dealing with Snow's own lived experience, they have narrative strength, and are useful documentary sources about life in the Civil Service, politics, and the universities. He rejoiced in the diverse social origins of the British élite. His own ascent from the working class to the peerage was a source of delight to him, and social mobility was a theme of his novels. They lack high art, the characterization is often shallow, and the prose pedestrian, showing little gift for wit, style, or literary craftsmanship. Yet, though he was dismissed like

W. Somerset Maugham as a mere story-teller, his novels were widely read, discussed, and enjoyed, and seen as a genuine insight into these important parts of national life. He was a perceptive and generous critic, revealing especially in his weekly article for the *Financial Times* a wide and deep knowledge of European literature, especially of the French and Russian masters, as well as an encyclopaedic knowledge of science, history, and current affairs.

Some of Snow's novels were produced as plays, notably *The Affair* (Strand theatre, 1961–2), and *The Masters* (Savoy and Piccadilly theatres, 1963–4), both adapted by Ronald Millar.

Snow was a generous and affable host, a kind friend, and a supporter of young writers, notably his Leicester friend Harry Hoff (William Cooper), who emulated his career as a scientific administrator and novelist. Snow's generous and broad sympathies led him to see the strengths rather than the weaknesses of people, and similarly of countries like the United States and the Soviet Union, in both of which as well as in Britain, he was honoured with numerous academic awards. He sought to be a sympathetic interpreter of different styles of life, and thus to extend mutual understanding. This was the origin of his Rede lectures at Cambridge in 1959, *The Two Cultures and the Scientific Revolution*, in which his theme was that ignorance by humanists of modern science was as barbaric as ignorance of the arts by scientists. This doctrine endorsed a fashionable view and was part of a feeling, widespread at the time, that Britain's relatively poor economic performance was due to the lack of scientific and technological knowledge in the ruling group. F. R. Leavis attacked the thesis with passion, asserting that his own interpretation of culture, based upon that of T. S. Eliot, as a knowledge of what great artists said of life, was in direct conflict with Snow's more pedestrian view of culture as knowledge. This controversy to some degree proved Snow's point, since he held that the imaginative insights formerly the monopoly of artists and religious thinkers had now become the prerogative of those who (like Newton) voyaged through strange seas of thought alone.

It was this enthusiasm for science, its intellectual excitement and its potentiality for good which, like H. G. Wells, he communicated. It also led him into further controversy such as that aroused by *Science and Government* (1961) and its *Postscript* (1962), covering his Godkin lectures at Harvard in 1960, in which he denounced as highly dangerous the influence in scientific matters during the 1939–45 war exercised by F. A. Lindemann (Viscount Cherwell) over (Sir) Winston Churchill, using as his argument the disagreements between the 'Prof' and Sir Henry Tizard on the development of radar and the effectiveness of the strategic bombing of German towns. Snow's sympathies were clearly with Tizard.

His later years, again like Wells, showed disillusion with the government's attempts to sponsor the technological revolution, and disappointment at the senseless violence abroad and in the streets of London. He always showed in his writing an inner pessimism of despair and death, faced with stoic determination by the men in his novels who were professionally successful.

Snow died in London 1 July 1980.

[*The Times*, 2 July 1980; R. Greacen (ed.), *The World of Snow*, 1962; S. Weintraub (ed.), *C. P. Snow—a Spectrum: Science, Criticism, Fiction*, 1963; David Shusterman, *C. P. Snow*, 1975; William Cooper, *C. P. Snow*, 1959; personal knowledge.]

JOHN VAIZEY

published 1986

STRACHEY (Giles) Lytton

(1880–1932)

Critic and biographer, was born in London 1 March 1880, the fourth of the five sons of Lieutenant-General (Sir) Richard Strachey, by his second wife, Jane Maria, second daughter of Sir John Peter Grant (1807–1893), of Rothiemurchus. He was first cousin of Sir Edward Strachey, fourth baronet, and first Baron Strachie, and of J. St. L. Strachey. Lytton Strachey evinced precocious taste and talent for literature, which were sedulously fostered by his mother. After a short period at Abbotsholme School, Derbyshire, and a longer at Leamington College, he was sent in 1897–1899 to Liverpool University College, where he studied history. This was followed by four years at Trinity College, Cambridge. Here, largely under the influence of Dr. George Edward Moore, he formed his ideas, and also made some distinguished lifelong friends, including John Maynard (later Lord) Keynes, Dr. Edward Morgan Forster, Mr. Desmond MacCarthy, Mr. Leonard Woolf, and Mr. Clive Bell. He won the chancellor's English medal in 1902, and obtained second classes in both parts of the historical tripos (1901, 1903). After failing to secure a fellowship, he took up residence in London, where he worked regularly on the *Spectator* under the editorship of J. St. L. Strachey and also contributed to the *Edinburgh* and the *New Quarterly Reviews*. This work, although he disliked it, trained him in his craft. Meanwhile he became a prominent member of the celebrated 'Bloomsbury' literary and artistic circle, composed mainly of his Cambridge friends with the addition of the daughters of Sir Leslie Stephen, Vanessa Bell and Virginia Woolf, and in which a culture of extreme refinement was combined with open rebellion alike against the beliefs and the habits of orthodox middle-class Victorianism.

Strachey's first book, *Landmarks in French Literature*, commissioned by H. A. L. Fisher for the 'Home University Library' series, came out in 1912. After this, his friends and family subscribed to make him financially independent of journalism, so that he might retire to the country and write books. His activities were not interrupted by the war of 1914–1918, for he was a conscientious objector; and *Eminent Victorians* appeared in 1918. This, although fiercely attacked as irreverent to the illustrious dead, at once put him in the front rank of contemporary authors. It was followed by *Queen Victoria* (1921), *Books and Characters, French and English* (1922), *Elizabeth and Essex* (1928), and *Portraits in Miniature, and Other Essays* (1931). The university of Edinburgh conferred upon him the honorary degree of LL.D. in 1926. In 1924 he settled at Ham Spray House, near Hungerford, where he was looked after by his friends Mr. and Mrs. Ralph Partridge until his death there from cancer 21 January 1932. He never married. *Characters and Commentaries*, a posthumous volume of collected studies, published and unpublished, appeared in 1933.

Strachey was a conspicuous figure wherever he appeared, with his wit and his silence, his tall, emaciated figure, and his red beard. Fastidious and ill-adjusted to the commonplace, he was in youth often melancholy; but literary success and the friendships which he cultivated so intensely made his later years agreeable. He was a sensitive, sensible critic, particularly remarkable for the work which he did in awakening Englishmen to the appreciation of the classical French authors, notably Racine. But his most memorable achievement was in biography. Here he sometimes showed the limitations of his civilized Voltairean rationalism, which made him unable to enter into the wild or mystical aspects of human nature. Nor was he a profound psychologist: before complex characters he was apt gracefully to confess himself baffled. But his economical mastery of design, his faculty of vivid story-telling, and the mingled elegance and vitality of his style are alike eminent; and they are made exhilarating by the continuous sparkle of an impish and adroit irony. He is also important historically, first, as the leader of that reaction against the Victorians which followed the war of 1914–1918, and, secondly, as the inaugurator of a new type of biography, brief and brilliant, in which fact and reflection are fused together into a work of art, individual and creative as a novel.

A portrait of Strachey by Henry Lamb is in the Tate Gallery, and a chalk drawing by Nina Hamnett belongs to the National Portrait Gallery.

Thomas

[Guy Boas, *Lytton Strachey* (English Association Pamphlet No. 93), November 1933; Sir (H.) Max(imilian) Beerbohm, *Lytton Strachey* (Rede lecture), 1943; private information; personal knowledge.]

DAVID CECIL

published 1949

THOMAS Dylan Marlais

(1914–1953)

Poet, was born in Swansea 27 October 1914, the only son and younger child of David John Thomas, English master at the Swansea Grammar School, by his wife, Florence Hannah Williams. 'Marlais', the name of a small stream in Carmarthenshire, links Thomas with his parents' native county. After the normal primary school education, Thomas entered the Swansea Grammar School, and its school magazine, of which he first became sub-editor then, in his final year, editor, bears ample testimony, in prose and verse, to the creative assiduity with which he applied himself to his editorial tasks. He left school with an undistinguished academic record in 1931 to join the *South Wales Daily Post* as a reporter but by the end of 1932 he had left the paper. This marked the beginning of his career as a professional poet.

In September 1933 the *Sunday Referee* printed his first poem to find publication in the London press, and in the next year he was awarded the paper's 'major prize' which led to the publication of his *18 Poems* (1934). These were marked by an impression of early maturity. The themes which were to sustain his poetic output to the end of his days are all found here: the 'Genesis' theme, the 'Adam' myth, and the creative 'Word'. These themes, continually developed throughout his career, and worked out with meticulous craftsmanship, justify his later claim that his poems were 'written for the love of Man and in praise of God'.

In November 1934 Thomas moved to London to work as a freelance and there he laid the foundations of the legend of the beer-swilling, roystering Bohemian, who behaved as some people imagined a poet should. At intervals he returned to Swansea where he spent the end of 1935 and the beginning of 1936 working on *Twenty-five Poems*, published in the latter year. In these poems he continues his probing into the nature of man, his beginning and end, and his place in the economy of creation. His essentially religious nature informs these poems, and his perceptive glimpse of the sacramental nature of the universe in the beautifully turned lyric, 'This Bread I Break', presages the change which was to be even more clearly discerned in *The Map of Love*, published in 1939. In the words of his close friend, Vernon Watkins, 'Each [poem] is an experience perceived and controlled by the religious sense, and each answers its own questions. He has pared his imagery without losing any of its force.'

In 1937 Dylan Thomas married Caitlin, daughter of Francis Macnamara; they had two sons and one daughter. At this time they settled in Laugharne. In 1939 *The World I Breathe* was published in America. It contained selections from *18 Poems*, *Twenty-five Poems*, *The Map of Love*, and additional new stories. In the following year, *Portrait of the Artist as a Young Dog* appeared—a thinly disguised autobiographical account of his boyhood in Swansea, Gower, and the Carmarthenshire countryside. In these stories we find the quintessence of Thomas's rich humour and sense of the comic, allied to a compassionate affection for all sorts and conditions of men.

During the war Thomas lived in London, interrupted by frequent spells in Laugharne and Swansea. He returned to Carmarthenshire in 1944, and in the autumn of that year settled in New Quay, Cardiganshire, moving back to London in September 1945, where he remained until March 1946 when he moved to Holywell Ford, Oxford. In 1947 he moved to South Leigh and in 1949 returned to Laugharne. The war period was perhaps the most fruitful of Thomas's whole career. Apart from his radio writing, collected posthumously in *Quite Early One Morning* (1954), he began to be used extensively by the B.B.C. as an actor and reader of poetry. His gifts as a reader were outstanding. At his best, he displayed a sensitivity which enabled him to ally himself, as it were, with the poet, in the very act of creating. There is little doubt that it was this gift for reading, which insinuated an ease of understanding into the most difficult of his own poems, that brought him his early fame and popularity. He confessed that his work for the B.B.C. and his public readings contributed towards that greater simplification and clarity which is displayed in his later work.

Apart from his work with the B.B.C., he was engaged in this period on script-writing for films—*Lidice*, *The Three Weird Sisters*, *These are the Men*, *Our Country*, *The Doctor and the Devils* (published 1953), *The Beach of Falesá*, and *Twenty Years A-Growing* (the last two published posthumously). Among his posthumous publications is *Adventures in the Skin Trade* (1955), an unfinished novel describing the arrival of a young poet in London, which was begun at some time prior to 1941. It is, like many of his stories, richly comic, and is all of a piece with his other writing. It was never completed, perhaps because of the war and the changed vision of this city of fire-raids and holocausts.

It was *Deaths and Entrances*, published in 1946, which sealed his promise, and secured for him a place in the English poetic tradition—in the direct line of his Welsh predecessors Donne, Herbert, and Vaughan. Although this volume contains a number of poems which arise from the great tragedy and holocaust of the war, yet it succeeds in conveying an impression of light and illumination. Here are the great poems of the holy innocence of childhood. This movement into light is accompanied by a simplifying of style, and an attendant gain in lucidity. In these poems, Thomas is a ritualist, celebrating the glory of the material order and his imagery takes on a 'Catholic' flavour, no doubt under the influence of Gerard Manley Hopkins, a poet whose work he loved.

The first of Thomas's four visits to America was made in the spring of 1950. There is little doubt that these trips were undertaken 'to make some money' which he badly needed. He was completely incapable of ordering the material side of his life, and even the prospect of 'making money' bored him. His account of one of his marathon tours is described in the hilariously funny broadcast talk 'Visit to America' and is a healthy antidote to J. M. Brinnin's lurid but one-sided account in *Dylan Thomas in America*.

Collected Poems was put together at the suggestion of his publishers in 1952, and contained all that he wished to preserve. The following January he was presented with the William Foyle poetry prize. When the time comes to make a final assessment of his work, his stature will be determined, not so much upon the strength of a handful of random poems, nor even on *Deaths and Entrances*, but on the *Collected Poems* seen as a unity, the fruit of a life of dedication to his 'craft and sullen art'. The 'Author's Prologue', a poem written expressly as an introduction to the *Collected Poems*, was to be his last completed poem and his final declaration of the relevance of his art to the human condition.

In January 1952 he made his second visit to America, and in April 1953 his third. Then came the final visit in the autumn of the same year when he arrived a sick man. He was scheduled to take part in the first performance of his 'play for voices', *Under Milk Wood*, on 24 October at the Poetry Center, New York. (The first part of this play had already appeared in *Botteghe Oscure* in 1952 under the title *Llareggub*, but it seems that Thomas worked on it right to the end. The final version was broadcast in the Third Programme of the B.B.C. on 25 January 1954.)

The presentation in New York was agreed by critics to be the finest performance of *Under Milk Wood*. It was his last appearance. Within a few days, after bouts of excessive drinking of hard liquor, he succumbed to alcoholic poisoning and died in New York 9 November 1953. His body was brought back to Laugharne and was interred in the burial ground of the parish church of St. Martin.

Portraits by Augustus John and Alfred Janes and a bronze bust, from a death mask, by David Slivka and Ibram Lassaw, are in the National Museum of Wales. The National Portrait Gallery has portraits by G. T. Stuart and Rupert Shephard and drawings by Michael Ayrton and Mervyn Levy. The Tate Gallery has a head painted by Eileen Agar.

[*The Times*, 10 November 1953; Dylan Thomas, *Letters to Vernon Watkins*, 1957; J. M. Brinnin, *Dylan Thomas in America*, 1956; J. A. Rolph, *Dylan Thomas: A Bibliography*, 1956; Augustus John, *Finishing Touches*, 1964; Constantine FitzGibbon, *The Life of Dylan Thomas*, 1965; *Poet in the Making: The Notebooks of Dylan Thomas*, ed. Ralph Maud, 1968; personal knowledge.]

ANEIRIN TALFAN DAVIES

published 1971

THOMPSON Flora Jane

(1876–1947)

Writer, was born in Juniper Hill, a hamlet in north-east Oxfordshire, 5 December 1876, the eldest child in the family of four daughters and two sons of Albert Timms, a stonemason, originally from Buckingham, and his wife Emma, a nursemaid, daughter of John Dibber from Stoke Lyne, an 'eggler', who took his pony and cart around local farms, collecting eggs and selling them in the market town. Her favourite brother Edwin, born in 1879, was to die in 1916 during the battle of the Somme. After elementary education at the village school in Cottisford she became, at the age of fourteen, an unofficial post-office counter clerk in the Oxfordshire village of Fringford. Until her marriage in 1903 she worked in post offices in Buckinghamshire, Essex, and Hampshire.

In 1911 she won a magazine essay competition and went on to write short stories, newspaper articles, and during the 1920s two long series of articles for the *Catholic Fireside* magazine. In alternate months she wrote nature articles and literary pieces. She was a dedicated if self-taught naturalist. An anthology of her nature articles called *The Peverel Papers* was published in 1986. The literary articles were the result of her home study of literature—she had grown up during the establishment of the free library system in Britain, which she used extensively to supplement her elementary education. Her first published book was *Bog Myrtle and Peat* (1921), a volume of poems which she was persuaded to submit for publication by her friend and literary mentor Dr Ronald Campbell Macfie. In 1938 she sent essays on her country childhood to the Oxford University Press. These were published as *Lark Rise* (1939), the story of the Oxfordshire hamlet where she was born. *Over to Candleford* (1941) was followed by *Candleford Green* (1943). These popular books were issued as the trilogy, *Lark Rise to Candleford* (1945), with a perceptive introduction by H. J. Massingham.

Flora Thompson was a reserved woman of little confidence who was astonished when reviewers praised her work and Sir Arthur Bryant rated her books as high as *Cranford*. The books, which have become classics of country writing, evoke the vigorous life of a hamlet, a village, and a country town in the England of the 1880s. They are social history but also the lightly disguised story of Flora Thompson's youth. Her last book, *Still Glides the Stream*, was published posthumously in 1948.

In 1903 she married John William Thompson, a post-office clerk and telegraphist from the Isle of Wight, son of Henry Thompson, formerly a chief petty officer in the Royal Navy. They had two sons and one daughter. In 1941 her much-loved younger son Peter was lost at sea when the ship on which he served was torpedoed in mid-Atlantic; she never recovered from this loss. She died 21 May 1947 in Brixham, Devon.

[Margaret Lane, *Flora Thompson*, 1976; Gillian Lindsay, *Flora Thompson: the Story of the Lark Rise Writer*, 1990.]

GILLIAN LINDSAY

published 1993

TOMLINSON Henry Major

(1873–1958)

Writer, was born in Poplar 21 June 1873, the eldest in the family of three sons and one daughter of Henry Tomlinson and his wife, Emily Major, daughter of a master gunner in the navy. His father was a foreman at the West India Dock, and as a boy Tomlinson became familiar with ships and seamen and the lure of the sea. After his father's death in 1886 he was taken from school and placed in a City shipping office at a wage of six shillings a week. He knew poverty and remembered it all his life; but with his mother's encouragement he soon began to read widely, especially in the history of travel and navigation, and in time he turned to the study of geology, to which he added botany, zoology, and mineralogy. In 1894 he was considered as a possible geologist for the Jackson–Harmsworth polar expedition, but, much to his disappointment, was advised that his health would not stand the strain.

Tomlinson grew increasingly restive in his office occupation although his frequent opportunities for visiting the ships and the docks were a source of inspiration for much of his future writing. It was not until 1904, however, that, after an office quarrel, he applied for a job with the radical *Morning Leader*, a paper to which he had already contributed. He was engaged as a reporter, and his love of the sea was soon turned to good account by his editor, Ernest Parke, who sent him to live for several weeks, in midwinter, with a fleet of trawlers on the Dogger Bank. An assignment to the naval manœuvres was a sequel. Parke later made him still happier by sending him, ostensibly as ship's purser, on a voyage to Brazil and two thousand miles up the Amazon and Madeira rivers in the first English steamer to make that passage. His first book, *The Sea and the Jungle*, followed in 1912. It was immediately hailed as a classic and subsequently appeared in many editions. The beauty of the prose and the descriptive writing showed Tomlinson to be a new author of unusual quality. He was also at this time contributing to the *English Review* edited by Ford Madox Hueffer (later Ford). When the *Morning Leader* was amalgamated with the *Daily News* in 1912 Tomlinson stayed on as a leader-writer; he became a war correspondent in Belgium and France in August 1914 and was official correspondent at British G.H.Q. in France in 1914–17. He was literary editor under H. W. Massingham of the *Nation* from 1917 to 1923.

Thoreau and Emerson helped to mould Tomlinson's thought and a style which was never that of a fashionable author but won the deep admiration of fellow craftsmen. In the post-war years he travelled widely and established himself as a writer of poetic essays and stories in collections such as *Old Junk* (1918), *Waiting for Daylight* (1922), and *Gifts of Fortune* (1926). *London River* (1921) was a moving book of personal memories and self-communings on the theme nearest his heart, while *Tidemarks* (1924) took the reader to the islands and straits of the Dutch East Indies. His first novel, *Gallions Reach* (1927), which was awarded the Femina Vie Heureuse prize, was acclaimed as an important work on both sides of the Atlantic. Yet, although Tomlinson was a born descriptive writer, he was not a born novelist. His next book, *All Our Yesterdays* (1930), a story of the war of 1914–18, demonstrated that he was more of a poet, journalist, philosopher, and student of humanity, than an inventor of plot and fictional character.

Tomlinson continued to produce novels until the end of his life. His writings became increasingly permeated by a hatred of war—specifically proclaimed in *Mars His Idiot* (1935)—but they also showed a redeeming belief in the supreme value of individual personality. Although his later work was somewhat uneven, he still conveyed his old mastery as an essayist in collections such as *The Turn of the Tide* (1945), while *A Mingled Yarn* (1953), a series of autobiographical sketches, displays him at his characteristic best in reminiscence and description. Tomlinson's gifts as a writer can be well studied here, and in the selection from his work made by Kenneth Hopkins (1953). In his last book, *The Trumpet Shall Sound* (1957), the story of the impact of the blitz on an English family, Tomlinson put into memorable words what many of those who lived through the war of 1939–45 thought only in their hearts.

Tomlinson was short of stature and his deeply lined face reflected a thoughtful and contemplative disposition. He suffered from deafness caused by a football accident in early youth and aggravated by gunfire on the western front. This handicap led people to think of him as a shy man, but he was constantly sought after by his many friends, who appreciated his fine sense of humour and fondness for good conversation in a small company. A keen naturalist, Tomlinson loved walking, and even in his later years thought nothing of taking long walks through the unspoiled Dorset countryside where he spent each summer.

In 1899 he married Florence Margaret, daughter of Thomas Hammond, ship's chandler, by whom he had one son and two daughters. Tomlinson received the honorary degree of LL.D. from Aberdeen in 1949. He died in London 5 February 1958 and was buried in the churchyard at Abbotsbury, Dorset. A portrait by Richard Murry became the possession of Mrs. Mary Middleton Murry; pencil drawings by William A. Wildman and Colin Moss and a bronze head by Sava Botzvaris are in the possession of the family.

[*The Times*, 6 and 14 February 1958; H. M. Tomlinson, *A Mingled Yarn*, 1953; Frank Swinnerton, *The Georgian Literary Scene 1910–1935*, 1935, and *Figures in the Foreground*, 1963; private information.]

DEREK HUDSON

published 1971

TYNAN Kenneth Peacock

(1927–1980)

Theatre critic, was born 2 April 1927 in Birmingham, the only son (a daughter had previously died in infancy) of Sir Peter Peacock, merchant and former mayor of Warrington, and Letitia Rose Tynan, a union kept quite separate from Peacock's accepted household and family in Lancashire. Tynan never met his much older half-brothers and half-sisters. From King Edward's School, Birmingham, he won a demyship to Magdalen College, Oxford, where he obtained a second class in English in 1948. At Oxford he embarked upon a systematic campaign to outshine or outrage all contemporaries as undergraduate journalist, actor, impresario, party-giver, and (despite a stammer) debater. If you were going to be a show-off in the midst of colonels, fighter pilots, and other heroes back from the war, he said later, you had to be a professional show-off. At the same time he was amassing enough serious and enthusiastic consideration of the theatre to provide him with his first book, *He that Plays the King* (1950), and a wider reputation.

After a spell as a repertory theatre director he seized the chance to become a professional theatre critic. Invited by (Sir) Alec Guinness to take the part of the Player King in Guinness's luckless production of *Hamlet* for the Festival of Britain, Tynan became the target of especially scornful remarks from the *Evening Standard*'s reviewer (Sir) A. Beverley Baxter. He replied with a letter to the editor so droll that according to legend he was immediately hired in Baxter's place. In fact some weeks elapsed, and he had in any case been writing about the theatre in the *Spectator*, but no doubt his flair for attracting attention played its part. With the *Evening Standard* (1952–3) and to a lesser extent with the *Daily Sketch* (1953–4) Tynan established himself as a funny and scathing writer on the theatre, if still one who wanted from it heroics and illusions. It was only after he was invited to join the *Observer* in 1954 that he started to apply to drama the political convictions which he was in the process of acquiring, with characteristic intemperance, about this time. 'I doubt that I could love anyone who did not wish to see it', he affirmed in a review of John Osborne's *Look Back in Anger* inspired as much by the play's tirades against respectability and authority as by its theatrical virtues. He went on to embrace socialism, nuclear disarmament, and the didactic drama of Bertolt Brecht.

His new-found beliefs did not prevent him from remaining a socializer as well as a socialist. He had married in 1951 Elaine, daughter of Samuel M. Brimberg, office equipment manufacturer, of New York. As Elaine Dundy she published two sparkling novels of the decade, *The Dud Avocado* (1958) in which a barely-disguised Kenneth Tynan appears, and *The Old Man and Me* (1964). Their Mayfair flat became a salon for celebrities passing through London, particularly from the United States. Tynan was fascinated by the outsize stars of Hollywood and Broadway. It was inevitable that he would be lured to America himself, as theatre critic of the *New Yorker*, though without severing his *Observer* connection. In the end he stayed only two years before returning to London in 1960.

Tynan was never averse to trying his hand in some production capacity as an adjunct to his criticism. He was story editor for Ealing Films in its last years (1955–7); produced two television programmes for ATV on the Stanislavskian method (1958) and dissent in America (1960), and edited the arts magazine *Tempo* for ABC Television (England) (1961–2). In 1963 came the invitation which was to tempt him away from his critic's seat altogether. Sir Laurence (later Lord) Olivier asked him to be literary manager of the National Theatre which was finally being set up in the temporary home of the Old Vic Theatre. Tynan threw himself into the task with energy and confidence. He disinterred forgotten classics, edited texts, and directly inspired such new works as Tom Stoppard's *Rosencrantz and Guildenstern are Dead* and Peter Shaffer's *Black Comedy*. These first seasons are generally regarded as having given the National's repertoire its stamp, but among the hits were one or two misfires, including a Brecht, which Tynan's critics could cite when in 1968 he clashed with the governors of the theatre over his determination to introduce *Soldiers*, by the German dramatist Rolf Hochhuth. The play alleged *inter alia* that Sir Winston Churchill had ordered the death of the wartime Polish leader General Sikorski. As a former colleague of Churchill's, the National's chairman Viscount Chandos was adamant that the production should not go ahead. Tynan responded by mounting the play himself in the commercial theatre and the following year resigned his post, though he remained a consultant until 1973.

There followed the exploit which prompts the most mixed feelings among Tynan's friends and admirers, the revue *Oh! Calcutta!* which he devised and produced first in New York, in 1969, and then in London. He had embraced the sexual 'liberation' of the era with the same enthusiasm he brought to its political concomitant, listing his recreations in *Who's Who* as sex and eating and in 1965 earning himself a footnote in the annals as the first Briton to say the word 'fuck' on television. *Oh! Calcutta!*'s mix of rather attractive nudity and distinctly seedy humour might have been designed to shock the bourgeoisie; ironically (if inevitably) it was a commercial success everywhere, and made Tynan well off.

He also ventured into film production with the 1971 version of *Macbeth* directed by Roman Polanski, but as the seventies wore on journalism reclaimed his energies, sadly beginning to dwindle as his health deteriorated. Mainly for American magazines he wrote a series of lengthy reflective profiles of actors and entertainers which, published in book form as *Show People* (1979), confirm Tynan's talent as a writer, his ability to conjure up time and place, people and performances, whether he is defining the extraordinary allure of Louise Brooks or conveying exactly what it was like to experience (Sir) Donald Wolfit and Frederick Valk (two of his heroes) in a barnstorming wartime production of *Othello*. He became FRSL in 1956.

He also published two collections of theatre reviews but disappointingly few original books. A long-planned memoir of his Oxford days materialized only in the form of his contribution to the television series *One Pair of Eyes* in 1968. Towards the end of his life he was planning an autobiography, but it was not to be realized. To lessen the ravages of the emphysema from which he suffered he was now living in Santa Monica, California. He died there 26 July 1980.

His first marriage had ended in divorce in 1964. There was one daughter. In 1967 Tynan married Kathleen, daughter of Matthew Halton, journalist and writer, herself a novelist and screenwriter; they had a son and daughter. Tynan was tall, slender, always elegant. In youth his habit of baring his teeth as he strove to overcome the stammer, coupled with flaring nostrils and a rather skull-like head, gave him the look of a startled rocking-horse. He matured into a relaxed and attractive human being, full of unexpected subsidiary enthusiasms (cricket, word games, bullfighting). His conversation, as Tom Stoppard put it, always had the jingle of loose change about it. When he died it was apparent that he had inspired quite exceptional affection in many who knew him. Whatever his enduring influence on the theatre may prove to be, he brought excitement, authority, and glamour to the business of writing about it.

[Godfrey Smith in *Sunday Times* (magazine section), 25 August 1963; Laurence Olivier, *Confessions of an Actor*, 1982; personal knowledge.]

PHILIP PURSER

published 1986

WALEY Arthur David

(1889–1966)

Orientalist, was born at Tunbridge Wells 19 August 1889, the second of the three sons of David Frederick Schloss, economist and Fabian socialist, and his wife, Rachel Sophia, daughter of Jacob Waley, legal writer and professor of political economy, whose surname the family adopted in 1914. He was the brother of Sir Sigismund David Waley.

Waley

Arthur Waley was brought up in Wimbledon and sent to school at Rugby (1903–6), where he shone as a classical scholar and won an open scholarship at King's College, Cambridge, while still under seventeen. He spent a year in France before going up to the university in 1907; he obtained a first class in part i of the classical tripos in 1910 but was obliged to abandon Cambridge when he developed diminished sight in one eye due to conical cornea. Rest and Continental travel saved the second eye from being affected and made him fluent in Spanish and German. Although he had got to know (Sir) Sydney Cockerell at Cambridge it was through Oswald Sickert, a brother of the painter, that he was led to consider a career in the British Museum. Sickert was one of a group of friends, mostly either on the museum staff or researchers in the library, who used to meet regularly for lunch in the years before 1914 at the Vienna Café in New Oxford Street, at which Laurence Binyon was one of the 'regulars'. In 1912 Sir Sidney Colvin retired from his keepership of prints and drawings and Waley was a candidate for the vacancy in February 1913, supported by both Sickert and Cockerell. In June he started working in the newly formed sub-department of oriental prints and drawings under its first head, Binyon. Waley's task was to make a rational index of the Chinese and Japanese painters represented in the museum collection; he immediately started to teach himself Chinese and Japanese. He had no formal instruction, for the School of Oriental Studies was not founded till 1916; but by that date Waley was privately printing his first fifty-two translations of Chinese poems, and in 1917–18 he added others in the first numbers of the *Bulletin* of the School and in the *New Statesman* and the *Little Review*. By 1918 he had completed enough translations of poems, mainly by writers of the classic T'ang period, to have a volume entitled *A Hundred and Seventy Chinese Poems* accepted for publication by Constable largely on account of a perceptive review in the *Times Literary Supplement* of the 1917 *Bulletin* poems. In 1919 (Sir) Stanley Unwin became his publisher and remained his constant friend and admirer.

During his sixteen years at the museum Waley's only official publications were the index of Chinese artists (1922), at that time the first in the West; and a catalogue of the paintings recovered from Tun-huang by Sir Aurel Stein and subsequently divided between the Government of India and the British Museum (1931). His *An Introduction to the Study of Chinese Painting* (1923) was a by-product of his unpublished notes on the national collection and its relation to the great tradition of Chinese painting. He also set in order and described the Japanese books with woodcut illustrations and the large collection of Japanese paintings. He retired from the museum on the last day of 1929 because he had been told that he ought to spend his winters abroad. Waley had started to ski as early as 1911 and he liked to get away into the mountains whenever he could, generally to Austria or Norway and not to the regular runs but as a lone figure on the high snow slopes.

In 1925 began the publication of Waley's largest and probably best-known translation—of the *Genji Monogatari* by Murasaki Shikibu, the late tenth-century classical novelist of Japan, the sixth volume of which did not appear until 1933. This was not the first of Waley's Japanese translations, for it had been preceded by two volumes of classic poetry, selections from the *Uta* (1919) and Nō plays (1921); in these he was more concerned with the resonances of the Japanese language, whereas in the *Genji* he aimed rather at an interpretation of the sensibility and wit of the closed society of the Heian court, described in the idiomatic English of his day. Inevitably this already shows signs of dating as the idiom itself becomes remote, but it may be long before it is again possible to enter so sympathetically into the spirit of that refined and élitist world.

The translations of Chinese poetry which he continued to produce for the rest of his life show Waley more as a creative poet, though his lives of Po Chü-i and Li Po show how closely he was aware of their milieux. In his verse translations Waley not only wanted to evoke the mood and intention of the original text but also to convey in the English mode the stresses of Chinese verse form. He denied the influence of G. Manley Hopkins in his use of 'sprung rhythm' but said that he was influenced by him in the phrasing of the Nō plays. In fact the level of his speech rhythm is naturally different from that of Hopkins, with none of its urgent acceleration but rather with the clear phrasing of the flute which he enjoyed playing.

Waley moved with the smooth grace of the skier, his gesture was courtly in salutation, but more characteristic was the attentive, withdrawn pose of his finely profiled head with its sensitive but severe mouth. His voice was high-pitched but low-toned and unchanging, so as to seem conversational in a lecture, academic in conversation. In later life he had a slight stoop which accentuated his ascetic appearance. He enjoyed meeting the sympathetic and their conversation but never spoke himself unless he had something to say; he expected the same restraint in others. His forty years' attachment to Beryl de Zoete, the anthropologist and interpreter of Eastern dance forms, brought out the depth of feeling and tenderness of which he was capable.

As a scholar Waley aimed always to express Chinese and Japanese thought at their most profound levels, with the highest standard of accuracy of meaning, in a way that would not be possible again because of the growth of professional specialization. He was always a lone figure in his work though he was not remote from the mood of his times. Although he never travelled to the Far East and did not seek to confront the contemporary societies of China or Japan, he was scathingly critical of the attitude of the West to their great cultures in the world in which he grew up: hence his scorn for the older generation of sinologists and his hatred of imperialism, as shown in his *The Opium War through Chinese Eyes* (1958).

For over forty years Waley lived in Bloomsbury, mostly in Gordon Square. Although he had many connections with the Bloomsbury group of artists and writers, he was never a member of a clique and his friendships with the Stracheys, the Keyneses, and with Roger Fry dated from his Cambridge days. He was elected an honorary fellow of King's in 1945 but was not often seen there. Other honours also came to him late, election to the British Academy in 1945, the Queen's medal for poetry in 1953, CBE in 1952, and CH in 1956. Aberdeen and Oxford universities awarded him honorary doctorates. After the death of Beryl in 1962 he went to live in Highgate where he was looked after by Alison Grant Robinson, an old friend from New Zealand, who was formerly married to Hugh Ferguson Robinson, and to whom he was married a month before his death at home from cancer of the spine 27 June 1966.

A volume of appreciation and an anthology of his writings was edited by Ivan Morris, under the title *Madly Singing in the Mountains* (1970), a phrase taken from a poem by Po Chü-i which Waley had translated in 1917 and chosen because of its 'joyfulness', as expressed in the lines:

'Each time that I look at a fine landscape:
Each time that I meet a loved friend,
I raise my voice and recite a stanza of poetry
And am glad as though a God had crossed my path.'

Two notes that Waley wrote on his own work when over seventy, while not factually reliable, contain his own assessment of his translations; that he had made them to the measure of his own tastes and sensibilities, in a 'recherche esthétique'. Forty years earlier he had written: 'If I have failed to make these translations in some sense works of art—if they are mere philology, not literature, then I have indeed fallen short of what I hoped and intended.' It can be asserted that his intention was fully realized.

A bibliography of Waley's work was published by F. A. Johns in 1968. A portrait drawing by Michael Ayrton is in King's College, Cambridge, and a pencil drawing by Rex Whistler is in the National Portrait Gallery.

[Introduction to the second edition of *170 Chinese Poems*, 1962; Ivan Morris (ed.), *Madly Singing in the Mountains*, 1970; *The Times*, 28 June 1966; L. P. Wilkinson in *King's College Annual Report*, 1966; private information; personal knowledge.]

BASIL GRAY

published 1981

WALLACE (Richard Horatio) Edgar

(1875–1932)

Novelist, playwright, and journalist, was born in Greenwich 1 April 1875, the son of Richard Horatio Edgar, an actor, and Mary Jane (Polly) Richards (née Blair), an actress. He was brought up by George Freeman, a Billingsgate fishporter, and his wife, kindly and respectable people who cared for the boy within their limited means. At the age of eleven he played truant to sell newspapers in Ludgate Circus a few yards from the site of the bronze plaque which now commemorates him, and from the age of twelve, when he left an elementary school in Peckham, he was successively employed as a printer's boy, as a newsboy, in a shoe shop, in a mackintosh cloth factory, in a Grimsby trawler, as a milk roundsman, and as a roadmaker and builder's labourer. At eighteen he enlisted in the Royal West Kent Regiment from which he transferred to the Medical Staff Corps and was drafted with it to South Africa in 1896. By this time he had produced his earliest work, a song for the comedian Arthur Roberts. In South Africa he wrote poems and articles for the *Cape Times* and other papers and later became successively a Reuter's correspondent and correspondent of the *Daily Mail*. In 1902 he became the first editor of the *Rand Daily Mail* in Johannesburg, and on his return to England again worked for the *Daily Mail*.

The first of the novels that were to make Wallace famous was *The Four Just Men* (1905), and this was followed by a series, most of which were sold outright for small sums, before he started on his West African stories, of which two were *Sanders of the River* (1911) and *Bones* (1915). Throughout his life he was interested principally in three activities; the stage, newspapers, and novel writing, and it would be true to say that he regarded them in that order of importance. His only relaxation was racing, and in the last few years of his life he owned and enjoyed a singularly unsuccessful string of racehorses. Graduating from music-hall songs and review sketches, he began to write plays, and his first dramatic success, *The Ringer* (Wyndham's Theatre, May 1926), marked the beginning of a phase in which his novels, such as *The Crimson Circle* (1922) and *The Green Archer* (1923), were being sold in their tens and hundreds of thousands, and he sometimes had two or three plays running in London at the same time. The novels for which he was most widely known were those detective stories in which, without the use of false clues or supernatural circumstances, a mysterious crime was solved and the criminals brought to justice: a simple formula on which the freshness and ingenuity of his invention worked a new pattern in every volume. His writing had simplicity, vigour, and pace, but it was the variety and originality of his plots that made his reputation: that, and his prolific output, since in twenty-eight years of authorship more than a hundred and seventy books of his were published. They were universally translated and his plays were produced in Europe, the British Empire, the United States of America, and the Scandinavian countries. His daily flow of magazine and newspaper articles was generally dictated to one of his secretaries, his novels were dictated to a dictaphone, and his plays were written by hand. He worked fast, and the best of his plays, *On the Spot* (1931), was written by him during a week-end.

Wallace married in South Africa in 1901 Ivy Maud (died 1926), daughter of William Shaw Caldecott, a Wesleyan minister, of Simon's Town, and had two sons and a daughter. Their marriage was dissolved in 1918, and in 1921 he married Ethel Violet King (died 1933), by whom he had a daughter. At the general election of 1931 he stood unsuccessfully as liberal candidate for Blackpool. He died suddenly 10 February 1932 at Hollywood, California, where he had been writing motion picture stories. The first of these, *King Kong*, was produced shortly after his death. He was chairman of the Press Club from 1923 to 1925, inaugurated the Press Club Fund, and was one of the founder members of the Company of Newspaper Makers.

A portrait of Wallace by Tennyson Cole is at the Press Club. A bust was made by Jo Davidson.

[*The Times*, 11 February 1932; Edgar Wallace, *People. A Short Autobiography*, 1926; Margaret Lane, *Edgar Wallace*, 1938; E. V. Wallace, *Edgar Wallace*, 1932.]

FRANK DILNOT

published 1949

WARNER Sylvia Townsend

(1893–1978)

Novelist and poet, was born at Harrow, Middlesex, 6 December 1893, the only child of George Townsend Warner, assistant master and later head of the modern side at Harrow School, and his wife, Nora Hudleston. She was, briefly, privately educated. After a short time working in a munitions factory in World War I she was from 1918 to 1928 a member of the editorial board of *Tudor Church Music* (Oxford University Press, 1923–9). During this period she began to write. Her first book of verse, *The Espalier*, appeared in

1925. In 1926 she published the novel *Lolly Willowes*. This deft and fanciful elaboration on the theme of witchcraft won her a loyal following in the United States as well as in Britain. In 1927 she became guest critic of the *New York Herald-Tribune*: in the next four decades the *New Yorker* would publish more than 140 of her short stories.

Warner's first literary connections in England were with David Garnett and other writers associated with Bloomsbury. A more important influence was T. F. Powys, who appreciated the strength of her individuality and introduced her to her lifelong companion Valentine Ackland (died 1969). With Ms Ackland she issued a book of verse *Whether a Dove or a Seagull* (1934), in which the separate authors of the poems were not identified. Her own second book of poetry, *Time Importuned* (1928) had found only a small, though discriminating, audience. The poems' formal sense, their assimilation of both Emily Dickinson and English seventeenth-century verse, were remarkable; but Sylvia Townsend Warner remains best known for her fiction. She published in all seven novels and eight collections of short stories. *Mr. Fortune's Maggot* (1927) is a bizarre tale in an imaginary island. It was followed in 1929 by *The True Heart*, a historical fiction with a background in rural Victorian Essex. Her most substantial novel, *Summer will Show* (1936), was once more historical, for its characters are caught up in the Paris revolution of 1848.

This is also a political book. From about 1933 Sylvia Townsend Warner was a committed though never narrowly partisan writer of the Left. Her association with *Left Review* led to a friendship with the writer John Edgell Rickword. In 1936 she visited Spain, returning there the following year to attend the congress of anti-Fascist writers. She also became a member of the Association of Writers for Intellectual Liberty. She felt *After the Death of Don Juan* (1938), a satirical political fable, to be one of the most personal of her books. But this novella, like other of her writings, was too easily regarded as 'miscellaneous' to be recognized as the product of a distinct literary imagination. *Opus 7* (1931), a short novel in verse, was overlooked: her short stories were collected but too seldom found a place in anthologies.

After World War II she published a further historical novel, *The Corner that Held Them* (1948), memorable for its depiction of a fourteenth-century nunnery and in part inspired by her study of early music, while a more acid social observation (so much part of her short stories) was found in *The Flint Anchor* (1954). This was her last novel. She had undertaken, but never brought to completion, a biography of her friend T. F. Powys. A love of her adopted county of Dorset led to an account of its neighbour *Somerset* (1949), and her literary and rural interests were reflected in selections from the writings of Gilbert White (1946) and in *Jane Austen* (1951). At the prompting of mutual friends she wrote a biography (1967) of T. H. White, a writer younger than herself whom she had never met. This unusual assignment called forth a subtle power of empathy surely nurtured by her fiction. She was also, in her late years, a distinguished translator, as is shown by her version of Proust's *Contre Sainte-Beuve* (1958). Her last complete work was both a new departure and a return to the folklore themes found in *Lolly Willowes* and much of her poetry: the stories of *Kingdoms of Elfin* (1977) are obstinately of fairyland. She resisted the suggestion that she write her autobiography, 'because I'm too imaginative', but a selection of her letters was published in 1982. She was a fellow of the Royal Society of Literature and an honorary member of the American Academy of Arts and Letters. She won the prix Menton in 1969.

She was unmarried. She died at home at Maldon Newton, Dorset, 1 May 1978.

[*Guardian*, 5 January 1977; *New York Times*, 27 March 1977; *The Times*, 2 May 1978; *P.N. Review*, vol. viii, No. 3, 1981; *Letters of Sylvia Townsend Warner*, ed. William Maxwell, 1982.]

ALEXANDRA PRINGLE

published 1986

WAUGH Evelyn Arthur St. John

(1903–1966)

Novelist, was born in Hampstead 28 October 1903, the younger son of Arthur Waugh, publisher and author, and his wife, Catherine Charlotte, daughter of Henry Charles Biddulph Colton Raban, of the Bengal Civil Service. The family originally came from the Scottish Lowlands, and Waugh's mother's family also came from Scotland, for she was directly descended from Henry, Lord Cockburn. Arthur Waugh, in the previous year to Evelyn's birth, had become managing director of Chapman and Hall, once famous as the publishers of Charles Dickens, although by the end of the century the firm had very much contracted, and Arthur Waugh did not have a particularly easy or lucrative life. Himself educated at Sherborne he had sent his elder son there. But the storm created by Alec (Alexander Raban) Waugh's novel based on his school days, *The Loom of Youth* (1917), made it necessary to find another school for Evelyn who was five years younger.

He was sent to the high Anglican public school, Lancing, after some happy years as a day boy at a preparatory school in Hampstead. At first he was unhappy, at a time when the privations of the war years were at their most severe, and when it was the general condition of new boys to be given a bad time at public schools. But he developed his artistic interests, in painting, drawing, and calligraphy, and became editor of the school magazine. He crowned his Lancing career by winning a history scholarship to Hertford College, Oxford, in December 1921. He chose Hertford in preference to his father's old college, New College, out of consideration for his father's strained purse, because the scholarship at Hertford was of greater value. He went up immediately in January 1922, and took happily to Oxford life. At first he was overshadowed by his brother's name, but he soon made many friends in many colleges, and lived a high-spirited life in which social and somewhat rowdy drinking played a larger part than academic study. He developed a lasting antipathy for his history tutor, C. R. M. F. Cruttwell, dean, and later head, of the college, who wrote him a severe letter when he obtained a bad third in 1924. Waugh subsequently used the name Cruttwell for derogatory characters in his fiction. Conversely, the origins of many of his characters were to be found in real people.

The next three years, the unhappiest of his life, saw Waugh in a succession of posts as an assistant master, first at a school in Denbighshire, caricatured in *Decline and Fall* (1928), then at Aston Clinton in Buckinghamshire, and finally for half a term at a day school in Notting Hill Gate. In his autobiography, *A Little Learning* (1964), he ends what was intended to be only the first volume with an account of a rather half-hearted attempt to drown himself towards the end of his time at the school in Wales. Leaving a Greek inscription on his clothes, he swam out to sea, only to find himself in a shoal of jellyfish which caused him to turn back and decide to live. As a schoolmaster he was easy-going and not unpopular with the boys, but had the candour to recognize that he was very unsatisfactory from the headmaster's point of view. He managed to pursue an active social life; he had made particularly close friends with the Plunket-Greene family and fell deeply in love with the daughter, Olivia, a devout Catholic. She did not reciprocate, but his close friendship with the family had a great influence on him.

While still a schoolmaster Waugh wrote an essay on the *Pre-Raphaelite Brotherhood* which was printed privately in 1926. It came to the notice of the publishing house of Duckworth who suggested that Waugh should write for them a book on Rossetti. By April 1927 Waugh and the teaching profession had had enough of one another. In the autumn of the year he decided to study carpentry seriously with a view to becoming a maker of fine furniture, and he always said that this work gave him greater pleasure than writing ever did. In December Waugh became engaged to Evelyn Florence Margaret Winifred Gardner, daughter of the late Lord Burghclere, whose widow (daughter of the fourth Earl of Carnarvon) was strongly against her daughter engaging herself to a young man with neither income nor occupation. His book on Rossetti was published in 1928 and received some good reviews, but did not solve any problems. It was made very clear to Waugh that if he wanted to marry he must earn some money, and this was the genesis of *Decline and Fall*. When Duckworths jibbed and wanted more alterations than the author would agree to, its publication was undertaken by Chapman and Hall in the absence of his father who might have hesitated to publish his son's work. The book was an immense success, enthusiastically praised, notably by Arnold Bennett who enjoyed a unique position as a critic of fiction, and Waugh's financial troubles were ended.

In the meantime Waugh had married Evelyn Gardner in June 1928 without the knowledge of her mother. The success of his first novel was soon soured by domestic trouble. While Waugh was writing his next novel, *Vile Bodies* (1930), which proved that he was not a man of one book, but a writer with a rich and developing talent, his young wife was unfaithful to him, and in 1930 he obtained a divorce. When in that year Waugh was received into the Roman Catholic Church by Father Martin D'Arcy at Farm Street, he was quite prepared to face the prospect that he could not, by the law of the Church, contract another marriage while his wife lived. It did not immediately dawn upon him that he had a very good case for arguing that the necessary intention of indissolubility on the part of both parties had not been present. His petition for an annulment made in 1933 was not granted until 1936, and it was not until 1937 that he made a second and enduring marriage to Laura Laetitia Gwendolen Evelyn (died 1973), a first cousin of his first wife, and youngest of the three daughters of the late Aubrey Nigel Henry Molyneux Herbert, half-brother of the fifth Earl of Carnarvon.

By that time Waugh had consolidated his position as a writer, and had produced what many critics regard as his finest achievement, in which, as he expressed it, he said all he had to say about a society without religion, a work of masterly construction, full of intensely comical situations which nevertheless illustrate a deeply serious theme. This was *A Handful of Dust* which came out in 1934. It was preceded by *Black Mischief* (1932), a high-spirited story made possible by a visit which the author made to Abyssinia in 1930 for the coronation of the Emperor Haile Selassie which he reported for the *Graphic* and as a special correspondent for *The Times*. He went on from Ethiopia to Aden, Zanzibar, Kenya, the Belgian Congo, and Cape

Town, recording his travels in *Remote People* (1931). As a war correspondent for the *Daily Mail* he witnessed Mussolini's invasion of Abyssinia in 1935 and returned there in 1936 to complete his account *Waugh in Abyssinia* (1936). These visits gave him material for a second novel with an Abyssinian setting, *Scoop* (1938). Meantime a visit to South America in 1932–3 resulted in another travel book *Ninety-Two Days* (1934).

When war broke out in 1939 Waugh was thoroughly established in the forefront of the younger novelists, with some entertaining travel books to his credit as well. Moreover he had written a biography of Edmund Campion (1935) which had won him the Hawthornden prize. All his profits from this he made over to Campion Hall, Oxford. He had a country house at Stinchcombe in Gloucestershire near the Severn, and a young wife and the beginning of what was to be a family of three sons and three daughters. But being of military age and aware of the dangers of a civilian job to his inventive talent, he immediately began seeking a commission. It was with great difficulty that he secured one in the Royal Marines; he was seconded for service in the Commandos in November 1940, officially transferring to the Royal Horse Guards in 1942. In 1941 he went to the Middle East and served as personal assistant to (Sir) Robert Laycock throughout the battle for Crete. By the end of the year he was back in England and he did not go overseas again until 1944. He was always a problem to his superiors who found his scepticism disruptive and he was never popular with the men under his command. These defects outweighed his marked physical courage and in March 1943 Laycock told him that he was 'so unpopular as to be unemployable'. It was Laycock, nevertheless, who had proposed him for membership of White's where Waugh had many friends.

In the early months of 1944 he was on leave and writing the novel which was to be very much the most successful of all his books in the United States, *Brideshead Revisited* (1945). Before that major undertaking, he had written, with a fluency and speed quite exceptional with him, *Put Out More Flags* (1942), in which in his best comic vein he developed the character of Basil Seal, whom his readers knew well from *Black Mischief*, who was now shown taking full advantage of all the opportunities which the early stages of the war provided for the advancement of his own fortunes. *Brideshead* was altogether more serious, shot through with a religious theme. It divided the critics, many of whom attributed its exceptional appeal to the American public to its detailed depiction of English aristocratic life.

But Waugh's military career was not yet ended. The prime minister's son, Randolph Churchill, was with Brigadier (Sir) Fitzroy Maclean's mission to Tito's Communist partisans in Yugoslavia, and he asked for Waugh for the sake of his company. In July 1944 Waugh joined the mission. Flying from Bari to Topusko the plane in which Churchill and Waugh were travelling caught fire on landing and as a result of their injuries it was not until September that they finally reached partisan headquarters. At close quarters, and with little to occupy him for most of the time, there was plenty of acrimony, sharpened by Waugh's dislike of the whole idea of co-operating to ensure that post-war Yugoslavia would be ruled by the Communists, thus placing the Catholic Croats and Slovenes under intolerant atheist masters. He took considerable risks of being court-martialled by reporting to the Vatican, and by the efforts he made to draw attention to what was happening, reporting on the religious situation to the Foreign Office and instigating questions in Parliament.

After the war ended, Waugh's talent lay fallow, although a short visit to Spain in 1946 with Douglas Woodruff resulted in a light-hearted satire, *Scott-King's Modern Europe* (1947), whose humour was applicable to many other government-sponsored commemorations beside that which was the purpose of this Spanish visit, the fourth centenary of the birth of the Dominican Francisco de Vittoria, who, his fellow countrymen maintained, was the real founder of international law and deserved the credit which the Protestant world had generally accorded to Grotius a generation later.

In 1947 Waugh visited Hollywood to discuss the proposed film of *Brideshead Revisited*. No film was ever made because he refused to alter the story as the producers wished, largely that they might satisfy the standards set by the very powerful Catholic Legion of Decency. But the visit was not barren. With time on his hands he became fascinated with Californian burial practices, and the result was *The Loved One* (1948) which, for all its macabre setting, was a highly successful light novel based on Forest Lawn. He made several further visits to America, went to Goa in 1952 for the four-hundredth anniversary of the death of St. Francis Xavier, to Ceylon in 1954, and to Jamaica in 1955.

Meantime in 1950 appeared what was in some ways Waugh's most ambitious work, his only venture into historical fiction, a novel about Saint Helena, the mother of Constantine the Great. He took great pains with this, and the book contains some of his best writing. He used to maintain that it should be read three times because more would be found in it each time.

After a long gestation Waugh's varied war-time experiences came out as a trilogy: in 1952 the first volume, *Men at Arms*, based on his experiences as a Royal Marine, and awarded the James Tait Black memorial prize; in 1955 the second, *Officers and Gentlemen*, drawn from his period with the Commandos and at the Allied reverse in Crete. Then, in 1961 came the final volume, *Unconditional Surrender*, with his experiences in Yugoslavia, the title reflecting the bitter irony that the adventure on which his hero, Guy Crouchback, had set out as on a crusade after kneeling at a crusader's tomb, had ended supporting atheistic Communism. It was only when the trilogy was issued in one volume under the general title of *Sword of Honour* (1962) that its structural unity and irony stood out in their full strength.

The fifties also saw a slight novel called *Love Among the Ruins* (1953); and in 1957 *The Ordeal of Gilbert Pinfold*, remarkable for the self-portrait of the author with which it begins, and for being based on severe hallucinations which had come upon him as a result of taking remedies for insomnia in too large quantities.

Waugh had found the restrictions of postwar Britain irksome and at one time had seriously contemplated moving to Ireland. It was characteristic of him that at a time when most people, if they moved, chose smaller houses, when he finally made his choice in 1956 it was to a house considerably larger and grander than Piers Court. This was Combe Florey House, six miles from Taunton, on high ground, with an imposing gate-house, and large rooms which he decorated in a flamboyant, Victorian manner. He had acquired a large collection of Victorian narrative paintings which could be bought, in the thirties and forties, for a few pounds, and subsequently greatly increased in value. With the proceeds of two lawsuits he arranged with the manufacturers at Wilton for a replica of one of the more startling prizewinning carpets of the Great Exhibition of 1851. Combe Florey was to be his home for the rest of his life, and was a source of great satisfaction to him. He travelled less abroad, but made one further visit with his daughter Margaret in 1961–2 to South America. When he published all that he wished to preserve of his travel books of the thirties it was under the general title *When the Going was Good* (1946).

Before he was sixty Waugh began to feel that he was growing old, and he rather enjoyed exaggerating the degree of deafness which was afflicting him, using his hearing-aid, generally a large, old-fashioned trumpet, in an aggressive manner, putting it down ostentatiously before an unwelcome speaker.

In 1957 Waugh's friend Monsignor Ronald Knox died after a long illness in which Waugh had shown great solicitude. He was Knox's executor and biographer and he immediately set about filling both offices with great thoroughness, even going out to consult Lady Acton in Rhodesia. The biography of Knox appeared in 1959 and was followed by *A Tourist in Africa* (1960), the result of a second visit to Rhodesia, and finally by the first volume of his autobiography. He never succeeded in completing the second volume. His writing life may be said to have ended before he was sixty, although he lived to be sixty-two. His last years were saddened by the course taken by the Second Vatican Council whose changes in the liturgy he hated. He dreaded the prospect of old age with diminishing faculties in an increasingly uncongenial world, but he was spared the ordeal. He died very suddenly on Easter Sunday 10 April 1966, after hearing Mass in the old rite. He was buried in the churchyard adjoining his home at Combe Florey where he had died.

Evelyn Waugh was of less than average height. As a very young man his friend (Sir) Harold Acton described him as faun-like with his reddish hair and light, quick movements; but in middle life he became inclined to portliness, with a reddish face and eyes which seemed to become more protuberant as he glared at the world. His exceptional intelligence brought with it the penalty that he was very easily bored, seeing to the end of situations and conversations before they began, and time hung heavily on his hands. Although he disciplined himself effectively, retiring to Chagford to write his novels, he had few hobbies beyond the collection of Victoriana, did not care for music, and took little interest in public events. But he was continually improvising variants in everyday life, himself writing reports to his children's schools at the end of the holidays as a riposte to the school report, inscribing on his gates 'No admittance on business', and engaging in practical jokes, or behaving quite unpredictably and often very rudely, in an attempt to make everyday life more interesting and amusing. This caused him to be very much discussed by his contemporaries, and gave him some slight relief from his habitual ennui and tendency towards self-hatred. He also did many secret acts of charity and generosity, and when reproached for uncharitableness always replied that without his religion he knew he would be so very much more unpleasant. He told Christopher Sykes that he looked with horror upon Dylan Thomas who in looks, dress, and conversation was in many ways a parody of Waugh: 'He's exactly what I would have been if I had not become a Catholic.' He carried on a large correspondence without employing a secretary, writing everything by hand, and he was as much addicted as Gladstone to the use of postcards which encouraged the economy of language in which he excelled. This was one of the few practical economies in his style of living.

A portrait of Waugh as a young man by Henry Lamb became the possession of Lady Pansy Lamb. A portrait bust by Paravicini is in the possession of the family. Waugh's manuscripts and letters were acquired by the university of Texas where a room has been set apart for them.

[Evelyn Waugh, *A Little Learning*, 1964, *Diaries*, ed. Michael Davie, 1976, and *Letters*, ed. Mark Amory, 1980; Alec Waugh, *My Brother Evelyn and Other Profiles*, 1967; Frances Donaldson, *Portrait of a Country Neighbour*, 1967; *Evelyn Waugh and his World*, ed. D. Pryce-Jones, 1973; Christopher Sykes, *Evelyn Waugh*, 1975; personal knowledge.]

DOUGLAS WOODRUFF

published 1981

Writer and painter, was born in Shanghai 29 March 1915, the youngest of the four sons (there were no daughters) of Arthur Joseph Welch, a wealthy English rubber merchant, and his American wife, Rosalind Bassett. After spending an itinerant early childhood he was educated first at an eccentric preparatory school intended for the sons of Christian Scientists, St Michael's in Uckfield, Sussex, and later at Repton, from where, at the age of sixteen, he ran away. When he was seventeen he returned to China for several months.

His original ambition was to be a painter, and in 1933 he enrolled at Goldsmith's College School of Art. Welch's spell as an art student came to an abrupt end, however, in 1935, at the age of twenty, when he was knocked off his bicycle by a motorist. He sustained appalling injuries, including a fracture of the spine. Long periods of enforced solitude as a semi-invalid threw him back on the resources of his own imagination, and after reading *Hindoo Holiday*, by J. R. Ackerley, he resolved to write a semi-autobiographical novel, based on Repton and China. The result, *Maiden Voyage* (1943), was acclaimed by (Dame) Edith Sitwell, who contributed a foreword in which she wrote: 'This is a very moving and remarkable first book and the author appears to be that rare being, a born writer.' Welch's second novel, *In Youth is Pleasure*, recalling a summer holiday at the age of fifteen, was published two years later, and was dedicated to the memory of his mother, who had died when he was eleven. A number of Welch's short stories, all in effect autobiographical, were published during his lifetime, by Cyril Connolly in *Horizon*, John Lehmann in Penguin *New Writing*, and Peter Quennell in the *Cornhill Magazine*. Within the space of only eight years, although desperately ill and while painting and illustrating as well, he completed some sixty short stories, all later published posthumously, three novels, and a quarter of a million words of journals.

Because he was so isolated physically, and knew only a handful of fellow artists—his friends did include John Minton, with whom he collaborated over the line drawings for *Vogue's Contemporary Cooking*, by Doris Lytton Toye, Keith Vaughan, and Graham Sutherland, a near neighbour in Kent—Welch never attached himself formally to any school of painting, yet he became an almost unconscious and very prolific exponent of the neo-Romantic movement. He provided quixotic endpapers for his own first editions, which later became collectors' items, and his paintings, in oils, water-colours, and pencil, crayon, and gouache, were exhibited in the

1940s at the Leicester Galleries. After his death many were given away or sold for a few pounds, and he was largely ignored as a painter until in 1987 six examples of his work were loaned to an exhibition entitled 'A Paradise Lost' at the Barbican Art Gallery, devoted to the neo-Romantic movement. There are self-portraits in the National Portrait Gallery in London and at the University of Texas in Austin.

As a writer, the quality, quantity, and character of Welch's output was inevitably circumscribed by his relative immobility and the restrictions this placed on the acquisition of new material and experience. But he was in any event fascinated by his childhood and adolescence, and by the time he died this juvenile field had been fruitfully tilled and probably exhausted. It is his interest in the minutiae of life and his shrewd and perceptive descriptions of people, places, and events that have left the most indelible impression on his admirers. His journals in particular constitute a moving memorial to a young man of integrity and moral courage, whose determination not to succumb to pain and humiliation was at times heroic. It took him four years to write his third, and posthumously published, novel, *A Voice Through a Cloud* (1950), an account of the accident itself and his struggle to convalesce. The manuscript was found beside his bed, complete except for about half a dozen pages, when he died, 30 December 1948, at Middle Orchard, Crouch, Kent. He was unmarried.

[Michael De-la-Noy, *Denton Welch: the Making of a Writer*, 1984.]

MICHAEL DE-LA-NOY

published 1993

WELLS Herbert George

(1866–1946)

Author, was born at 47 High Street, Bromley, Kent, 21 September 1866. His father, Joseph Wells, was the son of a Kentish gardener and his mother, Sarah, the daughter of George Neal, a Sussex innkeeper. She had been a lady's maid and was nearly forty-four when Herbert was born to her as her fourth child and third son; her daughter had already died. Joseph Wells had begun as a gardener but became a cricketer who, playing for Kent on 26 June 1862, bowled four Sussex batsmen in successive balls. His seasonal earnings as a cricket professional supplemented the slender takings of the shop in Bromley where he tried to sell china-ware, lamp-wicks, paraffin, and cricket accessories. He was an unsuccessful tradesman and the Wells household was continually overhung by the threat of insolvency.

The family circumstances into which Herbert George ('Bertie' in his family circle) was born and grew up were penurious to the verge of squalor. In that 'gaunt and impossible home' the prim little lady's maid became an incompetent and discouraged drudge whose anxieties about present poverty and future salvation were not assuaged by the likeable but easy-going traits of her husband.

Wells's origins and upbringing, like his adolescent vicissitudes and frustrations, profoundly influenced not only his novels but his social attitudes and explained much which seemed contradictory in his public character: the Socialist-individualist; the republican who repudiated titles but inherited from his mother a deference towards those who held them; the atheist who invoked God in *Mr. Britling Sees It Through*; the supranationalist who remained to the end so obviously English and cockney English at that; the pansophist with a snook-cocking disrespect for pedagogy; the philosopher who despaired of the wisdom of *Homo sapiens*, but gave a lifetime to the pursuit of a more perfect world; the hedonist, reacting against drudgery; the sensualist, revolting against piety.

By the standards of his later knowledge Wells was virtually self-taught. Mr. Morley's Commercial Academy, which he first attended, was a school, in a single room built over a scullery, for tradesmen's sons themselves destined for trade. To that end, it specialized in long-addition sums, book-keeping, and copper-plate flourishes which Wells retained to the last in his signature. Part boarding-, part day-school, its pupils were prepared for the examinations of the College of Preceptors from which body Wells at the age of thirteen was granted a certificate bracketing him, with another boy, first 'in all England' in book-keeping.

Wells, however, by an accident had been self-liberated from these narrow frontiers. He had been dropped at the age of seven by the son of the landlord of the Bell Inn and his leg was broken. The contrite landlady kept the victim supplied not only with delicacies unknown in his indigent home but also with books supplementing those which his father borrowed from the Literary Institute. He discovered books of travel and Wood's *Natural History* and 'that quite a number of things had happened and quite a number of interesting things existed outside the world of English affairs'.

When Wells was eleven his father broke his leg and the resultant limp put an end to his career as cricket coach. The chronic insolvency of the china-shop now became acute and after three years' struggle to make ends meet the home was broken up. Mrs. Wells returned as housekeeper to Miss Featherstonhaugh at Uppark, Sussex, where she had been lady's maid. The two elder brothers, Frank and Fred, were already journey-men drapers and Bertie became probationary apprentice with Rodgers and Denyer at Windsor. His book-keeping certificate did not compensate for his inattention and both he and his employers agreed that he was unfitted to be a draper. A courtesy 'uncle', headmaster of a national school at Wookey, Somerset, offered the fourteen-year-old the role of student teacher. He had to teach, with his fists, boys as big as himself, but he learned scepticism, an irreverence for religion, and something of sex before the authorities discovered that the headmaster had obtained his post by false pretences.

After an interlude at Uppark in which he made the most of a library which introduced him, then or later, to Voltaire, Tom Paine, and Plato, he went to a pharmaceutical chemist in Midhurst to attempt a new career. He found, however, that the cost of qualifying was well beyond the family means, and he knew no Latin. For Latin lessons he went to the headmaster of the local grammar school, Horace Byatt, for whom he formed a liking which was mutual.

Apprenticeship to pharmacy, however, still proving too expensive, Wells had to make a fourth start in life at the age of fifteen. Again it was drapery, this time at Hyde's Emporium, Southsea. For two years he rebelliously rolled blankets, huckaback, Turkey twill, and lace-curtains, ran errands, and kept the pin-bowls replenished. Yet 'living-in' included a library of several hundred books and even in the thirteen-hour working day there were opportunities—behind a pile of cotton goods—to study Latin.

With more than two years of his indentures to go he appealed des-perately to Byatt and received the offer of a student assistantship starting at £20 a year. His mother, who had already paid £40 of his £50 apprenticeship premium, refused to release him. Waylaying her as she was returning to Uppark with the procession of servants from church he persuaded his mother under threat of suicide to forfeit his indentures.

Midhurst (1883–4) changed the course of Wells's life. Under Byatt's eye he did some classroom teaching but he was also an earnest pupil. Since it was an endowed school, he had to be confirmed in order to retain his job. Having no faith he fiercely resented the hypocrisy thrust upon him. Byatt was entitled, under the science scheme of the Education Department, to organize evening classes and qualify for a grant. Wells was accordingly enrolled as a night student in the bogus science class designed to earn the headmaster £4 if his pupil gained an advanced first class in the examin-ations. To this end Wells crammed himself with elementary science, for the first time, and passed the examination with such success that he was offered a free studentship, with a maintenance grant of £1 a week, at the Normal School (later Royal College) of Science, South Kensington.

He was enrolled under T. H. Huxley who remained, for him, the greatest of all teachers. In his first year's study of biology, Wells distinguished himself, but continuing with physics and geology under other teachers he became lax and failed his third year examinations. He had hoped to become a research scientist: another false start due, in this instance, to truancy into literature and politics. He had spent more of his time in the library than in the laboratory and his evenings had been devoted to the pursuit of his new-found Socialism at meetings addressed by William Morris, Graham Wallas, and G. B. Shaw.

Wells next taught at Holt Academy, Wrexham, where he permanently damaged a kidney in a game of football and developed the symptoms of tuberculosis with haemorrhages which were to recur. This meant retirement to Uppark and fresh opportunity for reading. In 1889 he obtained a more congenial teaching post at Henley House School, Kilburn, kept by the father of A. A. Milne and where the future Lord Northcliffe had been a pupil. In 1890 he took his B.Sc. with a first class in zoology and a second in geology. A year later, as a full-time tutor on fees of £4 a week, at the University Tutorial College, he married his cousin Isabel Mary Wells in whose home he had lodged in London. He was already trying his hand at journalism on scientific subjects but his reading of (Sir) James Barrie's *When A Man's Single*, during a breakdown in health in 1893, encouraged him to attempt a more popular approach which was well received by editors.

In 1893 he left his wife for Amy Catherine Robbins (died 1927), one of his students at the Tutorial College whom he married when his divorce was completed in 1895. They had two sons, George Philip (who was to collaborate with his father and (Sir) Julian Huxley in producing *The Science of Life*) and Frank Richard.

Wells's writing period now began in earnest. He found a ready market for his short stories (such as *The Stolen Bacillus*, 1895) and proved himself a master of the technique. *The Time Machine* which in the hindsight of later years he regarded as one of his 'social fables' was received by the public in 1895 as a diverting extravaganza. It was the beginning of that long series of fantastic and imaginative romances which ranged from *The Invisible Man* (1897) to *The Shape of Things to Come* (1933): a series for which the adjective 'Wellsian' was coined (to become his private bugbear) and which gained him the reputation of prophet, a role he was willing to assume in such publications as *Anticipations* (1901). His foresight of the war in the air, of tanks, of the atomic bomb and 'the war of 1940' were to be remembered when his misses (like his discarding of the idea of a submarine) were forgotten. His ingenious knack was to seize upon some emerging scientific fact, such as the significance of radium, and fictionally to predict results like the artificial splitting of the atom: in that instance, in *The World Set Free* (1914), with a margin of error of a year. Although he might have to ignore gravity by inventing a substance like 'cavorite', there was usually a basis of scientific fact even in his most 'Wellsian' romances.

Alternating with such scientific excursions and, later, with his social tracts, were his 'real' novels beginning with *The Wheels of Chance* (1896), followed by *Love and Mr. Lewisham* (1900), *Kipps* (1905), *Tono-Bungay* (1909), *Ann Veronica* (1909), *The History of Mr. Polly* (1910), and continuing for the next thirty years. In popular esteem *Kipps, Tono-Bungay*, and *Mr. Polly* were the most successful and enduring of this genre of Wells's novels. They were rich in characterization and borrowed heavily from Wells's impressionable years: the running-down shop at Bromley, the drapers, the chemist's shop at Midhurst, or Uppark. Wells himself always had an attachment to *Mr. Lewisham* with the almost autobiographical account of Midhurst Grammar School, South Kensington college life, and Wells's drab little romance and first marriage. Nor did he understand the lack of popular appreciation of *The Bulpington of Blup* (1932) which, he thought, equalled Kipps in characterization.

Ann Veronica was notorious in its day and led to scandalized reviews and pulpit denunciations of its 'youthful heroine' who 'was allowed a frankness of desire and sexual enterprise, hitherto unknown in English popular fiction'. Wells was taken aback by the outburst because he was recording his times—and his experience. He pursued the topic of freer love, defiantly, in *The New Machiavelli* (1911) and *Marriage* (1912). He had already become the 'satyr-cupid' of Socialism by his Fabian address 'Socialism and the Middle Classes' (1906) in which he had argued the impermanence of the institution of marriage and advocated the endowment of motherhood as a service to the State. This was made a political issue in Manchester in 1906 when W. Joynson-Hicks (later Viscount Brentford) alleged that Socialists (e.g. Wells) advocated that wives should be held in common, a suggestion which Wells repudiated. Nevertheless, his frank behaviour offended many who regarded themselves as advanced thinkers, socially and politically, of whom Wells might otherwise have been the leader.

By now he had developed a 'drill' in his writing. He was producing argument-by-narrative books and following them up by fiction romanticizing his social theses. He called his novels 'social fables' and would point out that *Ann Veronica* was merely a version of some of his arguments in *A Modern Utopia* (1905). Sometimes the two genres became superimposed. His characters were liable to talk too much and his novels to become shapeless. By 1910 he had acquired a 'mission'. He was preoccupied with the future of mankind and with ideas of his 'New Republic' and 'The World State' and the political philosophy he was later to call 'The

Open Conspiracy'. He moved restlessly from one movement to another seeking the means of realizing his ideal. Despite his repeated and savage disappointments he maintained his optimistic belief in the perfectibility of the human race through scientific progress. He was searching for an instrument, an *élite* of leadership—the Fabian Society, the Samurai of *A Modern Utopia*; captains of industry in *The World of William Clissold* (3 vols., 1926); or the aviators in *The Shape of Things to Come*—which would rescue people from their own stupidities. And each time it was possible to note 'the same phases in the recurrent cycle of his questing mind, hope, disillusionment, bitter enmity'.

The outbreak of war in 1914 threw him into confusion. He found himself as emotionally involved as most people and professionally involved during an interlude at Crewe House preparing propaganda for Germany. It was to him *The War That Will End War* (1914), the prelude to his World State, and it entangled him in other ways. *Mr. Britling Sees It Through* (1916) was a powerful but conventional novel in which Wells returned to God and, when challenged by the rationalists, he went farther in *God The Invisible King* (1917). He was, subsequently, to recant his theism as he was to recant his vituperative attacks on those who had not wholeheartedly endorsed 'his' war. He took up the idea of the League of Nations but was presently assailing it as an institution which was thwarting him in his pursuit of the World State.

After the war he began his assault on education: to its failures he ascribed much of the misery of mankind. He entered upon his encyclopaedic phase with *The Outline of History* (1920), followed by *The Science of Life* (1931), and *The Work, Wealth and Happiness of Mankind* (1932). Despite many defects into which his desire for unification led him, these works were substantial and influential achievements on which Wells's reputation might have rested had he never written his scientific romances or his novels. 'If he had done nothing else, this great trilogy alone would have justified his title to be the greatest public teacher of our time.' (Sir Arthur (subsequently Lord) Salter, *Personality in Politics*, 1947). Nor did Wells expect them to achieve the world-wide success—and royalties—which they produced. They were his public-spirited attempt to transform history into 'human ecology' and to derive education for world citizenship from the common origins, problems, and purposes of mankind: an argument he elaborated in *World Brain* (1938) in which he maintained, on the eve of war, that civilization was a 'race between education and catastrophe'.

In politics, as in his social relationships, Wells was impatient, irascible, and unpredictable. He flounced in and out of party Socialism. He was the *enfant terrible* of the early Fabians who were nevertheless stimulated, if exasperated, by his clash with Shaw and the Webbs. Realizing that the leadership would not come his way, he resigned in 1908. He twice fought London University as Labour parliamentary candidate (1922, 1923) and he voted Labour in the last year of his life, but in the intervals he conducted violent guerrilla campaigns. He would subscribe to principles but was impatient both of personalities and of the slowness of the democratic processes. As a politician he had short use for details or programmes: his was the broad sweep. 'I can say bright things', he wrote, 'but I cannot manage stupid people.' With the disadvantage of a small piping voice which made him sound querulous he was a poor public speaker and had neither the tact nor patience to handle a committee. His recognition of his own inadequacy in political organization led him into his abortive search for chosen instruments which he discarded one after another, before they could fulfil his purpose. He was once described as a world optimist but a local pessimist. Politically he was naïve, as his two visits to Russia revealed. His interviews with Lenin and Stalin were a tribute to his world-wide acceptance as a major thinker, but his handling of them did not add to his reputation. The interviews were an anticlimax, as Shaw pointed out in a controversy which followed Wells's account of the second visit.

In the same year, 1934, there appeared his *Experiment in Autobiography* in two absorbing volumes written as if he were 'an observer rather than a participant' and with a self-critical freedom from vanity which did not conceal the fact that the writer was not entirely dissatisfied with H. G. Wells. But the book represented, especially in the first volume, a re-markable contribution to social history.

Towards the end of his life he turned to films as a medium and in 1936 wrote the script of *The Man Who Could Work Miracles* and the epic *Things To Come*. He also tried the radio in the hope that the microphone would compensate for the oratorical weakness of his voice, but he remained rather a broadcasting 'event' than a personality. His published works grew pessimistic and repetitive. He clamoured, urgently, for the world to listen, but his preoccupation with wide issues seemed too remote from the day-to-day problems of humanity to shape the action for which he pressed. His *The Fate of Homo Sapiens* (1939) was recriminatory, but he repented his despair and in 1940 called for a 'great debate' in *The New World Order, The Rights of Man*, and *The Commonsense of War and Peace*. The debate was launched on a world scale but was overtaken by the *Blitzkrieg*. A committee under Lord Sankey drafted the British version of a proposed declaration of human rights which to the last months of his life Wells was trying to universalize in correspondence with philosophers throughout the world. The episode of the human rights debate was characteristic of the con-tradictory personality of Wells. He despaired of individual reason but in-sisted on individual liberty. He defended free speech but tried, unsuccessfully, to impose the letter of his version of 'rights' on his distinguished colleagues. What seemed like embittered truculence would suddenly melt into chuckling acquiescence. His four-years' efforts to universalize it arose from the shock to his English reasoning of the pallid reception which the draft received in the Far East, due, as he discovered, to the inflexion of the rights being in the idiom of Western parliamentary democracy. So he turned from oriental translators to the Eastern philosophers. He did not live to see most of the declaration embodied in the United Nations' Convention of Human Rights but he would probably have resented the result as falling short of his own prescriptions.

Wells, with his injured kidney, his incipient tuberculosis, and, later, his diabetes, lived to be almost eighty, after a lifetime of intense productivity. His was an emotionally and intellectually turbulent life, at the end of which he felt the frustrations more than he realized the achievements. He underestimated his influence on the thinking of three decades because he could not recognize the mutations from the seeds which he had scattered and which had sprouted all over the world. And he was frustrated by never recognizing the reapers he sought so impatiently. It was his genius to stimulate imagination and to set people thinking about the possibilities of the world in which they lived. His own outlook was dictated by his materialistic interpretation of life, and thwarted by the inadequacies of the human material from which he wanted to shape his higher species. Protesting his belief in the common man, he found the clay too common for his purposes. He thought instead of mankind in terms abstracted from his own experience; yet even this depersonalized version proved reluctant to conform to his requirements. He came nearest to flesh-and-blood men in his earlier novels such as *Kipps* when he wrote of what he knew. His remarkable talent as a novelist was increasingly subordinated to his theories of scientific progress and education. Of Wells as a writer, it has been suggested, the tragedy was that 'having the power to become a great comic genius, fit for the company of Dickens, he declined the potentiality, preferring rather to become a minor prophet'. That may be an underestimate of his influence on his times and on events but it was a risk he took deliberately.

Wells's reputation for impatience, querulousness, petulance, and 'spoiled-childishness' set his public character. Maybe he even capitalized it, by calculated aggressiveness. Its origins were in his health, particularly in his diabetes, and those who knew him well knew his capacity (and craving) for friendship. He was always surprised and hurt when people took umbrage, or felt they had offended him, because of a fit of temper which he had quickly forgotten. He was indiscriminate in his kindnesses-by-stealth, encouraging do-gooders or sponsoring young authors or supporting movements which could only be an embarrassment to him. In his permanent relationships, with those who ignored his moods or his impishness, he inspired real affection. If he could on occasion be spiteful, he also suffered from spite.

He was appalled by the war of 1939–45 which he had himself predicted and through which he lived at 13 Hanover Terrace, Regent's Park, defying the high explosives and putting out incendiary bombs with the help of two women servants. There were personal frustrations too. He had received an honorary D.Lit. from London University (1936) and was an honorary fellow of the Imperial College of Science and Technology, but he desperately wanted to be a fellow of the Royal Society, somehow to redress that failure at South Kensington and to escape the gibe of 'Wellsian' and 'pseudo-scientist'. At seventy-eight he submitted a doctoral thesis on *The Quality of Illusion in the Continuity of Individual Life in the Higher Metazoa with particular reference to the Species Homo Sapiens* to the university of London and became D.Sc. He believed, wrongly, that this would prevail upon the Royal Society to give him the one honour which he really wanted. The books of his last years were postscripts to his once-vigorous thinking: the pathetic *Mind at the End of its Tether* (1945) and the more benign *The Happy Turning* (1945). He produced over a hundred books, and persisted in writing almost to the end which came in his sleep at his home in London 13 August 1946.

In appearance Wells was unimpressive: short, compact, and inclined to plumpness. His hands and feet were small, his arms short and ill-placed. His hair and moustache were light brown, skimpy and untidy, his grey eyes meditative or with an impish twinkle, his brow broad. He moved and spoke rapidly and, save on the platform, was a fascinating talker, especially in a small circle: at the corner table in the Reform Club or at the Savile; or with guests at his villa at Malagnou near Grasse on the Riviera where he wrote many of his books; and particularly with the young for whom he had a warm appeal and a patience which belied his public *persona*. Even so, like his own William Clissold, he could maintain that 'I have never given myself to anyone', and at the end he fulfilled the claim in his autobiography: 'I shall die, as I have lived, the responsible centre of my world.' He knew his limitations but resented being reminded of them. Yet he himself acknowledged in 1938, in one of his periodic moods of disgruntlement, that his epitaph would be: 'He was clever but he was not clever enough.'

Wells's literary remains were purchased by the university of Illinois. A sketch of Wells by Feliks Topolski is in the possession of Baroness Budberg. The National Portrait Gallery has a small plasticine medallion by Theodore Spicer-Simson. Of several drawings by (Sir) William Rothenstein one is reproduced in *Twenty-Four Portraits* (1920). A lithograph by Rothenstein is in the Bradford City Art Gallery.

[*The Times*, 14 August 1946; *Times Literary Supplement*, 19 July 1947 and 23 February 1951; J. D. Beresford, *H. G. Wells*, 1915; E. R. Pease, *History of the Fabian Society*, 1916; Ivor Brown, *H. G. Wells*, 1923; *The Book of Catherine Wells*, 1928; Geoffrey West, *H. G. Wells*, 1930; H. G. Wells, *Experiment in Autobiography*, 2 vols., 1934, and 'My Obituary' in the *Coronet Magazine*, 1937; G. B. Shaw, 'Wells' in the *New Statesman and Nation*, 17 August 1946; Beatrice Webb, *Our Partnership*, 1948; Vincent Brome, *H. G. Wells*, 1951; Wilson Harris, *Life So Far*, 1954.]

RITCHIE CALDER

published 1959

WEST **Dame Rebecca**

(1892–1983)

Author, reporter, and literary critic, was born Cicily Isabel in Paddington, London, 21 December 1892, the youngest of three daughters (there were no sons) of Charles Fairfield and his wife, Isabella Campbell Mackenzie. Her father, of Irish parentage, was a largely unsuccessful journalistic and entrepreneurial soldier of fortune, who abandoned his family in 1901 and died in poverty. Her mother, of Scottish stock, was a gifted amateur pianist, who earned her living before her marriage as a governess in a wealthy family, from whom she received an unsolicited and much needed allowance after the marriage broke up.

The fatherless family removed to the mother's native Edinburgh, where Cicily went to George Watson's Ladies' College; her future as a writer was signalled early, when, at the age of fourteen, she won the school's junior essay prize, and in the same year broke into print for the first time with a letter to the *Scotsman* on women's rights. (She was already, with her two sisters, an ardent feminist and socialist.)

Intent first, however, on a stage career, she trained for a year at the Academy of Dramatic Art in London, while beginning to write regularly for a new magazine which might have been created for her, the *Freewoman*. In 1912 she needed a pseudonym for her contributions; she chose the name of one of Henrik Ibsen's proud, rebellious, and independent heroines, and for the rest of her long life, to all the world except her close family, she was Rebecca West.

She made a literary reputation swiftly; her first book, a study of Henry James, appeared in 1916. But three years earlier she had sustained a wound that was never to heal, that indeed would bleed afresh after her death; she met H. G. Wells, then at the height of his fame as a writer, they became lovers, and she bore his unintentionally conceived child, a son, known as Anthony West.

The relationship with Wells was in any case both stormy and doomed, and inevitably petered out. She had a number of further liaisons both before and after her rather surprising marriage in 1930 to Henry Maxwell Andrews (died 1968), son of Lewis Henry John Andrews, of Wallace Bros., an East India merchant company; he was something of a scholar, and a not notably successful banker, but he clearly provided for her an ordered stability that she might never have found for herself. But nothing ever approached either the intensity or the influence of her love for Wells. She strove to absorb the experience and thus exorcize it, but the task was made more difficult by the deep antipathy that her son developed for her; he felt, not altogether without reason, that she had neglected him. Until she died they were constantly at loggerheads, sometimes legal ones, and after her death he took his revenge by publishing accounts of her, Wells, and himself which make wretched reading, whatever view is taken of the rights and wrongs of the matter.

There remains her literary achievement, much of which is certain to endure. None of her novels is wholly successful as a work of art, though perhaps *The Fountain Overflows*, published in 1957, comes nearest. It was intended to be the first volume of a trilogy in the form of a family saga; it is clearly based on her own youth, has a spontaneity that rings more true than in any of her other fiction, and is deservedly the most popular of her novels.

Her reportage is of an altogether different quality; at its best it has few equals in all journalism. *The Meaning of Treason* (1949) and *A Train of Powder* (1955) are the fruits of her attendance at such historic assizes as the Nuremberg tribunal and the post-war British treason trials, together with other notable episodes of our troubled world, particularly a gruesome murder. Her account of the case was published as 'Mr Setty and Mr Hume' in *A Train of Powder*. In these writings her omnivorous observation, brilliant sense of colour, and ruthless analysis combine to make a series of unforgettable pictures. But her undoubted masterpiece is *Black Lamb and Grey Falcon*.

It is drawn from a series of visits (telescoped into one for the purpose of the book) to Yugoslavia, or more precisely Serbia, that she made with her husband in the 1930s. She was overwhelmed by the country and its people, and this immense work (a quarter of a million words) is a tribute to both, bursting with their history, architecture, poetry, music, geography, literature, courage, flora, customs, religion, food, loves, hates, philosophy, rulers, and fate; the book was published in New York in 1941, just as Yugoslavia was experiencing the full weight of the Nazi assault.

The post-war tragedy of Yugoslavia's conquest by communism served to cement a hatred of that ideology which she had first felt at the Hitler-Stalin pact of 1939. Thereafter she was as implacable a foe of Soviet totalitarianism as of the Nazi one; her bitterness was accentuated by her knowledge that many of her friends in Yugoslavia who had survived the Nazis had fallen victim to Marshal Tito. But she never became fanatical or obsessed; her wisdom and balance enabled her to control her anger, the better to aim her deadliest darts at all those forces, external and internal alike, which threaten the free society.

Rebecca West was a woman of formidable, even daunting, personality, but with a warmth and understanding that made her company an enriching experience. She did not suffer fools gladly, or indeed at all; her wit could be savage, and the older she grew the less need she felt to restrain it. (Talking one day of a prominent man of undoubted gifts but *outré* beliefs, who affected a decadent air, she delivered a forceful judgement: 'He looks', she said, 'like a dead pimp.')

Her circle of friends was wide and varied; they gladly endured her quirks and occasional irascibility, and for all her temper she was not naturally quarrelsome, nor did she hug her wrath or bear grudges. Her strength began to ebb at the beginning of the 1980s; her last published article appeared in September 1982, but she fought death as tenaciously as she had battled with the demons all her life. She died 15 March 1983 in London. She was buried, according to her own instructions, in Brookwood cemetery, in Surrey.

She was appointed CBE in 1949 and DBE in 1959. She was made a chevalier of the Legion of Honour in 1957. P. Wyndham Lewis drew a portrait of her when she was forty, which now hangs in the National Portrait Gallery, London.

[Rebecca West, *Family Memories* (ed. Faith Evans), 1987; Victoria Glendinning, *Rebecca West*, 1987; *The Times*, 16 March 1983; personal knowledge.]

BERNARD LEVIN

published 1990

(1906–1964)

Novelist, was born 29 May 1906 in Bombay, the only child of Garrick Hanbury White, a district superintendent of police in the Indian Police Service, and his wife Constance Edith Southcote Aston, the daughter of a judge on the Indian circuit. His parents later divorced, and at the age of five White was sent to England to be brought up by his maternal grandparents in St Leonards, Hastings. In 1920 he went to Cheltenham College and in 1925 to Queen's College, Cambridge, to read English. He obtained a second class (division II) in part i of the English tripos (1927) and a first class in part ii (1929).

After contracting tuberculosis he spent a year in Italy, where he began to write a satirical novel, later published as *They Winter Abroad* (1932), under the pseudonym of James Aston. He returned to Cambridge and completed his degree course in 1929. In the same year he published *Loved Helen, and Other Poems*. For two years he taught at a preparatory school in Reigate, before being appointed head of the English department at Stowe by the school's headmaster, J. F. Roxburgh. White excelled in this role and for the rest of his life retained many of the attributes of the old-fashioned schoolmaster. He was a bachelor with (largely) homosexual instincts, melancholy and prone to drinking bouts, but with an enormous capacity for new interests and enthusiasms. ('The best thing for being sad', Merlyn says in *The Sword in the Stone*, 1938, 'is to learn something.') It was during his Stowe years (1932–6) that White acquired his passion for hunting, shooting, and fishing. Two early novels (*Earth Stopped*, 1934, and *Gone to Ground*, 1935), the satirical *Burke's Steerage* (1938), and *England Have My Bones* (1936) all have hunting and shooting themes. When he resigned from Stowe in 1936 in order to become a full-time writer, White spent some months in a cottage near the school experimenting with falconry, later describing the episode in his most successful book, *The Goshawk* (1951).

In 1938 White published *The Sword in the Stone*, the first instalment of what was to become an Arthurian tetralogy entitled *The Once and Future King*. It was a brilliantly imaginative, and in parts satirical, account of the boyhood of King Arthur, loosely based on the work of Sir Thomas Malory. White put himself into the character of Merlyn, passing on to the young king his knowledge of wildlife and hunting. He wrote the second instalment, *The Witch in the Wood* (1940), in Ireland, where he spent a fishing holiday at the beginning of 1939. In the event he stayed there for six years, immersing himself in the special atmosphere of rural Ireland which he found greatly sympathetic. At one time he intended to become a Catholic and even at one stage a priest. White's Irish impressions are to be found in *The Godstone and the Blackymor* (1959), illustrated by Edward Ardizzone, and *The Elephant and the Kangaroo* (1948), a fantasy about a second flood, with White as Noah.

White agonized about helping the war effort and in 1942 applied to join the Royal Air Force Volunteer Reserve (he had learned to fly before the war) but his attempts failed, thereby exacerbating his sense of guilt and isolation. A natural Tory, he abhorred the postwar Labour government and in 1947, after a surprise windfall of £15,000 when his children's book, *Mistress Masham's Repose* (1947), was chosen as the book of the month in the USA, exiled himself in the Channel Islands.

Although he was only in his early forties his writing days were almost over. He completed two books of historical essays, *The Age of Scandal* (1950) and *The Scandal Monger* (1952), and a translation of a medieval bestiary (*The Book of Beasts*, 1954), on which he had laboured for many years. In 1959 *The Once and Future King* was adapted for the stage as a musical called *Camelot*, by Alan Jay Lerner and Frederick Loewe. Starring Richard Burton and Julie Andrews, it opened on Broadway and was an immediate hit. This sudden acquisition of wealth finally put paid to White's writing career and he became more and more morose and more openly homosexual. Following a highly successful lecture tour of America in 1962, described in *America at Last* (1965), he died suddenly 1 July 1964 while crossing the Mediterranean. He was buried in Athens. He was unmarried.

White was a tall, distinguished, bearded figure, 'looking like one of the Sikhs at Queen Victoria's funeral' (his own description). As the child of a drunkard father and a hysterical over-possessive mother he suffered all his life from sadistic impulses, guilt, and irrational fears. He was a natural recluse who found all human relationships difficult. However, until his final period, he rose triumphantly above his handicaps. He was a master stylist, a sharp, satirical observer of the social scene with an unfailing capacity for taking up a variety of interests, and the ability to persuade his readers to share his enthusiasms, however out-of-the-way.

[Sylvia Townsend Warner, *T. H. White: a Biography*, 1967; David Garnett (ed.), *The White/Garnett Letters*, 1968; François Gallix (ed.), *Letters to a Friend: the Correspondence between T. H. White and L. J. Potts*, 1984.]

RICHARD INGRAMS

published 1993

(1886–1945)

Author and scholar, was born in London 20 September 1886, the only son of Richard Walter Stansby Williams, clerk, of Islington, by his wife, Mary, daughter of Thomas Wall, cabinet-maker, of London. He was educated at St. Albans School and at University College, London. In 1908 Williams joined the Oxford University Press as a reader, and remained a member of the staff, increasingly valued and much beloved, until his death. His duties, however, as literary adviser in a publisher's office, although carried out with enthusiasm and wisdom, occupied a relatively small place in his life. In 1912 he published his first book of verse, *The Silver Stair*, and, for the next thirty-three years, wrote, lectured, and conversed with a tireless and brilliant energy. In that time he produced, apart from anthologies, a number of prefaces and a rarely interrupted series of reviews, over thirty volumes of poetry, plays, literary criticism, fiction, biography, and theological argument.

Williams was an unswerving and devoted member of the Church of England with a refreshing tolerance for the scepticism of others, and a firm belief in the necessity of a 'doubting Thomas' in any apostolic body. More and more in his writings he devoted himself to the propagation and elaboration of two main doctrines—romantic love, and the coinherence of all human creatures. These themes formed the substance of all his later volumes, and found their fullest expression in the novels (which he described as 'psychological thrillers'), in his Arthurian poems, and in many books of literary and theological exegesis. His early verse was written in traditional form, but this he later abandoned in favour of a stressed prosody built upon a framework of loosely organized interior rhymes.

Many of Williams's contemporaries found him difficult and obscure. Although the charge angered him, it was not altogether unjustified, for he used the word 'romantic' in a sense that was highly personal and never fully defined. Its basis in his mind was Wordsworth's 'feeling intellect', and what he chiefly meant by it was the exploratory action of the mind working on the primary impact of an emotional experience. It was his view that the romantic approach could reveal objective truth, and this conviction, at variance with the normal implication of the word, led to much misunderstanding and doubt among his readers. In order to be fully equipped for the task of following the thought of any one of his volumes, it was not only necessary to have read the majority of its fellows, but to have spent many talkative hours in his company. The art of conversation and the craft of lecturing were his two most brilliant, provocative, and fruitful methods of communication. His influence on the minds of the young was salutary and inspiring, for he set his face against all vagueness of thought and pretentiousness of expression, and insisted, in all matters of literary commentary, upon a close and first-hand study of the texts. His favourite words of tutorial criticism were—'but that's not what he *says*'. The honorary degree of M.A. bestowed upon him by the university of Oxford in 1943 was a well-deserved recognition of two successive courses of lectures which brought brilliance and a climate of intellectual excitement into the atmosphere of Oxford in wartime.

About the relative importance of Williams's many books opinion must always differ. It is safe to say that the fullest expression of his mature views is to be found in criticism in *The English Poetic Mind* (1932), *Reason and Beauty in the Poetic Mind* (1933), and *The Figure of Beatrice* (1943): in poetry and drama in *Taliessin through Logres* (1938), *The Region of the Summer Stars* (1944), and *Thomas Cranmer of Canterbury* (the Canterbury Festival play for 1936): and in theology in *He Came Down from Heaven* (1938) and *The Descent of the Dove* (1939). Among his biographical works the most notable are *Bacon* (1933), *James I* (1934), *Rochester* (1935), and *Queen Elizabeth* (1936); and among his novels *War in Heaven* (1930), *The Place of the Lion* (1931), *Many Dimensions* (1931), *Descent into Hell* (1937), and *All Hallows' Eve* (1945).

In 1917 Williams married Florence, youngest daughter of James Edward Worrall Conway, ironmonger, of St. Albans, and had one son. He died at Oxford 15 May 1945.

[C. S. Lewis, Preface to *Essays presented to Charles Williams*, 1947; private information; personal knowledge.]

G. W. S. HOPKINS

published 1959

WILLIAMSON Henry

(1895–1977)

Author and journalist, was born 1 December 1895 in Brockley, near Lewisham, only son of William Williamson, bank clerk, of Parkstone, Dorset, and his wife, Gertrude, daughter of Thomas William Leaver. He was educated at Colfe's School, London.

On the outbreak of war he joined the army. His mind was scarred for life by the Christmas truce in 1914, when men who had been trying to kill each other for months past briefly fraternized, only to revert to war again. The Somme was always in his memory. He would not come to terms with the deadly phenomenon of incited patriotic fervour with its power to drive men into a hell of other men's devising. He felt that the land to which he returned at the age of twenty-three, at the end of the war, was in no way fit for heroes. Like many other young men who survived the test to destruction he could not adjust to the peace. He was emotionally burnt out, deeply depressed, and practically without money. He lived on a £40 a year war pension supplemented by what he could earn from newspapers and periodicals. It was then that he came upon *The Story of my Heart* (1883) by Richard Jefferies, the Wiltshire nature writer, and his spirit was invigorated. He went to Devon and began writing in an Exmoor cottage.

He wrote the four books that make up *The Flax of Dream* between 1918 and 1928 (1921, 1922, 1924, and 1928) but by 1924 had also produced two nature books, *The Lone Swallows* (1922) and *The Peregrine's Saga* (1923). On this theme came *Tarka the Otter* in 1927 which won the Hawthornden prize of 1928. There followed *The Wet Flanders Plain* (1929), *The Patriot's Progress* (1930), *Tales of a Devon Village* (1932), *The Gold Falcon* (1933), *Salar the Salmon* (1935), and then two books concerning Richard Jefferies.

As the years went by his books brought him security but he was deeply troubled by international trends. He saw it all happening again and, knowing how it had been, he clutched at any straw for peace, even the most unlikely. 'I salute the great man across the Rhine whose life symbol is the happy child', he wrote in 1936. Hindsight gives such a remark a sick absurdity but Williamson was far from alone in believing it. To some it seemed that Germany was rising from the ashes, firmly, hopefully, and in full employment, whereas in England the heroes still lived in slums and some men had never worked since before the war.

Such opinions, and his support of Sir Oswald Mosley did Williamson no good. When World War II broke out he was imprisoned briefly under defence regulations before being allowed to return to the Norfolk farm which he had owned for eight years and had 'brought from a state of near-dereliction' to full production. *The Children of Shallowford* came out in 1939, *The Story of a Norfolk Farm* in 1941, and six further books before *The Dark Lantern* in 1951 opened his fifteen-part saga *A Chronicle of Ancient Sunlight* which ended in 1969 with *The Gale of the World*, his last book. The *Chronicle* is a peerless social history and a damning indictment of war and his nature books most perfect of their kind, but his ill-conceived *affaire* with fascism was not forgotten and may have denied him honours.

In his narrative writing Williamson is thorough and painstaking and reveals a microscopic eye for detail; he speaks with authority and is always believable, often shockingly as in his war books. Yet much of his philosophy seems to be founded on original innocence. Here perhaps we may perceive an interaction between two great influences on his thinking; the effect of front line service on a sensitive mind and the subsequent discovery of Richard Jefferies's esoteric testament *The Story of my Heart*.

As a man Williamson was said to be often amusing, with a quick puckish humour, a conversationalist with holding power; at other times he could be perverse and irritating, touchy, unable to conceal boredom. He was a loyal and helpful friend. In his writing he was an obsessive perfectionist who wrote and rewrote, never sparing himself. Yet he remained vigorous until almost the close of his long life, striding across the placid hills and beside the clear rivers of the Devon countryside, to which he returned after leaving his Norfolk farm.

Williamson married first, in 1925, Ida Loetitia, daughter of Charles Calvert Hibbert; they had four sons and two daughters. The marriage was dissolved in 1947 and in 1948 he married Christine Mary, only daughter of Hedley Duffield, of Keswick; there was one son. The marriage was dissolved in 1968. Williamson died in a London hospital 13 August 1977.

[Brocard Sewell (ed.), *Henry Williamson: the Man, the Writings*, 1980; Daniel Farson, *Henry*, 1982; Williamson's autobiographical works; private information.]

RICHARD FRERE

published 1986

WODEHOUSE Sir Pelham Grenville

(1881–1975)

Writer, was born 15 October 1881 at 1 Vale Place, Epsom Road, Guildford, the third son of Henry Ernest Wodehouse, a magistrate in Hong Kong, and his wife, Eleanor, daughter of the Revd John Bathurst Deane. She was in England only for the birth of her child and quickly returned to Hong Kong taking him with her. Henry Ernest Wodehouse belonged to a collateral branch of the family of the Earls of Kimberley, being the son of the second son of Sir Armine Wodehouse (fifth baronet), whose descendants were created first Baron Wodehouse in 1797 and first Earl of Kimberley in 1866. His wife belonged to the equally ancient and extremely widespread family of Deane or Adeane.

When their eldest son was six the Wodehouse parents followed the custom of the time in sending him home to England to be educated. For reasons, which are not obvious and which have never been explained, they also sent his younger brothers with him (Pelham then aged two), taking a house in Bath and engaging a Miss Roper to look after them. This regime lasted for three years and then the boys were moved to a dame school in Croydon. Later they were sent to a small public school in Guernsey and finally Armine, the second son, and then Pelham (whose name had been shortened to 'Plum') went to Dulwich College. There were a large number of uncles and aunts on both sides of the family and they were sent to one or other of these in their holidays. Apart from a short period when he was fifteen, and when his parents returned to England and at first took a house near the school (later moving to Shropshire), Armine and Plum boarded at Dulwich.

Deprived so early, not merely of maternal love, but of home life and even a stable background, Wodehouse consoled himself from the youngest age in an imaginary world of his own. He said later in life that he never remembered the time when he did not intend to write and one small story, written when he was seven, remains to prove the skill with which he already handled language. When he went to Dulwich he achieved for the first time in his life some continuity and a stable and ordered life, and, because of the multiplicity of shared interests, he was able to communicate easily with his fellows without any great demands being made upon him. He repaid the happiness he felt there by a lifetime's devotion to the school which sometimes seemed almost obsessive. 'To me', he said in late life, 'the years between 1894 and 1900 were like heaven.'

He was in the school teams for cricket and rugby football and he had the good fortune to be at Dulwich with A. H. Gilkes, a distinguished headmaster and a renowned classicist, whose teaching must have been an important influence. His report for the year 1899 contained the following remarks: 'He has the most distorted ideas about wit and humour; he draws over his books and examination papers in the most distressing way and writes foolish rhymes in other people's books. Notwithstanding he has a genuine interest in literature and can often talk with enthusiasm and good sense about it.'

At first he worked for a scholarship at Oxford, but, when his brother, Armine, succeeded in this ambition (later winning the Newdigate prize), his father told him he could not afford to send them both. When he left school, he therefore went into the Hong Kong and Shanghai Bank. Here he was both unhappy and inefficient and he lived for the end of the day when, in 'horrible lodgings', he could spend his evenings writing. He left the Bank when (Sir) William Beach Thomas, lately a master at Dulwich, offered him a job (at first temporary but later becoming permanent) to write the 'By the Way' column on the *Globe* newspaper. From that time he supported himself by writing and his enormous output (written anonymously, under his own, other people's, and assumed names) included light verse, articles (some of which appeared in *Punch*), and short stories. Chiefly, however, this was the period of the school stories run as serials in the *Public School Magazine* or its rival, *The Captain*. In 1902 his first book, *The Pothunters*, was published by A. & C. Black and this was followed by six other volumes of school stories *Mike* (1909), the last of these, was distinguished by the entrance of a character called Psmith, an event which Evelyn Waugh said marked the date exactly when Wodehouse was touched by the sacred flame: 'Psmith appears and the light was kindled which has burned with growing brilliance for half a century.'

In 1904 he went for the first time to America, the country which would become his second home, and after that he often travelled backwards and forwards across the Atlantic. He soon began to set some of his novels in the American scene and to use the dialect of the New York gangs. He was in America in 1914 and he stayed there for the duration of the war. He had exceedingly bad eyesight and, although he attempted to register when America came into the war, he was rejected. He could not have served England in any military capacity but, more by his attitudes than by any action, he showed, as he would in the second war, how slight were his hold on reality and his ability to respond to abstractions such as country or tragedy on an impersonal scale.

In 1914 he married Ethel Newton (died 1984), the young widow of Leonard Rowley, of Dee Bank, Cheshire. She had one daughter, Leonora, whom he adopted and to whom he became as devoted as if she had been his own. Leonora later married Peter Cazalet. The Wodehouses were to have no children of their own. From the start Ethel Wodehouse was the dominant partner and she managed all their affairs, leaving him free to write. He had by now begun the extremely successful partnership in musical comedies with Guy Bolton and Jerome Kern, which led to a career in the theatre which seemed at the time as important as his career as a novelist and even more lucrative.

After the war he returned to England, but, although he had a house in London for some years, he still spent much time in America. In 1930 he made the first of two visits to Hollywood, causing a national sensation in 1931 by explaining in an interview that, although he had been paid enormous sums to write films, he had never been asked to do any real work. Finally, in 1934 he and his wife settled in Le Touquet.

In 1939 the Wodehouses remained in Le Touquet, and, when the Germans captured northern France, the writer was interned in Upper Silesia.

Wodehouse

On being released in 1941, he made five broadcasts to America from Berlin, and, although these were the equivalent of comic articles in his personal vein, and were made with the motive of reassuring all those people who had written to him or sent parcels, this was not understood at the time, particularly as the British propaganda machine was put to work to present him as a man who had served the enemy in return for his release from internment. Although this was proved to be quite untrue, it was held that he might, nevertheless, have committed a technical offence by speaking in wartime on an enemy wavelength, no matter what the content of his speech, and for many years he could not be guaranteed immunity from prosecution if he entered the jurisdiction of his own country. He accordingly went to America and, after settling down there, became an American citizen in 1955.

Because he wrote under other names and often turned novels into plays or plays into novels, it is difficult to be sure of his total output. He published under his own name ninety-seven books (including twenty-one collections of short stories), he wrote the lyrics or some of the lyrics for twenty-eight musical plays, and wrote or collaborated in the writing of sixteen plays. He wrote the scenario for six films and much light verse and innumerable articles. His work was translated into all the major languages of the world and his sales, which ran into many millions, cannot be estimated.

It seems likely that he achieved a permanent place in English literature. He was unique in that, although he wrote primarily for the general public, he had an inspired humour, and a prose style of so much freshness, suppleness, simplicity, and exactitude that, from such early admirers as Asquith, Hilaire Belloc and M. R. James, he has been the delight of generation after generation of writers and intellectuals, his name standing ever higher.

His most famous books are the Jeeves and the Blandings Castle series, and he achieved the ambition of every novelist in that at least two of his characters, Jeeves and Bertie Wooster, and possibly two others, Lord Emsworth and Psmith, have entered what Belloc called 'that long gallery of living figures which make up the glory of English fiction'. He also wrote more amusingly on golf than anyone before or since, *The Clicking of Cuthbert* (1922) and *The Heart of a Goof* (1926) being his masterpieces in this field.

In 1939 the University of Oxford made him an honorary D.Litt. and in 1975 he was created KBE. He died in a Long Island Hospital 14 February 1975, at the age of ninety-three, one of the most admired and probably the most loved of all the writers of his time.

[P. G. Wodehouse, *Performing Flea*, 1953 (autobiography); Richard Usborne, *Wodehouse at Work to the End*, 1977; Benny Green, *P. G. Wodehouse*, 1981; Iain

Sproat, *Wodehouse at War*, 1981; James H. Heineman and Donald R. Bensen (eds.), *P. G. Wodehouse, a Centenary Celebration*, 1982; Frances Donaldson, *P. G. Wodehouse*, 1982; David A. Jasen, *P. G. Wodehouse*, 1982; personal knowledge.]

FRANCES DONALDSON

published 1986

WOOLF (Adeline) Virginia

(1882–1941)

Novelist and critic, was born 25 January 1882 in Kensington, the second daughter of (Sir) Leslie Stephen and his second wife, Julia Prinsep, the widow of Herbert Duckworth. From early childhood, Virginia Stephen was distinguished by two characteristics which were to determine the course of her history: on the one hand a brilliant and imaginative creative intelligence, and on the other a nervous system of extreme fragility, which, under any severe intellectual or emotional strain, was liable to break down and throw her open to fits of suicidal manic depression. Too delicate for the rigours of regular school, she spent her childhood at her family's London house in Hyde Park Gate and country home at St. Ives in Cornwall. Her father taught her, talked to her, and gave her the run of his library. By the time she grew up, she was already one of the most richly cultured minds of her day. Her mother died in 1895; after this, she was looked after by her elder half-sister Stella Duckworth. Her half-brother, George Duckworth, attempted to launch her, at the age of nineteen, and her sister Vanessa in formal London society. With small success: although too aesthetically sensitive not to find food for her imagination in the world of fashion, Virginia was at once too intellectual and too unconventional to feel at home there. Meanwhile she had started writing and was soon contributing to the *Times Literary Supplement*. Her father's death in 1904 was followed by her nervous breakdown. After this Virginia, together with her sister Vanessa and her brother Adrian, settled in Gordon Square where they collected round them a group of brilliant young men whom their elder brother Thoby had got to know at Cambridge; notably Roger Fry, J. M. (later Lord) Keynes, Lytton Strachey, Dr. Edward Morgan Forster, Mr. Leonard Woolf, and Mr. Clive Bell. Thus was inaugurated the celebrated Bloomsbury circle, which stood for a point of view combining a rich and refined culture with declared opposition to the religious and moral standards of Victorian orthodoxy. Thoby's death in 1906 came as a blow

357

which threatened Virginia Stephen's mental stability for four years. She continued, however, to live in Bloomsbury, first in Fitzroy Square, and after 1911 in Brunswick Square, devoting herself to the study and perfection of her art.

In 1912 she married Leonard Sidney Woolf with whom she lived partly in London and partly in Sussex. In 1914 she had another serious breakdown, and although after a year she recovered, for the rest of her life her husband saw to it that she lived very quietly. Her condition was never secure: for literary work and the society of her friends, the two things in which she found most satisfaction, were, if over-indulged in, both liable to upset it. Finishing a book, in particular, always left her exhausted. Leonard Woolf's devoted care, however, was successful in preserving her for many years. It was during this period that her chief work was done and her fame established. Of her novels, *Voyage Out* appeared in 1915, *Night and Day* in 1919. They were in a relatively traditional form. *Jacob's Room*, in which Virginia Woolf's characteristic manner first fully revealed itself, came out in 1922, *Mrs. Dalloway* in 1925, *To the Lighthouse* in 1927, *The Waves* in 1931, *The Years* in 1937. She also published two fantasies: *Orlando* (1928) and *Flush* (1933); two books of critical and biographical essays, *The Common Reader* (first series, 1925, second series, 1932); a biography of Roger Fry (1940), and two gracefully written feminist pamphlets, *A Room of One's Own* (1929) and *Three Guineas* (1938). She also took an active part in the management of the Hogarth Press which was founded by her and her husband in 1917. During these years she lived partly in London, in Tavistock Square, and partly at Rodmell in Sussex. In 1939 the Woolfs moved to Mecklenburgh Square where they remained until the bombing of 1940, after which they retired to Rodmell. There in 1941 Virginia Woolf's nervous system suffered its final collapse under the strain of the war, and she drowned herself, 28 March. The following books were published posthumously: *Between the Acts*, a novel (1941); and *A Haunted House*, short stories (1943); four volumes of essays, *The Death of the Moth* (1942), *The Moment* (1947), *The Captain's Death Bed* (1950), and *Granite and Rainbow* (1958); and extracts from her diary, *A Writer's Diary* (1953).

In spite of her disabilities, Virginia Woolf contrived to make a strong and influential personal impression on some of the most distinguished minds of her time. Her closest literary friends were her oldest, notably Dr. Forster and Lytton Strachey; but she was also intimate with others, Lady Ottoline Morrell, Miss V. Sackville-West, and in later years Miss Elizabeth Bowen. She was shy in general society; and, even in congenial company, her personality could be formidable from its uncompromising fastidiousness. But it was also fascinating both for her ethereal beauty and for her conversation which combined fresh naturalness and an inexhaustible interest in other people with flights of whimsical fancy and a glinting satirical humour. As a writer she is in the first rank of English women. Her critical essays, at once so charming in form and so just and penetrating in judgement, are perhaps her securest achievement. But her most individual contribution to letters lies in her fiction. This shows the limitations of its author's personality: dramatic force and elemental human sentiment lie outside its scope. But it is distinguished by a subtle power to convey the processes of unspoken thought and feeling; by an extraordinary sensibility to the beautiful in nature and art; and by an original mastery of form that reveals itself alike in the intricate and musical design of her novels and in the shimmering felicities of her style. In Virginia Woolf the English aesthetic movement brought forth its most exquisite flower.

A small sketch in oil of Virginia Woolf by her sister, Vanessa Bell, is in the possession of the artist, who has also a small sketch in oil by Roger Fry, and a portrait and an ink drawing by Duncan Grant. The National Portrait Gallery has a chalk drawing by Francis Dodd and a lead bust by Stephen Tomlin. A portrait by J.-E. Blanche is believed to be in France.

[Personal knowledge.]

DAVID CECIL

[B. J. Kirkpatrick, *A Bibliography of Virginia Woolf*, 1957.]

published 1959

YEATS William Butler

(1865–1939)

Irish poet and playwright, the eldest son of John Butler Yeats, painter, by his wife, Susan, daughter of William Pollexfen, shipowner, was born in Dublin 13 June 1865. He was predominantly of Irish Protestant origin. His Yeats grandfather and great-grandfather had been Church of Ireland clergymen, and on his mother's side he sprang from a little community of shipowners and traders, long established in Sligo, with which county his father's family was also associated. Shortly after his birth his father, who possessed some small independent means, moved to London to study art. The children were frequently in Sligo with their Pollexfen grandparents, and the first verses which Yeats read with delight were from an Orange song-book found in his grandfather's stables. In 1877 he became a day boy at the Godolphin School, Hammersmith; but his holidays were spent in Sligo with his grandparents, and Sligo was the home to which his imagination constantly returned. In 1881 his father, now become a pre-Raphaelite portrait-painter, left London and took a house at Howth, near Dublin. Yeats's education was continued at the Dublin High School, where he was singled out as a clever and original lad, with a taste for natural history and English composition, but no scholar. He was about sixteen when he began to write verse under the eye of his father, who instructed him in Shakespeare and Balzac and directed his ambition towards dramatic poetry. The outlook of the elder Yeats, compounded of a humane aestheticism and the philosophy of J. S. Mill, did not wholly satisfy the spiritual needs of his son, who, while a student at the Metropolitan School of Art, fell readily into the company of a group of mystics. Of these the most remarkable was AE (George William Russell)—afterwards a collaborator in the Irish literary movement—and with AE Yeats began to study the lore of the East at a theosophical society which Madame Blavatsky had established in Dublin. Even then in his wanderings about Sligo his imagination had been enticed by the common people's stories of magic, clairvoyance, and ghost-seeing. An introduction to Irish saga in the poetry of Sir Samuel Ferguson and his friendship with an astrological uncle in Sligo were other notable influences of this period.

Soon after the publication of his first book, *Mosada*, a dramatic poem reminiscent of Spenser and Shelley (Dublin, 1886), Yeats joined his parents in Bedford Park, London, where they had again settled in 1887. He continued to write lyrics and plays, and received encouragement from W. E. Henley and William Morris, at whose houses he met many men of note. He also moved in theosophical and spiritualistic circles and wrote with E. J. Ellis a far-ranging interpretative work on the esoteric William Blake (*The Works of William Blake, Poetic, Symbolic and Critical*, 1893). He had to live very frugally, even when with the charming folk-stories of *The Celtic Twilight* (1893) and with his *Poems* (1895), he had gained a distinguished position among the younger imaginative writers. When in 1895 he took up quarters of his own, they were in a very modest locality near Euston; and indeed he was fifty years of age before his income from his books exceeded £200 a year.

After the death of Parnell there was a movement in Ireland towards imaginative nationalism, Gaelic, and the ancient stories, and Yeats tells in his *Autobiographies* (1926) how he hoped to create some new *Prometheus Unbound*, with Patrick, Oisin, or Fionn, in Prometheus' stead, and how on visits to Ireland he went about organizing literary societies among the Fenians and supporters of the Parnellite tradition. His Irish activities were greatly stimulated by friendships with two remarkable persons; the Fenian

John O'Leary, 'one of Plutarch's people', and Maud Gonne (Madame Gonne MacBride), 'a woman Homer sung', and the subject of his own love poetry. He figured with them in the '98 commemoration movement and was thus brought into contact with Irish revolutionary politics. As Henry Woodd Nevinson noted, 'violent rebellion to the dominating power was contrary to his nature'; yet such politics were not so far removed as might at first appear from Yeats's main preoccupation, for he looked for some accepted authority which would convince the people that 'the more difficult pleasure is the nobler pleasure'. His first concern was with culture and civilization, for which he perceived that some high code of morality was the necessary support, and he hoped to find that support in the Fenian tradition. In London, by contrast, his chief companions were men who were remote from active life, such as Arthur Symons, Lionel Johnson, and the aesthetes of the Rhymers' Club, whose masters had been Pater and Mallarmé. The mark of this companionship was apparent in some of the verse in his *Wind Among the Reeds* (1899) and in the stories *The Secret Rose* (1897), where the fresh Celticism of such lyrics as the well-known 'Lake Isle of Innisfree' and the 'Man Who Dreamed of Faeryland' had given place to something more stylized and sophisticated. 'Yeats took his small colleen to London', someone is made to say in the Irish trilogy *Hail and Farewell* by George Augustus Moore, 'and put paint upon her cheeks and dye upon her hair.' He was rescued from the fate of becoming a London-Irishman of letters by Isabella Augusta, Lady Gregory, who made a theatre of poetry in Dublin seem possible to him. By the social influence which she could exert and the moral impetus with which she took up his ideas, Lady Gregory brought about, with Edward Martyn and George Moore, two Irish writers interested in the stage, the first performance in Dublin of the poet's beautiful verse-play *The Countess Cathleen*, which had been published in the *Poems* of 1895. This event of 1899 marked the occasion of the foundation of an Irish theatre. It was also the occasion for Yeats of his first notable conflict with the opinions of his fellow countrymen, for the theme of the play aroused Catholic suspicion by seeming to imply an heretical purpose. O'Leary had told Yeats that to succeed in Ireland he must have either the Fenians or the Church on his side; in his subsequent experience as director of the celebrated Abbey Theatre—established by the generosity of an Englishwoman, Annie Elizabeth Fredericka Horniman—he encountered the hostility of the Fenians, or, as it seemed to him, their degenerate successors, whose literal patriotism was offended by J. M. Synge's pictures of peasant life. In giving so much of his energy to the defence of Synge and other prose writers Yeats perhaps renounced an ambition to found a great imaginative tradition in an Irish theatre. Although he provided the gifted Irish players with a series of short blank-verse plays on heroic subjects, it was not these but the work of younger men, social and political satirists, that finally established the Abbey Theatre as a national institution. His most popular play was an early one, his patriotic *Cathleen ni Houlihan*, first performed in 1902 when Maud Gonne, in the part of the old woman who is Ireland, seemed, as he wrote at the time, 'a divine being fallen into our mortal infirmity'. His later work for the stage, or that part of it which he wrote under the influence of the Japan *Noh* plays 'performable in the drawing-room', seemed designed to conceal his real dramatic gift from the multitude.

Yeats's sensibility changed and expanded as a result of his experience of 'theatre business and management of men'. In *Responsibilities* (1914) and *The Wild Swans at Coole* (1917) he seemed to repudiate the wavering moods and rhythm of the 'Celtic Twilight' school, as leader of which he had made his reputation, both in England and in Ireland. It had come to be his conviction that what currently passed as the Celtic note in literature reflected the sentimentality of the cities and was remote from the folk spirit, which is at once concrete and romantic. In this new work he kept close to particulars. He was no longer afraid of eloquence, and wrote of

> 'Merchant and scholar who have left me blood
> That has not passed through any huckster's loin;'

composed epigrams on Synge's enemies; and found themes in the Irish events in which he had figured. Donne (with his fury of self-control) and Landor had replaced Spenser and Shelley as his English masters. The Irish insurrection of Easter 1916, with its aftermath of executions, moved him and revived his tender feeling for his country:

> 'our part
> To murmur name upon name,
> As a mother names her child.'

For many years Yeats divided his time, when he was not occupied with the theatre in Dublin, between his London rooms (18 Woburn Buildings, later 5 Woburn Walk) and Coole Park, Lady Gregory's home in the county Galway plain. He spent many weeks each summer at Coole, praised for its hospitality to poets, scholars, and travellers in his two stately poems, 'Coole Park' and 'Coole and Ballylee',

> 'Where none has reigned that lacked a name and fame
> Or out of folly into folly came.'

In 1917, when he was fifty-two, Yeats married a young English girl, Georgie, only daughter of William Gilbert Hyde Lees, of Pickhill Hall, Wrexham, and settled temporarily at Oxford (4 Broad Street, since demolished). He now plunged into the astrologico-historical speculations which were subsequently embodied in *A Vision* (1925, revised edition 1937). These speculations had a genesis in what Yeats called 'an incredible experience'; but Plato, Plotinus, and modern idealist philosophies, as well as Spengler, were ingeniously introduced to corroborate the argument of the book, which was based in part at least on what appeared to be preternatural communications. To the experience and beliefs set out in *A Vision* are traceable certain dominant preoccupations of Yeats's later poetry, which reveal the monstrous impact of eternity in time. Such poetry as 'I saw a staring virgin stand ... And tear the heart out of his side', 'In Galilean turbulence', 'Those terrified vague fingers', and (his version of *The Magnificat*)

> 'The terror of all terrors that I bore
> The Heavens in my womb',

was religious in its vivid apprehension of supernatural forces, but certainly not Christian in tone.

The young men, almost all orthodox Catholics, who were building up the Irish Free State during the closing stages of the civil war of 1922–1923, overlooked Yeats's antinomianism and offered him in 1922 a position as a senator. He had seen something of the fighting from Ballylee in county Galway, where he had made a house out of an old Norman tower; and although the Irish senators at this moment ran some physical risks, he readily accepted the invitation. At the end of 1923 he was awarded the Nobel prize for literature, which he received in person at Stockholm, where he greatly impressed the audience by his fine manners. On his return to Dublin he became a diligent member of the senate, which certainly possessed in him its most distinguished figure. He liked to entertain in his house at 82 Merrion Square and discuss with the new politicians Irish problems from an imaginative and philosophical point of view. He did some useful work in committees; but in his speeches often threw discretion to the winds, notably in 1925, in a passionate and sardonic attack on a change in the divorce law, which he considered unjust to the Protestant minority—'the people of Burke and of Grattan', now represented by him as the true founders of Irish nationalism. He had gone on several American lecture tours and was a practised speaker. His voice was musical, touched with melancholy. When emphasis was needed he would introduce a hard metallic note, and this at moments of passion was like the clash of sword-blades. His myopic gaze as he spoke was turned within, looking into the darkness where, as he said, 'there is always something'. In appearance he was remarkable, having a pugnacious lower lip, olive complexion, and a magnificent head of hair which turned white in his sixties but never lost its vigour. He stood just over six foot, was careful if unconventional in his dress, and took regular exercise for his health, which had never been robust.

In 1928 Yeats's term of office as a senator came to an end, and he did not seek to renew it. In the same year he published *The Tower*; with this volume and *The Winding Stair* (New York, 1929) he was generally considered to have reached the peak of his poetic achievement. It was as if he had recovered his first vision, having become in the interval a great artist, master of many forms of expression, and possessed of many and varied themes. As compared with a Hardy, or a Housman, he had not a wide public, and did not command from his readers the same affection as these poets did from theirs. But the general consensus of critical opinion now assessed him not only as the greatest poet of English-speaking Ireland, but as one who would occupy a sure position among the greater poets of the English-speaking world. Most remarkable perhaps was the deference shown to him by members of the young modernist school. Writers who had grown up in a climate of opinion and feeling, the reverse of that which had prevailed in his youth, recognized in Yeats the most exciting and many-sided personality of the older generation of poets.

The honours which Yeats had won and his happy personal circumstances brought no complacency into his outlook, whether on himself or on society. The most rarefied and metaphysical lines of his poetry were interrupted by emphatic confessions that he found little consolation for the loss of the pride of youth in 'argument and abstract things', in the friendship of Plato and Plotinus ('I mock Plotinus' thought And cry in Plato's teeth'); and he sang of the eternal cross-purposes and the tragic ambivalence of all that touches man and of the impossibility of bringing life before the bar of reason. For an admirable prose play on Swift, *The Words upon the Window Pane* (1934), he wrote a preface in which he urged his countrymen, Catholic or communist, or both, to reject the belief in progress, 'the only myth of modern man', and admit the circular movement of history

> 'The Primum Mobile that fashioned us,
> Has made the very owls in circles move.'

The only politics to the immediate issues of which he had ever been attentive were Irish; but in his last years, when catastrophe loomed over the world, he was ready to discuss international questions, not wholly *sub specie aeternitatis*. As early as 1923 he had declared on a public occasion that 'we do not believe that war is passing away, or that the world is getting better and better', and in a poem of 1919, 'The Second Coming', he had associated a brazen winged beast with approaching public disaster.

In 1932, although in failing health, Yeats made a last lecture tour in the United States in the course of which he collected funds for the Irish Academy of Letters, which he and Mr. Bernard Shaw and Russell had founded in that year. His *Collected Poems* and *Collected Plays* were published in 1933 and 1934 respectively. Installed at home in a little country house near Dublin he frequently visited London. A few of his early English friends survived, and he found himself in imaginative understanding with some of the younger English poets, in particular Walter James Redfern Turner, the Sitwells, Lady Gerald Wellesley (later Duchess of Wellington). A meeting with an Indian religious man, Shri Purohit Swami, revived his old interest in Eastern philosophies, and at the beginning of 1935 he went to Majorca with the Swami, who was engaged under his eye in an English translation of the *Upanishads*. Here a dropsical condition clearly revealed itself. But no flagging of his mental powers could be detected and he remained to the end the indefatigable artist. He had dreamed since his youth of bringing poetry to the people by its recital to music without any loss of its immediate intelligibility; and two years before his death he began to supervise radio broadcasts of modern verse, 'In the Poet's Parlour', 'In the Poet's Pub', with the help of musicians who had a sensitive ear for the sound of words (see V. Clinton Baddeley's *Words for Music*, 1941). The spirited ballads, patriotic and amatory, which filled his last book (*Last Poems and Plays*, a posthumous publication, 1940) were no doubt conceived as a contribution to an art in which music should be the handmaid of poetry. At the end of 1938 his wife brought him to Cap Martin, near Mentone, where he had friends near by. He was his gay social self at a Christmas party; but wrote on 14 January 1939 to a friend that he knew for certain that his time would not be long. 'I am happy', he added, 'and it seems to me I have found what I wanted.' He died of myocarditis on 28 January at the little rock-town of Roquebrune, overlooking Monaco, and was buried in the cemetery there until in 1948 his remains were brought to the churchyard of his great grandfather's parish, Drumcliffe, near Sligo. He had a son and a daughter, who both survived him.

Yeats received honorary degrees from the universities of Dublin (1922), Oxford (1931), and Cambridge (1933). Among portraits in public galleries are a pencil drawing by John Butler Yeats, and a red chalk drawing by William Strang, in the National Gallery, Dublin, and paintings, by Augustus John in the Corporation Art Gallery, Glasgow, and in the Corporation Art Gallery, Manchester. A pastel by A. Mancini is in the possession of Mr. M. B. Yeats. Other portraits by John, Charles Shannon, and J. S. Sargent are reproduced in the *Autobiographies* and other of Yeats's books.

[*The Times*, 30 and 31 January 1939; John Eglinton (W. K. Magee), *Irish Literary Portraits*, 1935; Stephen Gwynn, *Irish Literature and Drama in the English Language*, 1936; Joseph Hone, *W. B. Yeats*, 1942; W. B. Yeats, *Autobiographies* (*Reveries over Childhood and Youth*, 1914, *The Trembling of the Veil*, 1922), 1926, and *Dramatis Personae*, 1935; F. L. MacNeice, *The Poetry of W. B. Yeats*, 1941; *Letters on Poetry from W. B. Yeats to Dorothy Wellesley*, edited by D. Wellesley, 1940; *London Mercury*, March 1939; personal knowledge.]

JOSEPH HONE

published 1949

YORKE Henry Vincent

(1905–1973)

Writer under the name of Henry Green, was born 29 October 1905 at Forthampton Court, near Tewkesbury, Gloucestershire, the third son and youngest of three children (the eldest died at the age of sixteen) of Vincent Wodehouse Yorke, who had manufacturing interests in the midlands, and his wife, Maud Evelyn, daughter of Henry Wyndham, second Baron Leconfield. He was educated at Eton and at Magdalen College, Oxford. After leaving Oxford early, under family pressure, he spent an apprenticeship in one of the firm's factories, and he thereafter looked after the firm's affairs from its London office.

Henry Green was one of the most original prose writers of his generation. He was the author of nine novels, one autobiographical book (*Pack My Bag*, 1940), and a number of shorter pieces which were published in various periodicals. The first of his novels, *Blindness*, was begun while he was still at Eton and published in 1926. He followed this in 1929 with *Living*, already remarkable for his prose style. After a ten-year interval came *Party Going* (1939). At the outbreak of war he joined the Auxiliary Fire Service, and his next novel, *Caught* (1943), was based on his experiences in the Fire Service during the London blitz. All his subsequent books also had one-word titles, *Loving* (1945), *Back* (1946), *Concluding* (1948), *Nothing* (1950), and *Doting* (1952). After the publication of the last-named he fell silent for the remainder of his life.

His novels show above all an extraordinarily acute ear for the way people talk in the most various walks of life; from the factory hands in *Living*, the domestic servants in *Loving*, the state bureaucrats in *Concluding*, and the upper-class rich in *Party Going*. His last two novels were deliberately created almost entirely out of dialogue. His prose style was distinctly his own and consisted mainly of very simple words and an idiosyncratic syntax, which might make the unwary reader embarking on one of his novels for the first time imagine he was dealing with a novice writer with little experience of language—until he gradually became aware of the extreme sophistication of the artifice, which concealed a hilarious sense of comedy and a capacity to rise to passages of pure poetic description, as in the extended dreamy metaphors which illuminate the scene of the overcrowded fog-bound railway terminus in *Party Going* and the glimpses the reader is given of the romantic flower-filled park surroundings of the State Institution (formerly a private estate) in the futuristic fantasy of *Concluding*.

His peak scenes of comedy nearly always arise from confusion and misunderstanding, as in *Loving* when Mrs Tennant confronts Mrs Welch, her drunken cook, about her mislaid sapphire ring, and, in *Concluding*, when there are muddled rumours about the disappearance of the student Mary and her doll. Henry Green revels in such confusions, and extracts the maximum of humour from them, while never giving the reader satisfactory explanations. Mary's disappearance remains a mystery, though it is hinted that some of the other young girls know the real answer. Henry Green seems in such scenes to suggest that there are puzzles in life which one can never solve however hard one enlists the aid of reason.

His use of symbolism is often closely connected with his sense of the irrational in human life. There seems no reason why Miss Fellowes's discovery of and concern for the dead pigeon should play such an important part in *Party Going* until one sees, or rather feels intuitively, what an effective foil it is to the behaviour of the stranded upper-class passengers locked in the hotel while the fog stops all trains. Birds appear again and again as his obsessive symbols: for instance, the peacocks in *Loving*, the starlings that gather in the trees of the park at sunset in *Concluding*, and Mr Rock's goose. There are other symbols, too, which he delights to introduce: he uses the word 'rosc' in *Back* to create a maximum of both confusion and poetic suggestion; and throughout his work roses and other flowers appear, to give the hint of another dimension to the foreground action.

Henry Green's novels, in fact, move us not only by their cunning mixture of comedy and poetry, their subtle strokes of characterization, and the bravura dramatic descriptions of human crisis, as in *Caught* and some of the shorter fire-fighting pieces, but also by their sense of the mystery and strangeness of life, which lingers like a haunting melody long after we have come to the last page.

Henry Green was an extremely lively conversationalist, and delighted in not always unmalicious gossip about his Eton and Oxford contemporaries who had become part of the literary world. He also told very amusing stories about his meetings with business delegates from abroad, particularly—during the war—from the Soviet Union. He seldom spoke about his work as a writer, and almost never about politics. In fact he gave the impression that he thought of politicians as rather inferior beings. He had a lasting dislike of being photographed full-face, with the result that nearly all the pictures that have survived are of the back of his head.

In 1929 he married Adelaide Mary, daughter of John Michael Gordon Biddulph, second Baron Biddulph. They had one son. Green was a bedridden invalid during his last years. He died in London 13 December 1973.

[Henry Green, *Pack my Bag*, 1940; personal knowledge.]

JOHN LEHMANN

published 1986